Sustainable Prosperity in the New Economy?

Sustainable Prosperity in the New Economy?

Business Organization and High-Tech Employment in the United States

William Lazonick

2009

W.E. Upjohn Institute for Employment Research
Kalamazoo, Michigan

Library of Congress Cataloging-in-Publication Data

Lazonick, William
  Sustainable prosperity in the new economy : business organization and high-tech employment in the United States / William Lazonick.
     p. cm.   *cor*
  Includes bibliographical references and index.
  ISBN-13: 978-0-88099-350-0 (pbk. : alk. paper)
  ISBN-10: 0-88099-350-2 (pbk. : alk. paper)
  ISBN-13: 978-0-88099-351-7 (hardcover : alk. paper)
  ISBN-10: 0-88099-351-0 (hardcover : alk. paper)
  1. Information technology—Economic aspects—United States. 2. High-technology industries—United States. 3. Labor market—United States. 4. Economic development—United States. I. Title.

  HC110.I55L39 2009
  330.973—dc22

                    2009023117

The facts presented in this study and the observations and viewpoints expressed are the sole responsibility of the author. They do not necessarily represent positions of the W.E. Upjohn Institute for Employment Research.

Cover design by Ace Creative.
Index prepared by Diane Worden.
Printed in the United States of America.
Printed on recycled paper.

To the memory of my parents, Louis and Pearl Lazonick.

Contents

Figures

Tables

x

Preface

As I write this preface in March 2009, the United States is in the midst of the worst economic crisis since the Great Depression. The Obama administration has established a massive stimulus package to get the economy back on track. As I show in this book, however, there are fundamental problems with the U.S. economy that predate the current crisis. Even in recovery, the U.S. economy will not generate stable and equitable growth—or what I call "sustainable prosperity"—unless these problems are fixed.

For the past three decades the distribution of income in the United States has become more unequal, with a hugely, and some might say grotesquely, disproportionate share of total national income now going to the very richest households. Over the same period, the U.S. economy has experienced an inexorable disappearance of "middle-class" jobs—stable employment opportunities that provide a decent standard of living. A key finding of this book is that even when economic conditions are generally prosperous, economic insecurity afflicts well-educated and highly experienced members of the U.S. labor force. Yet these are the people who should be best positioned to make a good living.

In this book, I analyze the ways in which the "New Economy business model" in the information and communications technology (ICT) industries has contributed to this instability and inequity. In the last decade, U.S.-based ICT companies have been replacing well-educated and highly experienced U.S. workers with qualified labor in lower-wage nations such as China and India. The contribution to the growth of these developing economies represents progress. The problem is that rather than use the profits from globalization to sustain and upgrade the employment of U.S. workers, companies like Cisco Systems, Hewlett-Packard, IBM, Intel, and Microsoft have been using these profits to repurchase billions of dollars annually of their own outstanding shares in an effort to boost their stock prices.

Underlying this mode of corporate resource allocation is the corporate governance ideology that contends that to achieve superior economic performance companies should "maximize shareholder value." In this book, I expose the fallacies of this argument, and I show how in practice shareholder-value ideology contributes to instability and inequity in the economy and tends to undermine the accumulation of innovative capability. This book provides an alternative perspective on how corporate resource allocation can contribute to the achievement of sustainable prosperity.

The research that underpins this book goes back some two decades, when I first started analyzing the financialization of the U.S. corporate economy and the consequent decline of what the eminent business historian Alfred Chandler called "managerial capitalism," or what I call the "Old Economy business model." In the last half of the 1980s, when my principal academic appointment was in the economics department of Barnard College at Columbia University, my work benefited greatly from my involvement with Al Chandler and "the Business History Group" at Harvard Business School. One result was the publication of *Business Organization and the Myth of the Market Economy* (Cambridge University Press 1991), a critique of the notion that the neoclassical theory of the market economy can comprehend the actual allocation of resources in the U.S. economy. Another result, published in *Industrial and Corporate Change* in 1992, was "Controlling the Market for Corporate Control: The Historical Significance of Managerial Capitalism," my first extended critique of agency theory and shareholder-value ideology.

Shortly thereafter, I met Mary O'Sullivan, a graduate of the Harvard Business School MBA program and a doctoral candidate in the Harvard Business Economics PhD program. Her insights into corporate finance, financial economics, and the evolution of the industrial corporation have contributed significantly to the analysis in this book. Our first major project, funded by the Jerome Levy Economics Institute, resulted in an edited volume, *Corporate Governance and Sustainable Prosperity* (Palgrave 2002), which focused on the disappearance of good jobs in the U.S. economy under a shareholder-value corporate governance regime. Among the contributors to this volume were Bob Forrant, Phil Moss, and Chris Tilly, my colleagues in the Department of Regional Economic and Social Development (RESD) at the University of Massachusetts, Lowell, with whom I have had ongoing discussions about employment and income distribution in the U.S. economy.

In 1993 I had been lured away from Columbia University to UMass Lowell by Chancellor William Hogan and Vice Chancellor for University Relations and Development Frederick Sperounis, both of whom were committed to a university-wide program of interdisciplinary research informed by an in-depth understanding of the realities of economic and social development. My RESD colleague John Wooding subsequently became provost in the Hogan administration. I would like to thank this trio for creating the intellectual environment and working conditions in which the type of research that is found in this book could be pursued.

Since the early 1990s I have sharpened my perspective on the distinctive evolution of U.S. capitalism through comparative research on corporate governance, innovation, and economic performance in Europe and Asia. An understanding of the European experience is important because of the persistence of distinctive corporate governance regimes across the European Union and the resistance of Europeans—to their ultimate benefit, I would argue—to the wholesale adoption of the U.S. shareholder-value model. An understanding of the Asian experience is important because, starting with Japan in the 1950s, the world's most dynamic developing economies have emerged in this region, with, as in the most recent cases of China and India, an increasingly heavy emphasis on the ICT industries as the engines of growth and the availability of highly capable labor forces to make that growth happen.

I am grateful to Keith Smith for introducing me, beginning in 1993, to the European collaborative research environment through my involvement in the Studies in Technology, Innovation, and Economic Policy Group in Oslo, Norway, when he was the director of that research institute. From 1996 to 2007 I carried out my research as a faculty member of INSEAD, the Institut Européen d' Administration des Affaires, or European Institute of Business Administration, in Fontainebleau, France. While at INSEAD, I led a major European Commission project, Corporate Governance, Innovation, and Economic Performance (CGEP), and was a participant in a subsequent EC project, European Socio-Economic Models of a Knowledge-Based Society (ESEMK), led by Yannick Lung of Université Montesquieu-Bordeaux IV. Research carried out under these projects has contributed to this book, as has work done with Henrik Glimstedt of the Stockholm School of Economics and Ulrich Jürgens of Wissenschaftszentrum-Berlin.

My research on Asia began in the early 1990s with a project with Kazuo Wada of the University of Tokyo and Takeshi Abe of Osaka University on the dynamic interaction of organization and technology in Japanese economic development. I greatly deepened my understanding of Japanese development when I was a visiting professor in the faculty of economics at the University of Tokyo in 1996–1997, as well as through a subsequent project on the Japanese enterprise led by Akira Kudo of the University of Tokyo and Glenn Hook of the University of Sheffield. I also benefited immensely from numerous discussions about Japanese and comparative capitalism with Ronald Dore, a person of remarkable knowledge and insight.

From 1997 to 1999, I was joined at INSEAD by my Harvard sociology student Qiwen Lu, whose pioneering book, *China's Leap into the Information Age* (Oxford University Press 2000), alerted me to the innovative capabilities being developed in China, a subject I address in Chapter 5 of this book. Sadly, Qiwen died just after his book manuscript was completed. Through Qiwen's work, I got to know Dic Lo of the University of London's School of Oriental and African Studies (SOAS) and Renmin University of China, who in 2006 hosted me on an illuminating trip to China. I have also learned much about China from my UMass Lowell graduate students, especially Hao Xie, Yue Zhang, and He Gao.

My firsthand insights into Indian development began in 1993 with a United Nations Development Programme project on the jute industry with my UMass

Lowell colleagues Michael Best and the late Sukant Tripathy. At the time there were tens of millions of educated unemployed in India. The rapid growth of the Indian information technology (IT) services industry from the late 1990s changed all that. In 2007 I made two trips to Bangalore, the center of the Indian IT services industry, to observe the economic transformation that had taken place. I owe special thanks to Parteii Sawyan of Shillong, who, through her friend, Naina Kidwai, CEO of HSBC India, helped me gain access to executives at a number of Indian IT services companies, including Infosys, Mindtreé, and Wipro. For sharing with me their knowledge of the Indian ICT industries, I am grateful to Arundhati Chakraborty, Amrita Dhindsa, and Sunil Swarup of HP India; Muthukrishnan Subramanian of IBM India; Somnath Baishya, Bikramjit Maitra, and Deependra Moitra of Infosys; Srini Rajam of Ittiam; Puneet Jetli, Krishnakumar Natarajan, and R.K. Veeraraghavan of Mindtree; Mohan Kumar of Motorola India; Swati Bhatia and Marion Leslie of Reuters India; and Ranjan Acharya, Jatin Dalal, Vinod Harith, Ashok Herur, Divakaran Mangalath, Sudip Nandy, Veena Padmanabhan, Jessie Paul, and Swapna Pillai of Wipro.

In the United States, I received a grant in the late 1990s from the Russell Sage Foundation to study how, in the Internet boom, Lucent Technologies, a major high-tech employer in Massachusetts, was coping with shortages of skilled production workers at its Merrimack Valley Works, which had 5,600 employees. As I was doing this research, however, boom turned to bust, and the project ended up being about the demise of a major high-tech manufacturing plant and the subsequent employment transitions of its displaced workers. Through this project, I came to know Edward March, director of engineering at Merrimack Valley Works, who subsequently was for a number of years a highly valued colleague of mine at UMass Lowell and who continues to enlighten me about the processes of technological change.

This plant-level study fed into a substantial research effort, initially in collaboration with Marie Carpenter and Mary O'Sullivan at INSEAD as part of the CGEP project, to analyze the impact of the New Economy business model, as epitomized by Cisco Systems, on strategy, organization, and finance at Old Economy communications equipment companies such as Lucent, Nortel, and Alcatel. INSEAD provided us with excellent access to executives at Alcatel, headquartered in Paris. I am especially grateful to François Béhague, Jean-Luc Corniglion, and Elizabeth Eastland for the time that they spent with us explaining the changes in organization and technology that occurred at Alcatel during the Internet boom and bust. Subsequently, in 2003, I also began to do research with Henrik Glimstedt on Ericsson, the Swedish communications equipment giant. With the extraordinary cooperation of Marcus Sheard, the company's vice president of worldwide compensation and benefits, we analyzed how Ericsson adopted U.S.-style employee stock option plans and then transformed their use to fit with the much more egalitarian Swedish business model.

Building on our research on the communications equipment companies, in August 2007 Marie Carpenter, Henrik Glimstedt, Ed March, and I organized a conference at INSEAD on innovation and competition in the global communications technology industry that brought together practitioners and academics. Besides providing material for this book, the conference led to an ongoing collaborative study of the global communications technology industry with Petter Kilefors and Martyn Roetter of Arthur D. Little consultants.

While all of this work has fed into *Sustainable Prosperity in the New Economy?* it was a grant from the W.E. Upjohn Institute for Employment Research that transformed a wide-ranging research agenda into a focused book. The Upjohn Institute's support for this project went far beyond funding. Susan Houseman encouraged me to apply for the grant and provided much-appreciated guidance and patience throughout the project. Two anonymous referees provided constructive comments on my original book proposal. Kevin Hollenbeck made excellent suggestions concerning the organization and editing of the book. Bob Wathen was a superb copy editor; he helped me to emphasize the bigger picture that I was painting while cleaning up my errant brushstrokes. The production of the book was then placed in Richard Wyrwa's very capable hands and Benjamin Jones did a great job of proofreading the galleys.

Since 2005 the material in this book has been presented at invited lectures in various venues around the world. Previous versions of some of the chapters have been published in various journals and edited volumes, in most cases with considerably more empirical detail than has been included in this book. These publications include *Internet and Digital Economics*; *The Future of Work in Massachusetts*; *Employee Pensions: Policies, Problems, and Possibilities*; *The Oxford Handbook of Information and Communication Technologies*; *Perspectives of Corporate Governance*; *Industrial and Corporate Change*; *Louvain Economic Review*; and *Capitalism and Society*.

Besides those people whose intellectual contributions I have already mentioned, in writing this book I have benefited from discussions with and/ or comments from Ron Adner, Sanjay Anandaram, Tosun Aricanli, Randy Barber, Ross Bassett, Christophe Belleval, Michael Best, Margaret Blair, Danny Breznitz, Eric Brousseau, Kristine Bruland, Bob Buchele, Leonardo Burlamaqui, Jose Cassiolato, Ha-Joon Chang, François Chesnais, Chris Clott, Andrea Colli, Tony Daley, Stephen Diamond, Yves Doz, Ciaran Driver, Steve Early, Jim Elliott, Dieter Ernst, Jan Fagerberg, Kaidong Feng, Tom Ferguson, Lou Ferleger, Patrick Fridenson, James Galbraith, Teresa Ghilarducci, Debbie Goldman, Margaret Graham, Leslie Hannah, Susan Helper, Ronil Hira, Ha

Hoang, Ken Jacobson, Martin Kenney, Bruce Kogut, Jackie Krafft, Sarah Kuhn, Kenji Kushida, Helena Lastres, Feng Lu, Robin Mansell, Stephen Marglin, Bill Mass, John Mathews, Mariana Mazzucato, Lars Mjøset, David Mowery, David Musson, Wim Naudé, Mario Pianta, Andrea Prencipe, Mike Prokosch, Dan Raff, Ravi Ramamurti, S.L. Rao, Petri Rouvinen, Mari Sako, Catherine Sauviat, Claude Serfati, Stefano Solari, Ed Steinmueller, Tim Sturgeon, Jomo Kwame Sundaram, Christian Weller, Chip White, Steven White, Cynthia Williams, Peer Zumbansen, and John Zysman. Among the research assistants who contributed to this book, Bob Bell, He Gao, Mustafa Erdem Sakinc, Oner Tulum, Hao Xie, and Yue Zhang have themselves become collaborators in my ongoing research projects. I would also like to thank Isa Cann, Tim Harrigan, Ben Hopkins, Sarah Johnson, Léah Lazonick, Mindy Lu, Paulsen Mrina, Dimitra Paparounas, and Susan Roe for their research assistance.

My daughters, Ashley, Léah, and Casey, heard me say all too often that the book was almost done. Now that it actually is finished, I want them to know how much their interest in their dad's work means to me. The person who heard me talk about this book-in-progress more than any other was Carol Oja, a brilliant musicologist and incredible human being, whose pertinent questions and insights helped me to clarify my arguments in my mind and on the written page. Finally, I would like to dedicate this book to the memory of my parents, Louis Lazonick (1914–1995) and Pearl Lazonick (1917–2005). Coming of age as they did in the Great Depression, they understood the importance of achieving stable and equitable economic growth.

1

What is New, and Permanent, about the "New Economy"?

THE END OF "THE ORGANIZATION MAN"

The Internet boom of the last half of the 1990s seemed to herald the arrival of a "New Economy" with its promise that, after the stagnation of the early 1990s, innovation in information and communication technologies (ICT) would regenerate economic prosperity. The sharp economic downturn in 2001–2002 called into question the New Economy's ability to deliver on this promise—and it even raised questions about whether there had really been anything "new" about the economy of the late 1990s after all. Perhaps the journalist John Cassidy (2002) was correct to title his book on the Internet boom *Dot.con: The Greatest Story Ever Sold*. If the New Economy was all smoke and mirrors, one would expect that, once the debris left behind by the storm of speculation and corruption had been cleared away, economic life would return to what it had been before the boom took place.

It is now clear that there was plenty of e-con in the New Economy. At the same time, however, there was something new, important, and permanent about the New Economy that transformed the economic lives of many from those they had led before. The core of that something new, important, and permanent is what I call the "New Economy business model" (NEBM), a mode of organizing business enterprises that has dramatically changed the ways in which, and terms on which, people in the United States are employed and, indeed, the way in which the U.S. economy operates.

NEBM emanated from Silicon Valley and spread to other regions of the United States. NEBM also affected employment relations in other areas of the world, especially Europe and Asia, as U.S.-based ICT companies extended their global reach and as high-tech companies based outside the United States sought to adopt elements of the new business model. With well-educated high-tech labor flowing into the United

States from abroad (especially from India and China) and with U.S.-based ICT companies offshoring various types of business activities to other countries (again especially to India and China), the ICT labor force had become vastly more globalized by the 2000s than it had been prior to the Internet revolution.

Although the Internet boom of the late 1990s made the New Economy a household phrase, the end of the boom did not result in the demise of NEBM. To the contrary, its characteristic features have become more widespread and entrenched in U.S. high-tech industries in the 2000s. With its start-up firms, vertical specialists, venture capital, and highly mobile labor, NEBM is a business model that remains dominant in the United States, and it is one that many national policymakers and corporate executives around the world seek to emulate.

At the same time, within the United States, it is a business model that has been associated with volatile stock markets, unequal incomes, and unstable employment, including the insecurity associated with the offshoring of high-skill jobs. If we define "sustainable prosperity" as a state of economic affairs in which growth results in stable employment and an equitable distribution of income, then U.S. economic prosperity would appear to be unsustainable. There is a need to understand the organizational and industrial dynamics of NEBM to determine how the tapping of its innovative capability might be rendered compatible with more socially desirable outcomes.

The "Old Economy business model" (OEBM) that dominated the U.S. corporate economy in the decades after World War II and into the 1980s offered employment that was far more stable and earnings that were far more equitable than employment and earnings in the NEBM era. The sociological foundation of OEBM was "the organization man." Popularized in the United States in the 1950s (Whyte 1956), the stereotypical organization man was a white, Anglo-Saxon, Protestant male who had obtained a college education right after high school, secured a well-paying job with an established company early in his career, and then worked his way up and around the corporate hierarchy over three or four decades of employment, with a substantial defined-benefit pension, complemented by highly subsidized medical coverage, awaiting him on retirement.[1] The employment stability offered by an established corporation was highly valued, while interfirm labor mobility was shunned.

The organization man could trace his origins back to the early decades of the twentieth century, and in the immediate post–World War II decades he was ubiquitous in the offices of U.S. corporate enterprises. Somewhat ironically, when formidable Japanese competitors confronted U.S.-based Old Economy companies in the 1980s, many U.S. observers of Japan's "lifetime employment" system viewed it as a mode of organization that was quite alien to the American way of life. During the first half of twentieth century, however, U.S. corporations had transformed the salaried professional, technical, and administrative employees who peopled the managerial structure into organization men. By the 1950s and 1960s, moreover, even unionized production workers, ostensibly paid on an "hourly" rather than salaried basis, found that collective bargaining protected their positions of seniority, so that they too experienced, and in a growing economy came to expect, lifetime employment as well as defined-benefit pensions and comprehensive health benefits, just like the salaried managers of the companies for which they worked.

From this historical perspective, NEBM can best be described as "the end of the organization man." It is not that New Economy companies have ceased to build complex and durable organizations. To attain and sustain competitive advantage, companies such as Intel, Microsoft, and Cisco—the blue-chip enterprises of the New Economy—need to integrate the labor services of tens of thousands of individuals who participate in complex hierarchical and functional divisions of labor. In an innovative enterprise, the role of an integrated division of labor is to develop and utilize new technologies. Indeed, one might argue that, given heightened technological complexity and intensified market competition in the ICT world of "open systems," the building of unique organizational capabilities has become more, not less, critical to the success of the enterprise (Lazonick 2008a).

Nor is it necessarily the case that employees who spend their entire careers with one company have become an endangered species. The leading industrial corporations still have low levels of employee turnover. Rather, what is new is the lack of a *commitment*, explicit or implicit, on the part of U.S. high-tech companies to provide their employees with stable employment, skill formation, and rewarding careers. When an employee begins to work for a company in the New Economy, he or she has no expectation of a career with that particular enterprise.

Nor does a person with high-tech capabilities necessarily want to work for one company for years and decades on end. Interfirm labor mobility can bring benefits to an employee, including working for a smaller company, choice of geographical location, a significant increase in salary, access to employee stock options, and new learning experiences. The NEBM represents dramatically diminished organizational commitment on both sides of the employment relation as compared with its Old Economy predecessor.

A corollary of this diminution in organizational commitment under NEBM has been an increased globalization of the types of labor that U.S.-based ICT firms employ. This globalization of labor has occurred through the offshoring of high-tech work and the international mobility of high-tech labor, neither of which is a new phenomenon, but both of which have intensified over the past decade or so. The employment relations of major U.S.-based ICT companies have become thoroughly globalized, based on corporate strategies that benefit from not only lower wages but also the enhancement of ICT skill levels in non-U.S. locations, especially in Asia.

While the extent of these impacts of NEBM on high-tech employment has become evident only since the last half of the 1990s, NEBM itself has taken a half-century to unfold. Indeed, its origins can be found in the mid-1950s, at precisely the time when the Old Economy industrial corporation was at the pinnacle of its power. The evolution of NEBM was integral to the microelectronics revolution. The development of computer chips since the late 1950s provided the technological foundation for the microcomputer revolution beginning in the late 1970s, which in turn created the technological infrastructure for the commercialization of the Internet in the 1990s. Although the U.S. government and the research laboratories of established Old Economy corporations played major, and indeed indispensable, roles in supporting these developments, each wave of innovation generated opportunities for the emergence of start-up companies that were to become central to the commercialization of the new technologies.

The regional concentration of these new ventures in what would become known by the beginning of the 1970s as Silicon Valley reinforced the emergence of a distinctive business model. From the late 1960s, venture capitalists backed so many high-tech start-ups in the vicinity of Stanford University that they created a whole new industry for fostering the growth of young technology firms. These start-ups lured "talent" from established companies by offering them compensation in the form of stock options, typically as a partial substitute for salaries, with the potential payoff being the high market value of the stock after an initial public offering (IPO) or the private sale of the young firm to an established corporation.

As these young companies grew, annual grants of stock options to a broad base of potentially highly mobile people became an important tool for retaining existing employees as well as attracting new ones. The subsequent growth of these companies occurred, moreover, not only by investing more capital in new facilities and hiring more people but also by acquiring even newer high-tech companies, almost invariably using their own stock rather than cash as the acquisition currency. In addition, wherever and whenever possible, ICT companies were system integrators that designed, tested, and marketed final products, while outsourcing the manufacture of components so that they could focus on higher value-added work. This outsourcing strategy became both more economical and more efficient over time as specialized contract manufacturers developed their capabilities, including their global organizations and highly automated production processes, for a larger extent of the market.

These features of the new ICT business model were already evident to industry observers in the late 1980s. It was only in the Internet boom of the last half of the 1990s, however, that this business model had a sufficient impact on new firm formation, product market competition, interfirm labor mobility, and productivity to give popular definition to a New Economy. In this book, I document the evolution of NEBM over the past half-century as a foundation for understanding the origins of the globalization of high-tech employment in the 2000s and its implications for high-tech employment opportunities in the United States.

NEBM has definitively replaced OEBM as the dominant mode of business organization in the ICT industries of the United States. NEBM has been, and continues to be, an important engine of innovation in the U.S. economy, and hence an important source of economic growth. The performance of an economy, however, is not measured by growth alone. Economists give high marks to an economy that not only generates growth but does so in a way that provides stable employment and an equitable income distribution—what I call "sustainable prosperity."

Yet over the past decade or so, NEBM has been an engine of innovation that, as I show in this book, has contributed to instability and inequity. ICT continues to help make the United States the richest economy in the world, in terms of both absolute and per capita income. The increased dominance of NEBM in the organization of the ICT industries, however, has meant increasingly insecure employment and incomes for most workers in this sector, and it has become an important factor in the trend toward greater employment instability and income inequality in the U.S. economy as a whole.

Following the Internet boom and bust, what has been particularly novel about the employment situation of the 2000s thus far is the extent to which this insecurity has afflicted highly educated and experienced members of the U.S. ICT labor force, as their former employers prefer to hire younger high-tech workers in the United States. At the same time, companies are also offshoring to lower-wage locations the types of high-skill jobs that Americans had thought could never be done abroad. In terms of their education and qualifications, the U.S. high-tech workers who suffer employment insecurity under NEBM are the types of people who in another era would have been the prototypical organization men, although they are no longer so uniformly white, Anglo-Saxon, Protestant, or male, as the organization men of the 1950s were apt to be. The public outcry against the "export of American jobs" in this first decade of the twenty-first century in effect laments the demise of the organization man.

In this book I explain the origins of this new era of employment insecurity and income inequality, and I consider what governments, businesses, and individuals can do about it. I ask whether the United States can refashion its high-tech business model to generate stable and equitable economic growth. Across the globe, government policymakers and corporate executives generally view the U.S. business model, with its innovative power, as one that, if only it could be implemented in their own nations and regions, would make their countries and communities big and strong. If the U.S. economy, including the business model that dominates the way in which it allocates resources, is to serve as an exemplar for the rest of the world, it is incumbent upon those of us who analyze its operation and seek to influence its performance to understand why it is failing to contribute to stable and equitable economic growth in the United States and what can be done to improve this record.

This book represents a step in my own quest to understand the institutional and organizational conditions under which an advanced economy—not only the U.S. economy—can achieve sustainable prosperity. Analogously, although I focus on the origins, operation, and impact of the dominant ICT industries, my interest is not in the operation and performance of the ICT sector per se. Rather, I have studied the ICT industries closely because they have been at the core of the innovative capability of the U.S. economy over much of the past century, especially over the past few decades. In order to grow, the economy needs innovation, which I define in economic terms as the generation of higher-quality, lower-cost goods and services than were previously available at prevailing factor prices. Innovation does not, however, necessarily result in sustainable prosperity. In this book I ask what types of national institutions and business organizations support the innovation process, and what are the implications of this national innovation system for employment stability and income equality in the economy as a whole.

INNOVATION AND GROWTH IN THE U.S. ECONOMY

The United States is the world's largest economy, with a gross domestic product (GDP) per capita that surpasses those of all other developed nations. Table 1.1 shows the growth of real GDP per capita from 1950 to 2006 (in 1990 international dollars) in the United States and other large advanced economies, some smaller advanced economies, and some of the most rapidly growing developing economies. These data show varying rates of change in GDP per capita, which suggests that the nation still matters as a unit of analysis for economic growth even in a globalized era (Lazonick 2007a).

The most dramatic success story of the last half of the twentieth century is that of Japan, which emerged from a state of devastation after World War II to become, in terms of total GDP, the second largest advanced economy by 1970 (see Maddison 2007). Japan became rich by transferring technology from abroad, primarily from the United States, and then developing and utilizing that technology to generate

Table 1.1 Real GDP per Capita in Selected Nations Compared with the United States, 1950–2006

	Real GDP[a]						
	1950	1960	1970	1980	1990	2000	2006
United States	$9,561	$11,328	$15,030	$18,577	$23,201	$28,403	$30,983
United States (298.4)[b]	100	100	100	100	100	100	100
Japan (127.5)	20	35	65	72	81	73	73
Canada (33.1)	76	77	80	87	81	79	80
France (61.7)	55	67	78	81	78	74	72
Germany (82.7)	41	68	72	76	69	67	65
Italy (58.1)	37	52	65	71	70	66	63
United Kingdom (60.6)	73	76	72	70	71	71	74
Finland (5.2)	44	55	64	70	73	70	75
Netherlands (16.5)	63	73	80	79	74	78	75
Norway (4.6)	57	64	67	81	80	88	90
Sweden (9.0)	70	77	85	80	76	72	77
Switzerland (7.5)	95	110	112	101	93	79	76
South Korea (48.8)	9	11	14	22	38	50	58
Taiwan (23.0)	10	13	20	32	43	60	64
China (1,310.8)	5	6	5	6	8	12	21
India (1,095.4)	6	7	6	5	6	7	8

a 1990 International Geary-Khamis dollars.
b 2006 population (in millions) in parentheses; United States = 100, for any year.
SOURCE: Maddison (2007); Conference Board (2008).

higher-quality, lower-cost products than the United States was capable of producing. What is remarkable about Japan's success is that, through innovation, it ultimately gained competitive advantage over the United States in the 1970s and 1980s in industries (such as mass-produced automobiles, consumer electronics, machine tools, steel, and semiconductors) in which the United States had reigned supreme in the 1950s and 1960s. Although low wages and long work hours (along with the oil crisis and the consequent demand for small, fuel-efficient cars) helped Japan capture U.S. markets in the 1970s, the proof that Japan had developed a highly innovative economy was its ability to extend its competitive advantage in the late 1970s and 1980s even as its wage rates rose substantially (as reflected in the GDP per capita figures in Table 1.1). Indeed, in the mid-1990s, the Japanese even began to work fewer hours per year on average than Americans (International Labour Organization 1999).

Since the 1980s, the Japanese challenge to U.S. dominance in high-technology and capital-intensive industries has been repeated by a number of other Asian economies, most notably South Korea, Taiwan, and China. In labor-intensive information-technology services, India has become a formidable competitor over the past decade as well. Critical to the development of these economies has been not only the transfer of technology from the United States but also, to an extent that was never the case for Japan, the development of the productive capabilities of nationals through graduate education and work experience in the United States—a phenomenon that I explore in considerable depth in this book.

While many of the Asian economies have been catching up, the United States remains a highly innovative economy in the 2000s. Real GDP per capita grew by an annual average of 3.04 percent in the 1960s, 2.18 percent in the 1970s, 2.10 percent in the 1980s, 1.86 percent in the 1990s, and 1.49 percent in the 2000s. Whatever problems there may be with the U.S. economy in the 2000s, they are not problems that, averaged over the whole population, result from a lack of productive power. At the same time, the United States has experienced a long-term trend toward a slower rate of increase in real GDP per capita alongside growing international competition from nations such as China and India that have developed enormous innovative capabilities but still have far lower wages than those that prevail in the United States. These changes may exacerbate tendencies to instability and inequity in the U.S. economy, thus making sustainable prosperity more difficult to attain.

Instability

From 1930 through 1941, the U.S. unemployment rate averaged about 17.4 percent, ranging from 8.9 percent in 1930 to 25.2 percent in 1933 (U.S. Bureau of the Census 1976, p. 126). It took the United States' entry into World War II to get the nation out of the Great Depression. After the war, Congress passed the Employment Act of 1946, which placed the federal government under obligation to pursue economic policies to secure conditions of full employment for American citizens. Since then, the civilian unemployment rate has not reached double digits, although it went as high as 9.7 percent in 1982 and 9.6 percent in 1983. As shown in Figure 1.1, the unemployment rate averaged 4.5 percent in the 1950s, 4.8 percent in the 1960s, 6.2 percent in 1970s, 7.3 percent in the 1980s, 5.6 percent in the 1990s, and 5.0 percent in the 2000s (through 2007).

Although government intervention has apparently eradicated the possibility of another Great Depression, the rate at which Americans can find employment is still far from stable over time, both within and across decades, as shown in Figure 1.1. Blacks and Hispanics experience much higher unemployment rates than whites, and in 1983 the black unemployment rate was at a Depression-level 19.5 percent. Moreover, as can also be seen in Figure 1.1, married men with spouses present, who as a group have among the lowest unemployment rates, also experience substantial fluctuations over time in the rate at which they are employed.

In the era of the organization man, lengthy tenure with one company became the foundation of employment security in the United States. In a recent survey of changes in job security, Henry Farber (2008, p. 1) stated that "there is ample evidence that long-term employment [with one company] is on the decline in the United States." Using Current Population Survey data for 1973–2006, Farber (p. 27) showed that, in the 1990s and 2000s, members of the U.S. labor force experienced shortened job tenure, with the impact being most pronounced for males. Moreover, education and experience are no longer the guarantors of employment security that they once were. Using Displaced Worker Sur-

Figure 1.1 U.S. Unemployment Rates, Percent of the Relevant Labor Force, 1947–2007

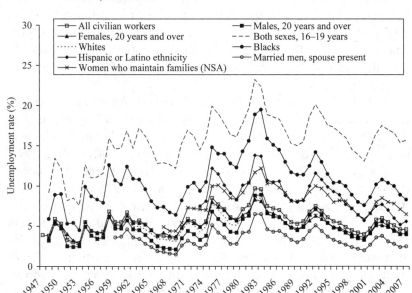

NOTE: Until 1972 the black unemployment rate included other races. NSA means not seasonally adjusted. The average annual unemployment rates for the U.S. civilian labor force were as follows: 1950s, 4.5 percent; 1960s, 4.8 percent; 1970s, 6.2 percent; 1980s, 7.3 percent; 1990s, 5.8 percent; 2000–2007, 5.0 percent.
SOURCE: U.S. Congress (2009, table B-42); U.S. Bureau of the Census (1976, p. 135).

vey data to analyze rates of job loss, Farber (p. 35) found that those with college educations had job loss rates 22 percent lower than those with high school educations in the 1980s, but only 12 percent lower in the 2000s. He also found that workers aged 45–54 had job loss rates 19 percent higher than workers aged 20–24 in the 1980s, whereas the job loss rates of the older age group were 58 percent higher than those of the younger age group in the 2000s.

If employment incomes have become more unstable over the course of one's career, so too have the financial returns on accumulated wealth. Large numbers of Americans have substantial wealth invested in the stock market, not only in direct holdings but also indirectly through their investments in mutual funds, pensions, and insurance policies.

In 1999 holdings of corporate equities in the U.S. economy were at a record 211 percent of GDP, about 3.5 times the percentage in 1990, and holdings of corporate equities per capita were at a peak of $86,994 in 2007 dollars (Board of Governors of the Federal Reserve System 2008, table L213). In 2007, holdings of corporate equities per capita were 41 percent higher in real terms than they had been in 1996, at the onset of the Internet boom.

In 1945 households directly held 93 percent of the value of corporate equities in the U.S. economy; by 2007 it was only 25 percent. Nevertheless, in 2007, on a per capita basis, the direct holdings of households in 2007 dollars were more than 88 percent greater than in 1945. Pensions (private and government) held only 6 percent of corporate equities in 1965, but they held 28 percent in 1985. Although this share stood at 23 percent in 2007, a steadily increasing proportion of savings has poured into mutual funds, which represented only 5 percent of corporate stockholdings in 1985 but 26 percent in 2007. The growth of mutual funds reflected the shift from defined-benefit to defined-contribution pensions and the trend toward the management of defined-contribution pensions through individual retirement accounts (IRAs; see Chapter 4). The mutual fund share of IRA assets grew from 17 percent in 1985 to 49 percent in 1999. In 1999, mutual funds absorbed 30 percent of defined-contribution assets but only 6 percent of defined-benefit assets, and they were heavily invested in equities (Engen and Lehnert 2000, pp. 802–803).

Stock market returns are very unstable, not only from year to year but also from decade to decade, as shown in Table 1.2 (which does not include the negative results for 2008). The extraordinarily high price yields in the 1980s and 1990s lured Americans into thinking that investments in the stock market could give them long-run financial security. High price yields may reflect real productivity gains made by innovative enterprises (as was indeed partly the case in those decades), but they may also reflect a high volume of speculative stock trading that imparts instability to the stock market. Furthermore, when innovation and speculation do not sustain increases in stock prices, corporate executives, encouraged by Wall Street, may seek to do so through manipulation. Hence, as I show in Chapter 6, with stock markets sluggish in the 2000s, U.S. companies, including leading high-tech enterprises, have turned to large-scale stock repurchases to boost their stock prices, thus

Table 1.2 Average Annual U.S. Corporate Stock and Bond Yields (%), 1960–2007

	1960–69	1970–79	1980–89	1990–99	2000–07
Real stock yield	6.63	−1.66	11.67	15.01	0.96
Price yield	5.80	1.35	12.91	15.54	2.09
Dividend yield	3.19	4.08	4.32	2.47	1.64
Change in CPI[a]	2.36	7.09	5.55	3.00	2.78
Real bond yield	2.65	1.14	5.79	4.72	3.34

NOTE: Stock yields are for Standard and Poor's composite index of 500 U.S. corporate stocks. Bond yields are for Moody's AAA-rated U.S. corporate bonds.
[a] Consumer price index.
SOURCE: Updated from Lazonick and O'Sullivan (2000a) using U.S. Congress (2009, tables B-62, B-3, B-95, and B-96).

redistributing income to shareholders from other stakeholders in the corporate economy. Yet I shall argue that, even for shareholders, stock-price appreciation based on stock repurchases is not sustainable over the long run.[2]

Inequity

A key characteristic of OEBM was the separation of asset owner-ship from managerial control over the allocation of corporate resources (Lazonick 1990, 1991). The salaries of those at the top of the corporate hierarchy were regulated much less by an external labor market for top executives than by the internal salary structure of the managerial orga-nizations over which they presided. Managerial personnel, who gener-ally had college educations, could look forward to promotion within the company over the course of their careers. When they retired, they would receive a guaranteed stream of income from a defined-benefit pension plan that rewarded years of service. Clerical and production workers, who generally had high school educations, could also look forward to spending their whole working lives with the same company, notwithstanding the fact that they were deemed to be "hourly" rather than "salaried" employees.

Research on the distribution of income in the United States has shown that there was a movement toward more equality in the immedi-ate post–World War II decades that came to a halt in the mid-1970s. A marked trend to more income inequality started with the recessionary years of the early 1980s and has continued to the present (see Autor, Katz, and Kearney 2008; Bradbury 1996; Danziger and Gottschalk 1995; Goldin and Katz 2008; Jones and Weinberg 2000; Levy and Murnane 1992; Moss 2002; Piketty and Saez 2003, 2006; Pryor 2007; Saez 2005). These movements can be seen in Figure 1.2, which charts the Gini coefficient for households from 1947 to 2007. The Gini coefficient is a measure of the amount of income inequality. The higher the Gini coefficient, the greater the extent of income inequality across households—the coefficient would be 0.0 if all households had the same income and 1.0 if one family had all the income and the remaining families had no income. An improvement in income equality is discernible until the mid-1970s, after which it became much worse.

A worsening in the distribution of income among households after the mid-1970s is also evident in Figure 1.3, which shows that the household income ratios of various higher to lower percentiles in the U.S. household income distribution have all trended upwards, with the

Figure 1.2 Gini Coefficient for All U.S. Families, 1947–2007

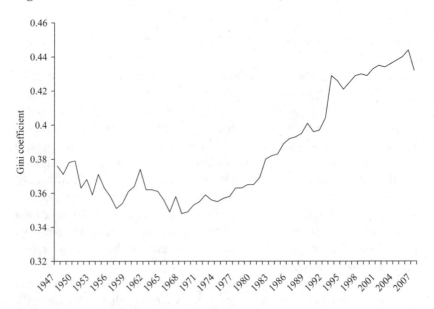

SOURCE: Table F-4 in U.S. Census Bureau (2009).

**Figure 1.3 Changes in the Relative Incomes of Selected Income
Percentiles in the U.S. Distribution of Income, 1967–2007**

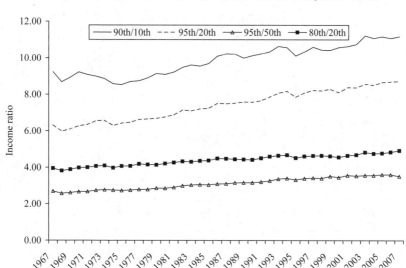

SOURCE: DeNavas-Walt, Proctor, and Smith (2008).

most marked upward trend occurring among the more extreme ratios
(90th/10th and 95th/20th). Figure 1.4, based on data collected by Piketty
and Saez (2006), shows that the top 1 percent of the income distribution gained a dramatically larger share of total income since 1985. The
next 4 percent (top 2–5 percent in Figure 1.4) have also increased their
share since the early 1980s. In 2004, 37 percent of all corporate equities
were held by the wealthiest 1 percent of households and 80 percent by
the top 20 percent in the wealth distribution (Allegretto 2006). And, as
we shall see, many if not most of the ongoing increases in top executive
pay have come from stock options as a mode of remuneration. If the
increased reliance of households, governments, and corporations on the
stock market has made the U.S. economy more unstable, the distribution of returns from the stock market has made the U.S. economy much
more unequal.

Figure 1.4　Shares of the Top Income Earners of the Total U.S. Income, 1913–2002

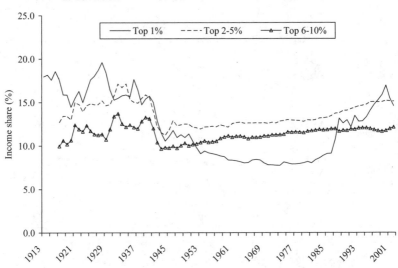

SOURCE: Piketty and Saez (2006, p. 201). Excel file available at http://elsa.berkeley .edu/~saez/ (accessed June 29, 2009).

ICT INDUSTRIES

What is a business model, and how do OEBM and NEBM differ? We can define a business enterprise by the product markets for which it competes and the ways in which it mobilizes capital and labor to compete for those markets (for an elaboration, see Lazonick 2007b). Hence, as shown in Table 1.3, a business model can be characterized by three components: 1) its *strategy*, the types of product markets for which a company competes and the types of production processes through which it generates goods and services for these markets; 2) its *finance*, the ways in which it funds investments in processes and products until they can generate financial returns; and 3) its *organization*, the ways in which it elicits skill and effort from its labor force to add value to these investments.

The evolution of NEBM has been intimately related to the development of the ICT industries in the United States. The U.S. Department

Table 1.3 Old Economy Business Model (OEBM) and New Economy Business Model (NEBM) in ICT Industries

	OEBM	NEBM
Strategy, product	Growth by building on internal capabilities; expansion into new product markets based on related technologies; geographic expansion to access national product markets.	New firm entry into specialized markets; sell branded components to system integrators; accumulate new capabilities by acquiring young technology firms.
Strategy, process	Development and patenting of proprietary technologies; vertical integration of the value chain at home and abroad.	Cross-license technology based on industry standards; vertical specialization of the value chain; outsourcing/offshoring of routine work.
Finance	Venture finance from personal savings, family, and business associates; NYSE listing; pay steady dividends; growth finance from retentions leveraged with bond issues.	Organized venture capital; IPO on NASDAQ; low or no dividends; growth finance from retentions plus stock as an acquisition currency; stock repurchases to support stock price.
Organization	Secure employment: career with one company; salaried and hourly employees; unions; defined-benefit pensions; employer-funded medical insurance in employment and retirement.	Insecure employment: interfirm mobility of labor; broad-based stock options; nonunion; defined-contribution pensions; employee bears greater burden of medical insurance.

of Commerce (2003) has defined ICT industries as those engaged in producing computer hardware, computer software and services, communications equipment, and communications services.[3] According to the department's report *Digital Economy 2003*, the output of ICT industries accounted for about 9 percent of U.S. GDP in 2000 at the peak of the Internet boom and about 8 percent in the early 2000s (Henry and Dalton 2003, p. 16).

Employment in U.S. ICT industries increased by 51.9 percent from 1993 to 2000, compared with a 20.8 percent increase for all business-sector industries. In 2000 these industries employed a total of 5.38 million people, representing 4.8 percent of employment by all U.S. business-sector industries. Although ICT employment declined by 0.6 percent in 2001 and by 10.7 percent in 2002, ICT industries still employed 4.78 million people, or 4.4 percent of employment in the U.S. business sector, in 2002 (Cooke 2003, pp. 21–22). According to Bureau of Economic Analysis (BEA) data, ICT-producing industries, which do not include communications services,[4] employed (in full-time equivalents) 4.68 million people in 2000, representing 4.4 percent of all business-sector employees in the United States, 3.67 million (3.5 percent) in 2003, and 3.76 million (3.5 percent) in 2006 (BEA 2009).

Figures 1.5 and 1.6 show the changes in employment and real wages (in 2000 dollars) in four main ICT industry classifications. As shown in Figure 1.5, employment in each of these four industry classifications increased substantially in the last half of the 1990s and peaked in 2001 with a total employment of 1,658,628, almost 2.4 times the number of employees in 1994. From 2001 to 2003, there was a net loss of just over 320,000 jobs, although more than 140,000 of these jobs were regained by 2006. Real wages in all of these classifications increased in the latter half of the 1990s, and then, for reasons that will be explained in Chapter 2, spiked in 2000—dramatically in the case of semiconductors and software publishing—before falling off sharply with the downturn of 2001 and showing little if any increase through 2006 (Fig. 1.6).

Employees in ICT industries earn, on average, much more than those in most other sectors of the economy. In 2006 the average annual incomes (in current dollars) of U.S. ICT employees were $111,212 in software publishing, $77,915 in semiconductors, $76,462 in custom computer programming services, $73,497 in computer system design services, and $62,620 in data processing, hosting, and related services

Figure 1.5 Employment in Four ICT Industrial Classifications, 1994–2006

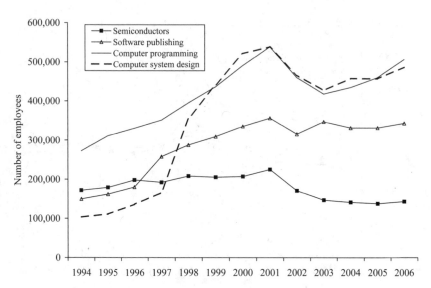

NOTE: SIC classifications for 1994–1997 and NAICS classifications for 1998–2006: Semiconductors and related devices: SIC 3674, NAICS 334413; Software publishing: SIC 7372, NAICS 511210 and 334611; Computer programming services: SIC 7371, NAICS 541511; Computer system design: SIC 7373 plus half of 7379, NAICS 54152.
SOURCE: U.S. Census Bureau (2008a).

(U.S. Census Bureau 2008a).[5] In 2006 a full-time equivalent employee in U.S. ICT-producing industries had 56 percent higher average compensation than a full-time equivalent employee in U.S. business sector goods-producing industries in general (BEA 2009). Following the ICT downturn in 2001–2002 and the "jobless recovery" of 2003–2004, ICT-producing industries had real growth in output of 13.3 percent in 2005 and 12.5 percent in 2006. The value-added of ICT-producing industries was 3.9 percent in 2006, contributing 14.2 percent of real GDP growth in the U.S. economy (Howells and Barefoot 2007).

Although the United States remains the world leader in ICT industries, it nevertheless has been running trade deficits in ICT goods, as shown in Table 1.4. The U.S. Census Bureau categorizes trade in Advanced Technology Products into 10 categories: Biotechnology,

**Figure 1.6 Real Wages (in 2000 dollars) in Four ICT Industrial
Classifications, 1994–2006**

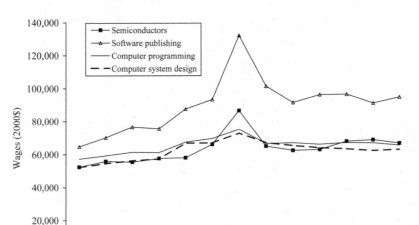

NOTE: See Figure 1.5 for SIC and NAICS classifications.
SOURCE: U.S. Census Bureau (2008a).

Life Science, Opt-Electronics, Information and Technology, Electronics, Flexible Manufacturing, Advanced Materials, Aerospace, Weapons, and Nuclear Technology. Except for Aerospace exports in 2006 and 2007, ICT exports have been greater than every other category of exports since 2002, and ICT imports have been five to seven times greater than the next largest categories, Electronics and Aerospace. A substantial portion of these ICT trade deficits reflect the globalization of investment and employment in ICT value chains, with U.S.-based multinational companies playing leading roles. It cannot, therefore, be assumed that the trade deficit measures a lack of competitiveness of U.S.-based companies in ICT industries.

Indeed, in the first half of the 2000s, U.S. ICT industries remained highly innovative. U.S.-based ICT firms accounted for 26.0 percent of all company-funded research and development (R&D) in the United States in 2000 and 31.2 percent in 2001 (Henry and Dalton 2003, p. 18). At the beginning of 2003, ICT companies employed 40 percent of

Table 1.4 U.S. Exports and Imports of ICT Products, Relative to All Advanced Technology Products (ATP), 2002–2007

	ICT exports ($b)	ICT imports ($b)	ICT trade balance ($b)	ICT as % of ATP exports	ICT as % of ATP imports	ICT as % of U.S. ATP deficit
2002	53.3	100.7	−47.4	29.6	51.8	285.6
2003	53.1	110.1	−57.0	29.5	53.2	212.4
2004	59.3	132.5	−73.2	29.4	55.6	198.7
2005	64.1	147.2	−83.1	29.7	56.7	190.2
2006	69.2	160.8	−91.6	27.4	55.3	240.3
2007	74.8	179.7	−104.9	27.4	55.0	196.2

SOURCE: U.S. Census Bureau (2008b).

the 1,075,500 full-time equivalent research and development (R&D) scientists and engineers in the U.S. business sector (National Science Foundation 2003). Table 1.5 shows R&D expenditures of the U.S. ICT companies that were among the top 100 globally in R&D spending in 2006.

Firm-level R&D spending is influenced by, among other factors, the technologies that a company develops and the product markets in which it competes. Note, for example, the high levels of R&D as a percent of sales for semiconductor companies such as Intel, Texas Instruments (TI), Qualcomm (the design of integrated circuits for code division multiple access [CDMA] wireless devices that the company pioneered represents a major part of its business), Advanced Micro Devices (AMD), and Broadcom. IBM and Hewlett-Packard (HP), the two largest ICT companies by total sales revenues, had by far the lowest levels of R&D as a percentage of sales and R&D dollars spent per employee. As we will see in Chapter 3, the limited extent to which IBM and HP allocate resources to R&D in the 2000s is the direct result of their transformations from OEBM to NEBM.

Whether they are U.S.-based or foreign, ICT companies are the leading patenters in the United States. IBM has been the top patenter every year since 1993, with Canon being either second or third. In 2007 IBM (USA) had 3,148 U.S. patents, Samsung (South Korea) 2,725, Canon (Japan) 1,987, Matsushita (Japan) 1,941, Intel (USA) 1,865, Microsoft (USA) 1,637, Toshiba (Japan) 1,549, Sony (Japan) 1,481, Micron Technology (USA) 1,476, and HP (USA) 1,470. Of these top

Table 1.5 U.S. ICT Companies among the Global Top 100 R&D Spenders, 2005 and 2006

ICT Company	Global rank		R&D expenditures ($m)		R&D as % of sales		R&D expenditures per employee ($000s)	
	2006	2005	2006	2005	2006	2005	2006	2005
Microsoft	5	7	7,121	6,584	13.9	14.9	90	93
Intel	12	14	5,873	5,145	16.6	13.3	62	52
IBM	14	11	5,682	5,378	6.2	5.9	16	16
Motorola	22	24	4,106	3,680	9.6	10.0	62	53
Cisco Systems	23	30	4,067	3,322	14.3	13.4	81	86
Hewlett-Packard	28	26	3,561	3,490	3.9	4.0	23	23
Oracle	48	55	2,195	1,872	12.2	13.0	29	33
Texas Instruments	50	51	2,190	2,015	15.4	15.1	71	57
Sun Microsystems	56	49	2,008	2,046	14.5	15.7	53	54
Qualcomm	66	89	1,516	1,011	20.1	17.8	135	109
EMC	77	90	1,254	1,005	11.2	10.4	40	38
Google	79	119	1,218	578	11.5	9.4	114	102
Advanced Micro Devices	80	77	1,205	1,144	21.3	19.6	73	116
Applied Materials	86	95	1,138	941	12.4	13.5	81	73
Broadcom	89	115	1,117	681	30.5	25.5	213	159
Electronic Arts	95	108	1,041	758	33.7	25.7	132	105

NOTE: Microsoft, Oracle, Sun Microsystems, and Electronic Arts all have fiscal years that end in the first half of the year. For these companies the data for 2006 are for the fiscal year ended in the first half of 2007 and the data for 2005 are for the fiscal year ended in the first half of 2006. In 2005 Freescale Semiconductor was ranked 74th and Lucent Technologies 75th among global R&D spenders. R&D expenditures as a percentage of sales were 20.3 percent at Freescale and 12.5 percent at Lucent. R&D expenditures per employee were $52,000 at Freescale and $39,000 at Lucent. In December 2006 Freescale was taken private and Lucent was acquired by Alcatel; hence comparable data for these companies for 2006 are not available.

SOURCE: Hira and Ross (2007).

10 patenters, Matsushita, Samsung, and Sony are partially in ICT, and the other seven, including the five U.S.-based companies, are primarily or wholly in ICT. Other U.S.-based ICT companies that were among the top 35 patenters in 2007 were TI (seventeenth with 752 patents), Sun Microsystems (twenty-sixth, 610), Cisco Systems (twenty-seventh, 582), Broadcom (thirty-first, 533), and Xerox (thirty-third, 517) (IFI Patent Intelligence 2008).

ICT products contribute to productivity throughout the U.S. economy. In a review of the book *Manufacturing Matters,* by Cohen and Zysman (1987), Robert Solow (1987) observed that, despite the authors' central belief that computerized manufacturing would produce a break with past patterns of productivity growth, how effectively U.S. industry would make use of computer automation remained an open question. Solow went on to remark that Cohen and Zysman, "like everyone else, are somewhat embarrassed by the fact that what everyone feels to have been a technological revolution, a drastic change in our productive lives, has been accompanied everywhere, including Japan, by a slowing-down of productivity growth, not by a step up." Solow then quipped, now rather famously: "You can see the computer age everywhere but in the productivity statistics."

Ultimately, however, the failure of the expansion of investment in and access to computers to result in productivity growth in the 1980s and early 1990s was replaced with an explosion of ICT-related productivity growth in the late 1990s and 2000s (Baily and Sichel 2003; Brynjolfsson and Hitt 2003; Gordon 2003; Jorgenson 2001; Oliner and Sichel 2002; Roach 2003). Why did it take so long for the "computer age" to make its mark on productivity growth?

The key to answering this question is the recognition that productivity depends on the *development* and *utilization* of technology. The development of technology in and of itself does not generate productivity. Indeed, the development of technology lowers productivity because it absorbs inputs into economic activity without generating valued outputs. An individual, enterprise, region, or nation that develops technology realizes productivity over time only when it actually utilizes that technology to sell products and generate revenues. In effect, through the utilization of technology, the high fixed costs of the development of technology can be transformed into low unit costs (see Lazonick 1991, 2006, 2008b). Developmental costs, which are included in the economist's conception of fixed costs, depend on both the size of the investment in productive resources that is made at a point in time and the duration of time over which the productive capability of those resources must be developed before they can generate financial returns.

It is for this reason that it is often necessary for a government to make developmental investments in physical infrastructure and a knowledge base in order to induce business enterprises (which by definition must generate profits to survive) to enter an industry that is based on new technology. The U.S. government played a fundamental role in funding the computer revolution. Without the backing of the developmental state, the microelectronics revolution would not have occurred (Braun and MacDonald 1982; Flamm 1987, 1988; Lécuyer 2006; Leslie 1993a,b; Mowery and Langlois 1996; National Research Council 1999; Tilton 1971).[6]

As they developed, the ICT industries created a demand for education and research in science and engineering, with externalities for other sectors of the economy in terms of access to advanced research and educated labor (e.g., Lenoir et al. 2003). The evolution in the 1960s of what would become known as Silicon Valley also created a demand for venture capital that, as I elaborate on in Chapter 2, had emerged by the early 1970s as an industry in its own right that was devoted to new firm formation.

The NEBM that was put in place in Silicon Valley in the 1970s and 1980s also depended on the investment decisions and productive resources of Old Economy companies, the most important of which was IBM. The world's leading computer company from the 1950s, IBM's development of the personal computer in the early 1980s based on an Intel microprocessor and a Microsoft operating system was the most important impetus to the emergence and consolidation of the vertically specialized industrial structure that came to characterize NEBM.

Even in the 1980s, when to a large extent (to paraphrase Solow), computers were everywhere but productivity nowhere, the two parts of ICT developed separately, with computer production and voice transmission having virtually nothing to do with each other as industries. It was only with the introduction of data communications based on packet switching that the information and communication technology industries came together, initially in the second half of the 1980s in the form of local area networks and then in the first half of the 1990s in the form of the Internet. Concomitantly, the wireless communications revolution was taking place, with "3G" (third-generation) convergence with information technology via the Internet in the 2000s. The contribution of the ICT industries to productivity growth from the mid-1990s on and the subsequent dominance of NEBM over OEBM in the ICT industries were part and parcel of the integration of information and communication technologies in the form of the Internet, giving meaning to the letters ICT.

THE TOP 20 OLD ECONOMY AND NEW ECONOMY COMPANIES

In 2005 there were 53 companies in the U.S. Fortune 500 that could be classified as ICT.[7] Combined, these 53 companies had $909 billion in revenues and 2.6 million employees. Of these 53 companies, 26, with $332 billion in revenues and 871,000 employees, could be defined as New Economy. Tables 1.6 and 1.7 list the top 20 Old Economy and top 20 New Economy ICT companies, respectively, by 2005 revenues and the number of people these companies had employed over the previous decade. For inclusion in Table 1.7 as New Economy, a company had to fulfill three criteria: 1) have been founded in 1957 or later, 2) not have been established by the spin-off of an existing division from an Old Economy company, and 3) not have grown through acquisition of, or merger with, an Old Economy company (as was the case for Electronic Data Systems, Comcast, and IAC, which are included as Old Economy companies).

I have chosen 1957 as the earliest date for inclusion in the New Economy list because that was the year that eight scientists and engineers left Shockley Semiconductor Laboratories in Palo Alto, California—itself founded just two years before—to launch Fairchild Semiconductor in nearby Mountain View. Fairchild Semiconductor was a division of Fairchild Camera and Instrument, based in Long Island, New York. As is well known, the creation of Fairchild Semiconductor sparked a chain reaction that resulted in the emergence of Silicon Valley as a center for the development of microelectronics (Berlin 2005; Kenney 2000; Lécuyer 2006; Lee et al. 2000; Lenoir et al. 2003). As I will show in Chapter

2, it was first and foremost in Silicon Valley, beginning in the late 1950s, that NEBM emerged as a viable, and ultimately dominant, business model. Note that 14 of the 20 New Economy companies listed in Table 1.7 are based in California, and 11 of those are in Silicon Valley.

Headed by the giants IBM and HP, six of the Old Economy companies in Table 1.6, including Xerox, Electronic Data Systems (EDS), First Data, and NCR, are strictly information technology companies.[8] The two semiconductor companies, TI and Freescale Semiconductor, supply chips to both the information technology and communication technology sectors of ICT but with an emphasis on communications applications. TI's major business is designing digital signal processing chips for the cell-phone industry, whereas Freescale is a 2004 spinoff of the wireless communications technology company Motorola. Along with Motorola in the communications equipment segment of ICT is Lucent Technologies, which was spun off from AT&T Corp. in 1996 and was merged with the French telecommunications equipment company Alcatel to become Alcatel-Lucent in 2006.[9]

The remaining 10 companies in Table 1.6 are communications service providers. Five of them are direct descendents of the old Bell System that, until its breakup on January 1, 1984, functioned as a regulated monopoly in the provision of local and long distance telephone services. AT&T, the parent company within the Bell System, included regional operating companies throughout the United States. AT&T's wholly owned subsidiary, Western Electric, manufactured equipment for the Bell System, while Bell Labs, the world famous research organization jointly owned by AT&T and Western Electric, engaged in basic and applied scientific research. The breakup of the Bell System separated seven regional Bell operating companies (RBOCs) from AT&T Corp., which now included Western Electric and Bell Labs within its internal organization as its AT&T Technologies division. The seven RBOCS were Ameritech, Bell Atlantic, BellSouth, NYNEX, Pacific Telesis (PacTel), Southwestern Bell Corp. (SBC), and US West. Subsequently Bell Atlantic and NYNEX were merged into Verizon; Ameritech, Pacific Telesis, and AT&T Corp. into SBC, which in 2005 changed its name to AT&T Inc.; and US West into Qwest. In December 2006 AT&T Inc. acquired BellSouth, so that in the 23 years since the breakup of the Bell System, AT&T Corp. and the seven RBOCs had become consolidated into three companies: AT&T Inc., Verizon, and Qwest.[10]

Table 1.6 Employment, 1996 and 2000–2005, at the Top 20 Old Economy Companies by 2005 Sales

Old Economy companies	2005 sales ($b)	Employees							2005 sales/employee
		1996	2000	2001	2002	2003	2004	2005	
International Business Machines (1911; NY; 10)	91.1	240,615	316,309	319,876	315,889	319,273	329,001	329,373	$277,000
Hewlett-Packard (1939; CA; 11)	86.7	112,000	88,500	86,200	141,000	142,000	151,000	150,000	$578,000
Verizon Communications (1885; NY; 18)	75.1	62,600	260,000	247,000	229,500	203,100	210,000	217,000	$346,000
AT&T Inc.[a] (1885; TX; 39)	43.9	61,540	220,090	193,420	175,400	168,950	162,000	189,950	$231,000
Motorola (1928; IL; 54)	36.8	139,000	147,000	111,000	97,000	88,000	68,000	69,000	$533,000
Sprint Nextel[b] (1899; KS; 59)	34.7	48,024	84,100	83,700	72,200	66,900	59,900	79,900	$434,000
Comcast[c] (1963; PA; 194)	22.3	16,400	35,000	38,000	82,000	68,000	74,000	80,000	$279,000
BellSouth (1885; GA; 106)	20.6	81,241	103,900	87,875	77,000	76,000	62,564	63066	$326,000
Electronic Data Systems[d] (1962; TX; 108)	20.5	100,000	122,000	143,000	137,000	132,000	117,000	117,000	$175,000
Xerox (1906; CT; 142)	15.7	86,700	92,500	78,900	67,800	61,100	58,100	55,200	$284,000
Qwest Communications (1885; CO; 160)	13.9	720	67,000	61,000	47,000	47,000	41,401	39,348	$353,000
Texas Instruments (1930; TX; 167)	13.4	59,927	42,481	34,724	34,589	34,154	35,472	35,207	$381,000
DirecTV Group (1932; CA; 168)	13.2	86,000	9,000	13,700	11,600	12,300	11,800	9,200	$1,435,000
First Data (1871; CO; 224)	10.5	40,000	27,000	29,000	29,000	29,000	32,000	33,000	$318,000
Alltel (1943; AR; 251)	9.5	16,307	27,257	23,955	25,348	19,986	18,598	21,373	$444,000
Lucent Technologies (1869; NJ; 255)	9.4	124,000	126,000	77,000	47,000	34,500	31,800	30,500	$308,000

Cox Communications (1898; GA; 273)	9.0	7,200	19,000	20,700	21,600	22,150	22,350	22,530	$399,000
IAC/InterActiveCorp[e] (1977; NY; 313)	7.1	4,750	20,780	16,900	23,200	25,700	26,000	28,000	$254,000
NCR (1884; OH; 357)	6.0	38,600	32,900	31,400	30,100	29,000	28,500	28,200	$213,000
Freescale Semiconductor[f] (1928; TX; 368)	5.8							22,700	$256,000
Averages (per firm, except sales per employee)	27.3	72,808	96,885	89,334	87,621	83,111	81,062	81,027	$391,000

NOTE: In parentheses: year of founding, state in which headquartered, and rank in 2006 Fortune 500 list. Included in the ICT industries are companies that the Fortune 500 2006 list classifies as being in the following industries: Computer Peripherals, Computer Software, Computers, Office Equipment, Financial Data Services, Information Technology Services, Internet Services and Retailing, Network and Other Communications Equipment, Semiconductors and Other Electronic Components, and Telecommunications. Blank = not applicable.

[a] In 2005 SBC Communications, founded in Texas in 1885 and ranked 33rd on the Fortune 500 list, acquired AT&T, founded in 1877 and ranted 56th on the 2005 list. SBC then changed its name to AT&T Inc. Employment figures for 1996 and 2000–2004 are for SBC. AT&T Corp.'s employment figures were: 1996, 130,000; 2000, 166,000; 2001, 117,800; 2002, 71,000; 2003, 61,000; and 2004, 47,565.

[b] In August 2005 Sprint, 65th on the Fortune 500 2005 list, acquired Nextel, founded in 1987 and 157th on the 2005 list.

[c] Comcast began its transformation into the largest Internet cable company in the United States through its acquisition of subscribers from AT&T Broadband in 2000–2001.

[d] General Motors bought Electronic Data Systems in 1984 and spun it off as an independent company in 1996.

[e] In 1998 HSN (formed out of Home Shopping Network) purchased USA Networks, which had been owned by Paramount and MCA. In the early 2000s, the company changed its name, first to USA Interactive and then to IAC/InterActiveCorp.

[f] In late 2004 Motorola spun off its semiconductor division as Freescale Semiconductor.

SOURCE: Fortune (2006); hoovers.com; S&P Compustat database.

Table 1.7 Employment, 1996 and 2000–2005, at the Top 20 New Economy Companies by 2005 Sales

New Economy Companies	2005 sales ($b)	Employees							2005 sales/ employee
		1996	2000	2001	2002	2003	2004	2005	
Dell Computer (1984; TX; 25)	55.9	8,400	36,500	40,000	34,600	39,100	55,200	65,200	$857,000
Microsoft (1975; WA; 48)	39.8	20,561	39,100	47,600	50,500	55,000	57,000	61,000	$652,000
Intel (1968; CA; 49)	38.8	48,500	86,100	83,400	78,700	79,700	85,000	99,900	$388,888
Cisco Systems (1984; CA; 83)	24.8	8,782	34,000	38,000	36,000	34,000	34,000	38,413	$646,000
Computer Sciences (1959; CA; 141)	15.8	33,850	58,000	68,000	67,000	90,000	90,000	79,000	$200,000
Apple Computer (1977; CA; 159)	13.9	10,896	8,568	9,603	10,211	10,912	12,561	15,810	$879,000
Oracle (1977; CA; 196)	11.8	23,111	41,320	42,297	42,006	40,650	41,658	49,872	$236,000
Samina-SCI (1980; CA; 198)	11.7	1,726	24,000	48,774	46,030	45,008	42,115	42,821	$273,000
Sun Microsystems (1982; CA; 211)	11.1	17,400	38,900	43,700	39,400	36,100	32,600	31,000	$358,000
Solectron (1977; CA; 227)	10.5	10,781	65,273	60,000	73,000	66,000	59,500	47,000	$223,000
EMC (1979; MA; 249)	9.7	4,800	24,100	20,100	17,400	20,000	22,700	21,000	$462,000
Amazon.com (1994; WA; 272)	8.5	151	9,000	7,800	7,500	7,800	9,000	12,000	$708,000
EchoStar Communications (1993; CO; 273)	8.4	1,200	11,000	11,000	15,000	15,000	20,000	21,000	$400,000
SAIC (1969; CA; 285)	8.0	20,931	39,078	41,500	40,400	38,700	44,900	43,800	$183,000
Jabil Circuit (1966; FL; 303)	7.5	2,649	19,115	17,097	20,000	26,000	34,000	40,000	$188,000
Applied Materials (1967; CA; 317)	7.0	11,403	19,220	17,365	16,077	12,050	12,960	12,750	$549,000
Google (1998; CA; 353)	6.1					1,628	3,021	5,680	$1,074,000

Advanced Micro Devices (1969; CA; 367)	5.8	12,200	14,696	14,415	12,146	14,300	15,900	15,900	$365,000
Qualcomm (1985; CA; 381)	5.7	6,000	6,300	6,500	8,100	7,400	7,600	9,300	$613,000
Yahoo! (1995; CA; 412)	5.3	155	3,259	3,000	3,600	5,500	7,600	9,800	$541,000
Averages (per firm, except sales per employee)	15.3	12,816	30,396	32,640	32,509	32,242	34,366	36,062	$424,000

NOTE: In parentheses: year of founding, state in which headquartered, and rank in 2006 Fortune 500 list. Included in the ICT industries are companies that the Fortune 500 2006 list classifies as being in the following industries: Computer Peripherals, Computer Software, Computers, Office Equipment, Financial Data Services, Information Technology Services, Internet Services and Retailing, Network and Other Communications Equipment, Semiconductors and Other Electronic Components, and Telecommunications. Blank = not applicable.

SOURCE: *Fortune* (2006); hoovers.com; S&P Compustat database.

In contrast, only three of the top 20 New Economy companies are clearly communications technology companies: Cisco Systems, which makes Internet routers and switches; EchoStar Communications, a major force in satellite television[11]; and Qualcomm, a wireless equipment manufacturer. Even so, Cisco's rise to dominance in its industry derives from its development of software that has enabled the convergence of information and communication technology—what is called the "triple play" of voice, data, and video—using the same infrastructures and equipment. The evolution of those infrastructures and equipment has depended critically on the development of ever more powerful, compact, and affordable computers—in short, the microelectronics revolution. At the center of this revolution were the hardware company, Intel, and the software company, Microsoft, both of which grew large supplying crucial inputs to the IBM personal computer (PC) and what used to be called its clones, including Dell Computer, no. 1 on the New Economy list. AMD, founded in Silicon Valley a year after Intel, sustained its growth for decades by serving as a second source for the supply of Intel chips, although in recent years it has increasingly been competing head-to-head with Intel with its own chip designs.

Applied Materials is the world's largest maker of semiconductor production equipment, while Solectron (since 2007 part of Flextronics), Sanmina-SCI, and Jabil Circuit are among the world's leading electronic manufacturing service (EMS) providers, supplying printed circuit boards and other components to companies such as IBM, HP, Dell, and Cisco. Other companies have established their own distinctive niches in the information technology sector, such as Apple in innovative computer products, Sun Microsystems in computer workstations, and EMC in information management and storage. Oracle is the leader in database management software, while Computer Sciences (CS) and SAIC line up behind "Old Economy" EDS in providing information technology services. Finally, Amazon.com, Google, and Yahoo! are, along with "Old Economy" IAC, in the *Fortune* industry classification "Internet Services and Retailing," which was newly created for the 2005 list. The revenues that each of them generated in 2005 put them on the top 20 New Economy list for the first time (compare Lazonick 2007b, pp. 67–68).

NEBM AS A FORCE FOR UNSTABLE AND INEQUITABLE ECONOMIC GROWTH

The basic thesis of this book is that the demise of OEBM and its replacement by NEBM together represent important parts of the explanation for the trend toward greater employment instability and income inequality in the U.S. economy over the past three decades—a reversal of the trend toward more stable and more equitable economic growth in the three decades after World War II. While NEBM has been evolving since the 1960s in ICT industries, the Internet boom and bust of the late 1990s and early 2000s was pivotal in the replacement of OEBM by NEBM as the dominant mode of business organization.

New Economy companies such as Intel, Microsoft, Oracle, Sun Microsystems, and Cisco Systems grew on the basis of NEBM. Among the major Old Economy companies, IBM led the shift to NEBM during the 1990s as it changed its product market strategy from lower margin hardware to higher margin software and services; its R&D orientation from proprietary technology systems to open technology systems, with extensive patenting as a source of leverage in cross-licensing and strategic alliances with other companies; its financial behavior from providing stable dividend yields to shareholders to boosting its stock price through massive stock repurchases; and its employment relations from its signature "lifelong employment" system with defined-benefit pensions to a focus on flexibility in the employment of labor, including the move to portable pension systems designed to be attractive to younger, highly mobile employees. During the late 1990s, other major Old Economy ICT companies such as Lucent, Xerox, Motorola, TI, and HP adopted aspects of NEBM, and with the sharp downturn of the early 2000s, NEBM became the norm for all ICT companies. In this book, I document this shift to NEBM in the ICT industries and analyze its implications for the possibilities for sustainable prosperity in the United States.

Chapter 2 provides a historical analysis of the rise of NEBM, from its origins in Silicon Valley in the 1960s to its consolidation as the dominant business model in ICT in the Internet boom of the late 1990s. I stress the role of the stock market in facilitating the reallocation of capital and labor from the security of the Old Economy in which established corporations dominated to the insecurity of the New Economy with its waves of start-ups. Facilitating the reallocation of capital was the emergence of NASDAQ (National Association of Securities Dealers Automated Quotations), a national electronic stock market with much laxer listing requirements than the Old Economy New York Stock Exchange (NYSE). Facilitating the reallocation of labor was the transformation of the employee stock option from a means of increasing the after-tax income of top executives under OEBM to a mode of luring a broad base of professional, technical, and administrative employees from secure employment under OEBM to insecure employment under NEBM.

Chapter 3 analyzes how major Old Economy companies—with a focus on the important cases of IBM, HP, and Lucent Technologies—restructured in attempts (in the case of Lucent unsuccessful) to make the transition from OEBM to NEBM. With its central positions in both Old Economy mainframes and New Economy PCs, in the early 1990s IBM proactively, dramatically, and successfully made the transition from OEBM to NEBM. So too did HP, beginning with its 1999 spinoff of Agilent—the original business that William Hewlett and David Packard had built—to focus on its open systems printer business, launched about 15 years earlier. In contrast, Lucent Technologies, the 1996 spinoff from AT&T that housed the famed Bell Labs and that was the largest telecommunications equipment company in the world in 1999, almost destroyed itself trying to adopt elements of NEBM and a decade later was a subsidiary of a French company, Alcatel-Lucent. All three cases in this chapter demonstrate the greatly heightened employment insecurity that the transition from OEBM to NEBM entails. In the cases of IBM and HP, we see that even when Old Economy corporations have made a successful transition to NEBM, employment insecurity increases. In the case of Lucent, we see the disastrous results of an Old Economy company in which top executives became fixated on the company's stock price as the measure of economic performance but failed to make the transition to NEBM.

Chapter 4 analyzes the relations between employment security and retirement security under both OEBM and NEBM. Under OEBM, the traditional nonportable, "back-loaded" defined-benefit pension plan encouraged employees to remain with a company for a career. In making the transition to NEBM, some Old Economy companies adopted portable but still defined-benefit cash-balance plans that favored the employment of younger workers, often as a prelude to replacing a cash-balance plan with a portable defined-contribution 401(k) plan. In contrast, most New Economy companies such as Microsoft, Oracle, Cisco, and Dell have offered their employees only defined-contribution plans over the course of their corporate histories. Many Old Economy companies have used existing defined-benefit pensions as a tool for downsizing the labor force by means of early retirement schemes that enhance the value of one's pension. By the mid-2000s, most Old Economy corporations offered only defined-contribution plans to new hires and, at some companies, even to all employees. The major exceptions can be found in those ICT companies in which industrial unions have remained strong as collective-bargaining agents. Under NEBM, members of the U.S. high-tech labor force confront a high-quality, low-wage globalized labor supply with no effective collective institutions to protect their conditions of work and pay.

Chapter 5 analyzes the forces that have underpinned the globalization of the ICT labor force. Since the 1960s the development strategies of national governments and indigenous businesses in many Asian nations have interacted with the investment strategies of U.S.-based ICT companies as well as U.S. immigration policy to generate a global high-tech labor supply. This process has entailed flows of U.S. capital to Asian labor as well as flows of Asian labor to U.S. capital. As a result, new possibilities to pursue high-tech careers, and thereby develop productive capabilities, have opened up to vast numbers of individuals in many Asian nations. By the same token, it is increasingly the case that members of the U.S. high-tech labor force must compete for jobs with highly qualified, but often much less expensive, labor situated halfway around the world. With the acceleration of offshoring in the 2000s, even well-educated and highly experienced members of the U.S. ICT labor force are facing unprecedented economic insecurity. Under these conditions, what is needed in the United States is the creation of employment opportunities that can make full use of the productive capabilities of educated and experienced U.S. high-tech labor.

Chapter 6 shows that, driven by a pervasive, but theoretically untenable, ideology that corporations should be run to maximize shareholder value, top executives of ICT companies have chosen to allocate corporate resources in a way that, at best, fails to support and, at worst, undermines the ability of members of the U.S. high-tech labor force to compete with a global labor supply without sacrificing their standards of living. Rather than use the profits of globalization to upgrade the capabilities of the U.S. high-tech labor and to create new opportunities for creative employment at home, top executives have become obsessed (if I may use such a psychological term) with allocating corporate financial resources to buying back their companies' own stock. I argue that the only purpose of stock repurchases is to boost a company's stock price, and that, as recipients of abundant stock option awards, the top executives who decide to buy back stock are themselves prime beneficiaries of these corporate allocation decisions.

Finally, Chapter 7 discusses the implications for sustainable prosperity of the rise and dominance of NEBM. With the transformation of employment relations, the globalization of the high-tech labor force, and the corporate commitment to maximizing shareholder value, well-educated and highly experienced members of the U.S. high-tech labor force are facing economic insecurity, even when the U.S. ICT corporations that could provide them with stable and remunerative employment opportunities are highly profitable. In terms of their accumulated capabilities, these ICT personnel should be among the best-positioned in the U.S. labor force to find stable and remunerative employment. Yet, notwithstanding the existence of older underemployed and unemployed high-tech workers, high-tech executives perpetually claim that there is a shortage of capable STEM (science, technology, engineering, and mathematics) labor in the United States. What these executives actually want is a large supply of younger workers who will work long hours for less pay.

These executives go on to blame an underperforming U.S. K–12 education system for failing to generate this abundant labor supply. The U.S. government does need to remain committed to investment in the nation's educational infrastructure. Government investment, however, will not in and of itself generate sustainable prosperity. The achievement of stable and equitable economic growth, both for existing members of the U.S. high-tech labor force and for those segments of U.S. society who have been left behind, will require a confrontation with the destructive "shareholder-value" ideology that currently guides the resource allocation decisions of U.S. business corporations.

Notes

1. In the early 1950s, the sociologist C. Wright Mills (1951) had written an influential academic treatise on the significance of the "white collar" employee. William H. Whyte, who wrote his best-selling *The Organization Man* while an editor of *Fortune*, later became a prominent urban sociologist. Whyte's characterization of "The Organization Man" has often been interpreted as pejorative, the victim of the bureaucratic suppression of rugged individualism. Whyte himself, however, denied this interpretation. In a 1982 interview, Whyte stated: "I didn't mean *The Organization Man* as a pejorative work. . . . After all, I've been an organization man myself in some very good organizations. And I don't think one loses grace by being a member of an organization. Yet many people interpreted this thing on its own, not having read it, as an attack on modern American life. That anybody who worked for a corporation had lost his soul. And I meant no such thing." Interview by Richard H. Heffner on "The Open Mind" October 15, 1982, available at http://www.theopenmind.tv/searcharchive_episode_transcript.asp?id=1509 (accessed June 26, 2009).

2. In Jeremy Siegel's well-known book, *Stocks for the Long Run*, now in its fourth edition, there is only one passing reference to stock buybacks (Siegel 2008, p. 98), notwithstanding the fact that, since the late 1990s, repurchases have become the major mode of distributing corporate revenues to shareholders.

3. The Department of Commerce (2003) described these industries as IT. I use the term ICT to describe the same set of industries in order to highlight the organizational separation of information and communication technologies in OEBM and the ongoing convergence of information and communication technologies that characterizes NEBM.

4. The BEA defines ICT-producing industries as consisting of computer and electronic products, publishing industries (includes software), information and data processing services, and computer systems design and related services.

5. U.S. Census Bureau (2008a, 1994–1997 data: http://censtats.census.gov/cbpsic/cbpsic.shtml; 1998–2006 data: http://censtats.census.gov/cbpnaic/cbpnaic.shtml).

6. See also Hambrecht (1984) for the views of a prominent Silicon Valley investment banker.

7. Given the gestation period of this book, I have organized collection of data around the top 20 OEBM and NEBM companies by revenues in 2005, taken from the Fortune 500 list published in 2006. The top 20 lists for 2007, taken from the Fortune 500 list published in 2008, have 15 of the same Old Economy companies and 18 of the same New Economy companies as in Tables 1.6 and 1.7, respectively. Gone from the Old Economy list in 2007 are BellSouth (acquired by AT&T Inc. in December 2006), Lucent Technologies (acquired by Alcatel in December 2006 to become Alcatel-Lucent), Cox Communications (taken private in December 2004 and included on the Fortune 500 list in 2005 but not thereafter), NCR (which with $6.2 billion in revenues in 2007 did not make the top 20 Old Economy list), and Freescale Semiconductor (taken private in December 2006). In place of these five

companies on the 2007 Old Economy list are Liberty Media (thirteenth), Automatic Data Processing (fourteenth), Liberty Global (fifteenth), Virgin Media (seventeenth), and Embarq (twentieth, a spinoff of Sprint Nextel's local telephone business in May 2006). Liberty Media, Liberty Global, and Virgin Media are all new companies with Old Economy roots. Gone from the New Economy list in 2007 are Solectron (acquired by Flextronics, based in Singapore, in October 2007) and AMD (which with $6.0 billion in revenues in 2007 did not make the top 20 list). Their replacements on the 2007 New Economy list are eBay (eighteenth) and Cablevision Systems (twentieth).

8. HP acquired EDS in August 2008 in a $13.9 billion deal.

9. In 2000, Lucent spun off Avaya, an enterprise networking company that, with $4.9 billion in revenues and 18,555 employees, ranked 434th in the Fortune 500 in 2005, and in 2001, it spun off Agere Systems, a communications chips company that, with $1.7 billion in revenues and 6,200 employees, ranked 904th in the Fortune 1000 in 2005.

10. With the growth of wireless communications, in 2001 AT&T Corp. spun off AT&T Wireless as a separate company, while in the same year, SBC and Bell South created the wireless company Cingular as a joint venture. In 2004 Cingular acquired AT&T Wireless. In December 2006, AT&T Inc. (formerly SBC) acquired BellSouth, and as a result Cingular, renamed AT&T Mobility, is now wholly owned by AT&T Inc.

11. On January 1, 2008, EchoStar Communications changed its name to DISH Network, while spinning off some of its businesses as EchoStar Corporation.

2

The Rise of the New Economy Business Model

ORIGINS OF THE MICROELECTRONICS REVOLUTION

Technologies that were discovered and developed by Old Economy corporations provided the essential foundations for the rise of the New Economy in ICT. During the post–World War II decades, AT&T, a regulated monopoly since 1913, dominated the communications industry. A U.S. government antitrust suit was launched in 1949 that sought to sever the exclusive relation between AT&T and Western Electric. The suit resulted in a 1956 consent decree that permitted AT&T to maintain exclusive control over its manufacturing company but barred the Bell System from competing in industries other than telecommunications. In addition, AT&T and Western Electric had to license their patents to other companies at reasonable fees (Lewis 1956). As a result, the R&D of Bell Labs, including the transistor invented there in 1947, supported the development of the ICT industries generally while the communications and computer industries remained organizationally distinct.

During the 1950s and 1960s, building on its overwhelming dominance of the punch-card tabulating machine industry, IBM came to dominate the computer industry. IBM introduced its first computer in 1952, and emerged as the undisputed leader of the computer industry within a decade. IBM grew from $166 million in revenues in 1950 to $1.8 billion in 1960, $7.5 billion in 1970, and $26.2 billion in 1980. By 1958 IBM was already the thirty-seventh largest industrial company by revenues in the United States, and a decade later it was the seventh largest. By 1963 IBM's dominance was such that its U.S. revenues of $1,244 million from data-processing computers were well over eight times those of its nearest competitor, Sperry Rand. Indeed, the eight companies that followed IBM had combined U.S. revenues of $539 million, or only 43 percent of IBM's (Chandler 2001, p. 86).

In the 1950s and 1960s, advances in computers, and in electronics more generally, came to depend critically on advances in semiconductors, the generic name for solid-state electronic devices. AT&T/Western Electric and IBM became important developers of semiconductors, but only for in-house use. Technology-rich and well-established Old Economy companies such as General Electric (GE), RCA, Raytheon, Sylvania, Philco-Ford, and Westinghouse entered the semiconductor industry. These companies were the leading manufacturers of the electronic vacuum tubes that were being replaced by the far smaller and less power-hungry semiconductor devices (Tilton 1971, chap. 4). On the face of it, GE was in a particularly strong position to dominate in microelectronics. In the early 1950s, GE's revenues were 9 to 10 times those of IBM, and GE Labs had been in existence since the beginning of the century. GE did hold 8 to 9 percent of the semiconductor market between 1957 and 1966 (p. 66), but thereafter GE, which is still among the largest and most powerful technology companies in the world, did not become a force in the commercialization of semiconductors.

The most successful merchant semiconductor companies in the latter half of the 1950s and in the 1960s were smaller firms, most notably Texas Instruments (TI), the leader with 17 percent of the U.S. market in 1966, Motorola, with 12 percent, and Fairchild, with 13 percent. TI remained the world leader in market share through 1984, and in 2007 stood in fourth place, with 4.3 percent of the world market, behind only Intel (15.0 percent), South Korea's Samsung (7.9 percent), and Japan's Toshiba (4.3 percent) (Gartner 2008). Motorola was second to TI in 1979 as the microcomputer revolution was unfolding, and the two companies remained neck and neck in 1984, when both had revenues from semiconductors that were almost twice those of Intel. From 1985 through 1990, Motorola was the top U.S. chip company. In 1991, it relinquished that position to Intel, which has been the world leader since 1992. In 2004 Motorola spun off its chip division as Freescale Semiconductor, which by 2007 had captured 2.1 percent of the world market.

Motorola and TI were founded just two years apart—Motorola as the Galvin Manufacturing Company in Illinois in 1928 and TI as Geophysical Service Inc. (GSI) in New Jersey in 1930. Over the ensuing decades, these companies became exemplars of OEBM, and employment relations at both Motorola and TI remained Old Economy in the 1980s (see Gutchess 1985a, pp. 280–281, and 1985b, pp. 62–66; Simison 1985).

An innovator in wireless communications technology, Galvin Manufacturing made the "Motorola" brand name of its car radios the company name in 1947, the same year it launched its television business and the transistor was invented at Bell Labs. In 1948 Motorola opened its own semiconductor research lab in Phoenix, Arizona, to develop devices for its electronic products. By 1954 the lab had evolved into a manufacturing facility that employed 800 people, and in the latter half of the 1950s, Motorola was selling not only transistorized radios, two-way radios, and pagers but also, as a distinct semiconductor business, germanium transistors. In 1958 Motorola hired Lester Hogan, a former Bell Labs researcher and at the time a Harvard applied physics professor, to head its semiconductor operations (Holbrook et al. 2000, p. 1024).

In the 1930s, GSI manufactured innovative seismic signal processing equipment for oil exploration (see Pirtle 2005, pp. 2–5). After shifting its headquarters from New Jersey to Dallas, Texas, GSI expanded during World War II as a defense contractor making submarine detection equipment. In 1951 GSI licensed the transistor from Bell Labs with a view to digitizing its seismic equipment. In the same year it changed its name to Texas Instruments. To lead the development of the semiconductors that it needed for its products, in 1953 TI lured away a prominent chemist, Gordon Teal, from Bell Labs by offering him the chance to run his own research lab in his home state of Texas (Teal 1991).

Within two years of joining TI, Teal and his team had developed the first commercializable silicon transistor. By 1957 TI had captured 20 percent of the semiconductor market. In 1958, a TI researcher, Jack Kilby, invented the integrated circuit, just ahead of Robert Noyce at Fairchild Semiconductor (Reid 1985). TI had $27 million in revenues and 2,100 employees in 1953, $233 million in revenues and 16,900 employees in 1960, and $828 million in revenues and 44,800 employees in 1970.

Given the prominence of companies such as Motorola and TI, the development of the U.S. semiconductor industry was not only a Silicon Valley phenomenon. The Silicon Valley semiconductor industry, however, gave rise to NEBM, and the key company in the evolution of Silicon Valley was Fairchild Semiconductor.

EVOLUTION OF THE NEBM

Strategic Characteristics

In September 1957 eight scientists and engineers left Shockley Semiconductor Laboratories in Palo Alto, California, to form Fairchild Semiconductor, a manufacturer of diffused silicon transistors, in nearby Mountain View. Just two years earlier, William Shockley, coinventor of the transistor, had recruited the "traitorous eight," as he later called them, to his new enterprise from different parts of the United States. The interfirm mobility of talented people to found or join start-ups was aided by a unique California law that prohibited employers from demanding that employees sign post-employment covenants not to compete (Gilson 1999). Over the following decades, this mobility became the defining characteristic of the dynamic regional economy that Shockley Labs and Fairchild Semiconductor inadvertently helped to create.

As shown in Figure 2.1, from 1959 through 1970, 42 new semiconductor firms—21 in 1968 and 1969 alone—were launched in the vicinity of Fairchild in what became known by the beginning of the 1970s as Silicon Valley.[1] By 1985 the number of Silicon Valley semiconductor start-ups since the founding of Fairchild totaled 125. Of these 125 firms, 32 were founded by at least one person who had left employment at Fairchild for that purpose, while another 35 companies were offspring from these "Fairchildren" (especially from National Semiconductor, Intel, Signetics, and Synertek). Fairchild was so important to the emergence of Silicon Valley because it not only drew people and knowledge from the established R&D labs of the electronic tube companies such as GE, RCA, Westinghouse, and Sylvania, but it also invested heavily in research, especially related to manufacturing processes for the mass production of diffused silicon transistors (Berlin 2005, chaps. 5–6; Lécuyer 2006, chaps. 5–6; Tilton 1971, p. 4).

Following the founding of Fairchild, the first wave of Silicon Valley semiconductor start-ups consisted of 10 firms launched between 1959 and 1964 oriented toward military markets. Between 1955 and 1963, the annual value of total U.S. semiconductor production rose from $40 million to $610 million, and the proportion that was for the U.S. military varied between 35 and 48 percent. In 1968, when the value of U.S.

Figure 2.1   Three Waves of Silicon Valley Semiconductor Start-Ups, 1955–1985

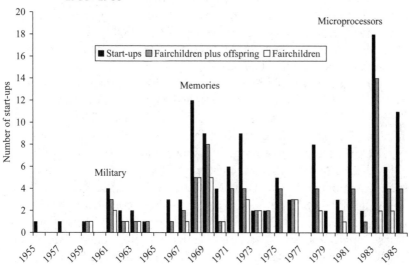

SOURCE: Semiconductor Equipment and Materials International (1995).

semiconductor production stood at $1.2 billion, the value of military production was still 25 percent of the total. By that time, integrated circuits accounted for 27 percent of the value of all U.S. semiconductor production, up from less than 3 percent five years earlier. Military demand was critical to the growth of this important product category, accounting for 94 percent of integrated circuit production in 1963 and 37 percent in 1968 (Tilton 1971, pp. 90–91).

Meanwhile, the price per integrated circuit declined from $31.60 in 1963 to $2.33 in 1968, thus dramatically increasing the economic viability of using integrated circuits for cost-conscious civilian markets (Tilton 1971, pp. 90–91). The realization of these commercial opportunities precipitated the second wave of Silicon Valley start-ups. From 1968 through 1972, the region hosted 40 semiconductor start-ups, 13 of which were Fairchildren and another eight of which were offspring of Fairchildren. Among these Fairchildren were Intel, founded in 1968 by Gordon Moore and Robert Noyce with Andrew Grove as their first employee, and Advanced Micro Devices (AMD), founded in 1969 by

Jerry Saunders, who brought with him seven other Fairchild executives (see Berlin 2005, chap. 7; Lécuyer 2006, chap. 7). When Moore and Noyce founded Intel to produce memory chips that could replace the magnetic coil memories then in use, they specifically declined to create a separate R&D lab and refused to accept government contracts for research (Bassett 2002, chap. 6).

The third wave of Silicon Valley semiconductor start-ups began in 1978, peaked in 1983, and continued to 1985. During these years there were 58 new firms created, of which seven were Fairchildren and another 26 offspring. In contrast to the dynamic random access memory (DRAM) and erasable programmable read-only memory (EPROM) chips that had underpinned the growth of the second-wave companies such as National, Intel, and AMD, third-wave firms such as VLSI Technology (1979), LSI Logic (1981), Cypress Semiconductor (1983), Cirrus Logic (1984), and Chips and Technologies (1985) focused on logic chips—microprocessors and application-specific integrated circuits (ASICs)—for which value-added lay in chip design rather than high-yield, low-defect mass production.

In pursuing this design-oriented strategy, the founders of these start-ups and their backers were taking advantage of new commercial opportunities opened up by the growth of consumer and business electronic product markets. Meanwhile during this third wave, integrated Japanese producers such as NEC, Hitachi, Toshiba, and Fujitsu that sold only a portion of the memory chips that they produced were taking command of the "commodity chip" markets that second-wave companies such as Intel and National had served (see Chase 1983; Patterson 1981, 1982). Underlying the formidable Japanese challenge were superior manufacturing methods that resulted in fewer defects and higher yields (see Burgelman 1994; Okimoto and Nishi 1994).

Around 1985 this Japanese challenge undermined the profitability of all the major memory producers, Intel included. So great was the Japanese threat in commodity chips that the most powerful U.S. semiconductor companies banded together to form SEMATECH (an acronym for Semiconductor Manufacturing Technology) with partial funding from the U.S. government, in an attempt to ensure that the United States would not lose indigenous capability in the production of semiconductor fabrication equipment as well (Browning and Shetler 2000; Grindley, Mowery, and Silverman 1994). By the beginning of the

1990s, however, Intel reemerged as the dominant U.S. competitor in the global semiconductor market, its revenues surpassing TI's starting in 1990 and Motorola's in 1991.

The foundation of Intel's success was the microprocessor, the "computer on a chip" that it had invented in 1971 and that became the major source of revenues for the company with the IBM-led PC revolution of the 1980s. In 1981 IBM announced its PC, with the operating system supplied by Microsoft and the microprocessor by Intel. Both Microsoft and Intel retained the right to sell these products to other companies. In 1982 IBM accounted for almost 14 percent of Intel's revenues (Chase 1983).

In 1982 IBM's PC sales were $500 million, and just two years later they were 11 times that amount, more than triple the 1984 revenues of its nearest competitor, Apple, and about equal to the revenues of IBM's top eight rivals. Subsequently, the very success of the IBM PC combined with open access to the Microsoft operating system and Intel microprocessor meant that, in the last half of the 1980s and beyond, IBM lost market share to lower-priced PC clones such as Compaq, Gateway, and Dell (Chandler 2001, pp. 118–199, 142–143).

Nevertheless IBM's strategy for entering the microcomputer market had consolidated and reinforced the vertically specialized structure of the industry in line with what can be viewed as the Silicon Valley model (Best 2001, p. 124; Grove 1996, chap. 3; Langlois 1992). The subsequent domination by Intel and Microsoft of the product markets for microprocessors and operating software, respectively, created an immense barrier to entry to actual and potential competitors who would *directly* confront the New Economy giants. At the same time, however, by defining the "open systems" standards for the computer industry, Intel and Microsoft opened up countless opportunities for new entrants to develop specialized niche products that conformed to the "Wintel" architecture (Borrus and Zysman 1997; Pollack 1985a).

Yet for the major Silicon Valley semiconductor companies in the 1970s, vertical specialization in chips was a competitive outcome, not a strategic choice. A 1979 *New York Times* article subtitled "The Cloning of I.B.M.'s Computers" observed, "It is almost axiomatic in the electronics industry that companies in the semiconductor business want to go into end-user businesses, in other words to vertically integrate into finished products and systems" (Schuyten 1979). As part of a strategy to integrate forward into consumer products, National Semiconductor and Fairchild started producing and marketing calculators (Sporck 2001, pp. 228–230). In 1972 Intel acquired a Silicon Valley digital watchmaker, Microma, which pioneered liquid crystal display watches. National Semiconductor and Fairchild Camera and Instruments (the parent company of Fairchild Semiconductor and by this time based in Silicon Valley) were also producing digital watches, as was TI (*BusinessWeek* 1976). Indeed, price competition from its semiconductor rivals led Intel to exit the watch business in 1978, taking a loss of $15 million on the venture (Manners 1997; Sporck 2001, pp. 185–187; Wharton 1990).

The semiconductor companies had somewhat more, but nevertheless limited, success integrating forward into capital goods. During the 1970s National manufactured checkout scanners and made money in that business before being outcompeted by IBM and NCR (Sporck 2001, pp. 230–231). Following the lead of Silicon Valley-based Amdahl, National had also entered the plug-compatible mainframe (PCM) market, producing clones of IBM's machines. By the early 1980s, however, all of National's PCMs were manufactured by Hitachi (*BusinessWeek* 1983), and in 1989, Hitachi and Electronic Data Systems bought National's mainframe business (Molloy 1989).

In addition, leading Silicon Valley semiconductor companies, including Intel, National, and Intel-spinoff Zilog, entered the minicomputer industry in the late 1970s and early 1980s, but they were outcompeted by not only the Japanese but also by firms in the Route 128 high-tech corridor to the north and west of Boston in Massachusetts, such as Digital Equipment Corporation (DEC) and Data General, as well as by IBM and HP. In 1981 Intel entered the microcomputer industry, one in which National was already engaged using Intel's 8086 microprocessor. Intel's director of corporate planning, Les Vadasz, argued that Intel's forward integration into microcomputers was strategic: "We develop products because they fit into our overall architecture of things" (*BusinessWeek* 1981a). But 1981 was also the year that IBM launched its PC, using Intel's microprocessor. IBM's success pushed Intel out of the microcomputer business and helped to ensure that the leading producer of microprocessors would grow to world dominance as a specialized semiconductor company.

The Silicon Valley semiconductor companies, therefore, had tried to integrate forward into final products, but competition from integrated

Japanese and U.S. rivals forced them to specialize in chips. Vertical specialization, however, did not stop there. A number of Silicon Valley design-oriented chip companies that entered the industry in the 1980s, and even more so in the 1990s, did so without investing in the manufacture of semiconductors. For example, many producers of programmable logic devices and graphics processors such as Altera, NVIDIA, and Xilinx turned to foundries to manufacture their chips. The Taiwanese in particular took advantage of the opportunity, as the Taiwan Semiconductor Manufacturing Company (TSMC) and United Microelectronics Corporation (UMC) became the largest semiconductor contract manufacturers in the world (Brown and Linden 2005, pp. 288–293; Leachman and Leachman 2004; Taiwan Industry Semiconductor Association 2007; Zerega 1999).

If a layer of vertical specialization emerged in the manufacture of chips, so too did it emerge in the assembly of chip sets, printed circuit boards, and, increasingly, even finished products (Sturgeon 2002). In the 1980s and early 1990s contract manufacturers, also known as electronic manufacturing service (EMS) providers, operated as job shops that took on extra work from integrated original equipment manufacturers (OEMs) in periods of peak demand. Then, during the mid-1990s, a few Old Economy companies—particularly IBM, HP, and Ericsson (in Sweden)—took the lead in selling existing plants to EMS providers (see Chapter 3). Meanwhile the newest New Economy companies, such as Cisco and 3Com, which engaged in internetworking, outsourced almost all of their manufacturing from the outset.

In the Internet boom of the late 1990s, the demand for EMS capacity soared. New Economy companies that did no manufacturing relied on EMS providers for not only assembly but also an increasing array of services including testing, design, documentation, and shipping (Curran 1997). Old Economy telecommunications equipment companies such as Motorola, Lucent, Nortel, and Alcatel also undertook major outsourcing programs to EMS providers; by 2000 there was a rush by these companies to offload manufacturing plants.

In the process, five dominant EMS providers emerged: Celestica, Flextronics, Jabil Circuit, Solectron, and Sanmina-SCI (Carbone 2000, 2002, 2004). From 1993 to 2003, the revenues of the largest EMS provider, Flextronics, increased from $93 million to $13.4 billion, and employment increased from 2,000 to 95,000. During the same period,

Solectron, the second largest EMS provider, saw an increase in revenues from $836 million to $11.0 billion and in employment from 4,500 to 66,000. Flextronics acquired Solectron in 2007. In 2007 dollars, the top five had combined revenues of $5.7 billion in 1994, $23.3 billion in 1999, $58.7 billion in 2004, and (including the combined operations of Flextronics and Solectron) $50.0 billion in 2007. Total employment at these companies was 90,000 people in 1999, 268,000 in 2004, and 356,000 in 2007.

Organizational Characteristics

These changes in industrial organization had far-reaching implications for the employment of labor. The start-up phenomenon and vertical specialization depended upon, and over time reinforced, the existence of industry-wide standards as distinct from the in-house proprietary standards that had characterized OEBM with its vertically integrated enterprises such as AT&T/Western Electric and IBM. The existence of industry-wide standards facilitated the movement of high-tech labor from one company to another over the course of a career. New Economy executives valued the industry-wide experience, including knowledge of the latest developments in technology and product markets, that new employees often brought with them to their company. The regional concentration of ICT firms in Silicon Valley further facilitated this movement of labor from one firm to another—one could change employer without relocating—while the networks created by regional concentration and interfirm mobility generated new learning to which participants in the regional labor force had privileged access relative to high-tech labor outside the region (Saxenian 1994).

The interfirm mobility of high-tech labor brought with it a new form of compensation—nonexecutive stock options—for attracting, retaining, and motivating a broad base of employees. The executive stock option had its origins in the United States from the late 1930s as high-level salaried corporate managers sought a form of compensation that would be subject to the 25 percent capital-gains tax rate rather than personal-income tax rates on the highest income brackets that reached 91 percent in the 1950s (Lazonick 2003a). The Revenue Act of 1950 transformed this possibility into reality (Pearson 1950), and over the course of the 1950s, top executives of U.S. corporations saw income from options become an important component of their total remuneration (Lewellen 1968).

In the late 1950s and early 1960s, however, a backlash of public sentiment against this enrichment of top executives led the U.S. Congress to place restrictions on the use of stock options as a mode of compensation. In 1959, the AFL-CIO issued a pamphlet in which it warned against an erosion of the New Deal legislation that sought to prevent the opportunity for "a handful of insiders to rig the game for their own ends" (Industrial Union Department, AFL-CIO, 1959, p. 4). In a much less strident article in the *Harvard Business Review*, Erwin Griswold, Dean of Harvard Law School, criticized the tax rules on stock options for favoring a special class of people who did not in any case make investments that justified capital gains (Griswold 1960). He argued that option grants focused the minds of executives more on the gamble of holding publicly traded stocks than on the requirements of managing large corporations.

Griswold's article provoked a vigorous academic debate (e.g., Baker 1963; Campbell 1961; Holland and Lewellen 1962; Lent and Menge 1962). Nonacademic participants in this discussion included Henry Ford II, CEO of Ford Motor Company; Thomas Watson, Jr., CEO of IBM; Nelson Rockefeller, governor of New York; and Albert Gore, senator from Tennessee. In a special message on tax reduction and reform delivered in January 1963, President John F. Kennedy advocated taxing executive stock options at ordinary income tax rates and thus "remove a gross inequality in the application of the income tax" (Washington Post 1963).

Gore championed this position in Congress, which revised the tax code in 1964 (Albright 1964; Cohen 1964; Gore 1965; Nossiter 1961). The "restricted" stock option of the 1950 Act became a "qualified" stock option; to qualify for capital-gains treatment, the option had to be exercised within five rather than 10 years, and, upon exercise, the acquired stock had to be held for three years rather than six months. In addition, the exercise price of the option had to be 100 percent of the market price, whereas previously it could be 85 to 95 percent. The new tax law also placed restrictions on the repricing of stock options should the company's stock price decline (Cohen 1964). Each of these changes reduced the probability that executives would realize as much in benefits from stock options as they had been receiving.

In 1969 and 1976, moreover, Congress raised the capital-gains rate and lowered the personal-income rate, thus mitigating the original purpose of options. Moreover, under the Tax Reform Act of 1976, Congress eliminated the capital-gains treatment of all future employee stock options. In 1978, Graef Crystal (1978, p. 145)—a compensation consultant who would later become a vocal critic of excessive executive pay (Crystal 1991)—stated that qualified stock options, "once the most popular of all executive compensation devices . . . have been given the last rites by Congress."

That was not the end of executive stock options, however. Congress subsequently lowered both the personal-income and capital-gains rates, and in 1981 restored the capital-gains treatment and relaxed the rules on the granting and exercising of stock options, thus resuscitating them (*BusinessWeek* 1981b; Noble 1981; Rankin 1981). In the forefront of lobbying Congress to bring back capital-gains treatment for stock options were the National Venture Capital Association (NVCA) and the American Electronics Association (AeA), both of which were nationwide organizations that emanated from Silicon Valley (Bacon 1981; Reiner 1989, chap. 6). In the 1980s and 1990s, stock options for both executives and nonexecutives would become a distinctive mode of compensation under NEBM.

The 1980s and 1990s witnessed an explosion in executive pay, driven by stock options. Between 1980 and 1994, the mean value of stock option grants to CEOs of large U.S. corporations rose from $155,037 to $1,213,180, or by 683 percent, while the mean value of their salary and bonus compensation rose from $654,935 to $1,292,290, or by 95 percent. As a result, stock options accounted for 19 percent of CEO compensation in 1980 but 48 percent in 1994 (Hall and Leibman 1998, p. 661).

A study of CEO remuneration in S&P 500 companies found that average compensation in 2003 dollars rose from $3.5 million in 1992 to a peak of $14.8 million in 2000, declining to $8.7 million in 2003 (Jensen, Murphy, and Wruck 2005, p. 33). The value of stock options accounted for 28 percent of this pay in 1992, 49 percent in 2000, and 38 percent in 2003. Of the change in pay from 1992 to 2000, 10.5 percent came from salaries, 15.4 percent from bonuses, and 56.7 percent from stock options. Of the decline in pay from 2000 to 2003, 14.1 percent came from salaries, 11.2 percent from bonuses, and 65.0 percent from stock options. It has been estimated that, largely as a result of gains from the exercise of stock options, the ratio of the pay of CEOs of major U.S. corporations to that of the average worker increased from 42:1 in 1980 to 85:1 in 1990 to 531:1 in 2000 (Dash 2006). Notwithstanding the less ebullient stock markets that prevailed in the first half of the 2000s, this ratio remained very high at 411:1 in 2005 and 364:1 in 2006 (AFL-CIO 2007).

With good reason, both academics and journalists who are critical of high executive pay have focused most of their attention on the excesses of executive stock options. Yet the vast majority of employee stock options in the United States have been issued to nonexecutive personnel as part of what became known as "broad-based" programs (Hall and Murphy 2003, pp. 51–53; Mehran and Tracy 2001; Oyer and Schaefer 2005; Sabow and Milligan 2000; Sesil et al. 2002). During the Internet boom, broad-based stock option programs diffused to many more companies, with top executives getting more of them and increasing numbers of nonexecutive employees getting them for the first time.

The significant use of stock options for nonexecutive employees originated in the 1960s when high-tech start-ups began to offer them to scientists, engineers, and managerial personnel at all levels, not just top executives, to lure them away from employment at established companies. Old Economy corporations could credibly promise secure employment to professional, technical, and administrative employees, with superior compensation taking the form of pay increases tied to promotion up the managerial hierarchy. Start-ups, their futures highly uncertain, could not realistically hold out the expectation of employment security. They could, however, use stock options, with exercise prices often at pennies a share, to attract well-educated and experienced personnel. If the start-up did an IPO or was sold to an already-listed company, these stock options would become very valuable.

The high concentration of start-ups in Silicon Valley meant that in the 1980s new ventures increasingly not only used stock options to induce high-tech labor to leave secure employment with established corporations, but they also competed among themselves for personnel, with an emphasis on stock options in their compensation packages. Besides attracting "talent" and giving these new hires a stake in getting the start-up to an IPO, ample stock options could substitute to some extent for cash salaries (e.g., see Uchitelle 1990).

At the same time, a company could also grant its employees non-qualified stock options on which ordinary taxes had to be paid at the time of exercise, but on which the company could claim a dollar-for-dollar tax credit without having to show the cost of stock options as an expense that would in turn reduce reported earnings (and as a result presumably place downward pressure on its stock price). In 2000, at the peak of the boom, this tax benefit from nonqualified employee stock options was worth $887 million to Intel, $5,535 million to Microsoft, and $2,495 million to Cisco.

Given the lowering of ordinary tax rates in the early 1980s, non-qualified options became a favored form of stock-based compensation, especially in Silicon Valley, where new ventures abounded. No longer were stock options viewed as an exclusive privilege of top executives. Rather, in the New Economy, stock options could be seen as necessary to attract "talent" to supply their expertise and effort to innovative new ventures that could drive the growth of the U.S. economy.

The growing importance of stock options to attract new employees placed pressure on high-tech firms to use options to retain them as well. For this reason, the practice evolved in New Economy firms of making annual option grants, with the vesting period for any annual block of option grants being 25 percent of the grants at the end of each of the first four years after the grant date. Once the options were vested, they could typically be exercised for a period of 10 years from the grant date, so long as one remained with the company. Without creating the Old Economy expectation among employees of "lifelong careers" with the company, the perpetual pipeline of unvested options functions as a tangible retention mechanism. Indeed, for most employees, the amount of options that an individual can expect to receive is tied to his or her position in the firm's hierarchical and functional division of labor, so that the retention function of stock options is integrally related to the employee's career progress within the particular company.

There is a widespread consensus among ICT firms that the prime function of stock options is to manage interfirm mobility on the labor market by attracting and retaining labor. As displayed in Figure 2.2, the importance that ICT compensation executives ascribed to the "attract" and "retain" objectives (along with the integrally related objective to "provide competitive total compensation") in the late 1990s and early 2000s is evident in their responses to the annual survey, conducted

**Figure 2.2 Objectives of Ongoing Stock-Option Programs, ICT
Companies Operating in the United States, 1996–2003**

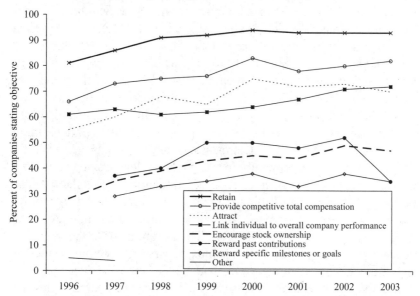

NOTE: The objectives were ranked in any given year by the percentage of companies
listing an objective as "most important" for their ongoing stock options plans. Companies gave multiple "most important" objectives, ranging from an average of 2.2 in
1996 to 3.6 in 2000. The ICT companies included in the survey changed from year to
year. Number of companies surveyed: 1996, 68; 1997, 68; 1998, 82; 1999, 81; 2000,
180; 2001, 166; 2002, 174; and 2003, 136. In 1996, "Rewarding past contributions"
was a frequent response in the "Other" category.
SOURCE: 1996–1997: iQuantic High-Tech Equity Practices Survey; 1998–2000:
iQuantic Equity Practices Survey for High Technology Industries; 2001–2002:
iQuantic-Buck Information Services Equity Practices Survey for the High Technology Industries; 2003: Mellon Equity Practices Survey for the High Technology Industries (April 2004).

by the consulting firm iQuantic, on the "most important" objectives
of ongoing high-tech stock option programs. Note the stability of the
relative rankings between 1996 and 2003, notwithstanding the fact, as
noted in Figure 2.2, that the number of companies that responded to the
survey varied markedly over this period, as did their average number of
"most important" responses.

In their early years, some Silicon Valley start-ups like Intel, Oracle, Sun Microsystems, and Cisco Systems granted stock options to substantial proportions of their employees. Many New Economy companies located outside Silicon Valley—for example, Microsoft, based in Washington State, and Dell, based in Texas—did so as well (Lazonick 2007b). During the 1980s and 1990s, New Economy companies maintained, and in some cases enlarged, their broad-based stock option programs even as they grew to employ tens of thousands of people.

By the 2000s, stock option awards outstanding accounted for a substantial proportion of the total common stock outstanding of the leading ICT companies (Table 2.1). Compensation professionals call this ratio the "overhang." The numerator in the overhang depends on the number of options awarded over the past decade (assuming that is the exercise period), changes in stock prices that make it worthwhile for employees to exercise these options, and cancellation of outstanding options when employees leave the company. The denominator in the overhang depends on the extent to which a company issues new common stock or retires outstanding common stock. In the 2000s the widespread practice of massive stock repurchases (as will be discussed in Chapter 6) tended to increase the overhang.

Microsoft, for example, started giving its 200 employees stock options in 1982, and four years later, with about 1,000 employees and $200 million in revenues, went public to provide liquidity to the shares that employees purchased when they exercised their vested options (see Lazonick 2003a). As the company grew to employ over 20,000 people in 1996 and almost 40,000 four years later, virtually all Microsoft employees got options. In May 2001, with stock prices tumbling, Microsoft doubled the option grants of all employees. Just over two years later, however, with 55,000 employees, the company announced that it would no longer award stock options. Since then, as Table 2.1 shows, Microsoft's overhang has been on the decline, despite its large-scale stock repurchases.

Until 1997 Intel awarded stock options to only about half of its employees. As the Internet boom heated up, and as the word spread among Intel's almost 50,000 employees that CEO Andrew Grove had raked in some $98 million from exercising stock options in 1996, the company expanded the program to include almost all of its employees. In contrast, Intel's main Silicon Valley rival, AMD, gave options to only

Table 2.1 Stock Options Outstanding as a Percent of Common Stock Outstanding, Selected U.S. ICT Companies, 2000–2007

	2000	2001	2002	2003	2004	2005	2006	2007
AMD	13.87	14.76	16.50	14.53	12.69	11.39	9.04	7.90
Cisco Systems	12.94	13.89	15.53	17.60	19.50	21.56	23.35	22.49
Dell	13.33	12.77	13.33	14.27	15.00	14.97	13.79	13.29
Hewlett-Packard	7.04	9.79	13.58	15.76	17.63	18.81	17.58	15.36
Intel	9.33	10.49	12.17	12.98	13.64	14.73	14.93	13.03
IBM	8.70	9.77	11.64	13.65	14.80	15.11	14.44	11.88
Lucent Technologies[a]	11.53	16.78	14.05	8.81	9.24	9.27	6.47	na
Microsoft	15.38	16.22	15.83	14.67	11.56	8.40	7.45	5.59
Motorola	6.14	8.37	11.02	12.73	13.40	12.20	10.20	9.90
Oracle	9.45	9.23	8.13	8.52	8.60	8.81	9.07	8.44
Sun Microsystems	13.87	14.86	16.29	17.67	18.09	17.18	15.61	13.33
Texas Instruments	8.39	8.92	10.24	12.10	13.61	13.81	14.69	14.61

NOTE: Fiscal years ending: January, Dell; May, Oracle; June, Microsoft and Sun Microsystems; July, Cisco Systems; September, Lucent Technologies; October, Hewlett-Packard; December, AMD, IBM, Intel, Motorola, and Texas Instruments.
[a] On December 1, 2006, Lucent ceased to exist when it was merged into the France-based company Alcatel to form Alcatel-Lucent.
SOURCE: Company 10-K filings.

11 percent of its 13,000 employees in 1983 and has never given options to more than 25 percent of its labor force, reaching that proportion in 1998, when it employed 12,800 people. Through the first half of the 1980s, AMD stood out in Silicon Valley as a company that had a "no-layoff" policy (Gutchess 1985b, pp. 24–27; see also McEnaney 1985).[2] Even in Silicon Valley, under certain conditions and for certain firms, the offer of employment security may have been more important than the offer of stock options in performing the retention function.

Cisco Systems, which had 10 employees as a start-up in 1984 and some 200 employees when it did its IPO in 1990, extended annual stock option grants on a systematic basis to virtually all of its employees over the course of the 1990s, even as its payroll reached 40,000 in 2000. With 66,129 employees at the end of fiscal 2008, Cisco still gives almost everyone options. Its overhang soared to almost 24 percent in 2006, but then, notwithstanding ongoing stock repurchases, declined in 2007 and then again in 2008 (to 20.16 percent) as the result of the exercise and cancellation of options. Like Cisco, Dell, Oracle, and Sun have histori-cally given options to all employees.

HP, an Old Economy company located in the heart of Silicon Val-ley, awarded stock options only to upper-level employees in the early 1980s, but then gradually extended stock options to a larger proportion of the labor force from the mid 1980s to 1998. In 1985 the proportion of HP employees holding options was only 8 percent, but it increased to 18 percent in 1990, 25 percent in 1995, and 30 percent in 1998. At the height of the Internet boom, this proportion jumped sharply, first to 57 percent in 1999 and then 98 percent in 2000. At the end of fiscal 2007, the proportion of HP employees holding options had declined to 58 percent, or 99,000 employees, but all regular HP employees have been eligible to receive options since 2000.

At the beginning of the 1990s, IBM, like most Old Economy com-panies, reserved stock options for top executives, but in making the transition to the NEBM (see Chapter 3), the company increasingly and substantially broadened the base of recipients. As can be seen in Table 2.1, the overhangs of HP, IBM, Intel, Motorola, and TI were on the rise in the first half of the 2000s, in large part because these companies have spent billions of dollars annually buying back shares in the 2000s, hence reducing the number of shares outstanding.

For NEBM employees, stock options are not only a potential form of remuneration for work but also, hopefully, a source of retirement savings. As will be shown in Chapter 4, almost all New Economy companies have defined-contribution rather than defined-benefit pension plans, often with a low level of contribution by the company. The expectation is that the accumulation of wealth through the exercise of stock options will form a much more significant financial foundation for retirement than the company pension plan per se.

During the Internet boom, at companies like Microsoft, Cisco, and Intel, income from broad-based stock options soared with speculative stock prices. Since 2001 a new reality has set in that includes lower levels of high-tech employment and wages that are based mostly on salaries. Using County Business Pattern (CBP) data, Figures 2.3 and 2.4 show the changes in full-time employment levels, and Figures 2.5 and 2.6 show the levels of real wages for two key ICT sectors—semicon-

Figure 2.3 Full-Time Employees in the Semiconductor Industry, Silicon Valley, Route 128, Dallas, and Oregon, 1994–2006

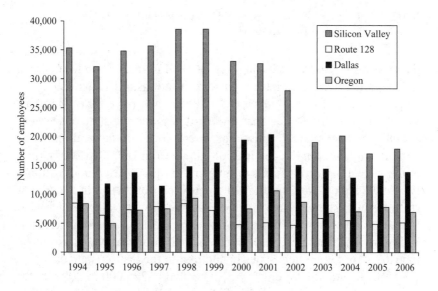

NOTE: SIC 3674 for 1994–1997; NAICS 334413 for 1998–2006.
SOURCE: U.S. Census Bureau (2008a).

Figure 2.4   Full-Time Employees in Software Publishing, Silicon Valley, Route 128, Dallas, and Washington State, 1994–2006

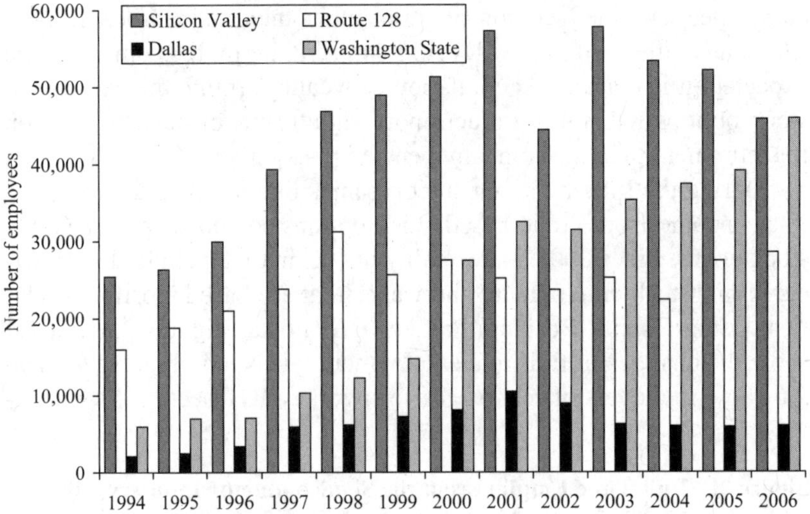

NOTE: SIC 7372 for 1994–1997; NAICS 511210 and 334611 for 1998–2006.
SOURCE: U.S. Census Bureau (2008a).

ductors and software publishing—from 1994 through 2006 for districts in the United States that have high concentrations of ICT workers.[3]

In the case of semiconductors, I have included data for Silicon Valley, Route 128, the Dallas area (home of TI), and the state of Oregon, which is Intel's main location for microprocessor fabrication. With 15,500 employees in Oregon in 2008 (down from 16,000 in 2005), Intel is the state's largest business employer, and the area around Portland has Intel's largest concentration of employees worldwide. In the case of software publishing, I have included data for Silicon Valley, Route 128, the Dallas area, and Washington State, which is the home of Microsoft. In Figures 2.5 and 2.6, I have included series of real wages for these industries for the United States in addition to the district/state data.

U.S. semiconductor employment peaked at 225,000 in 2001, but it was 39 percent lower in 2005 before increasing by 4 percent in 2006. Figure 2.3 shows that Silicon Valley dominated semiconductor employment in the United States from 1994 through 2006, but with a smaller

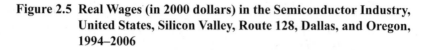

Figure 2.5 Real Wages (in 2000 dollars) in the Semiconductor Industry, United States, Silicon Valley, Route 128, Dallas, and Oregon, 1994–2006

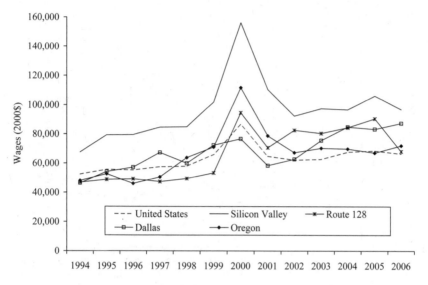

NOTE: SIC 3674 for 1994–1997; NAICS 334413 and 334611 for 1998–2006.
SOURCE: U.S. Census Bureau (2008a).

share of declining total numbers in the mid-2000s. Dallas increased its share to almost 10 percent in 2000 and maintained that share through 2006. Oregon's share was also higher in the first half of the 2000s than in the second half of the 1990s, largely because Intel kept its most advanced microprocessor design and fabrication in the United States while offshoring to other countries much of the less sophisticated semiconductor work that Intel had been doing at other locations in the United States.

U.S. software publishing employment increased dramatically in the second half of the 1990s, and, like semiconductor employment, reached a peak in 2001. The number of software publishing employees dropped by 41 percent in 2002, but subsequently recovered so that it was at 93 to 97 percent of its 2001 level from 2003 through 2006. Figure 2.4 shows that Silicon Valley dominated software publishing employment in the latter half of the 1990s, but that Washington was catching up because

Figure 2.6 Real Wages (in 2000 dollars) in Software Publishing, United States, Silicon Valley, Route 128, Dallas, and Washington State, 1994–2006

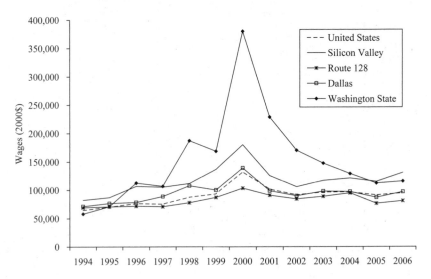

NOTE: SIC 7372 for 1994–1997; NAICS 511210 for 1998–2006.
SOURCE: U.S. Census Bureau (2008a).

of the growth of Microsoft. Indeed, in 2006, the number of software publishing employees in Washington surpassed the number in Silicon Valley for the first time. Route 128 had a larger share of software publishing employees in the second half of the 1990s than in the first half of the 2000s, with a recovery of share in 2005 and 2006 compared with 2001–2004.

As was shown in Figure 1.5, the largest numbers of ICT employees are in the computer programming and computer system design industries. Of the 506,321 people employed in computer programming in 2006, 9.1 percent were located in Silicon Valley and 3.6 percent along Route 128. Of the 486,523 people in computer system design in 2006, 5.0 percent were in Silicon Valley and 3.3 percent along Route 128.

Figure 2.5 shows that Silicon Valley led other areas in semiconductor wages by a considerable margin throughout the period. This differential probably reflects a combination of competition for labor among the large number of semiconductor companies in Silicon Valley and the high cost of living there. Note also the sharp spike in average real wages in Silicon Valley, Oregon, and Route 128 at the peak of the Internet boom. Indeed from 1996 to 2000, real wages in semiconductor employment in Silicon Valley almost doubled, from $79,600 to $156,300.

Even more dramatically, as shown in Figure 2.6, average real wages of software publishing employees in Washington more than tripled, from $112,600 in 1996 (already almost double 1994 real wages) to $380,038 in 2000. The reason—employees at companies such as Intel and Microsoft were cashing in on stock options at inflated stock market prices. In computer programming as well as computer system design employment, Silicon Valley wages were also higher than in other districts, and average real wages also moved up sharply in the boom.

The importance of the gains from the exercise of stock options indicated by the CBP data is confirmed when we calculate the gains from the exercise of stock options at the company level, using data from company filings to the Securities and Exchange Commission (SEC). In their proxy statements, companies provide data on the gains from the exercise of stock options of the CEO and the four other highest paid executives (the "top five"). Table 2.2 shows the average annual income per top five executive from the exercise of stock options from 1995 to 2007 at the same 12 ICT companies that are listed in Table 2.1.

In general, the gains peaked in fiscal 2000 or 2001, although Intel's top five experienced their peak in 1998. At Oracle each of the top five averaged almost $170 million from exercising stock options in 2001, although they reaped no gains in 2002, which was a relatively bad year for stock option gains at all of the companies. (Dell's fiscal year ends on January 31, and its 2002 average of $28.6 million primarily reflects options exercised in calendar year 2001.) Even before Microsoft ceased to award stock options, neither William Gates, its current chairman, nor Steven Ballmer, its current CEO, derived any earnings from the exercise of stock options, although in 2007 their stakes in Microsoft placed them at numbers 1 and 31, respectively, among the richest people in the world (Forbes 2007). Unlike most of the other companies, whose top five did very well from exercising options, Microsoft's top five averaged a paltry $5,180 in 2005 and zero in 2006, in sharp contrast to the $22.0 million (2005) and the $13.0 million (2006) that the top five received on average at Oracle, one of Microsoft's most important software rivals.

Table 2.2 Average Gains (thousand U.S. dollars) per Top Five Executive from the Exercise of Stock Options, Selected U.S. ICT Companies, 1995–2007

	AMD	CSCO	DELL	HPQ	INTC	IBM	LU	MSFT	MOT	ORCL	JAVA	TXN
1995	546	4,065	387	534	4,892	152	—	2,505	3,190	4,301	727	4,066
1996	2,011	15,790	820	1,074	24,585	5,383		0	1,038	8,302	2,786	0
1997	4,549	3,124	1,977	2,161	12,516	3,764	248	4,127	180	3,620	4,425	1,265
1998	190	5,972	14,417	1,114	40,137	10,239	15,597	3,271	0	3,752	11,515	1,492
1999	139	60,586	36,937	8,732	4,796	24,457	165	30,178	2,297	6,754	5,619	5,037
2000	20,080	51,302	98,791	4,360	32,063	13,293	6,100	50,653	607	83,504	25,180	15,048
2001	3,517	11,884	75,151	0	4,117	29,296	0	31,531	546	169,674	18,441	992
2002	16	805	28,612	127	3,514	943	1	1,405	114	0	5,406	0
2003	81	1,291	2,103	502	6,298	2,139	0	6,870	0	13,001	1,323	9,178
2004	115	14,207	14,019	182	6,338	2,876	0	8,564	808	8,633	1,432	493
2005	1,649	15,804	9,364	2,319	4,208	3,550	183	5	2,913	21,953	2,397	2,220
2006	4,746	17,614	31,466	4,903	2,929	3,210	—	0	8,178	12,998	564	7,286
2007	1	22,517	6,692	8,837	4,339	2,454		0	554	46,865	666	1,302

NOTE: AMD, Advanced Micro Devices; CSCO, Cisco Systems, DELL, Dell; HPQ, Hewlett-Packard; INTC, Intel; IBM, International Business Machines; LU, Lucent Technologies; MSFT, Microsoft; MOT, Motorola; ORCL, Oracle; JAVA, Sun Microsystems; and TXN, Texas Instruments. — = not available.
SOURCE: Company proxy statements.

In addition to the information on top five compensation, the notes to company 10-K financial statements provide data that permit an estimate of the average gains per company employee (including those who may not have received options) from the exercise of stock options. Hence, the ratio of the average gains of the top five to those of the average employee can be calculated.[4] Table 2.3 shows the average gains per employee (excluding the top five) from exercising options for the same 12 companies listed in Table 2.2. Very significant average gains were made by employees at these companies at the peak of the Internet boom, especially at Cisco, Dell, Intel, Microsoft, Oracle, and Sun, all of which awarded options to virtually all of their employees in the second half of the 1990s.

The gains that have been reaped more recently from the exercise of stock options pale in comparison to those achieved during the boom, even at Cisco, where a 60 percent increase in its stock price over the course of fiscal 2007 enabled its 55,700 employees to average $73,000 in stock-option gains. The cessation of new option grants at Microsoft from 2003 accounts for its sharp decline in average employee gains from 2005 to 2007.

At IBM the average gains from the exercise of stock options for the decade 1996–2005 were $95.9 million for the top five and $29,000 for the average employee. In the mid-1990s, IBM was beginning to transition from the Old Economy practice of awarding stock options only to upper-level executives to the New Economy practice of distributing options to a broader base of nonexecutive employees. The relatively low average gains per employee at IBM compared with the average gains at most of the other companies listed throughout the period 1995–2007 reflect the facts that 1) a smaller proportion of IBM employees received options; 2) with 386,558 employees at the end of 2007, IBM's headcount was more than three times that of Intel, the next largest employer among the 12 ICT companies; and 3) the movement of IBM's stock price was much more damped than those of most of the other companies during the Internet boom. At the height of the Internet boom, HP also substantially broadened the base of those who received stock options. The spike in average gains per employee to almost $18,000 in 2000 reflects the spike in HP's stock price as well as substantial increases in the number of stock options granted per option holder in the late 1990s.

Table 2.3 Average Gains (in U.S. dollars) per Employee (excluding the top five) from the Exercise of Stock Options, Selected U.S. ICT Companies, 1995–2007

	AMD	CSCO	DELL	HPQ	INTC	IBM	LU	MSFT	MOT	ORCL	JAVA	TXN
1995	1,086	60,894	3,833	2,362	18,746	671	—	51,829	—	—	2,468	2,136
1996	1,490	93,399	7,194	2,213	16,010	1,823	—	79,022	471	7,367	7,992	892
1997	5,075	85,159	11,219	3,156	25,295	3,615	1,019	154,196	1,058	6,588	7,626	2,932
1998	1,435	92,947	40,547	2,676	75,890	4,066	5,449	238,377	361	5,019	10,799	4,473
1999	1,687	193,476	126,639	6,613	56,589	5,790	7,505	369,693	4,055	5,650	27,477	47,880
2000	20,113	290,870	84,818	17,987	112,018	4,200	23,281	449,142	3,218	37,214	60,431	22,881
2001	2,115	105,865	76,122	1,498	18,235	4,011	828	143,772	415	88,723	46,763	6,767
2002	537	13596	33167	838	10413	1195	955	95310	334	6950	4550	4,650
2003	1,163	8,917	10,739	936	10,406	1,553	11	80,283	42	6,193	1,182	4,803
2004	5,103	32,804	12,216	638	8,405	1,842	486	50,690	1,381	7,908	1,960	6,144
2005	12,786	24,432	11,297	1,739	8,347	1,256	615	14,500	8,688	6,926	1,187	12,512
2006	18,197	25,487	8,724	6,809	3,396	1,857	558	6,208	3,852	9,514	1,249	11,142
2007	1,149	73,004	221	9,982	6,915	3,524		14,991	4,395	14,927	2,740	19,209

NOTE: See Table 2.2 for company ticker abbreviations. — = not available.
SOURCE: Company 10-K filings.

Table 2.4 Ratios of Average Top Five Gains from the Exercise of Stock Options to Average Gains of Other Employees, Selected U.S. ICT Companies, 1995–2007

	AMD	CSCO	DELL	HPQ	INTC	IBM	LU	MSFT	MOT	ORCL	JAVA	TXN
1995	231	60	83	202	232	200	—	45		—	221	14
1996	705	150	93	426	1,388	2,462	—	0	2,202	989	288	0
1997	482	33	149	623	440	909	212	25	170	487	506	4
1998	77	58	307	334	477	2,234	6,587	13	0	643	929	4
1999	48	202	252	1,186	75	3,755	19	74	566	949	175	1
2000	419	156	1,000	214	246	2,758	224	101	189	1,807	364	8
2001	651	94	835	0	194	6,442	0	192	1,316	1,575	324	2
2002	15	48	745	123	290	682	0	13	341	0	951	0
2003	43	119	175	452	531	1,268	0	77	0	1,728	834	22
2004	12	386	1,031	221	566	1,459	0	156	487	1,266	571	1
2005	72	585	745	1,077	454	2,557	298	0	335	2,709	1,527	2
2006	142	621	3,153	616	737	1,581	—	0	2,123	1,227	345	9
2007	1	227	10,475	504	366	439		0	78	2,245	157	1

NOTE: See Table 2.2 for company ticker abbreviations. — = not available.
SOURCE: Company proxy statements and 10-K filings.

Table 2.4 shows the ratios of the average top five gains from the exercise of stock options to the average gains of all other employees at each of the 12 companies in Tables 2.2 and 2.3, using the highest monthly stock prices to estimate the gains (see Note 4). As can be seen, the ratios have varied markedly not only from company to company for a given year but also from year to year for a given company. For example, in fiscal year 2006 (year ending January 31, 2006), the ratio for Dell was 3,153, as average options gains per employee fell to $8,724, the lowest level since 1996. Meanwhile, the average top five gains from exercising options stood at $31.5 million. In fiscal 2007, the Dell ratio soared to 10,475, as the top five averaged $6.7 million in gains from stock options while all of Dell's other employees—well over 85,000 of them worldwide—received an average of $221.

Just like the stock market boom from which the gains from the exercise of stock options flowed, the high levels of earnings could not be sustained when the ICT markets and the stock markets turned down. The decline in GDP that accompanied the end of the Internet boom lasted from March to November 2001. Subsequently, however, with the resumption of growth, there was a contraction in employment in the U.S. economy as a whole until the fourth quarter of 2003. In this jobless recovery, certain ICT occupational categories were hit particularly hard. Fourth-quarter surveys by the Bureau of Labor Statistics revealed that employment of computer programmers in the United States fell from 530,730 in 2000 to 501,580 in 2001 to 457,320 in 2002 to 403,220 in 2003, with average real annual wages declining from a peak of $65,517 in 2001 to $65,170 in 2003. Fourth-quarter employment of electrical and electronic engineering technicians fell from 244,570 in 2000 to 220,810 in 2001 to 194,960 in 2002 to 181,550 in 2003, although the average real annual wages of those who remained employed rose from $33,155 in 2000 to $46,190 in 2003 (U.S. Department of Labor 2008). The Institute of Electrical and Electronics Engineers (IEEE) estimated an unemployment rate for computer programmers of 6.4 percent on average in 2003 and 7.6 percent on average in the first half of 2004 (IEEE–Central Texas Section 2008). The problem, it was widely argued, was a marked acceleration in the 2000s of offshoring, especially to India (see Chapter 5), of what had been well-paying ICT jobs in the United States. Even in recovery, it seemed, the New Economy was failing to deliver on the promise of prosperity to many of the better-educated groups in the U.S. labor force.

Financial Characteristics

A major reason why stock options made such a significant contribution to the incomes of employees in Silicon Valley during the Internet boom was the competition for high-tech labor not only from established companies, but also from a proliferation of start-ups: stock options acted as the key to inducing interfirm labor mobility. From the beginning of the 1980s, start-ups found ample finance from venture capital, a mode of funding new firm formation in which Silicon Valley was far better provisioned than anywhere else in the world. In the period from 1995 to 2000, when start-ups became integral to the Internet boom, the San Francisco–Oakland–San Jose consolidated metropolitan statistical area (CMSA) accounted for 28 percent of the venture-backed deals and 24 percent of the venture-backed investments in the United States. By comparison, the CMSA around Boston accounted for 11 percent of deals and 9 percent of investments, while the CSMA around New York accounted for 10 percent of deals and 12 percent of investments (PricewaterhouseCoopers 2008a).

In its origins, however, the evolution of venture capital as a distinct industry for new firm formation depended on Old Economy money of East Coast origin. In the immediate post–World War II decades, the wealth of Old Economy families, including the Rockefellers, Mellons, and Whitneys, was an important source of venture capital funding (Wilson 1986, chap. 2). The first formal venture capital organization was American Research and Development (ARD), established in Boston in 1946 for the express purpose of supporting entrepreneurs in the founding of new firms to commercialize the accumulation of advanced scientific and technological capability that, as a result of military spending, had accumulated through World War II. Much of this capability could be found at the Massachusetts Institute of Technology (MIT). In the post–World War II decades, both MIT and ARD played important roles in the growth of the Route 128 high-tech corridor to the north and west of Boston (Hsu and Kenney 2005; Rosegrant and Lampe 1992, chaps. 2–4). From 1958 on, under the Small Business Administration, the U.S. government also supported the growth of venture capital by providing subsidies to small business investment corporations (Kenney and Florida 2000; Noone and Rubel 1970; Reiner 1989, chap. 5; Wilson 1986).

Meanwhile, also in the aftermath of World War II, Frederick Ter-man, dean of Stanford's School of Engineering, espoused a vision of a high-tech industrial district, anchored by a major research university, in the area surrounding Stanford in Palo Alto, California (see Berlin 2001; Lécuyer 2000; Leslie and Kargon 1996; Saxenian 1994). During the late 1940s and the 1950s, in the context of Cold War military spending, many start-ups were spun off from Stanford, and many established industrial corporations set up operations in the area, transforming Palo Alto and its environs into a major center for microwave and aerospace technology (Leslie 2000). Semiconductors came to the West Coast in 1955 after William Shockley, an inventor of the transistor at Bell Labs and a preeminent solid-state physicist, failed to work out a deal to set up a semiconductor lab at Raytheon, a leading military contractor in the Boston area with close ties to MIT. Instead Shockley secured the backing of Los Angeles–based Beckman Instruments to set up shop close to Stanford.

In 1957, a little more than a year after being hired by Shockley, eight scientists and engineers—Julius Blank, Victor Grinich, Jean Hoerni, Eugene Kleiner, Jay Last, Gordon Moore, Robert Noyce, and Sheldon Roberts—left Shockley Labs in search of funding. As Kleiner wrote in a now-famous letter to his father's broker at the New York investment bank Hayden Stone, they were looking for "a corporation interested in getting into the advanced semiconductor device business" in the lower San Francisco Peninsula (quoted in Lécuyer 2000, p. 163). At this time, there were some individuals involved in venture finance working for certain San Francisco financial institutions, most notably Reid Dennis of the Fireman's Fund and an informal circle of friends (Dennis 2000, pp. 182–183),[5] but there were as yet no firms on the West Coast specifically organized for the purpose of providing venture capital.[6]

Kleiner's letter asked where the "well-trained technical group" of Shockley defectors might get funding that "could get a company into the semiconductor business within three months." The broker to whom the letter was written passed it on to Arthur Rock, a young Hayden Stone employee with a Harvard MBA. Rock had already been involved in the venture financing, IPO, and sale of an East Coast semiconductor company, General Transistor (Lécuyer 2000, pp. 163–164).[7] Rock quickly responded, and after considerable time and effort, convinced Fairchild Camera and Instrument (a highly innovative company from

Long Island, New York) to fund Fairchild Semiconductor.[8] The eight Shockley defectors each received a 7.5 percent equity stake in Fairchild Semiconductor, with Hayden Stone holding 17 percent, and the other 23 percent reserved for allocation in hiring new managers. The deal was structured so that, at its option, Fairchild Camera could buy out the shareholders for $3 million at any time before the semiconductor company had three successive years of net earnings greater than $300,000 or for $5 million if the option was exercised between three years and eight years (Berlin 2001, p. 76; Lécuyer 2000, p. 166).

Fairchild Semiconductor experienced almost immediate success. In early 1958 the new enterprise landed a subcontract with IBM for semiconductors for the Minuteman missile. In 1958 Hoerni drew on Bell Labs research to perfect the planar process for the manufacture of silicon chips. Building on this breakthrough, the following year Noyce invented the integrated circuit (Berlin 2001, p. 64). In two years, the semiconductor company had grown from 13 to 700 employees and was highly profitable.[9] Its revenues for its second year through September 1959 were $6.5 million, 80 percent of which were military sales (Berlin 2001, p. 81). In October 1959, just two years after the launch of Fairchild Semiconductor, Fairchild Camera exercised its option to buy back the company for $3 million. The eight scientists and engineers who had founded Fairchild Semiconductor received publicly traded shares of Fairchild Camera and became employees of the company—now a division of the East Coast parent—that they once had collectively owned (*Wall Street Journal* 1959).

As for Arthur Rock, he was by no means finished with West Coast semiconductor start-ups or with the eight Fairchild Semiconductor founders. In 1960, while still a Hayden Stone employee, Rock arranged financing for two former executives of the West Coast conglomerate Litton Industries to launch Teledyne, a Los Angeles–based electronics firm. Rock remained actively involved in Teledyne's affairs, and in 1961, Hoerni, Kleiner, Last, and Roberts left Fairchild Semiconductor to found Amelco as a semiconductor division of Teledyne. In the same year, Rock left Hayden Stone and relocated to the San Francisco area, where he quickly teamed up with Tommy Davis, a local financier with a legal background and links with Stanford's Terman, to establish a venture capital firm, Davis and Rock. Among those who invested in the Davis and Rock venture fund were the eight Fairchild Semiconduc-

tor founders. When two of them, Moore and Noyce, decided to leave
Fairchild in 1968 to found their own company, Intel, they turned to
Rock for financing. Within days he had raised $2.5 million to fund the
start-up (Perkins 1994; Wilson 1986, p. 38).

 Rock was, therefore, a leading venture capitalist in both the first
and second waves of Silicon Valley semiconductor start-ups. As shown
in Figure 2.7, there was a coevolution between venture-capital firm
entrants in the Silicon Valley region and semiconductor start-ups. As
with the founding of semiconductor firms, the pattern of venture-capital firm entrants exhibits three waves of growing amplitude, the first
around 1958–1962, the second around 1968–1972, and the third around
1978–1983. With the exception of Rock, however, who himself had
become involved with West Coast start-ups while in the employ of an
East Coast investment bank, there was little involvement of San Francisco Peninsula venture capital with semiconductor start-ups until the
second wave.

**Figure 2.7 Coevolution of Venture Capital Entrants and Semiconductor
Start-Ups in Silicon Valley, 1957–1983**

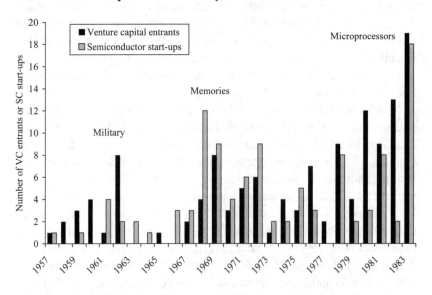

SOURCE: Semiconductor Equipment and Materials International (1995); West Coast
Venture Capital Genealogy Chart, available from Asset Management Company.

That involvement picked up slowly in the middle of the second wave, and toward the end of the period the semiconductor industry began contributing some of its well-known executives to the venture capital industry. In 1972 Donald Valentine, an engineer who had been head of marketing at Fairchild before joining National Semiconductor in 1967, founded Sequoia Capital, which became one of Silicon Valley's most successful venture capital firms. Also in 1972 Eugene Kleiner joined with HP executive Thomas Perkins to found a venture capital firm, Kleiner Perkins, which, renamed Kleiner Perkins Caufield and Byers in 1978, is commonly considered to be the exemplar of Silicon Valley venture capital. The firm's offices were located in a still largely vacant new complex at 3000 Sand Hill Road in Menlo Park, adjacent to Stanford and with easy access to the San Jose and San Francisco airports (Lane 1994). Sequoia also located there, as did many other Silicon Valley venture capital firms and the Western Association of Venture Capitalists, out of which grew the National Venture Capital Association (NVCA) in 1973. The second wave of semiconductor start-ups, therefore, not only gave Silicon Valley its name but also laid the foundation for an organized venture capital industry.

In the 1980s technology-oriented venture capital firms had become integral to both Silicon Valley and NEBM. These firms were organized as general partnerships of venture capitalists who handled five duties: 1) raised funds, largely from institutional investors such as pension funds, universities, and banks; 2) reviewed and selected the particular portfolio of industrial ventures in which to invest; 3) maintained control over resource allocation to these ventures, including the staging of funding as the venture evolved; 4) maintained control over resource allocation by these ventures, including the hiring and firing of executive personnel; and 5) sought to realize returns to the venture capital fund through either an IPO of the stock of the venture-backed industrial firms or a mergers and acquisitions (M&A) deal with an already-established corporation. It was Silicon Valley practice, which became the standard for U.S. venture capital by the 1980s, for the general partners of the venture capital firm to receive, in addition to a 2 percent management fee, a "carried interest" of at least 20 percent of the returns of a particular venture capital fund that they raised, distributing the remainder to the institutions or individuals who, as limited partners, provided the general partners with the capital for the fund (see Sahlman 1990).

It was the innovative capabilities of the companies in which venture capitalists invested that created the value from which money could be made. By the 1970s, the microelectronics revolution had resulted in a growing range of business and household product applications, and, coming out of the semiconductor revolution, the Silicon Valley venture capitalists had become part of the regional institutional environment. What was needed now was an adequate supply of capital for the investments in new ventures that could take advantage of the plethora of technological and market opportunities that the microelectronics revolution had opened up. Over the course of the 1970s, a number of changes in U.S. financial institutions encouraged the flow of capital into venture capital funds, thus favoring the growth of Silicon Valley and NEBM.

The launch of NASDAQ in 1971, with its much less stringent listing requirements than the NYSE, made it much easier for a young company to do an IPO, thus enhancing the ability of venture capitalists to use this mode of exit from their investments. In 1971, for example, less than three years after being founded, Intel did its IPO on NASDAQ, with a loss before extraordinary items of $513,000, offset by a gain of $1,427,000 for "sale of manufacturing know-how," for a net income of $914,000 (Intel 1973). Fourteen of the 20 New Economy firms in Table 1.7 are listed on NASDAQ: Intel (IPO in 1971), Applied Materials (1972), Apple Computer (1980), Microsoft (1986), Sun Microsystems (1986), Oracle (1986), Dell Computer (1988), Cisco Systems (1990), Qualcomm (1991), Sanmina (now Sanmina-SCI) (1993), EchoStar (renamed DISH Network in 2008) (1995), Yahoo! (1996), Amazon.com (1997), and Google (2004). The other six are listed on NYSE.

In 1975 the SEC barred stock exchanges from charging fixed commissions on stock-trading transactions, ending a practice that had prevailed on Wall Street since 1796 (*Wall Street Journal* 1974a). This change made it less costly for stock-market investors to buy and sell shares to realize capital gains as an alternative to holding the shares for the sake of a stream of dividend income. This change thus facilitated early IPOs of new ventures that were not yet profitable enough to pay dividends. It also favored the subsequent growth of the firm as a publicly listed company because of the willingness of capital-gains oriented stock-market investors to forego dividends, thus leaving more earnings in the company for internal investment.

In 1978, in response to intensive lobbying led by AeA and NVCA (both of which were dominated by Silicon Valley interests), the U.S. Congress reduced the capital-gains tax from as high as 49.875 percent to a maximum of 28 percent, thus reversing a 36-year trend toward higher capital gains taxes (Pierson 1978). In 1981 the capital-gains tax rate was further reduced to a maximum of 20 percent (Auten 1999). Venture capitalists saw lower capital-gains taxes as encouraging both entrepreneurial investment in new companies and portfolio investment by individuals in the publicly traded stocks of young, potentially high-growth companies.

During the 1970s, however, venture capitalists still faced constraints on the amount of money that they could raise for venture funds, mainly because of restrictions on their access to the vast accumulation of household savings held by pension funds. In the early 1970s, there was only a trickle of institutional money invested in venture capital, and even that flow dried up when the passage of the Employee Retirement Income Security Act (ERISA) in 1974 made corporations responsible for underfunded pensions and pension fund managers personally liable for breaches of their fiduciary duty to use the "prudent man" rule when making investments (Niland 1976). Under these circumstances, pension fund managers, who controlled the allocation of an ever-increasing share of U.S. household savings, avoided investment in venture capital funds. On July 23, 1979, however, the U.S. Department of Labor decreed that pension fund money could be invested not only in listed stocks and high-grade bonds but also in more speculative assets, including new ventures, without transgressing the prudent man rule (Ross 1979).

As a result, pension fund money poured into venture capital funds. Funds raised from pension funds (in 1997 dollars) by independent venture partnerships (the type that prevailed in Silicon Valley) were $69 million in 1978 (15 percent of all funds raised), $160 million in 1979 (31 percent), $400 million in 1980 (30 percent), and $421 million in 1981 (23 percent). By 1983, pension fund investment in independent venture partnerships had reached $1,808 million in 1997 dollars, of which private pension funds accounted for $1,516 million. Throughout the 1980s and 1990s, pension funds provided anywhere from 31 percent to 59 percent of the funds raised by independent venture capital partnerships, which in turn increased their share of all venture funds raised from 40 percent in 1980 to 80 percent a decade later (Gompers and Lerner 2002, p. 8).

Like the reduction in the capital gains tax rate, the clarification of ERISA did not just happen. Both the venture capital community and the managers of large corporate pension funds lobbied the U.S. government for the relaxation of the strictures of ERISA (Avnimelech, Kenney, and Teubal 2005, pp. 200–201). For example, in 1998, the NVCA gave its first Lifetime Achievement Award to NVCA cofounder David Morgenthaler for his seminal efforts in leading the NVCA in lobbying for the capital gains tax reduction as well as for the clarification of ERISA (Morgenthaler 2008).

As another example, in 1994 Janet Hickey, now comanaging director of Sprout Group, a venture capital affiliate of Credit Suisse, was one of the first inductees into the Private Equity Hall of Fame for her lobbying of the U.S. Department of Labor to permit pension funds to invest in venture capital at a time when she was involved in the management of General Electric's pension fund, one of the largest in the United States (Sprout Group 2009).

The massive infusion of capital into venture funds from the pension savings of U.S. households underpinned the third wave of entry of Silicon Valley venture capital firms. These venture capitalists in turn became much more active in funding semiconductor start-ups as well as those new firms producing the array of electronic products that silicon chips made possible. Semiconductor firms were supplying microprocessors and ASICs for a growing range of computer applications, which created a multitude of new opportunities in computer hardware and software that venture capitalists could fund, extending from video games and disk drives in the early 1980s to e-commerce and optical networking gear in the late 1990s.

Apple Computer's highly successful IPO in December 1980 is generally credited with setting off the start-up and IPO boom of the early 1980s. After achieving spectacular returns on its investments, averaging about 35 percent, between 1978 and 1983, the venture capital industry was punished for overinvesting, as its returns averaged less than 10 percent in the latter half of the 1980s. After 1990, returns moved up once again, soaring to almost 150 percent at the peak of the Internet boom before turning negative in the crash of 2001 and 2002 (Lerner 2002).

The Silicon Valley venture capital model spread to other parts of the United States, especially during the 1990s, with investments being made in many different locations and a wide range of industries. Measured in 2000 dollars, total venture capital investment in the United States rose from $9.1 billion in 1995 to $22.3 billion in 1998 before soaring to $55.9 billion in 1999 and $105.0 billion in 2000. After falling to $39.5 billion in 2001, venture capital investment averaged $21.4 billion per year from 2002 to 2007, including $25.3 billion in 2007 (or $30.5 billion in 2007 dollars; PricewaterhouseCoopers 2008b). Silicon Valley has remained, however, by far the world's most important location for venture capital (Gompers and Lerner 2002, p. 14; Green 2004).

Over time there have been shifts in the leading sectors for venture financing. Office and Computer Machinery was the leading sector from the second half of the 1960s through the first half of the 1980s, before being barely surpassed by the Communications and Electronics sectors in the latter half of that decade. In the first half of the 1990s, Biotechnology became important (Gompers and Lerner 2002, pp. 12–13; Green 2004). If we consider Media and Entertainment investments to be Internet related, the average share of ICT in venture capital investment was 69 percent in 1996–1999, 71 percent in 2000–2003, and 54 percent in 2004–2007 (PricewaterhouseCoopers 2008b). The 17-percentage-point decline in the ICT share of investment in 2004–2007 compared with 2000–2003 has been more or less offset by an increase in the shares of Biotechnology and Medical Devices. In 2004–2007 Biotechnology absorbed 17.6 percent of venture capital investment and Medical Devices 10.9 percent.

The importance of telecommunications and networking as recipients of venture capital in the 1990s and beyond reflects the evolution of converged information and communication technologies out of what had been, in the absence of networking, just information technologies. The origins of this convergence go back to the early 1970s when, at Xerox PARC, the Palo Alto–based research arm of the Old Economy copier company, Robert Metcalfe led a team that developed Ethernet, a technology that enabled computers to communicate with one another (Hiltzik 2000, ch. 13). When Xerox declined to commercialize this technology, Metcalfe sought to do so by cofounding 3Com—which stands for "computer, communication, and compatibility"—in 1979. With the widespread adoption of the IBM PC from 1982 on, 3Com was well positioned to be a leader in providing the hardware and software for local area networks (LANs).

After 3Com acquired the Silicon Valley company Bridge Communications in 1987, it became the largest supplier of LAN equipment, followed by Novell, based in Provo, Utah (Mulqueen 1989a). By this time, however, business, government, and nonprofit organizations that had installed LANs in geographically dispersed locations wanted bridges or routers that would link their LANs with wide area networks (WANs). The company that, by the beginning of the 1990s, was most successful in developing this internetworking technology was Cisco Systems.

In 1984 Leonard Bosack and Sandy Lerner, a husband-and-wife team, founded Cisco[10] and initially ran it from their living room. While working in computing in different parts of Stanford University, Bosack and Lerner had been involved in the development of the university's LANs and then had taken up the challenge of internetworking them. At the end of 1987, Cisco received an infusion of $2.5 million in venture funds from Sequoia Capital (Bellinger 1989; Mulqueen 1989b; Watson 1988). Yet with $10 million in revenues in fiscal 1988, venture finance was probably the least important of Sequoia's contributions to the growth of the firm. The case of Cisco exemplifies the *nonfinancial* role of Silicon Valley venture capitalists in developing a promising start-up into a going concern. The Sequoia partner most actively involved with the young company was Donald Valentine, who became a member of Cisco's board of directors. During 1988 Valentine directed the hiring of professional managers at Cisco, including John Morgridge as Cisco president and CEO. More generally, with over a quarter century of experience in Silicon Valley as first a semiconductor executive and then a venture capitalist, Valentine provided Cisco with business expertise that was based on an intimate understanding of the industrial environment in which the firm was trying to compete.

Morgridge stepped down as CEO in 1995 but remained Cisco's Chairman of the Board until 2006. Valentine also remained a member of the board until 2006. Beyond the initial professionalization of the company in the late 1980s, Morgridge and Valentine oversaw the phenomenal growth of Cisco from less than $28 million in sales in the year ending July 1989 to over $22 billion in sales in the year ending July 2001. The ways in which Cisco financed this growth as a publicly traded company exemplify NEBM.

Cisco's IPO in February 1990 netted the company $48 million which was used for working capital and cash reserves. Funds from operations easily covered the company's capital expenditures, not only in 1990 but also for every subsequent year. During its 18 years of existence as a public company, Cisco has collected $18.3 billion from its employees as they have exercised their stock options, a result of the fact that the company uses its stock as a compensation currency. But Cisco has never done another public stock offering. Rather, as will be detailed in Chapter 6, Cisco has also used its stock as a combination currency, doing 81 acquisitions for $38.1 billion from 1993 to 2003, 98 percent of which was paid in stock.

Typifying NEBM, Cisco has never paid any dividends. Of the 20 New Economy companies listed in Table 1.7, only five are currently paying cash dividends on an ongoing basis: Intel since 1992, Microsoft and Qualcomm since 2003, Applied Materials since 2005, and Jabil Circuit since 2006. Another four have paid dividends sporadically: Apple from 1987 through 1995, Computer Sciences once in 1998, EMC once in 2001, and EchoStar one time each in 2004 and 2008. Like Cisco, the other 10 leading New Economy ICT companies have never paid dividends.

In all 20 cases, no distributions to shareholders were made during the early years as public companies; all earnings were reinvested in the growth of the firm. Once these New Economy companies had reached a certain level of maturity, however, most of them began to distribute cash to shareholders by repurchasing their own stock. For the decade of 1998–2007, five of the companies did repurchases in every year: Microsoft (a 10-year total of $87.2 billion), Intel ($53.0 billion), Dell ($28.1 billion), Oracle ($25.5 billion), and Applied Materials ($8.9 billion). Cisco did repurchases every year from 2002 to 2007 for a total of $43.1 billion. In 2007 13 of the 20 companies in Table 1.7 did buybacks, averaging $4.1 billion. As I show in Chapter 6, the sole purpose of stock buybacks is to boost a company's stock price.

As we have seen in this chapter, the stock market played a major role in the emergence and growth of NEBM. As manifested by stock buybacks, by the 2000s, stock-price performance had become integral to the resource allocation decisions of top executives at these companies. In the boom years of the late 1990s, employees of these companies, as participants in broad-based stock-option plans, saw their compensation rise and in some cases soar as a result of the run-up in their companies' stock prices. Stock repurchases redound to the benefit of these employees, but only if they can keep their jobs. The main issue for high-tech workers in the 2000s is employment security under NEBM. If, in the 1980s and 1990s, these workers had responded to the lure of stock-based compensation by eschewing secure employment in Old Economy companies for insecure, but potentially more remunerative, employment in New Economy companies, in the 2000s they would find that their ticket across business models had been one-way. By the 2000s, as we shall see in the next chapter, the leading Old Economy ICT companies had made the transition from OEBM to NEBM and in the process had put an end to the tradition of "the organization man."

Notes

1. The first public use of the term "Silicon Valley" is credited to the journalist Don C. Hoefler in a series of articles that he wrote for *Electronic News* in 1971.
2. In 1986, however, amid the crisis among U.S. chip companies in the face of Japanese competition, AMD's no-layoff policy came to an end (see *Electronic Times* 1986).
3. Semiconductor employees are in SIC 3674 (semiconductors and related devices) for 1994–1997 and NAICS 334413 (semiconductor and related device manufacturing) for 1998–2006. Software publishing employees are in SIC 7372 (prepackaged software, which includes software publishing and reproduction of software) for 1994–1997 and NAICS 511210 (software publishers) plus NAICS 334611 (software reproducing) for 1998–2006. The proportion of NAICS 334611 employees to all software publishing employees is small, ranging from a low of 0.73 percent in 2003 to 1.57 percent in 1997. For the matching of SIC and NAICS classifications, see U.S. Census Bureau (1997).
4. Since the mid-1990s, companies have reported not only the number of options exercised in any given year but also the weighted average exercise price (WAEP) of the options exercised. To generate these estimates of employee gains from the exercise of stock options, I assume that employees exercise options evenly over the course of the year in all months in which the highest market price of the stock is greater than the WAEP for the year. I then use the difference between the mean market price and WAEP during each such month to derive the gains over the course of the year, shown in Table 2.2. For Table 2.3, I use the highest monthly market price rather than the mean market price to calculate the average gains per employee in order to avoid biasing the calculations of relative gains from exercising options in favor of high top five/employee ratios. I am grateful to Yue Zhang for her assistance in developing these estimates.

5. In 1957 Boston-based ARD backed the founding of Digital Equipment Corporation, taking 78 percent of the ownership for a $70,000 investment (Wilson 1986, p. 19). When the eight defectors from Shockley Labs did get funding to start Fairchild Semiconductor in 1957, Fairchild Camera's investment was $1.38 million. Even if these eight men had been willing to relocate to Route 128, it is unlikely that they would have been able to raise that kind of money through ARD.

6. The first firm in the San Francisco Peninsula devoted specifically to venture capital was Draper, Gaither, and Anderson (DGA), started in 1959; see *BusinessWeek* (1960), *New York Times* (1959), and Wilson (1986, p. 34). A product of the Cold War, DGA was founded by men who included two former generals in the U.S. Armed Forces, William H. Draper, Jr., and Frederick Anderson, and the former chairman of the Ford Foundation, H. Rowan Gaither, Jr., who was also the titular head of the committee that, in the wake of the Soviet launch of Sputnik in October 1957, produced the top secret Gaither Report, officially titled "Deterrence and Survival in the Nuclear Age," to advise President Dwight D. Eisenhower on the capability of the United States to respond to a nuclear attack (see Halperin 1961).

7. See Rock (2000, p. 141): "The reason I got so excited about Fairchild Semiconductor was because I'd already been in the semiconductor business through General Transistor."

8. The head of Fairchild Camera and Instrument, Sherman Fairchild, was no ordinary corporate backer. His father had been a founder and chairman of Computing-Tabulating-Recording Company, which in 1924 changed its name to International Business Machines. As a result, Sherman Fairchild ended up as IBM's largest single shareholder. He also invented the aerial camera, founded Fairchild Camera in 1920, and founded Fairchild Aviation in 1925 (see http://en.wikipedia.org/wiki/Sherman_Fairchild).

9. In announcing that his company would exchange Fairchild Camera shares for all of the Fairchild Semiconductor shares, President John Carter said the expansion of Fairchild Semiconductor's sales and profits would allow the company to grow without additional equity financing (*Wall Street Journal* 1959).

10. The company's name, short for San Francisco, was actually spelled "cisco," with a lower-case initial "c," until it went public in 1990.

3

The Demise of the Old Economy Business Model

OLD ECONOMY EMPLOYMENT RELATIONS IN THE 1980s

In the 1970s, even before the rise of NEBM, the postwar era of employment security at U.S. industrial corporations had begun to change (see Lazonick 2004a). Corporations that had acquired too many companies in too many unrelated lines of business in the conglomerate movement of the 1960s became impossible to manage strategically and began to unravel. Also in the 1970s, U.S. corporations that had provided secure employment faced new competitive challenges from the Japanese in the very industries that the United States had dominated. Furthermore, the 1970s saw the postwar prosperity of the 1950s and 1960s give way to "stagflation"—a partial cause of which was the breakdown of OEBM before a viable alternative business model could be put in its place. In 1978, Congress superseded the Employment Act of 1946 with the Full Employment and Balanced Growth Act, which focused not only on employment, but also on productivity, inflation, balancing the federal government budget, and achieving a balance of trade.

Then, in the 1980s, U.S. corporate executives began to invoke the ideology of "maximizing shareholder value" to legitimize downsizing the labor force and increasing distributions to shareholders in the forms of not only dividends but also stock buybacks. Among the prime beneficiaries of this "restructuring" process were the top executives themselves, who have seen their remuneration explode since the 1980s, mainly because of the gains on the bountiful stock options that their boards of directors have bestowed upon them. In the wake of the widespread corporate takeovers and plant closings of the 1980s in what became known as the Rust Belt, Harrison and Bluestone (1988) perceptively identified a "great U-turn" that had occurred in the distribution of income, from the trend toward greater equality in the post–World

War II decades to a trend toward greater inequality from the late 1970s onward. Some three decades later, as shown in Chapter 1, that trend toward inequality still prevails.

In the 1980s, however, ICT was far from the Rust Belt. Notwithstanding the Japanese challenge to U.S. industry in commodity chips, ICT was a dynamic growth sector in which U.S. companies continued to be world leaders. As a result, most of the top 20 Old Economy ICT companies listed in Table 1.6 were still able to hold out the promise to their employees of career employment with one company in that decade. IBM and HP—the two largest ICT companies by revenues in 2005—stood out in the 1980s as companies that had "no-layoff" policies (Gutchess 1985b, pp. 27–30, 38–44). In 1985, with revenues of $50.1 billion and more than 405,000 employees, IBM was by far the largest ICT company and ranked fifth on the Fortune 500 list. In 1985 HP had revenues of $6.5 billion, placing it at number 58 on the Fortune 500 list, and employed more than 90,000 people. The case of HP is of particular importance not only because its revenues surpassed those of IBM by 2007, but also because it is generally considered to be the pioneering company in the region around Stanford University, where, some two decades after HP was founded, NEBM began to emerge.

The second largest ICT company in 1985 was AT&T. The previous year AT&T had emerged out of the breakup of the Bell System as both a provider of long-distance telecommunications services, in competition with companies such as MCI and Sprint, and the leading telecommunications equipment company in the United States, in possession of the still-famous Bell Labs and the former Western Electric. AT&T employees were susceptible to layoffs both before and after the breakup of the Bell System. Nevertheless, AT&T retained Old Economy employment relations in the 1980s and 1990s, secured in part by the presence of a unionized workforce, unlike nonunion IBM and HP.

By the 2000s OEBM-style employment relations had met their demise at all of these companies, with the exception (to be considered in Chapter 4) of the unionized labor force of AT&T. By that time, however, AT&T was no longer a high-tech company. In what became known as the "trivestiture," in 1996 AT&T spun off its communications technology division as Lucent Technologies, which would now house Bell Labs, and its recently acquired information technology division as NCR. In this chapter, I will analyze the transformation of employment relations that occurred at IBM, HP, and Lucent from the mid-1980s to the mid-2000s. IBM and HP were successful in making the transition to NEBM, but Lucent was not. In 2006 it was absorbed by the French communications equipment company Alcatel. Yet, in all three cases, the demise of OEBM resulted in greatly increased employment insecurity for the high-tech labor force.

THE DESTRUCTION OF "LIFELONG" EMPLOYMENT AT IBM

IBM's proactive decision to begin a radical transformation from OEBM to NEBM in the early 1990s was a direct result of the business model that it had adopted in making its rapid and successful entry into the microcomputer industry in first half of the 1980s. The IBM PC consolidated the vertical structure of the microcomputer industry by outsourcing the microprocessor to Intel and the operating system to Microsoft. In the process, IBM played a major role in setting industry-wide standards that favored cross-licensing of technology and strategic alliances rather than in-house proprietary research. As a result, the retention of older employees with career-long experience with the company became much less valuable, and the recruitment of younger employees with experience at other companies much more valuable, to the company.

In 1985 IBM controlled more than 70 percent of the global mainframe computer market, and it was also the clear-cut global leader in sales in the minicomputer, microcomputer, and computer peripherals markets (Chandler 2001, pp. 118–119). At a time when Americans had come to see "permanent employment" as a key institution in the competitive success of Japan, Jack Kuehler, head of IBM's worldwide manufacturing operations, could state, "Our people when they come to this company work for life. They work as an IBM team, for the common goal to be very competitive. A lot of the things you read about Japanese management techniques, IBM has been doing for years" (Kotkin 1985).

Until the early 1990s, IBM was widely known as a company that offered both managerial and production personnel "lifelong employment," with a full array of benefits. In 1934 IBM gave all of its 7,600 employees access to group life insurance, and the company added survivor benefits in 1935. Two years later, it was one of the first major U.S. corporations to give employees paid vacations, in this case six days per year. Looking back, Thomas Watson, Jr., who succeeded his father, Thomas Watson, Sr., as head of IBM in 1956, said that his father had "tried to blur the distinction between white-collar and blue-collar workers," and that while he did not think that "his primary motive was to keep unions out, . . . that was one effect" (Watson and Petre 1990, p. 310).

The competitive success and sustained growth of IBM in the postwar decades helped to institutionalize a no-layoff policy. In 1952, when IBM employed almost 41,500 people, it was claimed that no employees had been laid off since 1921, and that the company had never experienced a slowdown or strike (Potter 1953). Moreover, treading in his father's footsteps, Watson, Jr., continued to "blur the distinction between white-collar and blue-collar workers." In 1958, with almost 89,000 employees, IBM was the first major company to place all hourly workers on salary (*Wall Street Journal* 1958).

IBM's lifelong employees could expect to be retrained and reassigned to new jobs within the company as its mix of products and processes changed. Between 1970 and 1975, a period of rapid technological change in the computer industry, IBM "retrained and physically relocated 5,000 employees as part of the most extensive corporate education program in the U.S." (*BusinessWeek* 1975). The same article quoted IBM chairman Frank Cary as saying: "If people are not worried about being laid off, they are flexible in making the changes we ask of them. We get a high degree of cooperation from the work force in making changes that are beneficial to the corporation. This is very important to us in a high-technology business."

One way in which IBM avoided layoffs was by staffing "lean," at 85 percent of the labor force that would be required to meet normal demand, and then using a combination of overtime (Saturday) work and subcontracting to bring supply up to the normal level when required (Gutchess 1985b, pp. 38–44). When demand was above normal, IBM would have the regular labor force work even more Saturdays and would also hire temporary workers. In periods of slack demand, IBM would produce for inventory, increase maintenance and repair work, and recondition equipment used by its sales force.

Throughout the 1980s, IBM touted its no-layoffs policy (see, e.g., the *Economist* 1986). As Watson, Jr., put it in his autobiography,

> [E]very IBM employee had job security, going back to the days when Dad had refused to fire people during the Depression. If a man proved ineffectual at his new assignment, he wasn't going to be put out on the street; instead we would assign him to a level where he could perform well. In doing this we would sometimes strip a man of a fair amount of his dignity, but we would then make a great effort to build his self-respect. We also abided by the IBM custom of promotion from within. As inexperienced as our executives might be in their new jobs, they had all come up from the bottom and knew what IBM stood for as well as they knew their own names. (Watson and Petre 1990, pp. 288–289)

Even in the last half of the 1980s, when IBM cut its total employment from a record high 405,535 people in 1985 to 373,816 in 1990, all of the reductions came through voluntary retirement schemes.

In the early 1990s, however, IBM took advantage of a slowdown in the computer industry to bring lifelong employment to an end. IBM's annual revenues dropped in 1991, 1992, and 1993. The average revenues during these three years were $64.0 billion, just over 7 percent less than 1990 revenues of $69.0 billion but greater than the company's average revenues for the years 1988–1990. Although this drop in revenues was not dramatic, especially in a nationwide recession, IBM had not experienced a year-to-year decline in revenues since 1946. With shrinking gross profit margins and losses totaling $15.9 billion in 1991–1993, IBM's top management portrayed the company as being in a crisis, and the general public came to view the world's leading computer company as an Old Economy "lumbering giant" (Burgess 1993; Kehoe 1991).

From 1990 to 1994, IBM cut employment from 373,816 to 219,839, reducing its labor force to only 59 percent of its year-end 1990 level. During this period, much of IBM's downsizing continued to be accomplished by making it attractive for its employees to accept voluntary severance packages, including early retirement at age 55. In 1993 and 1994, however, with CEO Louis Gerstner in charge, many thousands of IBM employees were fired outright.

IBM's losses of $15.9 billion in 1991–1993 included an $8.1 billion deficit in 1993, which was the largest annual loss in U.S. corporate history at the time. Workforce-related restructuring charges (including the cost of employee separations and relocations) accounted for 86 percent of these losses—in effect the cost to the company of ridding itself of its once-hallowed tradition of lifelong employment. Other restructuring charges, mainly for the consolidation of manufacturing capacity and elimination of excess space—both part and parcel of the massive downsizing process—amounted to $10.6 billion over the three years. Ignoring restructuring charges, IBM recorded positive net incomes before taxes of $939 million in 1991, $2,619 million in 1992, and $148 million in 1993. Although IBM continued to downsize at a torrid pace in 1994, most of it was done outside the United States and without voluntary severance provisions. During 1994 the company booked no restructuring charges and had after-tax profits of $3,021 million.

In March 1993 the company began involuntary layoffs, with 2,600 terminations that month (Ramstad 1994a). With the arrival of Gerstner as the new CEO on April 1, 1993, there was no longer any pretence of retaining IBM's tradition of employment security. Previously CEO at RJR Nabisco, Gerstner's own appointment was a departure from IBM's practice of promoting top executives from within. In May 1993 Gerstner hired Jerome York, Chrysler's chief financial officer, as his cost-cutting CFO. Then he hired Gerald Czarnecki, CEO of Bank of America–Hawaii, as his head of human resources, with a mandate (set in July 1993) to fire 35,000 people over the next year (Miller 1993).

Czarnecki was fond of telling IBM employees, "It's going to be painful for those who have one foot on the platform and one on the train, because the train is leaving" (Hays 1994a). Another of Czarnecki's quips to IBM employees: "If you don't enjoy what you're doing, you ought to work for someone else" (Lohr 1994). In January 1994, after having handed about 7,000 IBM employees one-way tickets out the door, Czarnecki was asked (presumably tongue-in-cheek) whether an employee could any longer assume "lifetime employment" at IBM (Lohr 1994). His response: "It's not that it's no longer sacred—it's gone, period." Indeed, by April 1994, after less than a year on the job, so too was Czarnecki, apparently taking his own advice. He said that he resigned because he did not enjoy this line of work (Hays 1994a), but CFO York reportedly axed Czarnecki for falling far short of the layoff objectives (Hays 1994b).

After further restructuring in 1994, IBM resumed its growth, with its revenues rising to almost $99 billion in 2007. The company increased employment from 219,839 in 1994, the lowest level since 1966, to 386,558 in 2007. The share of U.S. employees in IBM's worldwide employment declined, however, from 52.2 percent in 1996 to 32.8 percent in 2007. The net increase in IBM employees outside of the United States was 26,387 in 2006 and 37,961 in 2007.[1] One-quarter of IBM's 2007 employees worldwide were in Brazil, Russia, India, and China, with 74,000, or 19 percent of all IBM employees, in India alone (IBM 2008).

IBM employed 125,618 people in the United States in 1996 and 126,804 in 2007. Indeed, except for a net increase of six U.S. employees in 2006, the number of U.S. employees at IBM declined in every year from 2001 through 2007. Moreover, reflecting IBM's shift out of manufacturing and hardware, the types of employment that these U.S. workers performed changed dramatically. From 1996 to 2007, "technicians" fell from 10.0 to 7.6 percent of IBM's U.S. labor force, "office/clerical" workers from 7.1 to 3.7 percent, and "operatives" from 12.3 to 1.3 percent. During the same period, the proportion of the U.S. labor force employed in marketing increased from 12.6 to 32.2 percent.

Measured in 2007 U.S. dollars, IBM's sales per employee increased from an annual average of $257,000 in 1984–1990 to $383,000 in 1994–2000. In 2001–2007 real sales per employee fell back to an average of $294,000 ($264,000 in 2006 and $256,000 in 2007) as IBM increased its employment in India and other lower-wage areas of the world. Over the period from 1996 to 2005, IBM's annual net income averaged 8.2 percent of revenues, although it climbed to 10.3 percent in 2006 and 10.5 percent in 2007. The fact that this profit rate was well below the 13.7 percent average rate that IBM recorded from 1976 to 1985 reflects the much more competitive New Economy environment that IBM has faced since that time.

During the 1990s, IBM pursued a strategy of shifting its business out of hardware into services (Garr 1999; Gerstner 2002; Lazonick 2007b; Lohr 2004). Continuing a trend that began in the late 1980s, the share of revenues from hardware declined from 48 percent in 1996 to 25 percent in 2006, while the services share increased from 29 percent to 53 percent.[2] In December 2004 there was considerable publicity concerning IBM's sale of its PC business to Lenovo, an indigenous Chinese computer electronics company formerly known as Legend (see Chapter 5). The 2006 gross margins of 37 percent in hardware and 27 percent in services were virtually the same as in 1996. Software's share of revenues increased from 15 percent in 1996 to 20 percent in 2006, however, and the segment's already high gross margin of 74 percent in 1996 rose to 85 percent in 2006.

In the early 1990s, IBM was one of the first Old Economy companies, along with HP, to outsource manufacturing to Solectron, a company that became one of the largest electronic manufacturing service (EMS) providers before being acquired by Flextronics in 2007. Over the course of the 1990s, IBM rid itself of its manufacturing capacity. In the first transfer of an established production facility to the new breed of EMS provider, Solectron purchased IBM's electronic subassembly operations in France and North Carolina in 1992 and had IBM as its initial customer (Business Wire 1992). One of the top five EMS providers today is Celestica, which began life as IBM Canada and was spun off as a separate company in 1996.

These changes in product and process strategy were accompanied by significant reductions in IBM's R&D expenditures as a percentage of sales, reflecting the company's much greater orientation toward product development rather than basic research. The proportion of R&D to sales at IBM averaged 7.1 percent from 1981 to 1993, but it averaged only 5.6 percent from 1994 to 2007. IBM's total expenditures of $5.7 billion on R&D in 2006 placed it fourteenth among all R&D spenders globally. But its R&D expenditures of $16,000 per employee were lower than all but 22 other companies in the list of top 100 R&D spenders, far lower than fifth-place Microsoft's $90,000 per employee, twelfth-place Intel's $62,000, and twenty-third-place Cisco's $81,000 (Hira and Ross 2007). As the *IBM 2003 Annual Report* (IBM 2004, p. 49) stated, "A key transformation that has been taking place over the past decade and that continues today is the change in the focus and the culture of IBM's R&D organization to be more closely linked to and be primarily driven by industry-specific and client-specific needs."[3]

Integral to this strategy has been extensive patenting for the purposes of cross-licensing and intellectual property (IP) revenue generation (Chesbrough 2003; DiCarlo 1999; Grindley and Teece 1997). Cross-licensing has enabled IBM to gain access to technology developed by other companies rather than relying on in-house R&D. IBM sees its IP revenues, which averaged $1.3 billion per year over 2000–2004, as a direct return on its R&D expenditures, which averaged $5.3 billion over the same period. During the 1990s, as IBM scaled back its R&D expenditure rate, it ramped up its patenting activity. IBM was ninth in the number of U.S. patents awarded in 1989 and 1990, eighth in 1991, and sixth in 1992. With a 29 percent increase in patents awarded in 1993, IBM moved into the number one spot and has maintained that position in every subsequent year to the present (IFI Patent Intelligence 2008).

The company's new emphasis on services and software, as well as the vertically specialized structure of the ICT industry, which IBM itself had played a major role in creating, rendered the use of a fluid and flexible high-tech labor force much more desirable and possible than had been the case in the 1980s. Given the absence of in-house investments in proprietary systems, the organizational and technological rationales for Old Economy lifelong employment no longer existed at IBM. The company now favored younger employees, whose higher education was up-to-date and who had work experience at other companies within the ICT industries, over older employees who had spent their careers with IBM. In 1995 IBM rescinded the early-retirement offer that had helped it downsize its labor force; the offer had accomplished its purpose, and in any case, IBM no longer wanted to encourage all employees to remain with the company even until the age of 55 (Schultz 2000).

THE END OF "THE HP WAY"

Founded by William Hewlett and David Packard in Palo Alto, California, in 1939 to produce electronic test instruments, Hewlett-Packard, as HP was then known, grew to about 200 employees on the basis of military contracts during World War II. After the war, the company laid off most of the women who had been wartime production workers, bringing the employment level down to 111 in 1947. From that point on, HP's year-end employment level rose continuously for 38 years, until it reached 84,000 people in 1985. Employment declined by 2 percent in 1986 and by 6 percent in 1990–1991, with the reductions achieved through the offer of early retirement packages and relocations (Clark 1991; *New York Times* 1986; Ryan 1990). HP's employment level then grew to 124,600 in 1998, before dropping to 84,400 in 1999 when the company spun off Agilent, which contained its noncomputer-related businesses.

HP was able to sustain its no-layoff policy for more than half a century because, through continuous product innovation (see Packard 1995, Appendix 2), it was able to increase its revenues in every year from 1949 through 2000 (adjusting for the 1999 Agilent divestiture). Moreover, under Hewlett and Packard's leadership, the company avoided taking on long-term debt, which in the case of a downturn, could take employment decisions out of the company's control. Frank Williams, HP's manager of Corporate Personnel and Administration and Operations, said, "We try to operate the company in a manner that assures that everyone has a job" (Gutchess 1985b, p. 28).

The company adjusted to slower-than-expected growth as well as (infrequent) month-to-month declines by the use of subcontracting and a system of short-time working that became known as the "nine-day fortnight." First used for a few months in 1970 and then again for short periods in 1985 and 1992, the nine-day fortnight had every employee take off work every second Friday, with a 10 percent reduction in pay (Gutchess 1985b, p. 28; Mandel, Forest, and McWilliams 1992; McNerney 1996, p. 6; Moskowitz 1985; Packard 1995, pp. 133–134). HP also kept people employed by moving them around the organization to activities and locations in which more employees were needed. If a person did not want to move, he or she could get a voluntary severance package amounting to a half month's pay for every year of service with a minimum of four months (McNerney 1996). The company maintained its no-layoff policy through the 1990s, not by guaranteeing jobs but by ensuring that employees who were no longer required in certain types of jobs and certain locations would have the opportunity to find other employment within the company.

In his 1995 autobiography, *The HP Way*, Packard (1995, p. 134) cautioned that the company's employment policy did not represent "a commitment to providing absolute tenure status to our people." Yet in 1995 the company, with 105,200 employees, remained committed to its no-layoff policy at a time when most U.S. high-tech corporations had embraced "employability"—the notion that, by accumulating capabilities, a person could move from company to company and even from one type of job to another type in a constantly changing labor market. In a 1996 article in *HR Focus*, the human resources newsletter of the American Management Association, staff writer Donald McNerney (1996, p. 6) contrasted HP's ongoing "Old Economy" employment relations to the new norm among high-tech companies: "Not every firm buys into the new social contract with its emphasis on job cuts, mobile employees, and incessant churn. Hewlett-Packard, for one, rejects it outright." McNerney then quoted Tom Pierson, manager of HR planning, staffing, and relocations at HP's Palo Alto headquarters, as saying,

> I think [the employability doctrine] is just a rationalization for not being able to provide employment security . . . We feel very strongly about employment security. We still cherish careers [with the company] . . . We have a lot of our benefit and employee programs geared around length of service... And we've structured our total compensation package in a way that says: The longer you're here, the better off you are. (McNerney 1996, p. 6)

Pierson went on to argue that HP derived "a sizable return on investment" from employment security; the company could attract the best employees and keep turnover very low. After all, he observed: "[The HP Way] is Bill's and Dave's philosophy of how they started the company. They did not want to create a hire-and-fire organization." Clearly imbued with the spirit of Hewlett and Packard, Pierson concluded, "I have a real tough time wrapping my mind around the idea that, at the end of the day, I don't owe you anything and you don't owe me anything. That's not the way I want to run a company."

Unlike IBM, which deliberately and dramatically made the transition to New Economy employment relations in the first half of the 1990s, HP sustained its commitment to employment security through the 1990s. That this commitment lasted as long as it did is testimony to the legacy of the HP Way, a corporate philosophy whose life at the company was probably prolonged by the 1995 publication of founder David Packard's best-selling autobiography with this title.[4] By the mid-2000s, however, HP, with 150,000 employees, had become what Packard would have called a "hire and fire" company (see Wong 2006).

As was the case at IBM, HP's transition to NEBM, including the employment of a more mobile and flexible labor force, was encouraged by a shift from proprietary to industry technology standards that had begun to take root in the early 1980s. In the 1980s and 1990s, HP found itself at the center of the microelectronics revolution not only because of its location in Palo Alto, where it acquired iconic status as the pioneering Silicon Valley firm, but also because of a business strategy that focused increasingly on consumer-oriented computer products and peripherals. In 1983 computer products (including computers, calculators, printers, supplies, services, and support) accounted for 51 percent of HP's revenues while electronic test and measurement equipment—the business upon which HP had been founded—accounted for 37 percent.

In 1984, with the PC revolution in full swing, HP made a strategic decision to manufacture its computer products to comply with the open systems that had emerged in the IT industry (Beckman 1996; Deutschman 1994). As stated in HP's *1984 Annual Report* (Hewlett-Packard 1985, p. 11), "Because it recognizes how critical networking is to improving productivity, HP supports an 'open systems' concept whereby computer makers design their systems so that computers can 'talk' with those of other makers. It also supports industry standards that govern networks."

When, as a critical step in its move to open systems, HP introduced the first PC-compatible LaserJet printer in 1984, it had entered into an agreement, still in force in the 2000s, to purchase all of its printer engines from Canon. In the mid-2000s, Canon controlled more than 50 percent of the global laser printer market by selling its machines under its own name as well as to HP on an OEM basis (*Nikkei Weekly* 2005).

Based largely on this open systems strategy, HP's revenues increased from $4.7 billion to $47.1 billion from 1983 to 1998, representing an expansion of 6.1 times in real dollars. HP achieved this sixfold increase in real revenues, moreover, with an expansion in employment of only 1.7 times—from 72,000 to 142,600—with the result that sales per employee in 1998 dollars increased by 3.5 times, from $107,000 to $378,000.

In building its competitive strategy around open systems, HP acquired a greater interest in employing a labor force with industry-wide experience as distinct from one that had in-house experience in proprietary technology. HP's major Route 128 rivals in the minicomputer industry—Digital Equipment Corporation (DEC), Wang Laboratories, and Data General—all continued to adhere to proprietary systems, and all ceased to exist in the 1990s. In 1984 DEC had $1,527 million in minicomputer sales to HP's $950 million (Chandler 2001, pp. 118–119). In the 1990s, however, DEC fell victim to competition from ever more powerful and functional open-systems computers, and in 1998 DEC was acquired by Compaq—a company that, by cloning the IBM PC, had become a global leader in personal computers. What was left of DEC, a company that had a peak employment of 126,000 people, ultimately became a part of HP with the HP-Compaq merger in 2002.

In 1999 HP spun off its noncomputer-related businesses—test and measurement instrumentation, medical electronic equipment, and analytical instrumentation—as Agilent Technologies. Combined, these businesses had $6.5 billion of HP's $47.1 billion 1998 revenues and 43,000 of HP's 125,000 employees. Using a new business segment classification system, HP reported that "imaging and printing systems" represented 43 percent of revenues and 63 percent of earnings from operations in 1999, and "computing systems" 40 percent of revenues and 27 percent of earnings from operations. The only other important business segment (but one that HP was eager to expand) was IT services, with 15 percent of revenues and 13 percent of earnings from operations.

Although various types of computers, from handheld devices to engineering workstations, were important to HP's growth in the 1980s and 1990s, printers and the ink cartridges to supply them were the main drivers of the company's remarkable expansion. In 1995 HP had 61 percent of the U.S. monochrome laser printer market, which featured high-speed output, and 48 percent of the U.S. ink-jet printer market, which featured inexpensive machines for color printing (Business Wire 1996). In 2005 HP had about 50 percent of the "all-in-one" ink-jet printer market, an important segment for HP not only because of its rapid growth but also because it did not have to share the profits from these machines with Canon (K.S. Brown 2005; Morrison 2005).

HP's dependence on printers and ink refills would be even greater in the second half of the 2000s if it had not been for the company's merger with Compaq Computer in 2002. In 2007, imaging and printing generated 27 percent of total revenues and 43 percent of earnings from operations, while personal computer systems generated 34 percent of revenues but only 19 of earnings. HP has vied with Dell for world leadership in PC sales, with HP having a 18.9 percent share and Dell a 15.4 percent share in the first quarter of 2008 (Gonsalves 2008). Meanwhile, HP managed to expand its IT services from 12 percent of total revenues and 14 percent of earnings in 2000 to 16 percent of total revenues and 18 percent of earnings in 2007. That expansion took a great leap forward in 2008 when HP acquired Electronic Data Systems (EDS). With

$22.1 billion in revenues and 139,500 employees in 2007, EDS was, after IBM, the second largest U.S. IT services company.

Selling consumer-oriented products in markets in which price competition is intense, HP is no longer the "engineers' company" that Hewlett and Packard built. Like IBM, HP now allocates a much smaller percentage of sales to R&D than in the past. In 2000–2007, R&D expenditures were only 4.9 percent of sales, reaching an all-time low of 2.8 percent in 2008, compared with annual averages of 10.3 percent in the 1980s and 8.2 percent in the 1990s. At the same time, HP has advanced to the top ranks in patenting. When it launched its PC-compatible printers in 1984, HP had 63 patents in the United States, which placed it not even in the top 100 among all organizations and far behind second-place IBM (608) and sixth-place Canon (430). By 2004 HP had climbed to fourth place before falling back to tenth in 2007 (IFI Patent Intelligence 2008). Many of HP's patents are on its ink; the purpose of these ink patents is not only to improve product quality but also to block companies that cut into its revenues and profits by refilling and refurbishing empty print cartridges.

These changes in HP's product-market strategy over the past two decades have had far-reaching consequences for the company's employment relations. HP has no interest in making a commitment to provide careers within the company to the mass of its employees, as it did under OEBM. Another direct consequence of the move to open systems is that, since the mid-1980s, HP has been a leader among ICT companies in the outsourcing of employment to EMS providers. As in the case of IBM, HP's initial relations with EMS providers during the 1990s occurred when it transferred its manufacturing plants to them. The move to open systems facilitated the growth of EMS providers because now components became more modular, with standard interfaces for systems integration (Sturgeon 2002; Tully 1993). The transfer of manufacturing facilities from HP to EMS providers was integral to the process whereby HP transformed itself into a vertically specialized company that could generate extraordinarily high levels of sales per employee, reaching $608,000 in 2005–2007.

The 1999 spinoff of Agilent Technologies marked the beginning of the end of the HP Way. A few months after the Agilent spinoff, HP hired a new CEO, Cara Carleton S. Fiorina, an apostle of the New Economy recruited from Lucent Technologies (Burrows and Elstrom 1999). In her first analyst briefing as HP CEO, Fiorina was critical of her predecessors for failing to expand revenues fast enough and said that she was remedying the situation by dismissing sales representatives with poor records and revamping the compensation program (Fisher 1999). In November 2000 Fiorina altered HP's performance ranking system by ordering that 5 percent rather than the previous 1 percent of employees receive the lowest ranking, thus increasing the number of people who would have difficulty finding a new job within the company, should the positions in which they currently worked be eliminated (Poletti 2001a).

In early 2001, with economic recession setting in, HP announced that it would cut 1,700 marketing jobs and 3,000 of 14,000 management positions (Bergstein 2001a). The company continued to adhere to the traditional policy that gave these employees the opportunity to find another position within HP (Poletti 2001b). In late July, however—by which time 1,000 people whose jobs had been cut earlier in the year had left the company—HP announced that it would chop 6,000 jobs, amounting to 6.5 percent of its global labor force (Kirby 2001; Riley 2001). With 10,700 jobs having been eliminated within just seven months, displaced employees faced dim prospects of finding new positions within HP. When the announcement of 6,000 new layoffs was made, a company spokesperson commented, "Obviously people can't be happy when business isn't going well. But I think most people understand we are a business, and we have to do certain things to ensure our profitability" (Riley 2001). While HP's management never officially announced the demise of the HP Way, neither would it henceforth invoke it as the prevailing corporate philosophy.

Then, in September 2001, HP declared its intention to merge with Compaq Computer, the world's second largest PC producer and largest enterprise server producer, with a total of $33.6 billion in sales and 63,700 employees. HP was number four in both product markets, with a total of $18.2 billion in revenues. Given the downturn in ICT markets in 2001, it was clear that the merger of the two companies would entail a consolidation of operations that would mean a considerable loss of jobs. Indeed, it was the possibility of cost-savings through postcombination consolidation that made the merger financially attractive. HP's estimate for postmerger downsizing was 15,000 jobs (Bergstein 2001b). HP employees were subsequently told that any worker in the United States who was not selected for a position in the merged company would be given nine weeks with pay to find a new position within the company and, if unsuccessful, would then receive severance pay equal to a half-month's salary for every year of full-time service, with a minimum of four months and a maximum of 12 (Pimentel 2002a; *San Francisco Chronicle* 2002).

Sons of each of the company's cofounders sought to block the merger. Walter Hewlett voiced his opposition as a member of the HP board on the grounds that "the combination would dramatically increase Hewlett-Packard's exposure to the unattractive PC business and dilute current stockholders' interest in Hewlett-Packard's profitable printer business" (PR Newswire 2001). Hewlett was joined in opposing the merger by David Woodley Packard, who had been on the HP board until 1999, when he resigned to devote more time to his philanthropic foundation, the Packard Humanities Institute (Anders 1999). Packard's objection had to do with the fact that the merger would inevitably result in mass layoffs. As he put it,

> I am perfectly aware that HP has never guaranteed absolute ten-ure status to its employees; but I also know that Bill and Dave never developed a premeditated business strategy that treated HP employees as expendable. This new approach seems likely to affect the confidence and loyalty of the remaining employees. For over 50 years, one of HP's fundamental corporate objectives has been to provide long-term employment for its people. (Seipel 2001)

As the sole board member against the merger, Hewlett filed a law-suit in March 2002 in an attempt to block the deal. He argued that HP might have to lay off up to 24,000 employees after the merger rather than the announced figure of 15,000 (Seipel and Poletti 2002). In the end, a bare majority—51.4 percent—of HP's shareholders voted for the merger.

One year after the merger, employment at HP had declined from 153,500 to 141,400, the net result of 18,900 layoffs and 6,800 new hires (Takahashi 2003, 2004; see also Pimentel 2003). Fiorina stated that 16,600 of the terminations were "integration" layoffs; the other 2,300, done in February–April 2003, could, she claimed, be construed as "business layoffs." The low point for postmerger employment at HP was 139,800 in the summer of 2003, and the number of employees that HP reported at the end of fiscal 2003 was 142,000.

In early 2005 Fiorina was herself ousted from her job—with a $21.1 million severance package—because she, reportedly, "failed to slash costs and boost revenue as quickly as directors had hoped" (Konrad 2005). From the time of the merger with Compaq through 2006, HP laid off 45,000 employees, while hiring almost as many new employees (Wong 2006). The purpose of this "churn" was to reduce costs.

In the process, U.S. employees as a proportion of HP's worldwide employees declined from 48 percent in 2002 to 31 percent in 2007 (HP 2008, pp. 16, 134). HP's employment strategy has included substantial offshoring of production to China. HP had entered China in 1985 as part of the first Sino–U.S. high-tech joint venture (Ke 1998). Toward the end of 2006, HP employed 5,000 people in China, up from 3,000 in 2003, with immediate openings for more than 1,000 more, of which one-quarter would be R&D staff (Xinhua News Agency 2006).

HP set up a subsidiary in India in 1989, but it was not until 2002 that the company launched its first Indian research lab (Agence France-Press 2002). HP employed about 2,200 people in India just before its merger with Compaq (Dataquest 2002, 2003). At the end of 2003, after making an Indian affiliate, Digital Globalsoft, a wholly owned subsidiary, HP found itself with more than 10,000 employees in India, making it the nation's largest foreign employer, temporarily surpassing IBM (ZDNet UK 2003). By the end of 2006, HP had doubled that headcount to about 20,000 employees in India, or about 13 percent of its global labor force (CMP TechWeb 2005). In May 2008 HP announced the acquisition of EDS, which included its Bangalore-based subsidiary, MphasiS, and its 28,000 employees in India, potentially increasing HP employment in India to 59,000 (Kulkarni 2008).

The EDS acquisition was followed, however, with the inevitable integration layoffs. In September 2008 HP announced that it would cut 24,600 jobs worldwide—7.7 percent of the HP/EDS global labor force—with about half of the workforce reductions occurring in the United States (Bailey 2008; Robertson 2008). By 2008 such massive terminations had become the new HP way.

LUCENT'S FAILED TRANSITION TO NEBM

In 1999, at the height of the Internet boom, Lucent Technologies was the world's largest telecommunications equipment company.[5] With reported revenues of $38.3 billion, net income of $3.5 billion, and 153,000 employees for the fiscal year ending September 30, 1999, Lucent was far larger and more profitable than Nortel, Alcatel, and Ericsson, its three major global competitors. In 2006, however, Lucent's revenues were only $8.8 billion, and its employment level had dropped to 29,800. Both figures were lower than those of Lucent's three main rivals, even though all four companies had gone through wrenching declines in the early 2000s as the Internet boom turned to bust.

Indeed, Alcatel was almost twice the size of Lucent in terms of revenues and employees when the merger that created Alcatel-Lucent took place in December 2006, and Lucent Technologies became a wholly owned subsidiary of Alcatel. Lucent CEO Patricia Russo was named CEO of Alcatel-Lucent, but she occupied her new position at Alcatel headquarters in Paris.

Lucent could trace its origins back to Cleveland, Ohio, in 1869, when Elisha Gray and Enos Barton launched a company that manufactured telegraph equipment for Western Union. In 1872 the firm was reorganized as Western Electric Manufacturing Company, with its headquarters in Chicago. In 1881 American Telephone and Telegraph acquired a controlling interest in Western Electric. Subsequently, as AT&T's wholly owned subsidiary, Western Electric became its exclusive manufacturer of telecommunications equipment. In 1913 AT&T became a regulated monopoly for the provision of telephone service in the United States, thus making Western Electric in effect a monopolist in the provision of telephone equipment and infrastructures. In 1970 Western Electric had a peak employment of over 215,000 people, placing the company in seventh place among the largest employers in the Fortune 500.[6]

In the 1970s AT&T was challenged by new entrants into the long-distance business (in particular MCI) that demanded that AT&T provide them with access to its transmission infrastructure. In 1974 the U.S. Department of Justice launched an antitrust suit against AT&T, which resulted in the breakup of the Bell System on January 1, 1984. As we have discussed, the breakup separated seven regional Bell operating companies, or RBOCs, from AT&T Corp., which now included within its internal organization Western Electric and Bell Labs as its AT&T Technologies division. AT&T became a competitive long-distance telephone company but was excluded from entering local telephone markets, and the RBOCs continued to operate as regulated monopolies. The 1982 modification of the 1956 consent decree that underlay the breakup of the Bell System, however, left AT&T free to enter the computer industry. Toward that end, in a 1991 $7.4 billion hostile takeover, AT&T acquired NCR, a company that (as National Cash Register) itself dated back to 1884.

In September 1995 AT&T announced the "trivestiture." The direct impetus to the trivestiture was the pending passage of the Telecommunications Act of 1996, which would open up competition across all lines of business within the telecommunications industry. AT&T would now have a strong incentive to procure telecommunications equipment from suppliers other than its own manufacturing division, whereas AT&T's competitors might be reluctant to place equipment orders with AT&T Technologies while it remained a captive manufacturing organization. Meanwhile AT&T had failed to integrate NCR into its operations. Given that AT&T would now be a focused telecommunications service provider, it made sense to spin off NCR along with Lucent Technologies.

Lucent's IPO in April 1996 was the largest in U.S. history up to that time. Lucent executives were fond of saying that their company was a 127-year-old start-up that had well over $20 billion in annual sales. Running the company was Henry Schacht, an AT&T board member since 1981 who, in 1995 at the age of 60, had retired as chairman of Cummins Engine (Endlich 2004, chap. 3). Lucent's president and COO was 46-year-old Rich McGinn, a veteran of two decades in the Bell System who, despite having only an undergraduate degree in history, had risen to be head of AT&T's Network Systems group. It was generally recognized that McGinn was Schacht's heir apparent (p. 32), and indeed, in October 1997, McGinn took over from Schacht as CEO.

When McGinn became CEO, a press release quoted him as saying that he viewed "Lucent as a group of hot businesses, tightly focused on its customers, markets and competitors" (Business Wire 1997). These "hot businesses" consisted of four types: 1) core network products, including switching and access, optical networking, and wireless networking; 2) support businesses, including microelectronics, business communications systems, and network products; 3) new opportunity businesses, including the intellectual property group, the new ventures group, and data networking systems; and 4) software services, including communications software and global service provider business.

Lucent was able to take advantage of the Internet boom to increase its revenues at a compound rate of over 17 percent per year during the first four years of its existence. The core of Lucent's business in these years was its Systems for Network Operators division, which grew from $10.6 billion in revenues in 1995, when the company was still part of AT&T, to $23.6 billion, or 62 percent of revenues, just four years later. Most of Lucent's growth came from its "incumbent advantage" in supplying equipment to its traditional customers, AT&T and the RBOCs. During the latter half of the 1990s, these former Bell System service providers were buying equipment to provide multiple telephone lines to households and businesses to be used for dial-up Internet access across copper lines and increasing the capacity of local and regional networks to support escalating Internet traffic. The growth potential of this incumbent advantage eventually reached its limits, largely because of the advent of broadband Internet access via coaxial television cables as well as asymmetric digital subscriber line (ADSL) technology. At this point, Lucent faced the challenge of diversifying its customer base to supply equipment to the many newer entrants among the wireless and wireline service providers who were not encumbered by the sunk costs of legacy systems.

Two "next generation" service providers, Winstar and Global Crossing, that Lucent secured as customers in the late 1990s went bankrupt, and after 2000 Lucent remained heavily reliant on its traditional Bell System customers for revenues. In 2000, AT&T represented 10 percent of Lucent's revenues and Verizon 13 percent. In 2004–2006, Lucent's last three years of existence, Verizon's share of total revenues was about 28 percent. Lucent's most important non-Bell customer was Sprint, an incumbent long-distance provider, for which Lucent built much of its wireless network beginning in 1996. Sprint accounted for 15 percent of Lucent revenues in 2003, 11 percent in 2004, and 12 percent in 2005.

In the late 1990s, Lucent made a push into foreign markets that increased sales outside the United States from $6.7 billion in 1997 to $12.2 billion in 1999, an increase from 26 percent to 32 percent of total sales. Most of the increase in foreign revenues from 1997 to 1999/2000 was in Service Provider Networks, although the Enterprise Networks group, which would be spun off as Avaya in 2000, and Microelectronics and Communications Technologies (MCT), which would be spun off as Agere in 2001, also generated substantial increases in foreign sales during the Internet boom.

From the start, Lucent Technologies emphasized the role that Bell Labs could play in its efforts to compete as an independent company. Indeed, "Bell Labs Innovation" was inscribed on the company's logo. Under the system inherited from AT&T, Lucent's competitive strength was the quality of its products. The company was weak, however, in cost and time-to-market. Given the rapidity of technological change from the mid-1990s, Lucent needed to transform "Bell Labs Innovation" into commercial products at a much faster pace than in the past.

Rapid technological change in optical networking, wireless communications, and the "triple play" convergence of voice, data, and video during the second half of the 1990s led the major telecommunications equipment companies to look to acquisitions to fill critical gaps in their product portfolios as well as to give them instant access to new customers bent on investing in next-generation technologies. As will be detailed in Chapter 6, during the latter half of the 1990s, Cisco Systems engaged in growth through acquisitions, using its stock as the combination currency. Lucent (as well as Nortel and, to a more limited extent, Alcatel) followed suit (Carpenter. Lazonick, and O'Sullivan 2003). From 1998 to 2000, Lucent did 32 acquisitions valued at a total of $44.4 billion. Only 12 of these acquisitions were actually paid with Lucent's stock, but they accounted for 95 percent of the value of all Lucent's acquisitions and they absorbed 22.8 percent of Lucent's outstanding shares. (Lazonick and March 2008). Indeed, Lucent expended 13.5 percent of its stock for just one acquisition, Ascend Communications, in January 1999. Ascend's 1998 revenues (year ending September 30) were $1,478 million, or 4.9 percent of Lucent's, and it had shown a 1998 loss of $20 million.

Despite these acquisitions, Lucent failed to capitalize on the optical networking boom of 1998–2000. The company made all these acquisitions in the heat of a speculative frenzy that would not, and could not, last. Capital expenditures in the U.S. telecommunications industry went from $49.9 billion in 1998 to $60.7 billion in 1999 and $85.4 billion in 2000 before falling to $77.5 billion in 2001 and $36.4 billion in 2002 (U.S. Census Bureau 2008c). In 2000 these expenditures focused on optical networking infrastructures and equipment. Nortel was much better positioned than Lucent to take advantage of this optical networking boom. In the second half of the 1990s, Nortel had been much more aggressive than Lucent in developing high-speed optical networking equipment, while Lucent had remained much too reliant on demand from AT&T, which had already invested in inferior fiber optic cables incapable of supporting the dense wavelength-division multiplexing and OC-192 switches that next-generation carriers were demanding in 2000.

The five most expensive acquisitions in terms of cost per employee, given current stock valuations, were Chromatis Networks at $29.7 million per employee (a total of $4.8 billion); Spring Tide, $10.1 million ($1.3 billion); Nexabit, $7.4 million ($896 million); Ascend, $7.1 million ($21.4 billion); and Ortel, $5.5 million ($3.0 billion). The Chromatis acquisition failed to generate a commercial product and was shut down in August 2001, 15 months after it was acquired, with a $3.7 billion write-off. Spring Tide generated commercial products but was shut down in November 2002, with an impairment charge of $837 million. In July 2000, a year after the Nexabit acquisition, its founder left Lucent and set up as a competitor across the street. In October 2002 Lucent terminated the Nexabit product. Enriched by their shares of the $21.2 billion acquisition price, Ascend executives left in droves, many to start companies that competed with Lucent. Ortel became part of Agere, Lucent's microelectronics group spun off in early 2001. A few months later, Agere recorded a $2.7 billion impairment charge for Ortel, and sold it for $25 million in early 2003.

All of these acquisitions were made using Lucent stock as the mode of payment, thus giving Lucent the option under the then-prevailing Financial Accounting Standards Board (FASB) rules of treating the acquisitions as "pooling of interests" mergers rather than purchases. Lucent took the pooling-of-interests option for Ascend and Nexabit as well as for Kenan Systems (acquired for $1.5 billion in stock in January 1999 and sold for $300 million in cash in December 2001) and International Network Services (acquired for $3.3 billion in stock in August 1999 and sold for an undisclosed amount, possibly about $75 million, in July 2002). As a result, Lucent did not need to record the high acquisition valuations of these companies as assets on its balance sheet, and thus avoided the need to amortize these outlays in future years, which would have had a depressing effect on stated earnings. In addition, when these acquisitions lost value, the pooling-of-interests method meant that Lucent was not required to write off the investments and thus incur stated losses.[7] As a company based in Canada, Lucent's competitor, Nortel, could not avail itself of the pooling-of-interests obfuscation, and hence had to record the loss of $12.4 billion in write-downs on the four acquisitions that it made between January 2000 and February 2001. In July 2001, in the United States, FASB would outlaw the further use of pooling-of-interests methods of accounting for acquisitions (FASB 2001).

The failure of these acquisitions contributed little, therefore, to Lucent's stated losses of $14.1 billion in 2001 and $11.8 billion in 2002. Accounting tricks, however, could not change the fact that by 2001 Lucent had exhausted its incumbent advantage, the main source of its rapid growth from 1996 through 1999. With the RBOCs as its customers, Lucent had benefited from the 8 percent average annual growth in the number of telephone copper access lines in the United States from 1996 to 2000. From 2001 on, however, with the rapidly increasing adoption of coaxial cable and ADSL for Internet access, the number of telephone access lines actually declined and was 6 percent lower in 2005 than it had been in 1996, the year in which Lucent had come into existence (FCC 2007, chaps. 2 and 7).

All of the leading telecommunications equipment companies experienced significant declines in revenues, income, and employment in the Internet bust of 2001–2002. The fact that Nortel had been better positioned than Lucent to capture the booming optical networking market in 2000 only created for it greater exposure to the subsequent collapse of capital expenditures in the telecommunications industry (Carpenter, Lazonick, and O'Sullivan 2003). The question now was whether a particular company would have the capabilities and financial resources going forward to recover from the downturn and gain market share in the intensely competitive communications technology industry.

Like Nortel, where CEO John Roth was fired in November 2001, but not before raking in $100 million in remuneration (91 percent in stock options) the previous year, Lucent's decline was made much worse by the behavior of its top managers in 2000. Besides its ill-considered and costly acquisitions, Lucent's subsequent performance was adversely affected by its desperate attempt to meet Wall Street's expectations for continued growth in 2000. It was a year in which the telecommunications industry was still booming. Lucent, however, lacked the optical networking capabilities to share in that growth.

Lucent's executives engaged in excessive "vendor financing," which entailed making loans to customers to purchase Lucent equipment. It is a common practice in the telecommunications equipment industry for a vendor to secure business by offering to finance some of the purchase price of the equipment. The issue for the vendor is the risk of the loan going bad. In the Internet boom, with its young firms and unproven technologies, vendor financing could become very risky. At the end of fiscal 2000, Lucent had entered into agreements with customers to provide up to $8.1 billion in credit or loan guarantees. Lucent made provisions of what turned out to be bad debts to customers of $2.2 billion in 2001 and $1.3 billion in 2002.

In early 2001 Lucent was investigated by the SEC for "channel stuffing"—the booking of sales on shipped products preceded by private agreements with distributors that they did not have to pay for goods that they did not subsequently sell. More generally, there was great pressure on Lucent executives in 2000 to book sales before they were consummated in an attempt to meet quarterly revenue and earnings targets (Endlich 2004, chap. 8). In November 2000, after CEO McGinn was ousted, Lucent revealed that it had improperly booked $679 million in revenue during the 2000 fiscal year (Jander 2000, 2001). While the SEC took no action on this particular admission, in October 2002 it served notice to Lucent of a possible civil lawsuit over improper accounting in 1999 and 2000 to inflate its sales figures (Loomis 2003). In November 2000 the company was the target of two class action lawsuits from shareholders for misreporting its 2000 revenues and earnings (Johnson 2000). With Lucent's stock price in a free fall—in October 2002 it was just 1.5 percent of its value at its peak in December 1999—the number of lawsuits mounted, and in March 2003 the company agreed to an omnibus settlement of 54 separate lawsuits for a total of $420 million (PR Newswire 2003).

Lucent's revenues fell from $33.8 billion in 2000 to $8.5 billion in 2003, and the company booked losses for this three-year period totaling $26.8 billion. From 2000 to 2002, wireline revenues plummeted 66 percent, from $18.7 billion to $6.4 billion, while wireless revenues declined 21, percent from $6.8 billion to $5.4 billion. In the decline, the company shed assets and employees to stay afloat.

The first major disposal came at the end of fiscal 2000, when Lucent spun off its enterprise networks division, with revenues of $7.6 billion and 30,000 employees, as Avaya. In December 2000 Lucent sold its Power Systems business to Tyco International for $2.5 billion in cash. In April 2001 much of MCT would be spun off as Agere, which had 2000 external revenues of $3.1 billion and 16,500 employees worldwide. The IPO netted $3.3 billion for Agere, while the disposal left Lucent with a loss of $3.0 billion. In the first quarter of 2002, Lucent sold its Optical Fiber Solutions business to Furukawa Electric for $2.3 billion (of which about $2.1 billion was in cash).

In 2001, with revenues declining sharply from their 1999 peak, Lucent commenced a major downsizing program. By September 2002 Lucent had reduced its employment by 79,000 people, or by 63 percent of its labor force in 2000. The divestitures of the power business, fiber optic cable business, and microelectronics removed almost 28,000 people from the company. Most of remaining headcount reduction of 51,000 came through voluntary and involuntary terminations, including an early retirement program offered to 8,500 management personnel (Lucent Technologies 2002, pp. 3–4, 56; Prencipe 2001).

In addition, as a continuation of an outsourcing strategy begun in the boom but one that had become driven by the need to downsize in the decline, Lucent sold or leased some of its major manufacturing plants to contract manufacturers such as Solectron and Celestica. A prime example is the fate of Lucent's Merrimack Valley Works (MVW), located in North Andover, Massachusetts, about 30 miles north of Boston (see Lazonick, Fiddy, and Quimby 2002; Lazonick and Quimby 2007). MVW began operations in 1952 as the Western Electric factory that manufactured telecommunications transmission equipment for AT&T's Bell System, and it moved to its North Andover site in 1956. With 1.8 million square feet of manufacturing floor space, MVW had employed a peak of more than 10,000 people in the mid-1970s. In 1999–2000 MVW employed 5,600 people in jobs that were viewed as among the best in Boston's Route 128 high-tech region.

Among these employees were 250 engineers, as well as about 3,000 production workers represented by the Communications Workers of America (CWA). During the Internet boom, in response to the demands of rapid product development in the plant's optical networking products, MVW had been upgrading the skills of many of its production workers to function as testers, the highest-skilled shop-floor occupation. When MVW could not generate sufficient employees with the requisite capabilities internally to fill the demand for testers, its HR people searched New England community colleges for technically qualified recruits. With this combination of engineering and production capabilities, Lucent designated MVW as the company's "manufacturing center of excellence and global systems integration center" for optical networking products in June 2000 (Lucent Technologies 2000).

When that announcement was made, no one at Lucent imagined that within three years more than 80 percent of MVW's employees would be gone, with most of the layoffs occurring in 2001 and early 2002. In June 2002, with the telecommunications industry in a major slump, Lucent sold most of MVW's manufacturing operations to a contract manufacturer, A-Plus (owned by Solectron), which agreed to employ about 550 people from MVW. Lucent retained a product development staff of about 2,000 employees at MVW. By April 2003 A-Plus had ceased operations, and Lucent's MVW payroll was down to just over 1,000 people. In September 2003 the MVW campus was sold for $13.9 million to a local developer, with Lucent remaining as a tenant (Murray 2003a). In June 2007 Alcatel-Lucent announced that it would close the North Andover operations, which by then employed 475 people, and move production to Italy (McCabe 2007a).[8] Beginning in December 2007, Alcatel-Lucent began laying off the remaining 290 CWA members, with plans to transfer 190 managerial employees to the company's research center in Westford, Massachusetts (McCabe 2007b).

The CWA, which had represented some 3,000 workers at MVW as late as April 2001, had only 260 members employed by MVW in April 2003 (Murray 2003b,c). In September 1999, across its U.S. plants, Lucent employed 46,818 union members representing 40 percent of its U.S. labor force. Lucent employed only 6,800 U.S. union members in September 2002 and 2,800 in September 2006. Adding in the 2,800 union members at Avaya and the 26 U.S. union members at Agere, union-represented workers made up only 15 percent of the 38,199 U.S. employees of the three companies at the end of September 2006.[9]

Disposals of assets and downsizing of employment, however, were not sufficient to keep Lucent solvent. In the decline of 2001–2002, as its financial shortfalls mounted and its stock price plunged, Lucent was forced to go to the stock market as a source of finance, mainly because its downgraded bond rating made it impossible for the company to issue long-term debt. In August 2001 Lucent did a preferred stock issue that netted $1.83 billion (Lucent Technologies 2002, pp. 69–70), and in March 2002, when its bond rating had been cut for the fifth time in 16 months, it did a more complicated deal in which it set up a trust to issue preferred securities and then had the trust buy 7.75 percent convertible subordinated debentures from Lucent for a net cash inflow of $1.75 billion (Lucent Technologies 2003, p. 37).

The irony for a company like Lucent—and it applies to many other U.S. companies that experienced financial difficulties in the Internet bust—is that it could have used the speculative stock market of the New Economy boom to sell stock on the market to pay off debt or augment the corporate treasury (see Carpenter, Lazonick, and O'Sullivan 2003). After all, U.S. corporations had engaged in such refinancing in the speculative boom of the late 1920s (O'Sullivan 2004), and, in more recent history, major Japanese corporations had sold massive amounts of stock in Japan's "bubble economy" of the late 1980s (Lazonick 1999). Had it not been for this financial behavior, the adverse impacts on these corporations of the subsequent downturns—in the United States in the early 1930s and in Japan in the early 1990s—would have been more severe.

In the Internet boom, however, Lucent gave away the company's overvalued stock to do New Economy acquisitions that often impressed the stock market but that were more often than not shuttered or sold off at a large loss within a year or two, in some cases with the acquisition never having produced a commercializable product. In desperately shedding plants and people to survive in the Internet bust, moreover, Lucent disposed of well-developed capabilities that would be needed to compete in the 2000s. The spinoff of its microelectronics unit as Agere meant that Lucent lost any strategic advantage that it could have obtained from its microelectronics acquisitions as well as from Bell Labs device research investments that the company had made. The spinoff of its enterprise networks division as Avaya deprived Lucent of capabilities that would have been critical for competing for lucrative business communications services markets in the 2000s.

In accounting for fiscal 2006, its last year of operation as an independent company, Lucent split its Integrated Networks Solutions (INS) business into Multimedia Network Solutions (MNS) and Converged Core Solutions (CCS). This division reflected Lucent's responses to the challenges for the convergence of voice, data, and video in core transmission systems on the one hand and optical networking on the other. MNS revenues grew from $1,498 million in 2005 to $1,677 million in 2006, while CCS, once the backbone of Lucent's business, continued its dramatic decline, falling from $1,215 million in 2004 to $600 million in 2006.

Since CCS represented Lucent's "incumbent advantage," its decline did not necessarily reflect the company's failure to make the transition to NEBM. On the contrary, as we have seen in the cases of IBM and HP, their successful transitions to NEBM entailed shedding, or at least downsizing, old businesses and growing new ones. Lucent's problem in the 2000s was that it was unable to sustain revenue growth in those segments of the communications technology industry, most notably wireless communications, in which New Economy opportunities presented themselves.

In the boom years of 1998–2000, wireless products made up 18 percent of the Lucent's revenues. During the first half of the 2000s, as Lucent's overall sales lagged behind those of its main rivals, it nevertheless had considerable success in selling base stations, the central equipment for wireless infrastructures. From 2002 through 2005 Lucent steadily increased the number of installed base stations from 70,000 to 140,000, of which 35,000 were 3G in 2002 and 90,000 were 3G in 2005. All 20,000 base stations installed in 2005 were 3G.[10]

The problem was that all of the 3G base stations that Lucent installed were CDMA2000. Lucent failed to leverage the company's expertise in CDMA technology "to establish a strong position" in UMTS networks, as had been the company's expectation in 2002 (Lucent Technologies 2003, p. 10).[11] Lucent reported that it was conducting UMTS customer trials with Telefonica Spain, T-Mobile Germany, and AT&T Wireless in 2003 and with Cingular, China Netcom, and China's Ministry of Information Industry in 2004. Subsequently Lucent's reports were silent on the subject because the company had in fact failed completely in the commercialization of UMTS and, as a result, had lost out on sales to growing Asian and European markets. For example, the Chinese market, which had become important for Lucent's wireless products in the early 2000s, declined as a proportion of Lucent's total revenues from

11 percent in 2003 to 10 percent in 2004 to 9 percent in 2005 and then to only 4 percent in 2006. The decline in the Chinese market accounted for more than three-quarters of Lucent's $645 million decline in total revenues from 2005 to 2006.

Meanwhile in the 2000s, Lucent made its bottom line look better by adding "pension credits" to its income. As a "127-year-old start-up," Lucent had one of the biggest pension surpluses of any U.S. company, with additions to the surplus being generated year in and year out. Lucent's management allocated these pension credits to various operations, thus augmenting the bottom line. From 1996 through 2006, Lucent was able to claim $9.1 billion in pension credits, without which its total net income over its 11 years of existence would have been −$21.9 billion rather than −$12.7 billion.

From 2002 through 2005, as the company failed to reemerge as a viable competitor, Lucent chairman and CEO Patricia Russo received $39.6 million in compensation, even though none of it was from exercising stock options.[12] At what would be Lucent's last Annual General Meeting, in February 2006, two shareholders' resolutions were passed against the opposition of management, one that linked executives' stock-based pay to company performance and the other that precluded the company from basing performance pay for top executives on income figures that included the pension credit (Coughlin 2006; McKay 2006).

These rare triumphs of shareholder activism were, however, too little too late. On December 1, 2006, Lucent ceased to exist as an independent company. In 2008, about two years after the formation of Alcatel-Lucent, the merger was going quite badly, with net income negative in 2007 and the first half of 2008 (see Carpenter and Lazonick 2008; Hollinger et al. 2007; Keller 2008). In July 2008, Russo resigned as CEO, along with Alcatel-Lucent chairman Serge Tchuruk. Dragging down the French company, which had now become the world's largest in communications equipment, was the need to integrate an American company that had been badly damaged in its attempt to adopt NEBM.

SUCCESS AND FAILURE IN THE TRANSITION TO NEBM

Why were IBM and HP able to make successful transitions to NEBM, whereas Lucent was not? To succeed in global competition, a high-tech company must transform technology and access markets to generate higher-quality, lower-cost products than its rivals. In the 1990s, with the emergence of open technologies and deregulated markets, global competition became intense. As IT companies under OEBM, both IBM and HP had already competed in deregulated markets, but with proprietary systems. In the first half of the 1980s, both these companies made strategic decisions to take the lead in the development of open systems, with IBM focusing on microcomputers and HP focusing on computer peripherals. By the end of the 1980s, IBM dominated the PC market while HP dominated the laser printer market. Over the course of the 1990s, each of these companies then shed the proprietary technology businesses on which, under OEBM, they had been built, to focus on open systems businesses. Indeed, so successful was IBM in expanding its high-margin software business and its scalable service business that it decided to offload its now low-margin PCs in 2004.

In contrast, in its incarnations as Western Electric and a division of AT&T, Lucent Technologies had operated in highly regulated markets. Indeed, the impetus to the spinoff of Lucent from AT&T was the Tele-communications Act of 1996, which opened up competition in telecommunications, with two standards for digital multiplexing over optical fiber (SONET in North America and SDH in Europe) and two standards for 2G wireless transmission (CDMA in North America and GSM in Europe). Yet even in the boom years from 1996 to 1999, Lucent's prime customers remained AT&T and the RBOCs, which continued to build out and upgrade their legacy networks. As a result, Lucent's traditional business of supplying service providers with legacy wireline infrastructure, including network switches and copper access lines, remained central to its rapid growth. Meanwhile, in a telecommunications world characterized by rapid technological change, Bell Labs remained the global industry's leading corporate research lab. Given its history as a regulated monopoly, however, Lucent lacked the organizational capabilities to effect the rapid transformation of Bell Labs inventions into revenue-generating innovations.

At the peak of the Internet boom, Lucent tried to make up for these technological and market deficiencies by using large proportions of its stock to make New Economy acquisitions and by providing highly risky vendor financing to next-generation service providers. Indeed, Lucent's top executives sought to use these acquisitions and contracts to impress the stock market, cooking the company's books in the process to make Lucent's growth look better than it actually was. Some of the acquisitions did not yet have commercial products, and, most notably in the case of Ascend, the exorbitant price paid for a revenue-generating target led many key executives, and with them scores of technical and administrative personnel, to take their newfound wealth and walk out Lucent's door. When the telecommunications markets collapsed in 2001–2002, Lucent found itself in financial distress, and it lacked the resources to build revenues in the fast-growing wireless markets operating on different 2G and, eventually, 3G standards in different parts of the world.

From the perspective of the prospects for sustainable prosperity, Lucent's failure comes at a high cost for the U.S. economy. Bell Labs, the world's greatest corporate research lab, now part of Alcatel-Lucent, no longer does fundamental research (Berman 2003; Brumfiel 2008). In an industry that continues to grow rapidly on a global scale, the United States has lost tens of thousands of high-quality jobs with little prospect for their replacement, much less enhancement. A company that had excellent labor relations and in-house programs that enabled unionized shop-floor workers to upgrade their skill levels and in some cases even become university-educated engineers now, as Alcatel-Lucent, has a decimated union presence in the United States.

Even the successes of IBM and HP, however, come at a cost to the U.S. economy. The companies are the two largest ICT companies in the world, with long traditions of cutting-edge engineering, but neither company engages in basic research. In the 2000s both IBM and HP have had high and growing levels of employment, but most of these employees are based outside the United States. The trajectories of both companies strongly suggest that the number of U.S.-based employees will continue to decline absolutely as well as in proportion to the worldwide total. Among U.S. employees of IBM and HP, the expectation of career employment is dead and has been replaced by considerable employment uncertainty and even employee churn. In the 2000s both IBM and HP have been profiting immensely from their globalization strategies.

But, as we shall see in Chapter 6, their prime use of these profits has been to spend tens of billions of dollars repurchasing their own stock.

Notes

1. IBM employment data for the United States by type of employment as well as gender, race, and ethnicity of employees from 1996 through 2007 can be viewed at http://www-03.ibm.com/employment/us/diverse/employment_data.shtml (accessed July 6, 2009).
2. As of 2007, IBM changed its segment classification scheme so that one can no longer identify hardware sales.
3. All of the annual reports, 10-K filings, and global citizenship reports cited in this volume can be found at the respective company's Web site or at most business libraries.
4. Packard, who had retired as HP's chairman of the board in 1993, died in March 1996. Cofounder William Hewlett, who retired as CEO of HP in 1978 and as vice chairman of the board in 1987, died in January 2001.
5. The material in this section is based on my collaboration with Dr. Edward J. March, formerly director of Circuit Pack Engineering and Manufacturing, Optical Networking Group, Lucent Technologies, and currently visiting professor of engineering at Dartmouth College (see Lazonick and March 2008). I am grateful to Professor March for his permission to use the results of our joint work here.
6. In 1970 AT&T itself employed 773,000 people but as a service company was not included in the Fortune 500 list of the largest industrial companies based in the United States.
7. For Cisco's use of pooling-of-interests accounting for its acquisitions in the 1990s, see Donlan (2000).
8. For an analysis of what happened to the displaced MVW employees, based on training and reemployment data under a U.S. Department of Labor National Emergency Grant, see Lazonick and Quimby (2007).
9. In addition, Avaya added 2,970 union members outside of the United States as a result of its November 2004 acquisition of Tenovis Germany GmbH.
10. Starting in 2001, digital wireless telephony began to made the transition from 2G (or second generation) technology, which has limited and slow data transmission capabilities, to 3G (or third generation) technology, which enables cell phone users to make use of the services provided by high-speed Internet.
11. Within 3G technology, CDMA2000 is a network standard that is dominant in North America, whereas UMTS (of which the most widely used air interface is W-CDMA) is a network standard that is dominant in Western Europe. In the fast-growing Chinese market, both CDMA2000 and UMTS are employed, but in addition the Chinese government has supported the development of an indigenous 3G standard known as TD-SCDMA.

12. This is not to say that Russo did not have vested stock options that could eventually be exercised. Russo had been a career executive at AT&T/Lucent until she departed for a seven-month stint as president of Eastman Kodak in 2001. As an inducement to Russo to rejoin Lucent as CEO in 2002 and give up her unvested stock options at Eastman Kodak, she received 4.7 million stock options and 1.55 million restricted stock units (Klayman 2002). She then received 1.54 percent of all options that Lucent awarded in 2003, 4.86 percent in 2004, and 4.53 percent in 2005.

4

Pensions and Unions
in the New Economy

SECURITY THROUGH SENIORITY

The rise of NEBM and the demise of OEBM meant the end of employment relations based on careers with one company. In the post–World War II decades, such employment relations provided the fundamental foundation for stable and equitable growth in the U.S. economy. A "back-loaded" defined-benefit (DB) pension plan that rewarded years of service with the company ensured that the economic security enjoyed by "the organization man" would extend into one's years of retirement as well. Given the cost of employee turnover in mass production industries as well as the presence of strong unions to protect the seniority rights of older workers, even so-called hourly workers could expect to spend a career with one company and have a DB pension at the end.

Since the 1980s, employer-sponsored DB pension plans have covered a steadily declining proportion of business-sector employees. In 1980, 35 percent of business-sector wage and salary workers were active participants in DB plans insured by the U.S. government's Pension Benefit Guaranty Corporation. This proportion had fallen to 18 percent by 2004 (the latest year for which data are available). Even though the size of the U.S. business-sector labor force increased by 48 percent from 1980 to 2004, there were 6.6 million fewer workers active in an employer-sponsored DB plan in 2004 than in 1980 (Pension Benefit Guaranty Corporation 2007, Table S-33).

From 1985 to 2007, however, the assets in defined-contribution (DC) plans increased from 54 percent to 149 percent of the assets in DB plans. Over the past two decades, Individual Retirement Accounts (IRAs)—that is, nonemployer pensions—have become increasingly important as a form of retirement savings, rising from 20 percent of combined DB and DC assets in 1985 to 82 percent in 2007. In March 2008, 61 percent of all business-sector employees had access to one or more employee-sponsored retirement plans, with 21 percent having access to a DB plan and 56 percent having access to a DC plan (U.S. Bureau of Labor Statistics 2008a, Table 2).

Those business-sector employees who are still covered by DB plans tend to obtain that benefit by working for very large business corporations. Since the 1980s, about 80 percent of active participants in DB plans have been in single-employer plans, and the proportion of those in single-employer plans with 10,000 or more participants rose from 43 percent in 1985 to 65 percent in 2006, while the proportion of those in such plans with 5,000–9,999 participants stayed steady at about 11 percent (Pension Benefit Guaranty Corporation 2007, Table S-30). In the plans with 10,000 or more participants, there were a total of 12.7 million people in 1985 and 22.3 million in 2006; in the plans with 5,000–9,999 participants, there were 3.1 million in 1985 and 3.7 million in 2006.

Access to DB plans is particularly dependent on an employee's union status. In March 2008, 67 percent of union employees but only 16 percent of nonunion employees had access to a DB plan, whereas DC plans were available to 50 percent of union employees and 57 percent of nonunion employees (U.S. Bureau of Labor Statistics 2008a, Table 2). The proportion of the U.S. labor force that is unionized, however, has been in long-term decline. In 1983, 20.1 percent of employed wage and salary workers in the United States were union members, and in 2007 only 12.1 percent were (U.S. Bureau of Labor Statistics 2008b). In 2007 the rate of union membership rose with age, ranging from 4.8 percent of workers aged 16–24 to 16.1 percent of workers aged 55–64. It also differed markedly between the government sector, which had a rate of 35.9 percent, and the business sector, which had a rate of 7.5 percent.

A fundamental objective of the industrial unions that emerged from the Great Depression and which were widespread in the post–World War II decades was the protection of the seniority of their members. Even in the "nonunion era" of the 1910s and 1920s, employers in mass-production industries such as automobiles, consumer appliances, and steel recognized the high cost of turnover of the types of "semiskilled" workers who would in the 1930s become the bulwarks of the new industrial unionism. Even while, in the 1940s, employers successfully prevented these unions from having a voice in the running of the industrial corporations, their interest in low turnover led them to accede to union demands that collective bargaining contracts recognize a worker's seniority as both a basis for rewarding experience with higher pay and a protection against layoffs, which would be done on a "last hired, first fired" basis (Lazonick 1990, chaps. 7 and 8).

The extension of DB pensions to members of industrial unions, therefore, served the interests of both employers and employees in the industrial corporations of the post–World War II decades. In those ICT companies in which, in the 2000s, industrial unionism still prevails (such as is the case at AT&T, Verizon, and Qwest), workers have been able to maintain access to DB plans. In the 2000s, however, most Old Economy ICT companies do not have unions, and, with the exception of the janitorial labor force, collective bargaining has been virtually nonexistent in New Economy companies.

THE TRANSFORMATION OF PENSIONS IN ICT

Insofar as New Economy companies have offered pension plans, these plans have tended to be portable, reflecting the labor market reality of interfirm mobility. As Table 4.1 shows, 15 of the top 20 New Economy ICT companies in 2005 (see Table 1.7) have had only DC plans for U.S. employees throughout their histories. Two others—EMC and Sanmina—found themselves with DB plans when they acquired other companies, but they immediately froze those plans on completion of the acquisitions. The NEBM, against which Old Economy ICT companies increasingly had to compete in the 1990s, was one in which DC pensions overwhelmingly became the norm.

Of the top 20 New Economy companies in 2005, only two, Intel, founded in 1968, and Computer Sciences, founded in 1959 (the oldest company on the list), have had traditional noncontributory DB plans. In the manner of its Old Economy Silicon Valley neighbor, Hewlett-Packard, Intel established a DB plan that was originally meant to supplement its deferred profit-sharing scheme. One company on the New Economy list, SAIC, founded in 1969, was one of the largest employee-owned companies in the United States. In October 2006 SAIC did a $1.1 billion IPO, in part to enable its employees to sell their shares, which serve as their pensions, on the open market rather than to the company.[1]

Table 4.1 U.S. Pension Plans in 2005 of the Top 20 New Economy Companies by Sales

Company	Year founded	U.S. pension plan	Company 401(k) match	
			% of employee contribution that company matches	Maximum % of employee compensation matched
Dell	1984	401(k)	100	4
Microsoft	1975	401(k)	50	3
Intel[a]	1968	DB		
Cisco Systems	1984	401(k)	50	3
Computer Sciences[b]	1959	DB		
Apple[c]	1977	401(k)	50–100	6
Oracle[d]	1977	401(k)	50	6
Sanmina-SCI[e]	1980	401(k)	—	Discretionary
Sun Microsystems	1982	401(k)	—	4
Solectron	1977	401(k)	50	Discretionary
EMC[f]	1979	401(k)	Limited to $750/quarter	6
Amazon.com	1994	401(k)	Since 2003, using stock	Discretionary
SAIC[g]	1969	ESOP/401(k)	50	6
EchoStar	1993	401(k)	50, up to $1,000	Plus discretionary contribution
Jabil Circuit	1966	401(k)	—	Discretionary
Applied Materials[h]	1967	401(k)	"A percentage"	Discretionary
Google	1998	401(k)	Up to $2,200	
AMD[i]	1969	401(k)	50	
Qualcomm	1985	401(k)	"A portion"	6
Yahoo![j]	1995	401(k)	25	—

NOTE: Most of these companies have not provided postretirement medical benefits to their employees. In 1998 Intel began offering postretirement medical benefits in the form of dollar credits based on years of service. In 1999 Applied Materials began providing medical and vision benefits to retirees who are at least 55 and whose age plus years of service is at least 65 at the date of retirement, as well as coverage for a spouse or domestic partner until he or she becomes eligible for Medicare. Computer Sciences provided medical benefits and life insurance for employees until 1992. Blank = not applicable; — = not available. ESOP = employee stock ownership plan.

a Includes profit-sharing retirement plan begun in 1979.

b In 1988, Computer Sciences replaced a DB plan with a DC plan for its principle subsidiary, Associated Credit Services.

c Percentage contribution depends on years of service.

d Percentage of employee contribution that company matches is from Oracle's 2007 10-K.

e SCI had a noncontributory DB plan that was frozen when Sanmina acquired SCI in 2000. Unvested SCI employees were credited with years of service until vesting occurred but no additional benefits.

f Includes profit-sharing plan from 1983, supplemented by 401(k) from 1991. In 1999 EMC acquired Data General and then froze its DB plan.

g Company 401(k) match reported in 10-K for fiscal year ended January 31, 2007.

h Company match ranges from 20% after 2 years of service to 100% after 6 years.

i Company match was 50% of employee contributions to a maximum of 3% of compensation from 1992 to 1999.

j Employer contribution vests 33% per year of employment.

SOURCE: Company 10-K filings.

In the mid-1980s, as shown in Table 4.2, all but one of the companies (or their predecessors) that would be in the top 20 Old Economy
ICT companies in 2005 had traditional DB plans. The one exception
was Comcast, which would acquire DB plans for union workers along
with its purchase of Barden Cablevision in 1994 and AT&T Broadband
in 2002. IAC was not in existence in 1985, but its predecessors, Paramount and MCA, had DB plans. In the 1990s and 2000s, however, these
Old Economy companies found themselves competing against New
Economy companies, the vast majority of which never contemplated
the adoption of DB.

How did the Old Economy companies respond? In 2005, as can be
seen in Table 4.2, 12 companies still had DB plans for some or all of their
existing employees, as distinct from new hires. At five companies—HP,
Qwest, TI, Lucent, and NCR—only employees with a certain level of
seniority or those who had been employed with the company before a
stipulated date remained eligible for DB. At Qwest, however, the cutoff
date for DB applied only to salaried employees—all union members had
DB. Similarly, only union members had DB at Verizon and Comcast,
whereas at AT&T Inc. former SBC employees, both salaried and union,
had DB, while former AT&T Corp. employees, also both salaried and
union, had a cash-balance (CB) plan. Ten of the companies offered only
401(k) plans to new hires. At 13 of the 20 Old Economy companies,
only a 401(k) was on offer to salaried employees by 2005–2006.

During the 1990s, the CB plan, in various forms, came to serve as
a transitional type of pension plan between DB and DC. CB plans have
three features that are attractive to younger workers: 1) they can be structured to increase the accrual of pension benefits to younger employees,
although if the company's total pension costs are to remain the same,
this increase will be at the expense of the company's older employees;
2) they are portable, meaning that workers are not penalized by loss
of vesting rights when they change employers; and 3) they are DB,
with the company guaranteeing a specified rate of return on the accrued
cash balances of the individual employee. In the 1990s a number of
Old Economy ICT companies with DB plans made the transition to CB
plans because, in the new world of industry-wide technology standards
and interfirm mobility of high-tech personnel, they wanted to be able
to attract younger workers with education and experience in new technologies. By the same token, they found it less beneficial to retain older

workers who had the Old Economy expectation of lifelong employment with the company and tended to command higher pay. At the end of 2004, four companies—IBM, BellSouth, EDS, and Xerox—offered all existing employees CB plans, along with 401(k) plans, although Xerox employees could also opt for a DB plan.

IBM

In the 1990s and 2000s, the transitions from traditional DB to CB to DC plans in these Old Economy ICT companies were integrally related to transformations in their employment relations that reflected the adoption of some or all of the elements of NEBM. IBM is the most important case in point. In ridding itself of lifelong employment, as discussed in Chapter 3, IBM also rid itself of its traditional DB plans. Indeed the transformation of IBM's system of pension benefits in the 1990s and 2000s was, as we shall see, integral to the company's transition from OEBM to NEBM.

In 1989 IBM changed the vesting period for pension benefits from 10 years of service to five. Then in 1991 the company created a hybrid "Personal Retirement Plan" that included a CB feature to enable departing employees to take more pension benefits with them (Vosti 1992). In 1995, with IBM's massive downsizing having been completed, the company implemented a "Pension Equity Plan" (PEP) that placed CB front and center in the retirement plans that the company offered.

IBM's PEP was structured to favor midcareer employees. Donald Sauvigne, IBM's director of retirement programs, explained that in adopting PEP, "we were responding to the different makeup of the workforce. The reality is that fewer people will be spending their entire careers at IBM" (Geisel 1995). At the same time, IBM enhanced its 401(k) plan from a 30 percent company match on employee contributions up to 5 percent of pay to a 50 percent match on such contributions up to 6 percent of pay. At the beginning of 1995, when IBM had $28 billion in DB assets (including CB) and $7 billion in DC assets, Sauvigne stated that the company's goal was to "rebalance our delivery system to further encourage employees to recognize the importance of their responsibility to themselves" (Rohrer 1995).

Table 4.2 Retirement Plans in 1985 and 2005–2006 of the Top 20 Old Economy ICT Companies by Sales in 2005

Company	Retirement plans in place, 1985[a]	Retirement plan(s) in place, 2005–2006
IBM	DB (92%); 401(k) (8%), 30% to 5%[b]	Personal Pension (CB) Plan since 1999; 1/1/2005: new hires not eligible for Personal Pension Plan, only 401(k), with match ranging from 10% for most senior employees to 6% for recent hires.
HP	Profit-sharing DB (69%); supplemental DB (19%); 401(k) (12%), 33% to 12%	1/1/2006: no DB pension or medical benefits to new US hires; freeze on pension and medical benefits for employees without sufficient seniority; increase 401(k) match to 6%.
Verizon Communications[c]	Bell Atlantic, NYNEX: Bell System DB	1/1/2006: new management hires not eligible for pension benefits; 6/30/2006: salaried employees no longer earn pension benefits or service toward company retiree medical subsidy; salaried with less than 13.5 years of service not eligible for company-subsidized retiree health care or retiree life insurance benefits; 7/1/2006: salaried employees receive increased company match on 401(k).
AT&T Inc.[c]	SBC, Ameritech, Pacific Telesis, AT&T Corp.: Bell System DB; DC, 100% to 6%, for salaried employees	2005: SBC acquires AT&T Corp. and renames itself AT&T Inc.; SBC changes from CB to DB for salaried employees; AT&T Inc. changes back to DB for 55,000 salaried; AT&T Corp. keeps CB for both salaried and union workers (in 1998 CWA had agreed to a CB favorable to members of all ages).
Motorola	DB (30%); contributory 401(k)-sharing (70%)	1/1/2005: DB plan closed to new hires; profit-sharing component of 401(k) terminated; new hires get 401(k) match of 67% to 6% compared with 50% to 6% for those hired previously.

Sprint Nextel	GTE-Sprint: for salaried employees, 401(k), 50% to 6%, with extra 25% match based on company stock-price performance, with match in company stock; GTE, Southern Pacific, United Telecommunications: DB	12/31/2005: in wake of the merger with Nextel, Sprint DB plan amended to freeze benefit accruals for current employees, except those designated to work for Embarq (a local telephone spinoff from Sprint) and Sprint employees who were unvested prior to August 2005—they will be permitted to accumulate the five years of service credit needed for vesting, but pension accruals frozen after that; 1/1/2006: only Sprint Nextel pension plan is 401(k), 100% to 5%, no longer paid in company stock.
Comcast	None[d]	AT&T Broadband DB for "some union groups" (12/31/2005: Comcast had 4,000 union members); 401(k), discretionary company match.
BellSouth[c]	Bell System DB	CB (in 1998 CWA agreed to a CB favorable to members of all ages); 401(k), match determined annually.
Electronic Data Systems	General Motors division, 1984–1996: DB	CB; 401(k).
Xerox	DB with deferred profit-sharing component	Choice of DB or CB (in place since 1990); 401(k) 6 % match; 03/14/2005: only 401(k) for new union hires.
Qwest Communications[e]	Southern Pacific Railroad[e]: DB	DB for all union and salaried employees with 20 years of service by 12/31/2000 or service pension—eligible by 12/31/2003; CB for all others, based on 3% of pay while employed plus investment return.
Texas Instruments	DB (59%); profit-sharing (37%); 401(k) (4%), invested in company stock	For employees as of 11/1997 who declined enhanced DC plan: DB plus DC, 50% to 4%. For employees as of 11/30/1997 who chose enhanced DC plan and employees hired 12/1/1997 through 12/31/2003: DC, 2% of salary plus 100% to 4%. For employees hired after 12/31/2003: DC, 100% to 4%.

Table 4.2 (continued)

Company	Retirement plans in place 1985[a]	Retirement plan(s) in place, 2005–2006
DirecTV Group	GM Hughes Electronics as of 12/31/1985: DB[f]	DB plans for "many of our employees" and those who opted to participate in a DB plan prior to 1991; 401(k).
First Data	DB	DC, matching and discretionary company contributions.
Alltel	DB	Noncontributory profit-sharing DC plan and 401(k) for salaried employees, annual company contributions; DB plan frozen—no further accruals for salaried employees if under 40 as of 12/31/2005 or if 40-plus and with at least 2 years of service as of 12/31/2010.
Lucent Technologies[c]	AT&T Technologies: Bell System DB; DC, 100% to 6%, for salaried employees	CB for new hires; DB for employees on DB plan prior to 1/1/1999; 401(k), discretionary company match.
Cox Communications	DB; TRASOP[g]; PAYSOP[h]; 401(k), 25% to 5%	DB, 401(k), 50% to 6%; 2005: Cox went private.
IAC/InterActiveCorp	Paramount, MCA: DB	401(k), 50% to 3%.
NCR	DB (86%); profit-sharing (4%); 401(k) (11%), 25% to 6%; PAYSOP[h]	2005: DC plan for all new hires and employees less than 40 years old on and/or hired after August 31, 2004.
Freescale Semiconductor	Motorola: DB; contributory profit-sharing	401(k).

NOTE: The term "salaried" is used to mean managerial employees, nonbargaining unit employees, nonunion employees, and unrepresented employees.

[a] For IBM, HP, and Motorola, the italicized percentages in parentheses following different types of retirement plans represent assets in those plans as a proportion of total assets in 1986 (*Pensions and Investment Age* 1987); for TI, percentages are for 1987 (*Pensions and Investment Age* 1988); and for NCR, percentages are for 1988 (*Pensions and Investment Age* 1989).

[b] A term such as "30% to 5%" means that the company matches 30% of employee contributions up to 5% of the employee's annual salary or wages.

c With the breakup of the Bell System on January 1, 1984, AT&T Inc. and the seven RBOCS all had identical noncontributory DB plans with benefits based on years of service and average career earnings for managerial employees and a flat benefit per year for union employees. At the end of 1986, these DB plans represented 85–90% of the total retirement assets held by these companies.

d Comcast became an Old Economy company when it acquired AT&T Broadband (with a Bell System DB) in 2002.

e Denver-based Qwest Communications emerged in 1995 when privately owned Southern Pacific Telecommunications (SPT), a 1989 spin-off from the Southern Pacific Railroad, was renamed after acquiring Dallas-based Qwest Communications in 1995. In 1985 the Santa Fe Southern Pacific Railroad had a DB plan for all employees.

f For salaried employees, years of service plus salary history for managers; for hourly employees, flat amount per year of service plus supplement for retirement with 30 years of service before retirement age.

g Tax Reduction Act Employee Stock Ownership Plan.

h Payroll-Based Employee Stock Ownership Plan.

SOURCE: Company 10-K filings as well as various news articles and press releases.

That labor market logic was taken a major step further in 1999 when IBM announced that it was adopting a new CB plan, dubbed a "Personal Pension Plan," targeted at attracting younger, as distinct from midcareer, employees. Of the 141,000 people in IBM's U.S. labor force in 1999, 60,000 had joined the company since 1993. The 1999 plan paid every employee an annual amount equal to 5 percent of his or her salary for that year plus annual interest (based on market rates) on accumulated balances. IBM also moved to a similar type of CB plan for retiree health benefits (Geisel 1999).

In a communication to employees announcing the change in the pension plan, IBM's management wrote, "The fact that significantly fewer people are staying with one company their full careers means that, more and more, people are looking for opportunities to contribute and be rewarded sooner in their careers" (Lewis 1999). IBM employees were also told that "competition in our industry for skilled, talented employees has never been more fierce than it is today" (Frey 1999a). CEO Gerstner argued that "our old pension plan was created at a time when employees joined IBM for life. . . . [Now] we anticipate that only 10% of our new hires are likely to reach 30 years of service with IBM." Gerstner added that most of IBM's competitors "do not provide a pension plan at all" (Schultz 2000).

IBM did permit some 30,000 employees who were within five years of the 30 years of service required for retirement to remain on the traditional plan. The company also provided extra contributions to the CB plans of other employees age 45 or older. It was estimated, nevertheless, that these midcareer employees could lose 30 to 50 percent of their expected pensions (Lewis 1999; Lynn 1999).

Suddenly some of the IBM employees who would bear these losses became receptive to union organizing efforts, and three years later, 5,000 of them had joined Alliance@IBM, an affiliate of the Communication Workers of America, or CWA (Pimentel 2002b). Moreover, federal legislators also became involved. IBM was the biggest employer in Vermont, and Bernard Sanders, the state's lone member of the U.S. House of Representatives, charged that IBM's CB plan violated federal laws against age discrimination (Anand 1999; Maury and Shoaf 2001). Vermont Senator James Jeffords convinced IBM CEO Gerstner to permit those IBM employees who were at least 40 years old and had at least 10 years of service—some 65,000 people—to remain on the traditional DB plan (Affleck 2000; Kornblut 1999).

The SEC blocked IBM management's attempt to disallow a vote on the CB plan at the annual stockholders' meeting, thus rejecting IBM's claim that pension provision was a matter of ordinary business that did not require shareholder approval (Burns 2000). At annual stockholders' meetings from 2000 through 2007, shareholder proposals were put forward espousing that (in the words of the proposal text used from 2004 through 2007) "age discrimination in retirement policies will be ended by allowing all employees, regardless of age, to choose the promised pension and retirement medical insurance under the terms in effect before IBM adopted changes in 1995 and 1999." Management, of course, strongly and consistently opposed the resolutions, which went down to defeat eight times running. In 2000 the proposal received 299.7 million votes for and 755.4 million votes against, or 28.4 percent in favor, but thereafter the proposal failed to gain as much as 15 percent in favor (Affleck 2000; Alterio 2007; Arditi 2004; Bergstein 2006a; Drury 2005; Freund 2002; Fuscaldo 2001; Krishnan 2003). In 2007 there were 103.6 million votes for and 798.0 votes against, or 11.5 percent in favor (IBM 2007). The proposal was not on the proxy statement for IBM's 2008 annual meeting of stockholders.

IBM employees also looked to the courts for remedies. In July 2003 a federal district court judge ruled in favor of IBM employees in a class action lawsuit covering anyone who worked for IBM after December 31, 1994. The lawsuit charged that changes in IBM pension plans discriminated against older employees and hence violated ERISA (Tumulty 2003). In September 2004 IBM agreed to a settlement consisting of $320 million that was not subject to appeal plus another $1.4 billion should it lose its appeals of the lower court's decision (Dale 2004a,b; Wells 2004). In August 2006, however, on appeal, Judge Frank Easterbrook ruled in favor of the company, arguing that the CB plan was age-neutral because in every year it credited all employees with pension benefits equal to 5 percent of their pay regardless of age (Boehner 2006; Schultz and Francis 2006). Thus Easterbrook rejected the validity of the employees' charge that the plan entailed age discrimination, in effect deeming as irrelevant the fact that the change from DB to CB reduced the amount of benefits that older employees would be able to accumulate compared with the preexisting traditional back-loaded DB plan. In

January 2007, the U.S. Supreme Court refused an employees' petition for an appeal of the Easterbrook decision (Rugaber 2007).

IBM's position has been that the changes in its pension plans have reflected responses to changing labor and product market conditions (IBM 2006, p. 28). Indeed, it turned out that the adoption of CB was a first step in the eventual elimination of DB plans of any kind. In December 2004, IBM had announced that new hires would not be eligible for the CB plan. Instead the company would offer them a 401(k) plan (Crenshaw 2004). Then, in January 2006, IBM announced that as of 2008 it would freeze its existing CB plans (Bergstein 2006b; Crenshaw and Joyce 2006). Thereafter, the only employee pensions at IBM would be 401(k)s.

UNIONS

The Bell System Legacy

In its purpose and outcome, the industrial unionism that became widespread in the United States in the late 1930s and the 1940s was first and foremost about income security through employment followed by what the unions call "deferred wages" in retirement (Brody 1980; Ghilarducci 1992, chap. 3; Lazonick 1990, chaps. 8–10). Yet for decades after the rise of industrial unions, companies like IBM and HP demonstrated that, when sustained growth was combined with paternalism, a corporation could offer tens of thousands or even hundreds of thousands of corporate employees of all ranks the realistic expectation of long-term income security through employment and retirement without union representation. Indeed, as shown in Table 4.3, among the top 20 Old Economy ICT companies in 2005, the only ones with a substantial union presence were those that had evolved out of the Bell System: Verizon, with 140,000 union members (62 percent of its total labor force); AT&T Inc., with 121,000 union members (53 percent); BellSouth, with 53,000 union members (60 percent); and Qwest Communications, with 23,600 union members (60 percent). In 1999 Qwest, a nonunion company with 8,700 employees, had no choice but to become a unionized company after it engineered a successful hostile takeover

**Table 4.3 Union Membership in the Top 20 Old Economy ICT
           Companies, 2005**

	Employees	U.S. union members[a]
IBM	329,373	None
HP	150,000	None
Verizon Communications	217,000	CWA 74,251; IBEW 65,600; (99,800)
AT&T Inc.	228,350	CWA 108,547; IBEW 12,250
Motorola	69,000	None
Sprint Nextel	79,900	CWA 3,500; IBEW 3,500; (7,000)
Comcast	80,000	CWA (4,000)
BellSouth	88,666	CWA 53,151
Electronic Data Systems	117,000	None
Xerox	55,200	UNITE HERE 2,325; IAM and IUOE 225
Qwest Communications	39,348	CWA 23,642; (23,000)
Texas Instruments	35,207	None
DirecTV Group	9,200	None
First Data	33,000	CWA (1,100)
Alltel	21,373	CWA (1,387)
Lucent Technologies	30,500	CWA 2,708 (3,000)
Cox Communications	22,530	None
IAC/InterActiveCorp	28,000	None
NCR	28,200	None
Freescale Semiconductor	22,700	None

NOTE: CWA, Communication Workers of America; IAM, International Association
of Machinists and Aerospace Workers; IBEW, International Brotherhood of Electrical Workers; IUOE, International Union of Operating Engineers; UAW, United Auto
Workers; and UNITE HERE, merger of Union of Needletrades, Industrial, and Textile
Employees and Hotel Employees and Restaurant Employees International Union.
[a] Figure in parenthesis is the number of union members given in the company's 2005
annual report. CWA figures for 2005 are from the union's membership development
report for December 2005. Given that Cingular was 60 percent owned by AT&T Inc.
and 40 percent by BellSouth in 2005, the CWA figures of each of these parent companies include these proportions of Cingular's 21,469 CWA members in 2005. The
AT&T Inc. and BellSouth employment data include Cingular employees. Note also
that the 2005 union membership for AT&T Corp. includes 4,897 employees at the
formerly independent Southern New England Telephone Company (SNET), which
was acquired by SBC in 1998.
SOURCE: U.S. Bureau of Labor Statistics (2007); S&P Compustat database; Xerox
(2006, p. 63); information supplied by the CWA.

of US West, an RBOC with 70,800 employees, 36,000 of whom were CWA members (PR Newswire 1999a; Reuters News 1999a).[2] At Lucent Technologies, unions represented 46 percent of 98,000 U.S. employees when the company was spun off from AT&T Corp. in 1996. As was shown in Chapter 3, however, by 2006 union members were only 15 percent of a combined 38,000 U.S. employees at Lucent and its two major spinoffs, Avaya and Agere.

Since 1984 Verizon (with its origins in Bell Atlantic), AT&T Inc. (with its origins in SBC), and BellSouth (now part of AT&T Inc.) have been profitable, as was Qwest (as US West) until the 2000s. The traditional local wireline business has remained a very important source of revenues and profits for all these companies, although in the mid-2000s, AT&T Inc. and Qwest were far more dependent on wireline earnings than were the other two. Both Verizon and AT&T Inc. are now also leaders in the rapidly growing wireless segment of the U.S. telecommunications industry, and in 2005, for the first time, Verizon's wireless profits ($2.2 billion) surpassed its wireline profits ($1.9 billion). The directory (Yellow Pages) businesses of AT&T Inc., Verizon (spun off in 2006 as Idearc Media), and BellSouth, while relatively small, were always lucrative, with profit margins typically at 30 percent or more.

The wireline and directory businesses of these companies are the living legacies of their regulated monopoly status in the former Bell System. The Federal Communications Commission (FCC) and state public utility commissions regulate the return that RBOCs can obtain from their control of local telephone infrastructures. From 1984 through 1989 the RBOCs, as local exchange carriers (LECs), were permitted a maximum rate of return on assets of 12 percent, lowered to 11.25 percent in 1990. The following year the FCC changed the regulatory formula to a price cap that, after adjusting for inflation, annually lowered the maximum prices that LECs could charge by the expected rate of productivity growth (Arnold 1990; Kelly 1997). Companies that could exceed this expected rate, while maintaining quality of service, could capture additional profits. The Telecommunications Act of 1996 did not put an end to regulation of the local phone business, but it only required that, as a condition for the RBOCs to enter the long-distance markets, LECs had to make their local networks available at reasonable rental rates to any "competitive local exchange carrier" (CLEC) that might want to deliver local telephone service.

In 1989 AT&T Corp., whose long-distance service had previously been subject to a rate-of-return maximum of 12.2 percent, was placed under price cap regulation (Barry 1988; Starobin 1989). Unlike local telephone service, however, which the LECs still dominate, long-distance service became a highly competitive segment of the telecommunications industry during the 1990s, rendering rate regulation irrelevant. By the 2000s the long-distance segment was subject to extreme price competition both from resellers of overabundant long-distance capacity—the result of massive overinvestment in fiber optic transmission cables by companies such as Qwest and Global Crossing during the Internet boom—and from wireless companies that provided nationwide access as part of their service plans.

Highly dependent on the long-distance segment, AT&T Corp. saw its stand-alone consumer long-distance revenues, already in decline at the end of the Internet boom, plunge from $14.0 billion in 2001 to $5.2 billion in 2004, while its consumer bundled services revenues (based on local voice subscribers) only reached $2.7 billion from a very low base of $870 million three years earlier. From the perspective of the second half of the 2000s, two companies that emanated from the former Bell System came out on top—Verizon and AT&T Inc. They were able to build upon their regulated monopolies over local wireline exchanges and enter the expanding wireless industry without getting embroiled, as was the case with Qwest, AT&T Corp., and Lucent, in the speculative machinations of the late 1990s Internet boom.

The embeddedness of industrial unions in the Bell System in the decades prior to the breakup, and the ongoing regulation of the local wireline industry in the decades since, explain the high level of unionization that still prevails in this sector. At the end of 2005, Verizon, AT&T Inc., BellSouth, Qwest, and Cingular (now AT&T Mobility) together employed 573,000 people, almost 260,000 of whom (45 percent) were CWA members and another estimated 77,850 of whom (14 percent) were International Brotherhood of Electrical Workers (IBEW) members. The proportion of the potential labor force organized by the CWA in these companies was 94 percent at Verizon, 92 percent at AT&T Inc., 84 percent at BellSouth, 89 percent at Qwest, and 65 percent at Cingular.[3] Total employment at the former Bell System telecommunications service providers was down substantially from the 776,000 people employed by these companies (including the then-independent AT&T

Corp. and AT&T Wireless) in 2001. Nevertheless, in the mid-2000s, these companies remained bastions of business-sector union organization in the U.S. economy.

On occasion, CWA and IBEW have been able to secure "no-layoff" clauses in collective bargaining contracts with former Bell System companies, including with Pacific Telesis in 1986, NYNEX in 1994, Bell Atlantic in 1998 (followed by Verizon in 2000 and 2003), and SBC in 2004. That degree of employment security, however, has been the exception rather than the rule; both before the breakup of the Bell System and since, large-scale layoffs of union employees have been common at these companies. Nevertheless, seniority provisions in union contracts have meant that those union employees with the most years of service with a company have had, and continue to have, realistic expectations of continuous employment until retirement age, at which point they can count on retirement incomes secured from collectively bargained pensions. Notwithstanding the radical technological and organizational transformations that have taken place in the telecommunications industry since the mid-1990s, OEBM still prevailed at Verizon and AT&T Inc. in the latter half of the 2000s.

In sum, the high and steady revenues that the RBOCs have derived from their ongoing control over regulated local telephone exchanges have enabled these companies to maintain high (even if declining) levels of employment that in turn have provided employment security to large numbers of senior union members. In addition, the secure jobs available to union members are supported by two characteristics of RBOC employment that run counter to general employment trends in the ICT industries: 1) the RBOCs have not as a rule outsourced or offshored employment, and 2) RBOCs are not high-tech companies that employ mainly college-educated personnel.

As part of the regulatory structure, state public utility commissions have the right to demand that LECs maintain quality of service to their customers (Batt 1995, pp. 68–70). The companies must respond promptly and effectively to orders for new lines, repairs to existing lines, customer requests for modifications of service, and customer complaints. In-house control over the delivery of these services helps to assure high quality, as does the employment of a secure and experienced labor force.

How local that control needs to be to assure adequate quality of service is, however, another question. For example, in 2002 BellSouth decided that it would consolidate its 75 call centers into 28 facilities in 18 cities within the nine Southeastern states in which it operated, for a savings of $200 million over five years. As a result, an estimated 650–700 jobs would be lost (Bachman 2002). When BellSouth made the announcement, the Public Service Commissioner for North Louisiana objected to the fact that the consolidation would result in the loss of 103 local call-center jobs, which would be moved to South Louisiana. But the North Louisiana regulators had no way of blocking the closure of the call centers and the local loss of jobs that it would entail (*Baton Rouge Advocate* 2002). At the same time, in contrast to the growing practice among U.S. companies in the 2000s of outsourcing and offshoring call centers to low-wage areas of the world, in undertaking this large-scale consolidation, BellSouth was keeping call center jobs directly under its control and in the United States.

Also favoring the continued employment of union members at RBOCs is the fact that their revenue-generating activities are not high tech. To deliver telecommunications services, an RBOC needs a dedicated and trained labor force for sales, installation, repair, and customer support. It does not need scientists and engineers to research and develop new products. Indeed, as part of the postbreakup regulatory structure, the RBOCs were not permitted to design, fabricate, or assemble telecommunications products and equipment (Hearn 1991). Upgrades to the existing infrastructure and equipment are also done by the equipment suppliers.

In the old Bell System, basic research was carried out by Bell Labs and product development by Western Electric, both of which became the core of AT&T Technologies after the 1984 breakup and then of Lucent Technologies after the 1996 trivestiture. No longer having access to AT&T R&D after the breakup, the seven RBOCs set up a new cooperative research organization, Bellcore, located in New Jersey about 11 miles from the main Bell Labs campus, to serve their needs. Bellcore began with a $1 billion annual budget and 7,500 employees, about 4,500 of whom were scientists and technicians reassigned from Bell Labs (Berg 1985). From 1988 on, NYNEX, SBC, and US West established their own in-house research facilities to better absorb Bellcore innovations (Amparano 1988; Stroud 1988). In 1996, however, with the

Telecommunications Act opening up the possibility of interfirm competition among the RBOCs themselves in long-distance and wireless markets, the RBOCS agreed to sell Bellcore to SAIC (Cauley 1996; Horwitt 1996). Bellcore was later renamed Telcordia, and in 2005 was sold to a private equity group. Meanwhile AT&T Inc. (SBC), Verizon (Bell Atlantic), BellSouth, and Qwest did not try to maintain advanced technological capabilities, and since 1996 have recorded no expenditures for R&D.

Although the RBOCs have not employed scientists and engineers, they have employed large numbers of managerial personnel. Batt (1996, p. 60) has shown that, for the whole Bell System, excluding Bell Labs, the proportion of total employees who were managers rose from 13.7 percent in 1950 to 29.4 percent in 1980. Under the old Bell System, AT&T and its operating companies were expansive bureaucracies in which managerial personnel viewed themselves as public service employees. After the breakup, each of the former Bell companies began to restructure its organization to be better suited to the regulatory and competitive environment that each of them faced, given the resources that they had inherited from the Bell System. For example, AT&T and PacTel both downsized their labor forces significantly in the late 1980s while BellSouth, after reducing the size of its labor force by almost 4 percent in its first two years as an independent company, expanded it by more than 10 percent from 1986 through 1990.

In the first half of the 1990s, however, all eight former Bell companies downsized significantly, each one laying off large numbers of salaried managers as well as unionized workers. The recession of 1990–1992 was widely known as a white-collar recession, with U.S. corporations in general downsizing their salaried workforces to an extent that had no precedent in the post–World War II decades. The recessionary conditions, however, had little impact on the RBOCs, given their regulated rates and the relatively stable demand for local telephone service over the business cycle. Of much more importance in the downsizing decisions of the RBOCs was the move in 1991 to price-cap regulation, which meant that the RBOCs could reap the extra profits derived from a leaner labor force. As company-level research by Batt (1995, 1996, 1999, 2001) has shown, by the early 1990s, RBOC lower and middle level managers were working longer and harder, pressured by their superiors and fearful of termination.

Reinforcing this corporate response to the new regulatory mechanism was the fact that, beyond their salaries, the remuneration of top executives of AT&T and the RBOCs depended in part on annual bonuses and in part on gains from the exercise of stock options. For annual bonus awards, annual profitability was ostensibly the main performance criterion. In addition, in the latter half of the 1980s, for the first time, some of the remuneration of the top executives of the former Bell companies took the form of stock options (AT&T Corp. 1984; Maremont 1984).

For paying attention to profits and stock prices, the top executives of AT&T and the RBOCs were very well paid. For example, during the years 1992–1995, John L. Clendenin, chairman and CEO of Bell-South, received average annual compensation of $1,656,000, including averages of $659,000 in salary, $810,000 in bonuses, and $175,000 in gains from the exercise of stock options. These were the components of his annual pay. In addition, Clendenin received an annual average over these four years of $843,000 in long-term incentive pay, based on long-run profitability and stock price performance, and another $482,000 under a deferred compensation plan. In total, Clendenin's pay averaged $2,981,000 per year. Then there was, of course, an extremely generous pension awaiting him on retirement.

A prime way in which Clendenin and the other BellSouth top executives (who received smaller but nonetheless substantial rewards under these various pay categories) earned their keep in the first half of the 1990s was by reducing the number of people that their company employed. Early-retirement programs that made use of the company's pension plans were central to BellSouth's downsizing efforts. After the breakup, Bellsouth was the largest RBOC in terms of both sales and employees, just ahead of NYNEX. After trimming its labor force in 1985, in part through an early-retirement program, the company steadily increased both revenues and employment through 1990. From the end of 1990 to the end of 1996, however, BellSouth reduced its labor force from 101,945 to 81,241, even as its sales rose from $14.3 billion in 1990 ($17.2 billion in 1996 dollars) to $19.0 billion in 1996. With its management staff at about 29,000 out of 101,000 employees, in November 1990 and then again in May 1991, BellSouth announced that it would eliminate 3,000 management positions through early-retirement programs (Chester 1990; Husted 1991; Main 1991). In three previous early-retirement programs, including the one in 1985, about

4,000 managers had left the company (Elmore 1987a,b). The 1990 offer, for which BellSouth managers with 30 years of service or more were eligible, was taken by 1,146 people. The 1991 early-retirement offer came two months after the company announced that it would consolidate the headquarters of its two largest operating units, Southern Bell, with 46,000 employees, and South Central Bell, with 31,000 (Poole 1991). This time the company lowered the age and years-of-service thresholds for eligibility for the program, and another 3,100 managers took early retirement (PR Newswire 1991).

The downsizing of BellSouth, however, had just begun. In November 1992 the company announced that it would reduce its headcount by 8,000 by the end of 1996 through attrition, layoffs, and retirement offers targeted at individuals, but not through a company-wide early-retirement program as in the past (Ramirez 1992). BellSouth raised the total downsizing target through 1996 to more than 10,000 in 1993 and to as many as 16,000 in 1995, or 17 percent of employment at the end of 1992 (Guarisco 1995; McCash 1993). Indeed, at the end of 1996, Bell-South employed 81,241 people, 15,871 fewer than four years earlier.

Along the way, BellSouth also changed its pension plan for managers. In 1993, with the targeted reduction of 8,000 managers in process, BellSouth became the first RBOC to adopt a CB plan (BellSouth 1994, p. 50; Williams 1995; Wyatt 1996). Applicable only to nonrepresented workers, the BellSouth CB may have helped the company recruit younger salaried personnel, but given the downsizing context in which the plan was introduced, that was not its main purpose. Rather, with the stock of older managers eligible for early retirement having been substantially depleted by the departures under the 1990 and 1991 programs, BellSouth wanted to create an incentive to quit the company for midcareer managers who lacked the years of service to be eligible for early retirement. When the BellSouth CB went into effect in July 1993, the company employed 25,000 managers with an average age of 44 and average years with the company of 24 (Wyatt 1996).

In introducing the CB plan, BellSouth had a provision that employees who resigned before June 30, 1996, could have their choice of receiving the greater of two amounts: the CB account balance or the present value of an annuity (Anand 1994). The older managers who remained at BellSouth did not complain about the adoption of the CB plan because the percentage of pay credited to an employee's account increased from 3 percent to 8 percent with years of service, and employees who retired from the company before the end of 2005 would have their choice of the greater of the benefits under the CB plan or the traditional DB plan (Wyatt 1996).

BellSouth would be the first of six RBOCs to move to a CB plan, followed by Ameritech in 1995, Bell Atlantic and Pacific Telesis in 1996, and SBC and US West in 1997. All of these CB plans were for managerial personnel only; the RBOCs continued to bargain with the unions on DB plans. Among the original seven RBOCS, only NYNEX did not make the transition from DB to some form of CB for managers as an independent company (Williams 1997). After NYNEX was merged into Bell Atlantic in 1997, however, its managers also had a CB plan (Bell Atlantic 1997, p. 38).

The feature of BellSouth's plan that linked the company's annual percentage contribution to not only an employee's age but also his or her pay made this CB pension a "hybrid"; in a "pure" CB, such as IBM's 1999 plan, the company's percentage contribution is age-neutral, which, as we have seen, means that older employees who were on a traditional DB will see a reduction in their benefits. Earlier in the 1990s, as in the case of IBM, a number of companies that wanted to make the transition to CB adopted a PEP that distributed the accrual of benefits more evenly across workers at different stages of their careers.

Such was the case with the Ameritech CB plan, adopted in May 2005. Top management's motivation in introducing the PEP was not downsizing, as was the case with BellSouth's CB plan; Ameritech employment had already reached a low point at the end of 1994. Rather, Ameritech's PEP had the dual purpose of making its pension attractive to younger managers and reducing the incentive for older managers, under the back-loaded traditional DB plan, to stay with the company until they reached the "cliff" of dramatically increased benefits—i.e., when the age and service requirements of the pension were met. As Tim Meginnes, Ameritech's retirement plans manager, put it, "Benefit values increase steadily [with age under the PEP]. By smoothing out the cliff, employees' decisions on whether or not to stay can be made without focusing on an artificial milestone" (Geisel 1995). Gary Simko, director of Bell Atlantic Benefits Planning and Human Resource Communication, explained his company's change from DB to a hybrid CB at the beginning of 1996: "The telecommunications industry is undergoing immense change. Yet, our retirement benefits were designed years ago in a very predictable business climate when many employees spent most of their careers with one company. We needed to meet the needs of mobile employees, who make frequent moves from employer to employer" (M2 Presswire 1995).

As already mentioned, the new CB plans implemented by the RBOCs applied only to managerial personnel. They were apparently the "mobile employees" whose "needs" to "make frequent moves from employer to employer" a company like Bell Atlantic was so willing to assist. The fact is that top management of these companies introduced and implemented the new pension plans for their own strategic purposes, to the gain of some employees and the loss of others. As a group, "managers"—that is, salaried personnel—had no means of bargaining collectively with top management over the extent and distribution of the gains and losses that accompanied a change in pension plans.

Under certain economic conditions, however, managerial personnel might find a CB plan to be very advantageous. Such was the case at AT&T Corp., which adopted a CB plan for managers at the beginning of 1998. In late January, AT&T's chairman and CEO, C. Michael Armstrong, who had come to the company the previous November with a mandate for cutting costs, announced that over the coming year the company would eliminate 15,000 to 18,000 jobs, 10,000 to 11,000 of which would be achieved through pension incentives to managers under what was called the Voluntary Retirement Incentive Program (VRIP). The expectation was that the managerial ranks would be reduced by 25 percent (Burlingame and Gulotta 1998; Ribbing 1998). Indeed, as the designers of the VRIP put it, AT&T had adopted the CB plan specifically "to expose a broader group of people to an early retirement incentive program" (Burlingame and Gulotta 1998).

AT&T offered the VRIP to 43,000 AT&T managers. Older workers could get a 20 percent increase in their pension benefits. Eligibility for lifetime health benefits required that one's age plus years of service added up to 65, whereas previously it had been 75 (May 1998a). Up to certain limits, the pension benefits could be taken in a lump sum.

About 17,000 managers opted for the VRIP, an uptake that surpassed what AT&T's top management had hoped to achieve. The high response rate was attributable to both the value of the VRIP offer and the ease with which a departing AT&T manager could expect to land another well-paying job in the boom conditions of 1998. To avoid losing key people in key areas, top management had put limits on the number of people in specific departments who could be offered the VRIP. As a result of these restrictions, AT&T turned down 1,700 applications. For not being given the opportunity to quit their jobs, these people subsequently filed a lawsuit against AT&T, but it was thrown out of court (May 1998b, 1999).

By the end of 1998, 14,700 of the 15,300 VRIP managers had already left AT&T, with the remaining 600 leaving in early 1999. The company paid out a total of $4.6 billion in lump sum settlements, an average of over $300,000 per VRIP recipient (AT&T Corp. 1999, p. 64). AT&T's management pension fund could afford this cash flow; at the end of 1997, it had a surplus of more than $12.5 billion.

With pension money so plentiful, even the unions jumped on the CB bandwagon. In mid-1988, the CWA and IBEW negotiated a contract that included a CB plan. With about 50,000 union employees at AT&T, this CB was thought to have been the largest ever to cover union members (*Business Insurance* 1998).

In 1999, as a result of the negative reaction on the part of IBM employees to the company's new CB plan, the United States Senate Committee on Health, Education, and Pensions held hearings on hybrid pension plans. There to give testimony was Morton Bahr, president of the CWA. Bahr (1999) said that his experience with the issue of the conversion of DB to CB went back to 1992 when, late in the negotiation process, AT&T had proposed a CB plan (Brown 1992). Lacking a good understanding of the attributes of such a plan, the union rejected the proposal. Then in 1995 AT&T had once again proposed a CB plan in union negotiations, but it was rejected by the CWA because it would harm older workers.

In 1998, however, AT&T was willing to remedy this problem. According to Bahr (1999), "our agreement increased the value of pension benefits for employees at every stage of their careers." Now union members had the benefit of "pension portability in case of downsizing or change in career plans." At the same time, as of June 30, 1998, retiring union members with 15 years or more of service with AT&T could choose to receive benefits based on either a traditional DB plan, enhanced by 7 percent immediately and another 8 percent by 2000, or a CB plan (*Business Insurance* 1998; Fulman 1998). It is not clear how many union members took advantage of the negotiated CB plan to leave AT&T, but at the end of 1998, the company employed 42,036 CWA workers, down from 48,787 a year earlier. The number of CWA members employed at AT&T continued to decline steadily over the subsequent years, falling to 14,920 in 2004. At that point, AT&T Corp., the parent company of the old Bell System, was taken over by one of its former regional subsidiaries, SBC, and became AT&T Inc.

Other Unionized Old Economy Companies

Beyond the legacy of the CWA and the IBEW from the old Bell System, only two other top 20 Old Economy ICT companies in 2005 (Table 1.6) had a history of significant union representation—NCR and Xerox. These two cases illustrate the limits of union power in a world of changing technology and global competition. They also show the ways in which business strategy can confront (NCR) or engage (Xerox) the collective organization of employees in the construction of a company's business model.

Although NCR was a nonunion company in 2005, such was not always the case. Founded as National Cash Register in Dayton, Ohio, in 1884, NCR was a pioneer in welfare capitalism, and, unlike Old Economy ICT companies such as IBM, HP, Motorola, and TI, it had had a long history of unionization. In 1901 a strike shut down NCR's factory in Dayton, and 2,000 workers walked off the job (*Chicago Daily Tribune* 1901). That strike would be the last to take place at NCR for 67 years.

NCR continued to engage in collective bargaining, and under the National Labor Relations Act from the late 1930s the NCR Employees Independent Union became the workers' representative at NCR's Dayton plant (Stark 1940). In the early 1950s, with 33,000 employees, NCR, still based primarily in Dayton, was 60 percent unionized (*Monthly Labor Review* 1965). By 1968, NCR's employment level had reached 91,000, and at the end of the next year it would attain an all-time peak of 102,000. The Dayton plant alone had 14,863 union members in 1968, when workers on piece-rates staged a strike after being informed by the union that only workers on hourly rates had gained in recent pay negotiations (*New York Times* 1968). Sanctioned by the union, the strike lasted a week and led to negotiations over not only wage rates but also retirement pay and vacations.

The 1968 strike, however, marked the beginning of the end for the workers at the Dayton plant and ultimately for unions at NCR. In 1971, NCR's 17,000 union members (18 percent of the company's 95,000 total employees) opted for representation by the United Auto Workers (UAW) instead of the NCR Employees Independent Union. In the 1970s, however, NCR made the transition from a company that manufactured electromechanical business machines to one that made digital electronic business machines (Anderson 1991; Rosenbloom 2000). In the process, as an early example of the runaway shop, which was to become widespread among U.S. companies in the 1980s and beyond, NCR built its new electronics facilities in places other than Dayton, employing a nonunion labor force, and ran down its unionized operations.

The Dayton plant had employed 15,700 factory workers in 1969, but by 1977 it had only 850, most of them low-paid assemblers (Anderson 1991, pp. 192–194; *Business Week* 1977; Rosenbloom 2000, p. 1098). In contrast, by the mid-1970s NCR employed 18,000 field engineers—25 percent of its labor force—to market its electronic business machines (Rosenbloom 2000, p. 1099). In 2000, the 70 remaining UAW workers at NCR, most of them making $10 per hour and having an average of 17.4 years of service to the company, lost their jobs when NCR outsourced their work, which was in shipping, receiving, building maintenance, and food service (*Dayton Daily News* 2000).

Unlike the NCR experience, unions have survived to the present at Xerox, although with neither the membership nor the influence that they once had. Xerox had been founded in 1906 in Rochester, New York, as the Haloid Company, which, based on its development of the "xerography" process for photocopying, changed its name to Haloid Xerox in 1958 and then to Xerox in 1961. It grew from $37 million in revenues in 1960 to $1.7 billion a decade later. At that point Xerox controlled 96 percent of the market for photocopiers. The Amalgamated Clothing Workers (ACW) had organized Haloid in 1937 and, at the beginning of 1960, represented 586 Haloid Xerox workers out of a company total of 1,894 employees. With the success of Xerox in the 1960s, membership in ACW Local 14A, based at the Webster, New York, plant near Rochester, multiplied. Throughout the 1970s, the ACW, which became the Amalgamated Clothing and Textile Workers Union (ACTWU) in 1976, had more than 4,500 union members at Webster and 5,500–6,000 at all of Xerox's U.S. operations.

During the early 1980s, Xerox went through a major reorganiza-
tion in which the company emulated Japanese practices, such as rapid
product development, rationalization of supplier relationships, and
statistical quality control (*BusinessWeek* 1984; Jacobson and Hillkirk
1986; Prokesch 1985). In the process, ACTWU and Xerox management
became engaged in cooperative efforts to generate innovation, enhance
productivity, and save jobs at the Webster plant. The framework for these
efforts had its origins in 1980, when, as part of the collective bargaining
agreement, Xerox management and ACTWU established a Joint Company–Union Employee Involvement Committee "to investigate and
pursue opportunities for enhancing employees' work satisfaction and
productivity" (Pace and Argona 1989).[4] The agreement covered 5,000
union employees in three locations, most of them at the Webster plant.
The implementation of Employee Involvement (EI) entailed the formation and training of problem-solving teams (PSTs), each composed of
six or seven union members and a supervisor. By the mid-1980s, the
Webster plant had 150 PSTs.

In August 1981 Xerox announced that it would be outsourcing up
to 200 blue-collar jobs in the Webster wire harness assembly plant to
Mexico for an annual savings of $3 million (Costanza 1989; Pace and
Argona 1989; *Washington Post* 1982). The union asked for the formation of a study team that could determine whether cost-savings could be
achieved that would enable wire harness assembly to remain in Webster. The study team came up with $4.2 million in cost reductions that
kept the jobs at home. Subsequently, union-management cooperation at
Xerox became a textbook case of the role of EI from the shop floor up in
sustaining the competitive advantage of blue-collar jobs in a high-wage
economy (Cutcher-Gershenfeld 1991, 1992; Jacobson 1988; Lazes et
al. 1991; Pace and Kelly 1998; Swoboda 1992). In 1989, for example,
EI and ACTWU received credit for helping Xerox win the Malcolm
Baldrige National Quality Award (Holusha 1989; PR Newswire 1989).

At the same time as the union was cooperating in EI programs,
however, Xerox was downsizing its labor force, and blue-collar, along
with salaried and contract, employees constantly faced the threat of job
loss. As a condition for its continued participation in the EI program,
the union demanded that employment security be made part of the collective bargaining agreement. The 1984 contract provided the 3,300

members of Local 14A a guarantee of no layoffs for economic reasons during the three-year life of the pact. In return, the union agreed to the containment of wage growth, a reduction in some benefits, stricter absenteeism control measures, and a replication of the wire harness study in any type of work in which management deemed the Webster plant to be uncompetitive (Pace and Argona 1989). Subsequent union contracts in 1986, 1989, and 1992 renewed the guarantee of employment security for three years each, while the 1994 contract (negotiated a year early), covering 6,200 workers, renewed it for seven years.

During this period, however, the influence of the union at Xerox declined. The ACTWU represented 3,850 employees at the Webster plant in 1994 but only 1,955 in 2002, when the Union of Needletrades, Industrial and Textile Employees, or UNITE—the result of the 1995 merger of the ACTWU with the International Ladies Garment Workers Union—concluded its next contract with Xerox. When UNITE HERE—the product of the 2004 merger of UNITE with the Hotel Employees and Restaurant Employees International Union—signed the recently expired four-year contract in March 2005, it covered 1,517 employees, or not quite 25 percent of the number covered 11 years before.

With its incentive for outsourcing vastly increased in the 2000s, Xerox's management decided that the study-team arrangement had become a relic of the Old Economy. In the collective bargaining agreement signed in 2002, the union got the same employment earnings guarantees as in the 1994 contract along with a package of wage increases, improvements in medical and dental coverage, and an increase in the company contribution to 401(k) accounts. What the union lost, however, was the right to form joint study teams to seek ways of keeping work in the plant that would otherwise be outsourced.

When that contract came up for renewal in March 2005, the study-team arrangement was not even a subject of collective bargaining. The new contract did stipulate, however, that workers at the Webster plant would continue to do final assembly and testing of specific Xerox printers, copiers, and digital presses. The one concession that the union had to make was that any new union hires would not be eligible to receive the choice between the DB and the CB plan that had been available to existing employees since 1990. Instead the new hires would be offered a 401(k) plan with the 6 percent company match (Tyler 2005). Given the union's employment trajectory at Webster since the early 1990s, however, it is unlikely that, going forward, there will be many new hires to whom the new pension regime will apply.

THE ABSENCE OF UNIONS IN NEBM

Organized labor in the United States has never been strong among the types of college-educated professional, technical, and administrative (PTA) employees who, with the automation and offshoring of operative and clerical work, constitute an increasing majority of employees at ICT firms. The most significant example of PTA unionism in the United States is the Society of Professional Engineering Employees in Aerospace (SPEEA), which has almost 24,000 members and has represented engineers and technicians at Boeing (founded in Seattle in 1916) in collective bargaining for more than six decades. Indeed, in 2000 SPEEA staged the largest white-collar strike in U.S. history against Boeing, with wages and health benefits at issue (Morrow 2000a,b). Organizing PTA workers is, however, especially difficult in the New Economy, where, to use Albert Hirschman's (1970) terms, employees have depended on "exit" via the labor market rather than "voice" via union representation to exercise influence over their conditions of work and pay.[5]

Silicon Valley, as the birthplace of NEBM, has always been an anti-union environment. In 1985, when the Silicon Valley semiconductor industry was beset by Japanese competition, Gordon Moore of Intel was quoted as saying, "Our industry changes so rapidly, and the nature of the jobs changes continuously. I think [the lack of unionization] has served the industry well" (Malone 1985). Similarly, in his book, *Spin-off*, Charles Sporck (2001, p. 271), CEO of National Semiconductor and a major figure in the semiconductor industry, contends that "unions have a way of evolving into extremely stubborn obstacles to innovation. We were constantly changing assignments around to make best use of individual talents and skills. It would have been impossible to move ahead with the rapidly developing technology of semiconductors in an organization hampered by union formalities."

Whether or not one accepts these judgments by Silicon Valley's top executives on the incompatibility of unions with NEBM, the fact is, as

Sporck (2001, p. 271) put it, "no semiconductor facility in Silicon Valley was ever unionized." In the mid-1970s, the UAW had gotten as far as a representation ballot at one of Intel's plants, but four out of five eligible employees rejected the union (Jackson 1997, chap. 16). Attempts by U.S. unions to organize Silicon Valley employees in the mid-1980s came to naught (Miller 1984; Sawyer 1984).[6]

The most notable attempt to organize U.S. high-tech employees in the 1990s stemmed from Microsoft's practice of employing contingent workers (Van Jaarsveld 2004). In 1990 the Internal Revenue Service had ruled that Microsoft had been misclassifying regular employees as independent contractors to exclude them from benefits such as the employee stock purchase plan and savings plan. In 1992 these workers launched a class action lawsuit (*Vizcaino v. Microsoft*) which was finally settled in December 2000 with a payment from Microsoft of $97 million.

The lawsuit mobilized contingent workers at Microsoft to form, in 1998, the Washington Alliance of Technology Workers (WashTech), a union that affiliated with the CWA.[7] While WashTech has been unsuccessful in gaining union recognition at Microsoft or any other employer, it has wielded a certain amount of political influence in Washington State and has participated in CWA training initiatives (Van Jaarsveld 2004, pp. 373–379). In 2000 WashTech came to the aid of customer service representatives who had been laid off at Amazon.com and was reportedly able to pressure the company into granting them better severance packages (Wilson and Blain 2001). Also affiliated with CWA is Alliance@IBM, formed in 1999 in response to IBM's adoption of a CB pension plan, which significantly reduced the pension benefits of older IBM employees (Frey 1999b; PR Newswire 1999b).

In Silicon Valley, the only occupational group that has won collective bargaining agreements has been janitors. In 1992 Hewlett-Packard agreed to employ a janitorial contractor whose employees were represented by the Service Employees International Union (SEIU) (U.S. Newswire 1992). By 1996 an SEIU official announced that "every major high-tech company is cleaned by a union janitorial company except for Intel" (Holmes 1996). By the end of the decade, amid the affluence of the high-tech boom, there was a general acceptance among Silicon Valley's high-tech employers that the people, most of them Hispanic immigrants, who cleaned their facilities needed collective bargaining to bolster their meager pay. Even Intel, which remained adamantly non-union, paid its janitors at the union rate (Kirby 2000).

As for the college-educated members of the ICT labor force, their power vis-à-vis employers has resided in individual mobility in the labor market rather than in collective bargaining at the place of work. For many ICT employees, the power of individual labor mobility served them well in the Internet boom of the late 1990s, especially when they entered into employment at companies with generous stock-option plans. Recall from Chapter 2 the enormous average gains of employees at companies like Microsoft and Cisco in the Internet boom. It has been claimed, quite plausibly, that the Internet boom created 10,000 stock-option millionaires at Microsoft alone (Harden 2003).[8]

In the 2000s, however, the U.S. ICT labor market has changed in ways that have greatly diminished the power of individual mobility, especially for educated and experienced high-tech workers in their 40s and 50s. As we shall see in the next chapter, even college-educated members of the U.S. ICT labor force now face competition from large and growing supplies of highly qualified but much less expensive high-tech labor in developing nations, especially India and China. Yet in a dynamic industry whose continued, and generally rapid, growth is based on innovation, heightened global labor-market competition need not necessarily mean a paucity of stable and remunerative jobs for educated and experienced high-tech employees in the United States. The problem, as I show in Chapter 6, is that the top executives of leading high-tech companies that have been profiting handsomely from globalization have been far more interested in allocating corporate resources to boost their companies' stock prices, and thereby their own compensation, than in creating or even maintaining stable and remunerative employment opportunities for high-tech workers in the United States.

Notes

1. Although about 19 percent of SAIC's common shares were floated in the IPO, employees retained 98 percent of SAIC's voting rights (Cowan 2006).
2. Qwest had emerged in 1994 through the combination of a telecommunications subsidiary of Southern Pacific Rail and Qwest Communications, which had built a digital microwave system in the southwest (Business Wire 1994).
3. At the end of July 2008, CWA membership was as follows: Verizon, 59,825 (74,251 in 2005); AT&T Inc., 161,342 (161,698 in 2005, including BellSouth and Cingular union members); and Qwest, 18,415 (23,642 in 2005). In addition, there were 1,747 at Idearc, the 2006 spinoff of Verizon's Yellow Pages business, and 869 at Dex Media, the 2002 spinoff of Qwest's Yellow Pages business. I am grateful to Debbie Goldman and Beatriz Woods of CWA for making these membership data available to me.
4. Larry Pace and Dominick Argona were internal consultants to the employee involvement initiative, and Argona was also manager of the employee involvement function within the human resources department. Anthony Costanza was the shop chairman of ACTWU Local 14A from 1981 to 1986 and was subsequently international vice president of ACTWU.
5. For the problems of unionism in the "boundaryless workplace," see Stone (2004).
6. For a history of attempts to organize workers in high-tech industries in Silicon Valley, see Bacon (2006).
7. See WashTech (2008). For useful works that focus on the roles of contingent employment and flexible labor markets in Silicon Valley, see Benner (2002) and Hyde (2003).
8. For the distribution of stock options at Cisco in 1999, see O'Reilly and Pfeffer (2000).

5

Globalization of the
High-Tech Labor Force

OFFSHORING

By the 2000s, employment relations in U.S. ICT industries had changed dramatically from those that had prevailed into the 1980s. The interfirm mobility of labor, facilitated by industry standards as opposed to proprietary standards, and the vertical specialization of the value chain, including the outsourcing of manufacturing activity, set the stage for a vast globalization of the high-tech labor force. In the first half of the 2000s, "offshoring" entered the American lexicon as U.S.-based companies moved large numbers of jobs overseas, with India and China as prime locations. Many of the engineering and programming jobs that have been offshored in the 2000s are ones that observers of U.S. high-tech industry thought could not be done abroad. The development of sophisticated products and processes generally requires interactive learning that is both collective and cumulative. Workers engaged in interactive learning have to be in close communication with one another. With the United States at the center of the ICT revolution, the assumption was that these jobs could not be relocated to low-wage developing countries.

Indeed, precisely because the United States dominates ICT, it is the place to which people come from around the world for ICT-related higher education and work experience. Why would many of the best ICT jobs be migrating to India and China if Indian and Chinese people are migrating to the United States to study and work in ICT? The answer to this question is important for understanding the impact of globalization on the economic insecurity of high-tech workers in the United States in the 2000s. The demise of career employment with one company would be much less of a source of insecurity for U.S. high-tech workers if the U.S.-based companies that are globalizing were creating more and better jobs at home.

In fact, many major U.S.-based ICT companies that have been expanding their worldwide employment in the 2000s have been reducing employment in the United States. From 2001 to 2007, IBM increased its worldwide employment by 21 percent, from 319,867 to 386,558, but its U.S. employment fell by 17 percent, from 152,195 to 126,804. Similarly, from 2002 to 2007, HP's worldwide employment expanded by 22 percent, from 141,000 to 172,000, but its U.S. employment fell by 21 percent, from 67,350 to 53,519. In 2007 Intel's worldwide employment of 85,187 was 2 percent higher than in 2001, but its U.S. employment of 46,186 was 15 percent lower.[1]

Some U.S.-based companies that have increased U.S. employment in the 2000s have expanded non-U.S. employment at a faster rate. Microsoft doubled its U.S. employment from 27,000 in 2000 to 55,000 in 2008, but the U.S. share of worldwide employment fell from 69 percent to 60 percent. Cisco Systems increased its U.S. employment from 25,000 in 2000 to 37,400 in 2008, but the U.S. share of worldwide employment fell from 74 percent to 57 percent.[2]

Offshoring by U.S. high-tech companies is by no means new. For decades U.S. ICT companies have been routinely offshoring production activities, usually through foreign direct investment (FDI). Previously offshoring had been driven mainly by the search for low-wage labor to perform relatively low-skill work. New in the 2000s was the extent to which offshoring represented a search for low-wage labor to perform relatively high-skill work. In the 2000s U.S. ICT companies have been able to access an abundance of such labor in developing countries, especially India and China.

Since the 1960s the development strategies of national governments and indigenous businesses in Asian nations have interacted with the investment strategies of U.S.-based ICT companies as well as U.S. immigration policy to generate a global labor supply. This process has entailed flows of U.S. capital to Asian labor as well as flows of Asian labor to U.S. capital. As a result, new possibilities to pursue high-tech careers, and thereby develop productive capabilities, have opened up to vast numbers of individuals in Asian nations. Many found the relevant educational programs and work experience in their home countries. But many gained access to education and experience by following global career paths that included study and work abroad, especially in the United States.

For Asian nations in the process of development, these global career paths have posed a danger of "brain drain"—the career path could come to an end in the United States (or another advanced economy) rather than in the country where the individual had been born and raised. For nations such as South Korea, Taiwan, China, and India, however, which have experienced brain drain at certain stages of their development, the education and experience that their nationals received in the United States created valuable "human capital" that could potentially be lured back home. A major challenge for these Asian nations has been the creation of domestic employment opportunities, through a combination of FDI, strategic government initiatives, and the growth of indigenous businesses, to enable the career paths of global nationals to be followed back home, thus transforming a potential "brain drain" into an actual "brain gain."

EDUCATION AND GROWTH IN ASIA

Between 1970 and 2000, real GDP per capita increased 7.5 times in South Korea, 5.4 times in Taiwan, 4.7 in Singapore, and 3.7 in Hong Kong. In the process these four nations became known as the "Tiger economies." During this period, Japan, starting from a much higher base than the four Tigers, saw its real GDP per capita rise 2.2 times, while the United States saw its rise 1.9 times. Over these three decades, Japan's GDP per capita increased from 35 percent to 75 percent of that of the United States, South Korea's from 13 percent to 51 percent, Taiwan's from 20 percent to 59 percent, Singapore's from 30 percent to 79 percent, and Hong Kong's from 38 percent to 76 percent (Maddison 2007). The increases in wages that these higher levels of GDP per capita both permitted and reflected did not undermine the competitive advantage of Japan or the Tiger economies in ICT. On the contrary, by further mobilizing the skills and efforts of the indigenous labor force as well as increasing the extent of domestic product markets that enjoyed a degree of protection, rising wages were integral to the dynamics of economic growth.

These cases of rapid growth entailed active and purposeful government initiatives to build communications and educational infrastructures and to develop domestic high-tech knowledge bases. National and local governments also provided subsidies to business enterprises, both foreign and domestically owned, to make use of these infrastructures and knowledge bases to generate products that could ultimately be competitive at home and abroad (e.g., Amsden 1989; Amsden and Chu 2003; Branscomb and Choi 1996; Breznitz 2007; Ernst 2002; Hobday 1995; Jomo, Fulker, and Rasiah 1999; Kim 1997a; Lazonick 2007c; Lu 2000; Mathews and Cho 2000; Saxenian 2006; Wade 1990). These government and business investments in high-tech capabilities created large numbers of indigenous high-tech employment opportunities. Insofar as these investments generated higher productivity than previously, they contributed to the economic growth of the nation. In general, a portion of these productivity gains accrued as higher returns to labor, thus eliminating to some extent the low-wage advantage that the nation may have had. Given the presence of other lower wage nations in the process of developing their productive capabilities, economic growth that results in higher wages creates an imperative to "upgrade" employment opportunities by moving into higher value-added activities. As part of a dynamic national investment strategy, the emergence of ever more remunerative high-tech employment opportunities may be both cause and effect of sustained economic growth.

The most fundamental, and expensive, expenditure of a government that seeks to support economic development is investment in a system of primary, secondary, and tertiary education. In the case of Japan, investments in education that began in the late nineteenth century laid the foundations for the nation's economic transformation from the 1950s on. Because of laws dating back to 1886 that made primary education universally free and compulsory, 98 percent of all Japanese school-age children went to primary school by 1909 (Koike and Inoki 1990, pp. 227–228). Japan also developed a system of higher education from the late nineteenth century onward that sent its graduates into industry (Yonekawa 1984). Additionally, starting in the late nineteenth century, Japanese companies engaged in the practice of sending university-educated employees abroad for extended periods of time to learn about Western technology (Fukasaku 1992; Matsumoto 1999). Of utmost importance to Japan's post–World War II development was the fact that Japanese industrial enterprises had made university-educated engineers integral to their managerial organizations for decades (Morikawa 2001, pp. 62–63).

These investments in education meant that only 2.4 percent of Japan's population aged 15 and over had no schooling in 1960, and that on average Japan's population had 7.8 years of schooling (the U.S. figures were 2.0 percent with no schooling and an average of 8.5 years of schooling). By contrast, in 1960 the no-schooling proportion of the population was 42.8 percent for South Korea, 37.3 percent for Taiwan, 46.2 percent for Singapore, and 19.7 percent for Hong Kong; the average years of schooling were between about 4 and 5 in all of the countries (Barro and Lee 2000). A major challenge that faced the would-be Tigers, and other Asian nations such as Malaysia, Indonesia, the Philippines, and Thailand, was to transform their national educational systems into foundations for industrial development.

South Korea dramatically transformed its educational system after 1960. The average years of schooling of South Korea's population aged 15 and over rose from 7.9 years in 1980 to 10.8 in 2000, surpassing Japan's 2000 figure of 9.5 and not far behind the U.S. figure of 12.0. By the late 1990s, South Korea had the highest number of PhDs per capita of any country in the world (Kim and Leslie 1998, p. 154).

India—a nation with 680 million people aged 15 or over in 2000 compared with South Korea's 37 million—has not experienced such a dramatic transformation of its mass education system. In 1960 the population aged 15 and over included 72.2 percent with no schooling and had on average 1.7 years of schooling. By 2000 India's no-schooling figure remained high (43.9 percent), and the average for years of schooling was only 5.1. With one-sixth of the world's population in the first half of the 2000s, India had over one-third of the world's illiterates (EFA Global Monitoring Report 2007, pp. 276, 278, 284–287).

Yet, at the same time, India has become a leading source for supplying engineers and programmers to the global ICT labor force. The stage was set by government investments made in the 1950s and 1960s, of which the decision to create Institutes of Technology, modeled on the Massachusetts Institute of Technology, stands out (Bassett 2005; Sebaly 1972). The first Indian Institute of Technology (IIT) was founded at Kharagpur, West Bengal, in 1952 (Bassett 2005; Shenkman 1954, p. 28). A 1959 Act of Parliament established IIT Kanpur, which became the leading technological institute in India. From 1962 to 1972, IIT Kanpur received assistance from the Kanpur Indo-American Programme (KIAP), through which a consortium of nine U.S. universities assisted in setting up research laboratories and academic curricula.

In the late 1960s, India was second only to the United States in the number of students in universities, even though the number of university students in India was extremely low on a per capita basis (Ilchman 1969, p. 783). Notwithstanding the important contribution of the IITs to the creation of an elite corps of engineering graduates, Indian graduates were more numerous in the natural sciences. India's 1,907,944 bachelor's degrees in natural sciences from 1975 to 1990 represented more than 97 percent of the U.S. total, and by the late 1980s India was granting more such degrees annually than the United States. India's output of undergraduate engineers was less prodigious but nonetheless significant, rising from 35 percent to 45 percent of the annual number of U.S. engineering graduates from 1975 to 1990 (National Science Foundation 1993, Appendix Table A-3).

China, by contrast, focused much more on producing engineers than natural scientists. The total Chinese output of undergraduate engineers for the period from 1982 to 1990 (the period for which Chinese data are available) exceeded the 1975–1990 totals of Japan by 29 percent, the United States by 35 percent, and the combined numbers of Taiwan, South Korea, and India by 72 percent. From 1975 to 1990, South Korea quadrupled its annual output of engineering bachelor's degrees, while those of Taiwan and India both doubled. Between 1990 and 2000, India increased its total enrollments in engineering from 258,284 to 576,649 (Government of India 2002, 2003) while China increased the number of undergraduate engineering degrees awarded from 114,620 to 212,905 and South Korea from 28,071 to 56,508. Perhaps more significantly, in the first four years of the 2000s, China more than doubled its undergraduate engineering degrees, awarding 442,463 in 2004. Over the same period South Korea increased its undergraduate engineering degrees to 70,034 (National Science Board 2004, Appendix Table 2-34; 2008, Appendix Table 2-38).

Table 5.1 shows the number of science and engineering doctorates awarded per 100,000 in population aged 25–34 years for the most recent year available in five leading Asian countries and the United States. While, by this measure, the United States outstrips the five Asian nations in the physical and biological sciences, it lags behind South

Table 5.1 Doctoral Degrees Awarded per 100,000 Population, Aged 25–34, Most Recent Available Year, for Selected Asian Countries and the United States

Country	Year	All science and engineering fields	Physical/ biological sciences	Engineering
China	2004	10.1	3.1	5.5
India	2003	4.6	3.3	0.6
Japan	2005	41.3	8.3	21.1
South Korea	2004	44.0	9.8	25.4
Taiwan	2005	37.0	7.2	20.2
United States	2006	66.2	25.1	14.6

SOURCE: National Science Board (2008, Appendix Table 2-40); population statistics from U.S. Census Bureau (2008d).

Korea, Japan, and Taiwan in engineering. At a much lower level of doctorates per capita, China and India are about even in the sciences, but China is far ahead of India in engineering.

The U.S. figures, however, include large proportions of people, especially from Asia, who were not U.S. citizens or permanent residents. Already in the period from 1964 to 1970, there were an average of 25,656 foreign engineering students on nonimmigrant visas studying in the United States, of whom 18.6 percent were from China and Taiwan, 16.2 percent from India, and 2.5 percent from South Korea. In 2003–2004, of the 279,076 foreign graduate students in the United States, 66.0 percent were from Asia, with 22.6 percent of the total from India, 18.2 percent from China, 8.9 percent from South Korea, and 5.4 percent from Taiwan (Institute of International Education 2005). In 2005 foreign citizens on temporary visas earned 43.6 percent of the engineering master's degrees awarded in the United States, compared with 33.9 percent in 1995 and 38.2 percent in 2000, and they also earned 58.6 percent of the engineering doctoral degrees, compared with 42.1 percent in 1995 and 46.0 percent in 2000. In 2005, in mathematics and statistics, foreign citizens on temporary visas earned 38.6 percent of the master's degrees and 50.0 percent of the doctoral degrees, while in computer sciences, these figures were 42.0 percent and 52.7 percent, respectively (National Science Board 2008, Appendix Tables 2-30 and 2-32). In 2007, among graduate students in the United States on temporary visas, Indian and Chinese students represented 44.0 percent and 20.3 percent, respectively, in engineering, 10.5 percent and 41.5 percent in mathematics, and 55.2 percent and 15.0 percent in computer sciences (Appendix Table 2-24).

In 2002–2005, of all non-U.S. citizens who received U.S. engineering doctorates, 46 percent had "definite plans to stay" in the United States after graduation, compared with 51 percent in 1998–2001. The proportion of Chinese with these intentions was 56 percent and that of Indians was 63 percent, compared with 62 and 70 percent in 1998–2001 (National Science Board 2008, Appendix Table 2-33). The greater ease with which graduates on temporary visas were able to secure green cards from the late 1990s may also have been a factor in keeping these numbers high (Vaughan 2003). Insofar as foreign university graduates stayed in the United States to pursue careers, they became part of their home country's brain drain.

BRAIN DRAIN

An investment in high-tech education can only make an immediate contribution to the growth of a developing nation if there are employment opportunities in the domestic economy that can make productive use of the educated labor. Employment experience in turn augments the productive capabilities of the domestic labor force, especially in industries that make use of sophisticated technologies. The problem of high-tech brain drain occurs when a developing nation invests in the education of scientists and engineers, but the most attractive employment opportunities for these university graduates are abroad rather than at home.

The science and engineering brain drain was a major problem in the 1960s and 1970s for the developing Asian economies (Adams 1968; Fortney 1970; Pernia 1976; Van der Kroef 1968). In the late 1960s, Asia surpassed Europe as the main source of scientists and engineers coming to the United States from abroad (Schmeck 1973). The United States stood accused of taking the best that the newly industrializing countries had to offer, thus building U.S. high-tech capabilities at the expense of economies that could ill afford it.

Encouraging the Asian brain drain was the U.S. Immigration and Naturalization Law of 1965 that abolished the national quota system in favor of preference to people whose skills could be "especially advantageous" to the United States (Fortney 1970, p. 217). Of the 41,652 professional, technical, and kindred workers who immigrated to the United States in 1967, engineers, at almost 21 percent of the total, represented the largest single group. In 1966 the 4,921 new immigrant engineers were equivalent to 9.5 percent of the new graduates of U.S. engineering institutions (p. 219). Fortney (p. 218) summed up the change: "The old law discriminated severely against all residents of 'coloured' countries, especially those of Asia. Immigrants from Asia in the professional, technical, and kindred worker category more than doubled between 1965 and 1966 (2,078 to 5,628) and again between 1966 and 1967 (5,628 to 12,282)."

Over 30,000 college graduates went abroad from Taiwan between 1956 and 1972, with only 2,586 returning (Ho 1975, p. 40). Nearly 60 percent of those who left Taiwan had science or engineering educations, and they tended to be the best students, thus exacerbating that nation's loss. In the 1950s and 1960s, South Korea also had a serious brain drain. In the period between 1953 and 1972, 10,412 students, 5,376 of whom were in science and engineering, requested permission from the Korean Ministry of Education to study in the United States, and more than 90 percent did not return after graduation (Yoon 1992, p. 6). Between 1974 and 1988, the number of immigrant scientists and engineers as a proportion of all scientists and engineers in the United States increased from 5.8 percent to 10.5 percent, with the five leading sources being India, the UK, Taiwan, Poland, and China (Arnst 1991; North 1995, p. 6).

The Immigration Act of 1990 increased the annual number of employment-based visas that could be issued (including family members) from 54,000 to 140,000. The "employment-based preferences" (EBP) class represented 11.6 percent of the immigrants admitted from 1996 to 2000 and 15.7 percent from 2001 to 2004, notwithstanding a large but temporary decline in EBP admissions in 2003. From 1996 through 2004, 454,000 Indians received green cards, 190,000 of whom were EBP admissions. Indians received 8.4 percent of the EBP visas in 1996, but that rose to an average of 24.7 percent from 2002 to 2004 before falling to 12.3 percent in 2007 (Immigration and Naturalization

Service 1999, 2000, 2002a,b, 2003; U.S. Department of Homeland Security 2003a, 2004a, 2006a,b, 2007, 2008). Before 1998, China had been the largest recipient, with 13.9 percent in 1996 and 15.4 percent in 1997, but that fell to 6.8 percent by 2007.

H-1B and L-1 nonimmigrant work visas have also been of great importance in enabling the flow of educated Asians to the United States for high-tech employment. India has been the top nation in terms of numbers of H-1B visas issued since 1993, when it surpassed the Philippines (U.S. Department of State 2009). From 2000 to 2003, Indians received 57.0 percent of the 547,000 initial H-1B visas and 48.0 percent of the 457,000 continuing visas issued (U.S. Department of Homeland Security 2003b, 2004b, 2006c). China was a distant second with 9.5 percent of the initial and 7.7 percent of the continuing visas. Over the 12-year period from 1997 to 2008, Indians received 45.7 percent of all H-1B visas issued, followed by the Chinese with 5.8 percent and the British with 4.9 percent.

Indians have also been the leading recipients of L-1 visas since 2000, when they surpassed both the Japanese and the British. Traditionally multinational companies (MNCs) based in advanced nations have dominated the L-1 visa category. The proportion of L-1 visas that went to Indians climbed dramatically from 4.4 percent in 1997 to 47.7 percent in 2008 (U.S. Department of State 2009). The next closest in 2008 were the British with 7.5 percent, the Japanese with 6.4 percent, and the French and the Germans with 3.5 percent each. Indians, therefore, have become the leading source of both immigrant and nonimmigrant entrants to the United States in search of work as well as education.

H-1B visas are predominantly high-tech visas. For FY2000–2003, 98 percent of H-1B visas were issued to people with at least bachelor's degrees. In FY2003, 50 percent had bachelor's degrees, 31 percent master's degrees, 12 percent doctorates, and 6 percent professional degrees. At 39 percent of the total, the largest occupational category among visa holders was "computer-related," followed by "architecture, engineering, and surveying" (12 percent), "education" (11 percent), and "medicine and health" (11 percent) (U.S. Department of Homeland Security 2003b, 2004b, 2006c).

Under the Immigration Act of 1990, which amended earlier legislation, an H-1B visa is issued for an initial period of three years, with the possibility of reapplying for extension for another three years. H-1B visa holders can apply for permanent resident (i.e., immigrant) status, and employers of H-1B visa holders often sponsor the nonimmigrant for permanent resident status. Under the American Competitiveness for the 21st Century Act of 1998, H-1B visa holders can obtain one-year extensions while waiting to become permanent residents, prompting some to contend that H-1B is a "preimmigrant" rather than "nonimmigrant" program. In 2001 more than 228,000 nonimmigrant visa holders became permanent residents (Vaughan 2003). Alternatively, former H-1B visa holders who have been out of the United States for at least one year can take a job with a new H-1B visa, valid for three years, again with the possibility of a further three-year extension (Yale-Loehr 2003a).

Created in 1970, the L-1 visa category enables an MNC, whether U.S. or non-U.S., to bring foreign employees from abroad to work for the company or an affiliate in the United States. The sponsoring firm must have employed an "intracompany transferee" continuously for one year in the previous three years "in a managerial or executive position or in a position where she gained specialized knowledge" (Yale-Loehr 2003b). Executives and managers enter on an L-1A visa and can work in the United States for up to seven years, whereas employees with specialized knowledge enter on an L-1B visa and can work for up to five years.

There is no limit to the number of L-1 visas that can be issued. Such was also the case with H-1 visas prior to the Immigration Act of 1990.[3] During the 1980s H-1 visas began to be widely used. The number of H-1 visas issued doubled from about 10,000 in 1969 to 20,000 in 1979 and then climbed to almost 49,000 in 1989 (Lowell 2000, p. 3). In October 1990, prior to the passage of the 1990 Immigration Act, *Electronics Weekly* (1990) reported that "U.S. electronics companies are worried about proposed changes in U.S. immigration laws that will limit the number of foreign staff they can hire. U.S. electronics companies rely heavily on electronics engineers and other skilled staff from abroad."

The British magazine *Computing* warned, "Jobs for thousands of UK programmers/analysts threatened by immigration bill limiting work visas." The article quoted Charles Sporck, CEO of National Semiconductor, as saying that in some parts of his company "at least a third of the staff are from overseas," and also cited a Microsoft representative as saying his company relied heavily on foreign programmers (Foremski 1990).

Then as now, the issue of whether or not there was a high-tech "labor shortage" was a highly politicized issue (see U.S. House of Representatives 1990). In the late 1980s, a National Science Foundation prediction of an impending shortage of scientists and engineers bolstered high-tech industry's demand for an accommodating policy for employment-based immigrant visas and H-1B and L-1 nonimmigrant visas (see Weinstein 1998). In the Congressional hearings that preceded the Immigration Act of 1990, labor economist Vernon Briggs advocated limits on the availability of high-tech visas. "I believe strongly that labor shortages are wonderful, and we should never do anything to eliminate that pressure," he said, "because it is forcing us to ask all the right questions about education and health, antidiscrimination policy, all the right policies are in place" (U.S. House of Representatives 1990, p. 298; quoted in Weinstein 1998).

Michael Teitelbaum, a demographer serving as a program officer at the Alfred P. Sloan Foundation, argued against legislation that would succumb to declarations by business interests that they faced critical labor shortages. "What many employers and non-experts call 'labor shortages,'" he said, "are really mismatches between the skills needed and those being provided by U.S. educational systems; hence the focus should be on educational and on-the-job training systems, to make them relate more effectively to labor demands, as do those in Germany and Japan" (U.S. House of Representatives 1990, p. 572; see also Teitelbaum 1996).

In the ultimate passage of the Immigration Act of 1990, however, business interests prevailed. The bill that was enacted set the annual cap of initial H-1B visas at 65,000, about 16,000 more than the number issued in 1989, rather than the 25,000 cap that labor interests had been advocating. The change was influenced by lobbying efforts from the business community (e.g., see Szabo 1989). Upon his election as president of the American Immigration Lawyers Association in 1988, H. Ronald Klesko declared, "This will be the year of business immigration. We will focus on creating a business immigration coalition composed of business leaders, chambers of commerce, human resource groups, corporate counsels, state development agency leaders and the immigration bar" (PR Newswire 1988). In November 1990, on the eve of the signing of the new Immigration Act by President George H.W. Bush, Harris N. Miller, coordinator of the Business Immigration Coalition, representing 250 companies and business associations formed to lobby for the new bill, told a *New York Times* reporter, "We're very concerned about shortages of skilled people, particularly in the sciences and engineering, computer science and mathematics" (DePalma 1990). In 1991, with the Immigration Act in place, Miller remarked, "We were successful because we refashioned the debate from the jobs displacement issue, where we always lost, to the competitive issue" (Lee 1991).

To the present, Miller has remained a key figure in lobbying for the free flow of the global ICT labor force into the United States. In 1995 Miller became president of the Information Technology Association of America (ITAA), a position he retained until 2006, when he quit to stage an unsuccessful campaign for the Democratic nomination in Virginia as a candidate for the U.S. Senate. As a leading trade association for the ICT industries, ITAA was in the forefront of lobbying efforts that resulted in securing the American Competitiveness and Workforce Improvement Act of 1998. This legislation raised the annual H-1B cap to 115,000 initial visas in fiscal years 1999 and 2000.[4] The American Competitiveness for the 21st Century Act of 2000 raised the annual cap to 195,000 initial visas in FY2001–2003. As of October 1, 2003, the annual cap of 65,000 was restored, but with an extra 20,000 visas available to foreign-born professionals who have an advanced degree from a U.S. institution of higher education (U.S. Citizenship and Immigration Services 2005).[5]

In 2007 and 2008, Congress debated an increase in the H-1B cap. Any changes in the H-1B cap, however, would now have to be enacted as part of comprehensive immigration reform, legislation that includes a process for legalizing the status of illegal immigrants, almost all of whom are poorly educated and low-paid. In effect, high-tech business interests found their efforts to have the H-1B cap raised stalled by the failure in Congress to secure the votes for reform of illegal immigration laws.

Advocating the H-1B increase was Compete America, an association that among its 16 company members includes Analog Devices, Cisco Systems, Google, HP, Intel, International Rectifier, Microsoft, Motorola, National Semiconductor, Oracle, Qualcomm, and TI (Compete America 2008). In congressional hearings in 2007, Bill Gates of Microsoft argued the case for more H-1Bs as follows:

Unfortunately, America's immigration policies are driving away the world's best and brightest precisely when we need them most. The terrible shortfall in our visa supply for the highly skilled stems not from security concerns, but from visa policies that have not been updated in over a decade and a half. We live in a different economy now. Simply put: It makes no sense to tell well-trained, highly skilled individuals—many of whom are educated at our top colleges and universities—that the United States does not welcome or value them. For too many foreign students and professionals, however, our immigration policies send precisely this message. (Elstrom 2007)

An argument against raising the H-1B cap came from information released by two U.S. Senators, Charles Grassley of Iowa and Richard Durbin of Illinois, which showed that Indian IT services companies represented four of the top five and 10 of the top 20 users of H-1B visas in 2006.[6] The top four India-based companies—Infosys Technologies, Wipro, Tata Consultancy Services (TCS), and Satyam Computer Services—held a combined total of 14,836 H-1B visas. In 2007 H-1B visas were more widely distributed, but Infosys still led the list of successful applicants with 4,559 petitions approved, and Wipro was second with 2,567, Satyam third with 1,396, and TCS sixth with 797—a four-company total of 9,319. These companies were also large-scale users of L-1 visas, with TCS leading with 4,887 visas in 2006. Cognizant Technology Solutions, a New Jersey–based spinoff of Dun and Bradstreet that employs about three-quarters of its workforce in India, was the second largest user of L-1 visas in 2006 and the sixth largest user of H-1B visas (Press Trust of India 2007). Indeed, almost all of the U.S.-based ICT firms that employ large numbers of nonimmigrants on H-1B and L-1 visas in the United States have significant numbers of employees in India as well.

THE HISTORICAL ROLE OF U.S. FDI IN STEMMING THE ASIAN BRAIN DRAIN

Over the last four decades of the twentieth century, the career paths of vast numbers of well-educated people from around the world, especially Asia, took them to the United States for specialized education and specialty occupations. The challenge facing the developing nations that experienced this brain drain was to create employment opportunities that could bring these people, with their enhanced capabilities, back home, or, alternatively, to create employment opportunities at home so that educated individuals would not need to go abroad to develop their capabilities and establish a high-tech career.

Historically, a key source of these employment opportunities in the nations of Asia occurred starting in the 1960s, when U.S. microelectronics companies offshored semiconductor assembly operations. As we have seen in Chapter 2, subsequent to the invention of the transistor at Bell Labs in 1947, and with the support of Cold War military spending, an array of U.S. companies, including Western Electric, Raytheon, GE, RCA, Westinghouse, IBM, TI, Motorola, and, after 1957, Fairchild Semiconductor, made the United States the center of the global semiconductor industry (Tilton 1971). From the late 1950s on, however, U.S. companies began to feel competitive pressure in the production of transistors from the Japanese, who had successfully transferred the technology from the United States (Flamm 1985, p. 70). By the early 1960s, U.S. semiconductor manufacturers began to consider the option of doing labor-intensive assembly work in low-wage offshore locations.

In his memoir, Charles Sporck (2001, p. 95), who had been head of manufacturing at Fairchild Semiconductor from 1961 to 1967 before becoming CEO of National Semiconductor, recalled how Fairchild had pioneered offshoring the assembly of transistors to Asia in the early 1960s: "Fairchild's establishment of a Hong Kong facility in 1963 was the first Southeast Asian manufacturing venture of any American semiconductor company. The plant provided an immediate cost advantage in both direct labor and overhead, and overnight it challenged the wisdom of most investments in assembly automation by TI, Motorola and others. In fact, we started a trend toward assembly plants in Southeast Asia that was adopted by many other companies as time went by."

By 1971 a United Nations research report stated, "Every established United States semiconductor firm appears to be engaged in some offshore assembly" (Chang 1971, p. 17). The report listed 33 offshore facilities established from 1963 to 1971 by 22 different U.S. semiconductor companies. Eight of these companies, with 16 offshore plants among them, were based in Silicon Valley (pp. 19–20). After 1972, Malaysia became a favored location for semiconductor assembly, with HP and Intel being among the first to open plants in the new Free Trade Zone in Penang. In 1974 Malaysia hosted 11 U.S.-owned semiconductor facilities, South Korea nine, Hong Kong eight, Taiwan three, and the rest of Asia six, and there were 15 U.S. facilities in Latin American countries, primarily Mexico (Davis and Hatano 1985, p. 129).

By 1970 almost all of the assembly work in semiconductors that still remained in the United States was automated. But rapid changes in technology that rendered automated processes obsolete combined with the availability of hard-working, low-wage labor favored the use of labor-intensive methods in a number of developing countries. By the first half of the 1980s, U.S.-based merchant producers did 80 percent of their semiconductor assembly offshore, and much of the assembly operations that remained in the United States were for military purposes (Davis and Hatano 1985, p. 129).

U.S. tariff policy facilitated the offshoring movement. Sections 806.30 and 807 of the Tariff Schedule of the United States permitted goods that had been exported from the United States for foreign assembly to be imported with duty charged only on the value added abroad. In 1967 dollars, "806/807" imports of semiconductors to the United States increased from $130 million in 1969 (accounting for 95 percent of all semiconductor imports into the United States) to $2,267 million in 1979 (79 percent) to $3,368 million in 1983 (69 percent) (Flamm 1985, p. 74).

As late as 1974, Mexico was the most important single national location for 806/807 semiconductor exports, but its share eroded sharply after 1975 (Flamm 1985, p. 76). In 1970 the average hourly wage for semiconductor assembly in Singapore, Hong Kong, and South Korea was less than one-tenth that in the United States, and about half that in Mexico (Chang 1971, p. 27; Sharpston 1975, p. 105). The relatively high value and low weight of semiconductor products meant that the proximity of Mexico to the United States did not offer an appreciable transportation advantage over an Asian location (Davis and Hatano 1985, p. 129; Flamm 1985; Moxon 1974, pp. 35–36). Within Asia during the 1970s and early 1980s, there was a marked shift of 806/807 activity from Hong Kong to Malaysia and the Philippines, while South Korea and Singapore sustained substantial market shares. In 1985 there were

63 U.S. semiconductor plants in Asia, employing just under 100,000 people (Henderson 1989, pp. 54, 59; Scott 1987, pp. 145, 147).

Although the impetus to offshore chip assembly was the search for low-wage labor, the lowest-wage Asian locations, such as Indonesia and Thailand, did not dominate. Other considerations, most notably political stability and the productivity of labor, entered into plant location. In 1967, for example, James Stokes, the head of Signetics Korea, was quoted as saying, "If we had been looking only for cheap wages, we could have gone to Africa" (*New York Times* 1967). George Needham, director of Motorola's assembly plant on the outskirts of Seoul, told plant visitors in 1970 that a Korean female worker could be taught to assemble semiconductors in two weeks less than her American counterpart. "The girls here are more motivated," Needham was quoted as saying. "Life is tough in this country. These people really need this work." He claimed that production costs in South Korea were one-tenth of those in a similar Motorola plant in Phoenix, Arizona, the headquarters of the company's semiconductor operations (Shabecoff 1970, p. 57).

In the 1960s and 1970s, however, South Korea and many other Asian nations had more to offer MNCs than just low-wage, hardworking female labor for assembly operations. Of great significance for the persistence of these offshored investments even as wage levels rose was the fact that when, in the 1960s and 1970s, foreign semiconductor companies employed relatively low-wage (female) labor to perform low-skill production jobs, they could find relatively low-wage (male) labor to perform high-skill engineering and managerial jobs. By the mid-1980s, all of these Asian economies were on the way to transforming themselves from relatively low-wage to relatively high-wage economies. The availability of an indigenous supply of high-skill labor was critical for upgrading productive capabilities so that the ICT industries of these nations, and the offshored facilities, could remain competitive in a higher wage environment.

The importance of this high-skill labor, even in the early 1960s, is evident in Charles Sporck's follow-up to his statement, quoted above, about Fairchild's 1963 entry into Hong Kong in search of low-wage assembly workers. "Although we went to Hong Kong for direct labor savings, we found that we could hire engineers and other overhead people at dramatically lower costs as well," he said. "In many cases, they had been educated and trained in the United States and they were highly capable technicians and supervisors. Their availability and their overall caliber made the decision to go offshore immediately success-ful" (Sporck 2001, p. 95).

The fact that qualified indigenous engineers were available to the U.S. semiconductor companies when they offshored their assembly operations in the 1960s and 1970s is of great importance for understand-ing what the World Bank (1993) would call, with considerable mystifi-cation, "the East Asian miracle." The type of economic transformations that occurred in Asia depended on the availability of both a highly edu-cated, high-tech labor force and employment opportunities that would enable the members of this labor force to contribute to the growth pro-cess. The transformations in productive capabilities that occurred in South Korea, Taiwan, Hong Kong, Singapore, and Malaysia from the 1970s onwards and in the world's two most populous nations, India and China, from the 1980s onwards were the results of the interaction of the investment strategies of developmental states, innovative enterprises, and educated individuals in the pursuit of high-tech careers.

SOUTH KOREA'S REVERSAL OF THE BRAIN DRAIN

In its 1993 report on the development of Asia's human resources in science and technology, the National Science Foundation (1993, p. 1) stated, "Asian countries with high technology economies will compete with the United States for the Asian-born graduates of U.S. universi-ties. Though Asian scientists and engineers will continue to contribute to the U.S. labor force, more will probably return to Asia." South Korea in particular was very aggressive from the late 1960s onwards in the implementation of various policies designed to reverse the brain drain. In his study of the process, Bang-Soon Yoon (1992, p. 5) argued that "the Korean model of RBD [reverse brain drain] is without precedent in the world and has been highly successful. . . . Brain drain is no longer considered a social problem by [Korean] policy-makers."

How was such a reversal achieved? By the 1990s the successful development of South Korea and Taiwan in the ICT industries had cre-ated employment opportunities that entailed sufficiently high salaries and sufficiently challenging jobs to lure back large numbers of nationals who had acquired high-tech education and experience abroad. In the well-documented case of Taiwan, this amounted to an annual average of more than 6,000 people from 1993 to 1996 (Saxenian and Hsu 2001, pp. 905–906). As a dynamic historical process, the reversal of the brain drain was an effect as well as a cause of successful industrial development. It could not have occurred but for the investment strategies of developmental states and innovative enterprises that had upgraded the quality of higher education and employment opportunities available to indigenous high-tech labor since the 1960s and 1970s.

Foreign Direct Investment

From the outset, MNCs that had come to South Korea and Taiwan in search of low-wage labor for labor-intensive assembly operations in the 1960s and 1970s created a demand for university-educated labor. Over time, as these companies invested in higher value-added activities, the high-end employment opportunities increased. Encouraged by this transfer of technology through FDI, national governments made investments in research institutes and graduate programs to build an indigenous knowledge base. These institutes and programs, which themselves generated attractive domestic high-tech employment opportunities, in turn supported the emergence of indigenous Korean and Taiwanese companies as world-class competitors. In many cases, highly educated and very experienced Koreans or Taiwanese who had been pursuing successful careers in the United States played key roles in building indigenous research institutes and companies (for the case of Taiwan, see Saxenian 2006, chaps. 4 and 5). The vast majority of the employees of these indigenous companies were, however, homegrown.

Among the pioneering U.S. MNCs in South Korea, Motorola made the most significant contribution to reversing the brain drain (Lee 1998). Motorola trained a group of 50 Korean engineers to start up Motorola Korea (MK) in 1967 with a total employment of 300 people. By 1972 MK was Korea's largest electronics company, both in terms of sales and exports (Bloom 1992, p. 38). Two years later MK had 5,000 employees, including two-thirds of the original 50 Korean engineers (Behrman and Wallender 1976, pp. 267, 299). As Behrman and Wallender (p. 270) put it in their detailed case study of the transfer of technology within Motorola to MK, the Korean subsidiary "is run virtually by Korean engineer-managers, since all manufacturing units are under Koreans and the only American is the general manager, who has a financial background. . . . The Korean managers have almost all been 'promoted from within' as the company expanded, and nearly all are in their early thirties and have been given such responsibility because of their education and abilities."[7]

Automation reduced MK's headcount to 3,800 in 1988, including about 2,100 employees in its semiconductor operations. In December 1988, in the midst of labor demands for better pay and work conditions that marked South Korea's transition from its "newly industrializing" stage, MK closed its plant after a group of workers, carrying cans of gasoline, had occupied a computer room and threatened to set themselves on fire (Reuters News 1988). A nonunion company around the world, Motorola had agreed to recognize the union but had balked at some of the union demands. The plant was reopened within a week (*Electronic Buyers' News* 1989).

In May 1989, a *BusinessWeek* article asked, "Is the era of cheap Asian labor over?" and answered that "rising wages and union strife are sending some companies packing" (Yang and Nakarmi 1989). Among the U.S. chip companies, National Semiconductor, in the midst of rationalizing its global capacity, closed down its Korean facility, laying off 250 employees (Clark 1990; Electronic World News 1989). Motorola, however, never considered leaving South Korea, in part because it was building a major presence there in wireless communications. As of the end of 1993, MK employed 2,500 people and had shipped $3.2 billion in electronics products since it had opened in 1967 (*Business Korea* 1994).

In 1996 MK began construction of a state-of-the-art manufacturing complex for wireless products and semiconductor packaging at Paju, 40 kilometers north of Seoul (*Korea Economic Weekly* 1999). Then, in 1998, in the wake of the Asian financial crisis, Motorola pledged to invest $300 million in South Korea over the next three years. The first stage of this new investment package was a software design center at its Paju chip plant that began operations with 50 Korean software programmers (*Korea Herald* 1998).

In 1999, as part of its global strategy to outsource manufacturing, Motorola sold the Paju plant, which had 880 employees, along with another Motorola facility in Taiwan, to Advanced Semiconductor Engineering (ASE), a Taiwanese company. Despite the sale, Motorola remained committed to South Korea; by that time, semiconductors represented only 30 percent of Motorola's business in Korea, and in any case MK had a long-term supply agreement with ASE (Flannery 1999; *Korea Economic Weekly* 1999; *Korea Times* 1999).

In 2004 Motorola spun off its entire semiconductor product division as Freescale Semiconductor. As an independent company, Freescale had plants in Hong Kong and Malaysia but no Korean operation. In May 2005, however, Freescale announced that, attracted by Korea's expertise in mobile technology, it would open an R&D center in Seoul, with six engineers. Freescale was not the only U.S. semiconductor company navigating back to South Korea in search of high-skill labor for high-end work. National Semiconductor, absent from the country since 1989 when it closed its assembly facility in the midst of labor unrest, came back to South Korea in 2005 to launch both a design center and an R&D center (Wohn 2005).

In the 2000s, there is no question that South Korea has the research capability to serve the high end of the high-tech market. Not only has the brain drain been reversed, but with MNCs now locating in South Korea to access highly skilled ICT labor, it can no longer be taken for granted that the center of the world of high-end work is the United States, or even Japan. Beginning in the second half of the 1960s, as we have seen, MNCs in search of low-wage labor played a critical role in beginning the reversal process by offering Korean engineers and managers opportunities to accumulate ICT experience while staying at home. In the process they transferred considerable technology to, and developed considerable capability in, South Korea.

Repatriation

The investments that permitted the economic transformation of South Korea did not come, however, from MNCs alone. Building on the capabilities that FDI brought to South Korea, as well as on the capabilities of Koreans who had been studying and working abroad, the Korean government and indigenous businesses made the investments in ICT that transformed South Korea into a leading "career path" location. Of particular importance, more in terms of quality than quantity, was the repatriation of Korean scientists and engineers who had worked abroad.

In 1968 some 2,000 Korean scientists and engineers lived abroad (Kim and Leslie 1998, p. 168). The very existence of these expatriates presented an opportunity for South Korea to build indigenous high-tech capabilities if only the brain drain could be reversed. Since the latter half of the 1960s, the Korean government saw the creation of an industrial research complex as a way to lure back some of those expatriate Koreans so that they could contribute to the development of South Korea's knowledge base (Bloom 1992, p. 54; Yoon 1992). Specifically, the desire by South Korea's policymakers to transform the nation's brain drain into its brain gain served as both opportunity and impetus in the establishment of two seminal knowledge-creating institutions, the Korea Institute of Science and Technology (KIST) and the Korea Advanced Institute of Science and Technology (KAIST).

KIST came into being in 1966 after the U.S. Agency for International Development (USAID) funded a team of U.S. scientists to visit South Korea in May 1965 to offer advice on the formation of a national institute for scientific research. Headed by Donald Hornig, scientific advisor to President Lyndon Johnson, the team included James Fisk, president of Bell Labs, and Bertram Thomas, president of Battelle Memorial Institute (Bloom 1992, p. 54; Kim and Leslie 1998, pp. 159–161). These discussions led KIST to opt for the Battelle contract research model, which entailed ongoing interaction with industry, rather than the Bell scientific research model. The U.S. government provided substantial initial funding, including a $3.1 million contract to Battelle to provide technical advice.

In 1967 the Korean government ensured KIST's autonomy in research and management and its financial stability through special legislation, the Assistance Act of the Korea Institute of Science and Technology (Yoon 1992, pp. 16–17). The same year saw the creation of the Ministry of Science and Technology (MOST) (Bloom 1992, p. 54). A 1975 MOST document described KIST as "the bridge between domestic industry and advanced technologies of foreign countries" (quoted in Kim and Leslie 1998, p. 161).

In conducting a search for its first scientists and engineers, KIST's ideal profile was someone with an undergraduate degree from Seoul National University, plus a graduate degree and five years of work experience abroad. In its first year, 1969, KIST had 494 employees, of whom 18 were repatriated scientists and engineers (14 with doctorates) (Yoon 1992, pp. 13–14). To attract key personnel from abroad, KIST paid high salaries and offered perquisites such as relocation expenses, free housing, and education expenses for children. Such compensation packages subsequently became the norm in government repatriation initiatives (Yoon 1992, pp. 14–16). By 1975, out of a total of 984 employees, KIST had 137 repatriates, 69 of whom had returned permanently to Korea (Yoon 1992, p. 13).

During the 1970s there was a proliferation of government research institutes in South Korea, some of them spinoffs of specialist departments of KIST (Lee, Bae, and Lee 1991). The Korea Institute of Electronics Technology (KIET) emerged in 1976 to conduct research into semiconductor design, processes, and systems. At the head of each of KIET's three research divisions was a Korean with research experience in the U.S. semiconductor industry (Bloom 1992, p. 56; Mathews and Cho 2000, p. 118).[8] In a joint venture with the Silicon Valley chipmaker VLSI Technology, KIET put in place Korea's first VLSI (very-large-scale integration) pilot wafer-fabrication plant in 1978, and launched a fully operational 16K DRAM (dynamic random access memory) fabrication plant by 1979 (Mathews and Cho 2000, p. 118).

Overall, from 1968 through 1980, MOST-sponsored repatriation programs brought back home 130 overseas Koreans on a permanent basis and 182 on a temporary basis to public R&D institutes (Yoon 1992, p. 10). The repatriates brought knowledge, experience, connections, and leadership to South Korea. Given the rapid growth in demand for scientists, engineers, and technicians in South Korea from the late 1970s on, however, the vast majority of those employed by the public research institutes had to be homegrown.

The number of researchers in South Korea grew from 14,749 in 1978 (0.40 researchers per 1,000 population) to 18,434 in 1980 (0.48) and to 28,448 in 1982 (0.72). The government's share in R&D expenditures constituted 49 percent of the total in 1978 and 52 percent in 1980, before falling to 41 percent in 1982 as business enterprises began to invest heavily in their own R&D (Arnold 1988, p. 439).[9] Government investments in indigenous R&D capability demanded complementary investments in indigenous academic institutions to generate a homegrown supply of high-tech labor. Analogous to KIST, the keystone educational investment was the founding of the Korea Advanced Institute of Science (KAIS), the nation's first specialized graduate school of science and engineering, in February 1971. KAIS admitted its first master's students in 1973, its first doctoral students in 1975, and its first undergraduate students in 1986.[10] Along the way, KAIS became KAIST when KIST and KAIS were merged at the end of 1980. The name of the academic institution remained KAIST when the two organizations demerged in 1989 as KAIST (the former KAIS) moved its campus 100 miles south of Seoul to become the centerpiece of Taedok Science Town (Kim and Leslie 1998, pp. 178–180).

KAIS was the brainchild of a 30-year-old Korean physicist, KunMo Chung, working in the United States (Kim and Leslie 1998). In October 1969 Chung submitted a document titled "The Establishment of a New Graduate School of Applied Science and Technology in Korea" to John A. Hannah, head of USAID and Chung's former thesis advisor at Michigan State University. Hannah handed off the proposal to USAID's Korean division, which forwarded it to the Korean Economic Planning Board (Kim and Leslie 1998, p. 165). The board in turn interested MOST in the concept, and in April MOST invited Chung to Korea to present his plan to key political leaders. With President Chung-Hee Park's support, by July 1970 KAIS had won legislative approval.

As with KIST, USAID provided financial assistance and advice. To bring KAIS to fruition, Lee DuBridge, Science Advisor to President Nixon, appointed a five-man committee of engineering educators headed by Frederick Terman, provost of Stanford University and the academic visionary behind the emergence of Silicon Valley. Among the other committee members were two of Terman's protégés and Chung (Kim and Leslie 1998, p. 167). In writing his original proposal for KAIS, Chung had been influenced by a recent report by Terman on the reform of engineering education in New York State (Kim and Leslie 1998, pp. 165–169). In effect, therefore, from conception to founding, KAIS reflected Terman's ideas, including a "Steeples of Excellence" strategy to provide outstanding graduate education in a few high-priority fields (Kim and Leslie 1998, p. 168).

The government provided all KAIST students with tuition, room and board, a stipend, and a conversion of the normally compulsory three years of military service into three years of work in a government research facility subsequent to receiving their master's degrees (Kim and Leslie 1998, p. 169). From its inception through 1996, KAIST awarded a total of 3,108 bachelor's degrees, 9,566 master's degrees, and 2,647 doctoral degrees. Of the master's recipients, 43 percent went into industry, 17 percent to government research institutes, and an estimated 34 percent into advanced training. Of the doctoral recipients, 45 percent went into industry, 27 percent to government research institutes, and 26 percent into academic positions (Kim and Leslie 1998, p. 174).

Indigenous Innovation

By the 1990s there were plenty of good employment opportunities for these graduates in South Korea, not only with MNCs such as MK or government research institutes such as KIST, but also, and indeed primarily, with Korean *chaebol* such as Samsung, Hyundai, and LG (Lucky-Goldstar), which through indigenous innovation had transformed knowledge from abroad into world-leading products in a number of high-technology sectors. In no Korean industry was this transformation as dramatic as in semiconductors. In 1980 semiconductors represented 2.5 percent of Korea's production and 2.5 percent of exports; in 1990 they represented 7.3 percent of production and 7.0 percent of exports (Byun 1994, p. 709).

In semiconductors, no Korean company was as successful as Samsung. With $20.5 billion in revenues and 7.5 percent of the market, Samsung was the world's second-leading supplier of semiconductors in 2007, behind Intel ($33.8 billion) and ahead of Toshiba and TI ($11.8 billion each) (Gartner 2008). Samsung is the world leader in the flash memory market and shares the world lead in the DRAM market with South Korea's Hynix Semiconductor, formerly Hyundai Electronics.

Samsung entered the semiconductor industry in 1975 when it bought Korea Semiconductor Company (KSC), a just-launched semiconductor firm that had run into financial trouble. The founder of KSC, Ki-Dong Kang, a Korean-American PhD who had worked in semiconductor design at Motorola, now provided Samsung with his knowledge. Samsung also took over the assets of an abortive transistor joint venture between Goldstar and National Semiconductor (Mathews and Cho 2000, p. 116). Thus, in 1975 Samsung acquired the capability to fabricate wafers and produce LSI (large-scale integration) chips for consumer electronics products just as the Korean government promulgated a six-year plan to promote the semiconductor industry (Kim 1997b, p. 88).

In 1982 Samsung started its Semiconductor R&D Laboratory to reverse-engineer semiconductors from Japan and the United States. At the same time Samsung organized a task force to formulate a strategy for entering into the production of VLSI chips. After six months of information-gathering and analysis, the team spent a month on a fact-finding trip to the United States, where it especially sought advice from Korean-Americans with semiconductor expertise. The major semiconductor companies in the United States had already rebuffed Samsung's requests to license 64K DRAM technology, so the task force identified smaller companies strapped for cash that would make the technology available. One such company was Micron Technology, founded by former TI engineers in 1978, which had just generated its first revenues from its new fabrication facility in Idaho in 1982 (Spaeth 1984). As part of the deal, Samsung sent its engineers to Micron for training. Subsequently, in 1985 Samsung was also able to buy an advanced high-speed MOS (metal-oxide-silicon) process for $2.1 million from Zytrex, a 1983 Silicon Valley start-up that had just gone bankrupt (Chira 1985; Pollack 1985b).

In 1983 Samsung announced a massive investment in designing and producing 64K VLSI chips. As the biggest *chaebol* in South Korea, Samsung was able to fund the investments in semiconductors from earnings from other divisions. It was also able to avail itself of government subsidies. The product development process involved two parallel groups. One was in Silicon Valley and employed 300 American engineers led by five Korean-Americans with PhDs and design experience at major U.S. chip companies. The other was in South Korea, and it was led by two Korean-American scientists who had developed 64K DRAMs at U.S. companies as well as by Korean engineers who had run Samsung's LSI operations and received VLSI training at Samsung's U.S. technology suppliers. Samsung's Silicon Valley unit also trained the company's Korean engineers as part of the process of transferring technology from the United States to South Korea (Byun 1994, p. 711; Kim 1997b, pp. 89–93).

When Samsung released its 64K DRAM in 1984, it lagged behind the United States chipmakers by 40 months and the Japanese by 18 months. Samsung repeated this product development process for its

256K chip released in 1985, further reducing the technology gap with the United States and Japan, as it continued to do with the 1M DRAM in 1987, the 4M in 1989, and the 16M in 1992, at which point it had caught up (Byun 1994, p. 713).

Between 1980 and 1994 the company's sales soared from 2.5 billion to 115.2 billion won (the South Korean currency). In the process Samsung Electronics increased its R&D as a proportion of sales from 2.1 percent in 1980 to 6.2 percent in 1994. In 1980 the company employed 690 R&D staff, who produced only 18 local patent applications, four local patent awards, and no foreign patent applications or awards in that year. By 1994 the company had 8,919 R&D staff who could claim credit for 2,802 local applications, 1,413 local awards, 1,478 foreign applications, and 752 foreign awards. The generation of one local patent award for Samsung Electronics required 116.8 R&D staff in 1985, 10.4 in 1990, and 6.3 in 1994, while the generation of one foreign patent award required 992.5 R&D staff in 1985, 52.2 in 1990, and 11.9 in 1994 (Kim 1997b, p. 95).

As a result of the employment opportunities that Samsung and other leading *chaebol* such as Hyundai and LG had created, by the late 1980s the brain drain had been reversed. Indeed, in 1989 a *Wall Street Journal* article titled "Costly Exports" announced, "Reverse 'Brain Drain' Helps Asia but Robs U.S. of Scarce Talent—Korea in Particular Benefits as Scientists Return to Take Top Jobs" (Yoder 1989). The Koreans now took a very different view of the estimated 6,000 scientists and engineers in the United States than they would have two decades before. To wit, the article quoted Chin Hai Sool, a director general at Korea's Ministry of Science and Technology, as saying that Koreans in the United States "have become a precious resource for us."

In sharp contrast to the Korean perspective was that coming from those concerned with the implications of the reverse brain drain for the supply of scientists and engineers in the United States. "'We've been counting on foreign graduates to stay here and fill our needs because we haven't been filling our own needs for a long time,' says Betty Vetter, executive director of the Commission on Professionals in Science and Technology, in Washington. 'There's nobody to replace these people.'" (quoted in Yoder 1989).

By the early 1990s South Korea had developed to a stage at which it could quickly tap this "precious resource." Of the 13,878 foreign science and engineering doctorate recipients with temporary visas from U.S. universities in 1990–1991, almost 56 percent were from China (2,779), South Korea (1,912), Taiwan (1,824), or India (1,235). In 1995, 47 percent of the 1990–1991 recipients were working in the United States, including 88 percent of the Chinese, 79 percent of the Indians, and 42 percent of the Taiwanese, but only 11 percent of the Koreans—a proportion even lower than the 13 percent of the 227 Japanese doctoral recipients (Johnson and Regets 1998).

MALAYSIA'S FDI-DRIVEN DEVELOPMENT

Not all of the Asian nations that have built up significant ICT capabilities since the 1960s have been able to engage in indigenous innovation in the manner of South Korea (for the case of Taiwan, see Breznitz 2007, chap. 3; Mathews 1997; Saxenian 2006, chaps. 4 and 5). Malaysia in particular has become a world center for electronics manufacturing over the past three decades based on FDI. From 2003 to 2007, the Malaysian economy grew at about 5.5 percent per year, with electronics dominating its manufacturing base and exports (see Index Mundi 2008; more generally, see Best 2001, chap. 6). The fact that Malaysia has prospered on the basis of FDI implies that MNCs have been successfully upgrading their productive capabilities there, thus making it possible to pay employees higher wages and still remain globally competitive. And indeed, such has been the case.

Since the 1960s, U.S. MNCs have employed nationals rather than expatriates in host countries. Data from the early 1980s on employment in the Bayan Lepas Free Trade Zone (BLFTZ) in Penang confirm the overwhelming reliance of MNCs on indigenous labor at all levels of the local organization. In 1982, 27 electronics/electrical factories employed a total of 24,446 people, of whom 5,389 (22 percent) were male and 6,625 (27 percent) were nonfactory workers. Only 34 of these employees were expatriates. For the BLFTZ as a whole, there were 226 expatriates out of 52,073 employees, representing 0.43 percent of the total, 1.16 percent of males, and 1.55 percent of nonfactory workers (Salih and Young 1987, p. 184). Given the small absolute number of expatriates—just 1.26 per electronics/electrical factory in 1982—the indigenization of the labor force at the MNCs obviously extended high up the organizational hierarchy. A survey done in the mid-1990s found that National Semiconductor's only expatriate in Penang was the managing director. Texas Instruments (2,800 employees) and Motorola (4,000 employees) each had only three expatriate managers in Malaysia (Ismail 1999, pp. 27–28).

Intel's history in Malaysia from the early 1970s to the present illustrates the upgrading of indigenous capabilities by a U.S. MNC in the semiconductor industry. Intel was one of the first semiconductor manufacturers to offshore to the BLFTZ when Malaysia launched it in 1972, and as the company itself was only founded in 1968, the Penang facility was Intel's first offshore plant. In 1974 Intel employed about 1,000 people in Penang (*Wall Street Journal* 1974b) and about 2,000 a decade later. Over the next 10 years, Intel's Penang production tripled, but its labor force remained at about 2,000 because of automation of labor-intensive assembly processes. In 1980 engineers had represented only one out of 40 Intel employees in Penang, but by 1994, one in six employees was an engineer (Ismail 1999, p. 27; Zachary 1994). Over time Malaysia became Intel's main source of expertise on assembly operations. In the mid-1980s, when Intel was setting up its assembly line in its automated chip factory in Chandler, Arizona, it brought in its Malaysian experts from Penang as consultants (Dreyfack and Port 1986). In 1990, when Intel set up a design optimization lab at the Penang facility, it sent 10 engineers to Silicon Valley for training. At that time, Intel announced that it would continue to invest in automation in Penang, with the goal of attaining zero-defect production (Dennis 1990).

In July 1992 Intel decided to shift its entire microcontroller design, manufacturing, and marketing operations out of the Chandler facility to its Penang plant, a move that Lai Pin Yong, Intel Malaysia's managing director, called a milestone for the local electronics industry. "This is the first time in Malaysia," Yong said, "that a multinational is giving its offshore plant total responsibility of an important product." As a result, Intel Malaysia expected to add another 50 engineers to the 300 that it already employed (*Electronic Times* 1992a). In preparation, a team of 30 Malaysians had been receiving training in the United States and Japan for two to three years. When the Intel Penang Design Centre opened in November 1992, it was said to be the first of its kind in Southeast Asia (Leow 1992; see also Ismail 1999, pp. 32–33).

In 2003, with US$2.3 billion invested in Malaysia since 1972, Intel Malaysia employed about 1,000 Malaysians in R&D and had secured 21 U.S. patents. In August 2003 Intel added to its Malaysian R&D capabilities by opening a design and development center, with a focus on manufacturing processes and packaging technology for Intel's various products. On a visit to Penang in August 2003 to open the new center, Intel CEO Craig Barrett (as paraphrased by a *Business Times* reporter) commended "the Malaysian Government and business leaders for their work in stimulating IT research and innovation through university research grants and efforts to strengthen education programmes," while warning that "a critical factor to the impact of Intel's investment hinged on the continued availability of talent to sustain design and development efforts locally" (*Business Times* 2003).

In December 2005, with almost 10,000 employees (about 10 percent of its global labor force) at five sites in Malaysia, Intel announced plans to invest $230 million in a 2,000-person assembly and test site, along with a design and development center, in Kulim (Ismail 2005; Yee 2005). On the occasion of this investment, Craig Barrett, who had become Intel's chairman in May of that year, stated, "Intel is working with the Education Ministry to help grow Malaysia's globally competitive ICT workforce. Through the Intel Teach to the Future programme, we have trained more than 30,000 Malaysian teachers to use technology to improve student learning.

"Effectively integrating technology into the classrooms," Barrett continued, "opens up new and exciting learning opportunities, giving young people the knowledge and skills to compete in an increasingly complex world" (Ismail 2005).

EVOLUTION OF IT SERVICES IN INDIA

In the wake of a Memorandum of Agreement on high-technology transfers from the United States to India, signed after years of negotiation in May 1985, the Indian Department of Electronics announced its intention to build "technology parks" that would permit foreign companies to be wholly owned for the purpose of developing and exporting large-scale software systems (Tenorio 1985). In June 1985, TI began exploratory talks with the Indian government about establishing a software development center in Bangalore. Two key conditions for TI were 100 percent ownership of the facility and permission to connect to an internal global communications network (Mitchell 1986). The Indian government acceded to both demands.

In the mid-1980s, TI was a global company with an Asian presence in Japan, Taiwan, Singapore, and Malaysia. It was, however, like other U.S. semiconductor companies, facing a major competitive challenge from the Japanese in commodity memory chips. TI's future lay in custom chips, particularly ASICs (application specific integrated circuits) and VLSI (Mitchell 1986). These products called for substantial software programming, using computer-aided design.

Robert Rozeboom, vice president of TI's semiconductor group design automation department, told a reporter in August 1985 that TI had "started to look at India seriously in 1984 as a potential site for software development for our computer-aided design. Software development is critical to our semiconductor operations. India has such a strong educational system in the sciences and it has such a large number of graduates who are underemployed, it became an obvious choice for us" (United Press International 1985). The U.S.-India technology transfer agreement created an opening for TI to locate a software development center in India. It was a small investment for TI—$5 million out of total 1986 capital expenditures of $446 million.

TI India employed 16 engineers and programmers when it began operations in 1986. This number increased to 85 in 1990, 275 in 1995, 500 in 2000, 1,300 in 2005, and 1,800 in 2007, which was almost 6 percent of TI's worldwide labor force (Indo-Asian News Service 2007). All of these employees in India were engaged in R&D, and all were Indian.

In 1997 an article in *Electronic Engineering Times* called TI India "a dream company for local engineers" (Bindra 1997). A report issued in 2003, when TI India topped "India's first ever list of Top 25 Great Places to Work," stated, "TI India, a subsidiary of TI Inc, employs 832 people in a single site in India. It has eight women at senior management level. Staff turnover is at seven percent. The company has 170 employees who have completed five years with the company. It has 18 employees who are over 44 years of age" (*Business World* 2003).

About 75 percent of TI India's employees were working on digital signal processing (DSP) chips, used in cell phones, modems, MP3 players, digital still cameras, and Voice over Internet Protocol phones (Business Line 2002). In DSP, the mainstay of TI's overall semiconductor business, TI India had become, according to a company press release, "the research base for its parent company." By the end of 2003, TI India had garnered 225 U.S. patents (Rai 2003).

Almost two decades after it had been the first MNC to locate in Bangalore, TI was not alone in viewing India as a prime location for software programming and R&D (see Mitra 2007). By 1992, 30 other MNCs, including Motorola and IBM, had set up software programming facilities in Bangalore (O'Reilly 1992). IBM, which had left India in 1978 over issues of foreign ownership, returned in 1992 after India's 1991 liberalization reforms (Chatterjee 1994; Tarrant 1991; Tripathi 1992). HP set up a subsidiary in India in 1989 but waited until 2002 to launch its first Indian research lab (Agence France-Press 2002). In April 2004 AMD announced a $5 million investment in a microprocessor design center that would employ 120 chip designers and development engineers by the end of 2005 (Sharma 2004). In the first half of 2005, both Intel and Microsoft set up advanced research centers in Bangalore (Dudley 2004; Subramanyam 2005). In October, as part of a $1.1 billion expansion in India over three years, Cisco broke ground on a $50 million, one-million-square-foot R&D campus in Bangalore that would double to 3,000 the number of people on Cisco payrolls in India (CMP TechWeb 2005). A month later, Cisco's rival, Juniper Networks, announced a new $8.5 million development center in Bangalore that would increase its employment in India from 325 to 675 (*Business Standard* 2005). In December Intel said that it would spend $1 billion in India over the coming years, including $800 million on education and community programs and the remainder primarily for the expansion of its R&D center in Bangalore (*Computer Reseller News* 2005).

By the mid-2000s, however, the growth of indigenous IT enterprises made Indians far less reliant on MNCs for high-tech employment than in the past. For the year ending March 31, 2008, the five leading Indian IT companies—Tata Consultancy Services (TCS), Wipro, Infosys, Satyam, and HCL Technologies—generated a total of $18.7 billion in revenues and employed a total of 368,000 people worldwide, up from a combined $2.4 billion in revenues and 46,000 employees in 2001.[11]

TCS is the largest of these five companies, with $5.7 billion in revenues in fiscal 2007 (year ending March 31, 2008). Based in Mumbai as part of Tata Group, India's largest industrial conglomerate, TCS began supplying offshore IT services in 1968. Besides engaging in software development in India, during the 1980s TCS became a leading "body shop," sending engineers and programmers to do projects abroad (Head 1989).TCS increased its employment from 2,000 people in 1991 to 16,800 in 2001. Employment has soared in the 2000s, reaching 111,407 in March 2008, and the company planned to add 30,000–50,000 people over the next year (Dow Jones International News 2008). More than 90 percent of TCS employees are Indian nationals (TCS 2008, pp. 32–33). The company generates 56 percent of its global revenues in North America, 29 percent in Europe, and 9 percent in India.

Following TCS are Wipro and Infosys, both based in Bangalore, with revenues for the year ending March 31, 2008, of $4.9 billion and $4.2 billion, respectively. H.M. Hasham Premji founded Wipro (an abbreviation of Western Indian Vegetable Products) in 1946 as a vendor of cooking oil. He died in 1966, but his son Azim, just short of receiving his undergraduate degree in electrical engineering at Stanford University, returned to India to run the business. Wipro entered the computer business in the late 1970s after IBM left the country rather than submit to government regulations that required 60 percent Indian ownership of foreign affiliates. Subsequently Wipro expanded into IT services and software. In 1992 the company had 1,640 employees (*Economist* 1991). Ten years later, Wipro employed more than 14,000 people, and by March 2008 it employed 82,122.

Infosys Technologies was founded as a software development company in 1981 by N.R. Narayana Murthy, the company's CEO until 2002, and six other software engineers, including Nandan M. Nilekani, the current CEO. Murthy had an undergraduate engineering degree from the University of Mysore and a master's degree in electrical engineering from IIT Kanpur, while Nilekani had an undergraduate degree in electrical engineering from IIT Mumbai. During its first decade, the company gained a reputation for high-quality offshore design and development for companies such as GE, DEC, Reebok, and Nestlé. In 1992 Infosys employed more than 300 software engineers (Zintner 1993). The company grew to 5,389 employees in 2001 and then surged to 52,715 employees in March 2006, 72,241 in March 2007, and 91,187 in March 2008. Almost 75 percent of the new hires in this period were beginning their careers. The average age of these "Infoscions," about 93 percent of whom are described as "software professionals," is 26 years old (Infosys 2008, pp. 5, 132, 135).

INDIGENOUS INNOVATION IN CHINA

Whereas India's emergence as a force in the world of ICT has been focused mainly on IT services, China's development path has been much more diverse. In entering a full range of industries with different levels of skill, China has had the advantage over India of a much more extensive system of mass education, as shown in Table 5.2. Note that India had a much higher proportion of the population who had completed postsecondary education in both 1980 and 2000, although in each of the nations, the group that attained this level of education represented an elite. At the university level, as we have seen, an important difference between China and India in the 1980s was that China emphasized undergraduate degrees in engineering while India emphasized undergraduate degrees in science. In terms of the supply of college-educated personnel, therefore, China was much better positioned than India in the 1990s to absorb technology from the advanced nations and adapt it to indigenous industrial uses.

In the 1980s and 1990s, to unleash these productive capabilities to support industrial development, China quite deliberately transformed the relation between its science and technology (S&T) infrastructure and high-tech enterprises that competed for growing commercial markets. China had developed considerable S&T capability under the central planning system prior to the economic reforms in the late 1970s (Conroy 1992; Gu 1999; Sigurdson 1980; Suttmeier 1975). Until the 1980s, however, the evolution of the S&T infrastructure was driven exclusively by government demand, much of it for military purposes. A prime task of the reform process was to transfer national S&T resources to businesses that could innovate in producing goods for commercial markets.

The transformed S&T infrastructure consisted of national programs, ranging from basic research to industrial R&D, and public

Table 5.2 Highest Levels of Educational Attainment, Percentage of the Population 25 Years Old and Over, China and India, 1980 and 2000

	China		India	
Highest level of educational attainment	1980	2000	1980	2000
No schooling	44.9	20.9	72.5	44.5
1st level (primary education)	32.3	40.7	11.3	33.2
	(12.2)[a]	(15.3)	(4.2)	(12.4)
2nd level (secondary education)	21.7	35.7	13.7	17.4
	(5.6)	(14.1)	(5.1)	(6.5)
Postsecondary (higher education)	1.0	2.7	2.5	4.8
	(0.9)	(2.3)	(1.7)	(3.3)
Average years of school	3.6	5.7	2.7	4.8

[a] % who completed level in parentheses.
SOURCE: Barro and Lee (2000).

research institutes that interacted with industrial enterprises to develop technologies for domestic and, increasingly, international product markets. It included National Key Laboratories for basic research, National Engineering Centers for applied research, and Corporate R&D Centers and Experimental Zones for New Technology Industries for the commercialization of technology (Gu 1999). What turned this S&T infrastructure into a "national system of innovation" in the 1980s and 1990s was the emergence of highly autonomous business enterprises that were successful in the commercialization of technology. The most notable successes occurred in ICT. The institutionalization of organizational relations among government institutes and business enterprises not only permitted China to develop new productive capabilities but also ensured that these capabilities would be utilized to meet new demands for industrial application.

The importance of ICT to China's development in the late twentieth and early twenty-first centuries is clear in the trade data. During the 1990s and into the 2000s, China became both a major exporter and major importer of electronic office machines, IT products, and telecommunications products, as world trade in electronics became increasingly based on a vertically specialized international division of labor (Amighini 2004). In 1992 China had about 2 percent of world trade in office machines, less than 1 percent in IT products, and 2 percent in telecom products. In these different ICT groupings, China lagged far behind nations such as the United States, Japan, Germany, Singapore, and Hong Kong. By 2003, however, China had become the world's leading exporter in all of these groupings, with 18 percent of world trade in office machines, 18 percent in IT products, and 11 percent in telecom products (pp. 207–208).

ICT figures especially prominently in China's trade relations with the United States. U.S. exports of advanced technology products (ATP) to China increased from $5.5 billion (representing 2.4 percent of all U.S. ATP exports) in 2000 to $20.3 billion (7.4 percent) in 2007.[12] Meanwhile U.S. ATP imports from China rose from $10.7 billion in 2000 (5.5 percent of all U.S. ATP imports) to $88.0 billion in 2007 (26.9 percent). In 2003 U.S. ATP imports from China surpassed those from Japan, and by 2007 ATP imports from China were more than three times those from Japan. U.S. ATP exports to China exceeded those to Japan by 2.6 percent in 2007, after being 8.7 percent lower the year before.

U.S. ATP imports from China are highly concentrated in ICT, while U.S. ATP exports to China are spread across a wider range of industrial sectors. In 2007, 88.5 percent of U.S. ATP imports from China were classified in the information and communications grouping, with another 9.3 percent in the optoelectronics and electronics groupings. Of U.S. ATP exports to China in 2007, aerospace made up 35.4 percent, electronics 32.3 percent, information and communications 16.5 percent, flexible manufacturing 7.1 percent, and life sciences 5.5 percent.

As was the case in the analyses of the development of South Korea, Malaysia, and India, a key to understanding China's progress in ICT is the dynamic interaction among investments by the Chinese government, indigenous enterprise, and MNCs in the development of productive capabilities. A pioneer in carrying out this type of research for the case of China was the late Qiwen Lu, with whom I collaborated closely (see Foreword to Lu 2000; Lazonick 2004b; Lu and Lazonick 2001). In his book, *China's Leap into the Information Age*, Lu (2000) did in-depth case studies of the evolution of four leading indigenous computer companies: Stone, Legend, Founder, and Great Wall. Lu documented the transfer of technological capabilities developed within the S&T infrastructure to indigenous business enterprises and the transformation of these capabilities by these enterprises, often in collaboration with MNCs, into innovative products.

In May 2005, one of these companies, Lenovo—known as Legend Group Limited until a year earlier—acquired IBM's PC operations for $1.75 billion, with the right to use the IBM name on its products for five years.[13] IBM retained an 18.9 percent stake in Lenovo (reduced to 4.7 percent by July 2008), which it viewed as beneficial to its own expansion plans in China. For its part, Lenovo located its headquarters in the United States along with most of the design and development work (Poletti 2004).

In 2004, prior to the deal with IBM, Lenovo had already been China's largest PC producer, with a 25.1 percent market share, followed by Founder with 9.9 percent, Tsinghua Tongfang with 7.8 percent, Dell with 7.2 percent, and IBM with 5.1 percent (Associated Press Newswires 2005). With $3.0 billion in revenues and 11,400 employees in fiscal 2004, Lenovo took control of a loss-making division of IBM that, nevertheless, had $9 billion in revenues and 10,000 employees, about 40 percent of whom were working in China. With the IBM acquisition, Lenovo became, after Dell and HP, the third-largest PC maker in the world, with a 7.2 percent global market share. It also increased its share of the Chinese PC market to over 33 percent (Industry Updates 2006). In 2007 Lenovo was fourth in global PC shipments, with a 7.5 percent share, having been surpassed by the Taiwanese firm Acer, which had acquired the U.S. company Gateway (Deffree 2008). During fiscal year 2008, Lenovo had revenues of $16.4 billion and before-tax profits of $513 million, and it employed 23,100 people worldwide as of March 31, 2008.

The history of Legend/Lenovo, as analyzed by Lu (2000, chap. 3), exemplifies the ways in which the complementarity between indigenous enterprises and MNCs has become ever more important to China's development. The rapidly expanding U.S. trade with China in advanced technology reflects in part imports from and exports to the United States by U.S. MNCs, such as Cisco, Dell, HP, IBM, Intel, Microsoft, Motorola, Oracle, and Sun Microsystems, that have offshored to China. Some of these companies, for example Dell in computers, have competed for Chinese markets with indigenous companies such as Lenovo and Founder. U.S. ICT companies have also set up shop in free trade zones, such as the Pudong district in Shanghai, from which they have produced for export, employing highly qualified but still relatively low-cost Chinese ICT labor. U.S. ICT companies have also been prominent in joint ventures with Chinese companies, often as a means of developing relations with Chinese businesses and governments that will yield new investment opportunities and product markets in the future. Increasingly in areas such as chip manufacture and packaged software in which U.S. ICT companies still have distinct competitive advantages, these companies are investing in new facilities in China to supply inputs to Chinese ICT companies that are growing rapidly by serving the burgeoning Chinese domestic markets.

Intel is a prime example of a world leader in ICT that began to make significant investments in China in the last half of the 1990s and that has accelerated its direct investment in China in the 2000s. Intel's first major business deal with China came in late 1984 when it sold the Chinese government 1,000 microcomputers with the Intel 8088 processor (*Wall Street Journal* 1984). Less than a year later, Intel opened up a two-person marketing office in Beijing, run by William Huo, a 25-year-old Taiwan-born American with a Princeton degree in electrical engineering and computer science. Sales agreements still had to be approved at Intel's Far East headquarters in Hong Kong. Under the auspices of China's State Education Commission, Huo's job was to set up microprocessor development labs at 100 Chinese universities, where engineers would be taught how to program Intel processors (Sabin 1986).

When, in June 1986, Li Tieying, the Minister of Electronics Industry, came to Palo Alto as the first Chinese official to attend a trade meeting of the U.S. semiconductor industry, he complained that, despite many visits by U.S. executives to China, there had thus far been no foreign investments in chip manufacturing. The major problem, he was told, was China's unwillingness to protect intellectual property (*Electronics Weekly* 1987). In addition, COCOM—the Coordinating Committee for Multilateral Export Controls—had embargoed the exports of military-related technology, including advanced semiconductors, to Communist regimes (Bozman 1990; Parker 1994a,b).

In September 1988, however, Motorola launched the first semiconductor facility in China that was established as a wholly owned venture. At the time, Intel was among a number of chip companies said to be contemplating similar investments. It appeared that Intel would make its first move into Chinese production in 1991, when it reportedly entered into a joint venture with the state-owned China Electronics Corporation (CEC), the nation's largest electronics enterprise group, and the Hongkong Corporation to produce microprocessors for the Chinese market (Xinhua News Agency 1991).

In September of the following year the Intel head office instructed Intel Technology Malaysia to enter into negotiations with the Chinese authorities about opening a semiconductor plant in China (*Electronic Times* 1992b). In March 1994 Intel signed a contract with CEC whereby CEC would promote Intel's products as the standard PC architecture in China, while Huajing Electronics, a CEC subsidiary and China's largest semiconductor producer, would assemble and test Intel 386SX microprocessors and Intel microcontrollers (Johns 1994; Kehoe 1994).

In September 1994 Intel supported this initiative by launching a wholly owned subsidiary, Intel Architecture Development Limited (IADL) in Shanghai. With 25 Chinese engineers initially, IADL would develop software that would make PCs, and Intel chips, more applicable to Chinese needs (Riley 1994; *Shanghai Star* 1994). A month later IADL signed a Memorandum of Understanding with Jitong Communications, a key ICT vendor attached to the Ministry of Electronics, to exhibit and sell Intel products (*Electronic Times* 1994).

Enabling Intel's more aggressive stance toward selling its more advanced products in China was the end of the Cold War and the disbanding in March 1994 of COCOM. Included among the products that had been embargoed by COCOM was Intel's Pentium chip. In December 1994 Intel held seminars in Beijing, Shanghai, Guangzhou, Chengdu, and Xian to reveal, in the words of a Reuters reporter, "the Pentium's sensitive operational guts to Chinese software developers" (Parker 1994b).

On his trip to Shanghai to launch IADL, Andrew Grove, Intel's CEO, announced that the company was exploring the possibility of opening up a wholly owned chip factory in China (Pei 1994), and by the following June plans for such a plant had been hatched (Newsbytes 1995). One report on the project noted that "Intel is planning to pull out its expatriates as soon as possible in view of installing Chinese in key executive positions. Hence, management training is expected to become a priority for the American company" (ESP Report on Engineering Construction and Operations in the Developing World 1995).

Run by Intel Technology (China) Company Limited and located in Shanghai's Pudong Development Zone, the facility went into operation at the beginning of 1998, assembling and testing flash memory chips for export. The plant quickly became the largest exporter among MNCs in Pudong and had 800 employees by 2000. Construction was underway to increase Intel's Shanghai factory space from 120,000 to 500,000 square meters (Asia Pulse 2000), and by the time the expansion came on line, Intel had spent about $500 million on it (AsiaPort Daily News 2001). In 2004 Intel had three assembly and test facilities in Shanghai with 2,000 people on their payrolls out of a total of 2,400 Intel China employees across the country (Heim 2004).

In 1997 Intel had moved its regional sales functions from Hong Kong to Beijing to better position itself to tap into China's growing market opportunities (LaPedus 1997). The following year, also in Beijing, the company set up Intel China Research Center (ICRC), its first research facility in the Asia-Pacific region. According to Intel's Web site, the mission of ICRC is to "empower the future of the digital world through research and platform innovations, and drive strategic technology collaborations with Chinese government, academia and industry" (Intel 2008a).

One such collaboration, begun in 1999, was with Legend Holdings to expand the use of the Internet in China. Legend was the first Chinese PC maker to which Intel supplied chips; the two companies had been working together closely since the mid-1990s, with Intel pushing Legend to increase the power of its PCs. Indeed, in 1998 Legend ceremoniously presented its millionth PC to Intel CEO Andrew Grove (O'Neill 1998). Now the two companies would work together to upgrade the speed of computer terminals as well as the capacity and applications of servers in China's broadband network (Reuters News 1999b). They took the collaboration further when, in 2003, they opened the Intel-Lenovo Technology Advancement Center in Beijing for home networking and security applications (Xinhua Financial Network 2003). Nevertheless, less than a year later, Lenovo announced that it would use microprocessors from AMD, Intel's longtime rival, in two of its new consumer PCs (Asia in Focus 2004). At the time Lenovo said that it was not considering using AMD chips for commercial PCs and servers. In 2006, however, Lenovo did just that as it used AMD microprocessors in PCs designed for businesses (Evers 2006).

In 2000 Intel placed IADL (now called Intel Architecture Labs), ICRC, and other Intel support centers under the umbrella of Intel China

Labs (Asiainfo Daily China News 2000; Hou 2000). By the mid 2000s, Intel was involved in a wide variety of government, academic, and industrial collaborations, many of them focused on wireless technology. In June 2005 the company created the $200 million Intel Capital China Technology Fund to invest in Chinese technology companies in areas related to Intel's strategic interests (Business Wire 2005). In September 2005 Intel launched Asia-Pacific Research and Development Limited in Shanghai's Zizhu Science Park, with prospective employment of 1,000 people by the end of 2006 (M2 Presswire 2005). In January 2006, Intel China established an "Innovation Alliance," initially with 22 Chinese high-tech companies including 10 computer manufacturers and 12 software vendors and content providers. The innovation alliance, open to all Chinese ICT companies, would be used by Intel to offer member enterprises technical support and consulting services related to market surveys, product design, and application software (China Industry Daily News 2006).

In 2001 Intel had 90 percent of the Chinese microprocessor market (Young and Lin 2006). In 2002 the Chinese market became Intel's second largest, trailing only the United States (Young 2003). During the 2000s China has been the company's fastest growing market, notwithstanding the fact that it has lost significant market share to AMD. In 2004 Intel's China market share had fallen to 74 percent, down 16 points from 2001, while AMD's increased from 5 percent to 18 percent over the same period (Young and Lin 2006). In 2007 AMD became the leader in microprocessors in China, with over a 50 percent share (*China Daily* 2007).

In an interview in Beijing in 2004, Craig Barrett, Intel's CEO, pronounced that people in China "are capable of doing any engineering job, any software job, and managerial job that people in the U.S. are capable of doing" (Heim 2004). In 2005 Intel employed more than 5,000 people in China, about 5 percent of its global labor force and a doubling of the Chinese employment level from 2004 (Wallace 2005). Most of these people worked in Intel's four assembly and test factories—three in Shanghai and a fourth in Chengdu, in the southwestern province of Sichuan, which began operations in December 2005. In March 2005, Intel announced that it would build a second plant in Chengdu to come on line in 2007 (AFX International Focus 2005).

As in Malaysia, virtually all of the people who Intel employs in China are homegrown. An article published in 2006 in the *Wall Street Journal* provides an excellent description of how, in Chengdu—a low-cost location but one with little history of high-tech manufacturing—Intel recruited and trained, in collaboration with local universities, a labor force for its first chip plant, and was in the process of doing the same for the second one (Ramstad and Juying 2006). The article also noted that with the completion of the second Chengdu plant, "the company has said it will build its next factory in yet another place where no other chip manufacturing exists: Vietnam."[14]

GLOBAL LABOR FLOWS AND NATIONAL ECONOMIC DEVELOPMENT

I began this chapter by asking, "With so many educated people coming from Asia to the United States for further graduate study and work experience, why are so many high-tech jobs going from the United States to the places from which these people are coming?" The answer is that the flows of people from East to West and jobs from West to East are complementary movements in the globalization of the high-tech labor force as a dynamically evolving process. At an early stage of development, people go from East to West for graduate education and work experience through which they can build careers in a way not possible at home. Meanwhile jobs go from West to East in search of low-wage but nevertheless productive labor. Over time, through MNC investment in higher value-added activities, the quality of the indigenous labor force improves. As living standards rise in the East, some of its expatriates, now more educated and experienced from their time in the West, are lured back home. Indeed some of them will make the return trip to the East as employees of the companies for which they had worked in the West. If and when indigenous companies emerge in the East as global players, the need to go abroad for education and experience will be further reduced, while many of the most educated and experienced expatriates working in the West will come back home to assume leadership posts.

Focusing mainly on Asian entrepreneurs who have spent time starting or managing companies in Silicon Valley, Saxenian (2006, pp. 18–
21) has characterized these flows as "brain circulation," an apt characterization for the global career paths that increasing numbers of Asians
are pursuing. As these "brains" circulate, their capabilities accumulate.
What I have outlined in this chapter are the historical forces, beyond
the desire of talented individuals to pursue challenging and rewarding
careers, that created the global ICT labor force and that have enabled
nations such as South Korea, Taiwan, India, and China to reap the
returns on national investments in education by bringing large numbers of educated and experienced people back home. More important
quantitatively, the growth dynamic that has been set in motion in these
nations has generated domestic employment opportunities that are sufficiently challenging and rewarding that it is increasingly unnecessary
for ambitious college graduates to go abroad to pursue careers.

These historical forces cannot be understood as "market forces."
Rather, as I have illustrated, their essence resides in a triad of investment strategies of MNCs engaged in FDI, national governments that
construct indigenous S&T infrastructures, and indigenous companies
that build on the investment strategies of foreign companies and domestic governments to become world-class competitors in their own right.
This triad takes as its historical starting point the existence of a national
education system that created a highly educated labor supply in advance
of domestic employment demand. In the absence of jobs at home, market forces, aided by changes in U.S. immigration policy, directed this
labor abroad, with brain drain as the result. By means of the investment
triad, nations such as South Korea and Taiwan in effect confronted these
market forces and helped to generate a dynamic of indigenous job creation that reversed the brain drain and transformed expatriate scientists
and engineers from wasted investments into valuable resources. China
and India are now doing the same.

The particular cases that I have examined reveal distinctive development paths, depending on the relation over time of investment by
foreign and indigenous enterprises. In the cases of Motorola in South
Korea, Intel in Malaysia, and TI in India, U.S.-based MNCs invested
early and then upgraded and expanded their investments over substantial
periods of time. In addition, great emphasis was placed on the almost
exclusive employment of indigenous engineers and managers in each

case, creating some of the first attractive opportunities for nationals to pursue high-tech careers at home.

In the case of South Korea, indigenous investments by government and business have driven the development of domestic high-tech capabilities since the late 1980s. Samsung in particular has emerged as a world leader in ICT. In the 2000s these indigenous investments are creating new opportunities for high-end investment by MNCs in South Korea, including new investments by a company, Motorola, that has been doing business there for more than 40 years. In contrast, in the absence of leading indigenous ICT companies, Malaysia's growth still remains highly dependent on the upgrading strategies of MNCs such as Intel, with scant impetus for indigenous innovation.

For U.S. high-tech MNCs, the inducement to invest in India was never low-wage, low-skill labor. What first attracted TI to India in the mid-1980s was the availability of highly educated engineers and programmers who also happened to have relatively low wages. Over time TI expanded and upgraded its Indian operations, employing larger numbers of educated workers to design increasingly complex products. Two decades after TI came to Bangalore, India is experiencing a growth dynamic in which, with both skill levels and wages rising, indigenous companies such as TCS, Wipro, and Infosys are taking the lead, and in which MNCs continue to be attracted to India more for the high quality of its ICT labor supply than for its low cost.

A similar process of indigenous innovation has been taking place in China, but with the difference being that indigenous Chinese companies such as Lenovo and Founder, the leading Chinese electronic publishing company (Lu 2000, chap.4; Lu and Lazonick 2001), have emerged to serve the growing Chinese consumer and business markets, drawing upon the capital goods expertise of MNCs such as Intel, TI, Motorola, and HP to develop higher-quality, lower-cost products. Lenovo and Founder are prime examples of indigenous companies that have become leading competitors not only in China but also internationally. In the communications technology sector, Huawei Technologies and ZTE are doing the same (Feng and Zhang 2008). Although there are large numbers of Chinese ICT employees who have acquired higher education and work experience in the United States, the vast majority have been receiving that education and experience in China.

Given the growth dynamic that has taken hold in these nations, sheer size ensures that Indians and Chinese will dominate the expansion of the global ICT labor supply. Combined, the population of India and China is 33 times that of South Korea and Taiwan. India and China have rapidly growing home markets that both provide domestic demand for the products of indigenous companies and give their governments leverage with MNCs in gaining access to advanced technology as a condition for FDI. While India and China offer indigenous scientists and engineers rapidly expanding employment opportunities at home, vast numbers of their educated populations are studying and working abroad. Aided by the liberalization of U.S. immigration policy, the global career path is much more of a "mass" phenomenon for Indian and Chinese scientists and engineers than it has been for the Koreans and Taiwanese. History tells us that more and more Indian and Chinese high-tech labor, following global career paths, will migrate back to the places whence they came. The globalization of the high-tech labor force and the sustained development of India and China have gone, and will continue to go, hand in hand.

What are the implications of the globalization of the ICT labor force for employment opportunities in a high-wage country such as the United States? "Offshoring" has been a major political issue in the United States in the 2000s (see Hira and Hira 2005) precisely because of the globalization of the ICT labor force, whose evolution I have just analyzed. Responding to a reporter who in late 2003 asked what job prospects in Silicon Valley would look like in three years, the ever-quotable Craig Barrett stated, "Companies can still form in Silicon Valley and be competitive around the world, It's just that they are not going to create jobs in Silicon Valley" (Merritt 2004). In 2004 Barrett had this to say:

> As CEO of Intel, my allegiance is to the shareholders of Intel and to the success of the company. We go after the most cost-effective resources around the world, no matter where they are. [However,] as an American citizen, I would have to be worried about whether jobs that are created are created outside the U.S. . . . As a citizen, I see all these resources and I think this puts my country in danger. (Heim 2004)

Subsequently Barrett served as a member of the U.S. National Academy of Sciences' Committee on Prospering in the Global Economy of the 21st Century (CPGE), which delved into deficiencies in the development of science and engineering capabilities in the United States (CPGE 2007). Notwithstanding his obvious concern about these problems from a public policy perspective, on a radio talk show in February 2006 Barrett remarked, "Companies like Intel can do perfectly well in the global marketplace without hiring a single U.S. employee."[15]

Notes

1. These data are drawn from the companies' global citizenship reports, available on their Web sites.
2. These data are drawn from 10-K filings.
3. The H-1 visa for foreigners of "distinguished merit and ability" became known as the H-1B visa when a special category of H-1A visas was created for registered nurses under the Immigration Nursing Relief Act of 1989 (Mailman and Yale-Loehr 2003).
4. The relevant fiscal year runs from October 1 to September 30.
5. Of the 65,000 visas that can be issued annually, 6,800 are set aside for Chile and Singapore under the terms of U.S. trade agreements with those countries. If any of these 6,800 visas are unused, they are added to the next year's visa cap.
6. This information is available at Senator Grassley's Web site at http://grassley .senate.gov/issues/upload/03072008.pdf.
7. Behrman and Wallender (1976, pp. 300–302) provide details on the internal career paths followed by managers of the manufacturing units between 1967 and 1974.
8. In 1985 KIET merged with the Korea Electrotechnology and Telecommunications Research Institute to become the Electronics and Telecommunications Research Institute (ETRI).
9. Over this four-year period, total Korean R&D expenditures tripled while GNP more than doubled, with R&D expenditure as a proportion of GNP rising from 0.67 to 0.95 (Arnold 1988).
10. See the KAIST Web site: http://www.kaist.edu/as_intro/as_nt_facts/as_ft_gnr/as_ ft_gnr.html. There is also an English link to an overview of KAIST at http://www .kaist.edu/edu.html. The undergraduates went to Korea Institute of Technology, which merged with KAIST in 1989.
11. The end of the fiscal year is March 31 for Infosys, Satyam, TCS, and Wipro, and June 30 for HCL. Note that given the accounting fraud scandal at Satyam that came to light in January 2009, the Satyam revenue and employment figures may be overstated.
12. ATP trade data are available from the U.S. Census Bureau (2008e).
13. For a study of the evolution of Lenovo that is complementary to the earlier study by Lu (2000, chap. 3), see Xie and White (2004).
14. See also Hopfner (2007). Intel's $1 billion plant in Ho Chi Minh City, with a capacity for 600 million chip sets per year, was slated to begin production in Sep-

tember 2009 with 500 engineers, increasing to 1,000 by the end of 2009. After a three-year ramp-up, Intel expects to employ 4,000 at the Vietnam plant.

15. Craig Barrett, interviewed by Tom Ashbrook, *On Point*, WBUR, February 11, 2006.

6
The Quest for Shareholder Value

NEBM AND THE STOCK MARKET

The globalization of the ICT labor force need not necessarily create employment problems for members of the U.S. ICT labor force. A nation such as the United States is in a prime position to both contribute to and gain from globalization. With taxpayers' money, the U.S. government has supported, and continues to support, the building of the world's most formidable high-tech knowledge base. The United States has, and will continue to have, the world's leading universities for research and education in science and technology. Based in the United States are many of the world's most powerful high-tech companies. In the 2000s these high-tech companies have in general been very profitable, in part because of their ability to take advantage of the opportunities opened up by globalization. As the rest of the world develops, a combination of government investments in the knowledge base and business investments in innovative products and processes should be able to create employment opportunities in high-value-added activities that can make full use of the productivity and creativity of the U.S. high-tech labor force.

But what happens if the ideology prevails that only the private sector makes productive contributions to economic growth, thus undermining the longstanding developmental role of government in the United States? And what happens if the ideology prevails that the primary if not sole purpose of the so-called private sector is to create value for shareholders, thus distributing corporate resources to those participants in the corporate economy who (as I will show in this chapter) contribute least? Indeed, what happens if the executives who run these corporations find that by allocating resources in ways that purportedly "maximize shareholder value," they can become superrich even as many of the well-educated and experienced people who have worked long and hard for these companies face employment insecurity and the erosion of their accumulated human capital?

"What happens?" has happened. We see it in the explosion, and reexplosion, of top executive pay, which has been a topic of socioeconomic conversation for the past three decades. We see it in the Bush administration's tax cuts for the rich through the Jobs and Growth Tax Relief Reconciliation Act of 2003, a piece of legislation that in its very title promised that a reduction of the dividends and capital gains tax rates to 15 percent would redound to the benefit of the U.S. economy as a whole. We see it in the trillions of dollars of stock repurchases that U.S. companies have done in the 2000s in an effort to jack up their stock prices. And we see it in the decline of the middle class, including educated and experienced men and women in their 40s, 50s, and 60s whose careers were supposed to lift them into the upper middle class or beyond.

The underlying economic ideology that has supported this mode of resource allocation is the argument—now taken as a law of nature within the U.S. business community—that maximizing shareholder value results in superior economic performance. It is an ideology that came to the fore in the 1980s as overextended Old Economy companies restructured in the face of new global competition (Lazonick and O'Sullivan 2000a). In doing so, these corporations shifted from a "retain and reinvest" resource allocation regime, in which they retained corporate employees in career jobs and reinvested corporate revenues in new products and processes, to a "downsize and distribute" regime, in which they downsized their labor forces and distributed corporate revenues to shareholders to an unprecedented extent in the forms of not only cash dividends but also stock buybacks.

If Old Economy downsize-and-distribute had been the only allocation regime in town, the sustainability of this mode of allocating corporate revenues would have reached its limits in the early 1990s—as indeed seemed to be the case in the white-collar recession of the early 1990s and the jobless recovery that followed. The longest stock market boom in U.S. history could not have been sustained if it had depended solely, or even primarily, on the downsizing of the labor force and the distribution of corporate revenues to shareholders. Over the long run, the superior performance of the corporation, as reflected ultimately in a sustained upward movement of its stock price, requires innovation.

Fortunately for the growth of the U.S. economy, there was another allocation regime being practiced in the emerging New Economy. It was a variation of the retain-and-reinvest regime that had been in force in the Old Economy, with the major difference in the 1980s and 1990s being that New Economy companies retained almost all of their profits to invest in corporate growth, often not even paying cash dividends. These companies did not, however, retain their labor forces in systems of career employment. Rather, for the economic and technological reasons that I have explained in this book, NEBM favored the employment of younger workers, using flexible employment arrangements.

The performance of New Economy companies in the 1980s and the 1990s gave Americans reason to believe in the possibility of sustainable prosperity. As we have seen, during these decades U.S. households became more dependent on the stock market as a source of income, especially for the retirement years. Given this dependency, the notion that business corporations should maximize shareholder value sounded like a slogan that was good for people's wealth. It was the rise and consolidation of NEBM in the most innovative sectors of the economy that ensured the ultimate triumph of this ideology of corporate resource allocation.

Not only did New Economy innovation sustain the stock market boom in the 1980s and 1990s but it also, as I showed in Chapter 2, fostered a mode of business organization in which the stock market played a number of central functions in mobilizing capital and labor as well as in enabling the growth of the firm. A highly liquid stock market was an inducement for venture capital to invest in highly uncertain products and processes. To help ensure a high level of returns from these investments, the high-tech lobby, representing the AeA and the NVCA, has led the successful fight for a lower tax regime in the name of innovative enterprise since the late 1970s. The stock market also made possible, in the form of broad-based employee stock option plans, the key mode of remuneration that New Economy start-ups used to attract professional, technical, and administrative employees away from secure employment at established Old Economy companies. Having thus mobilized capital and labor, a high-tech start-up then sought to develop a product that would enable it to do an IPO. Once listed on the stock market, New Economy companies reinvested their earnings in the growth of the firm. When successful, their stock prices rose, thus making their stock a more valuable "currency" for not only attracting and retaining employees but also acquiring other, typically even younger, technology firms without expending cash.

That was the story of the 1980s and 1990s. That is not the case in the 2000s. The leading New Economy companies, as well as companies such as HP and IBM that successfully made the transition to NEBM, have ample productive capabilities. The allocation of resources in these companies no longer, however, follows a retain-and-reinvest regime, even of the NEBM variety. Rather, these companies, now considered mature, are in the forefront of a mode of corporate resource allocation that focuses on buying back their own outstanding shares for the sake of supporting their stock prices. As I will show in this chapter and the next, it is the American middle class that is paying the price (see also Lazonick 2008c,d).

MAXIMIZING SHAREHOLDER VALUE

In all of the richest economies, business corporations are repositories of large, and in many cases vast, quantities of resources over which corporate managers, rather than markets, exercise allocative control. Indeed, it can be argued that corporate control, as distinct from market control, of resource allocation represented the defining institutional characteristic of twentieth-century capitalist economies (Chandler 1977, 1990). Whereas the conventional theory of the market economy maintains that markets should allocate resources to achieve superior economic performance, the actual pervasiveness of corporate control over resource allocation demands a theory of the ways in which corporate governance affects economic performance.

During the 1980s and 1990s, the argument that maximizing shareholder value results in superior economic performance came to dominate the corporate governance debates. This shareholder-value perspective represents an attempt to construct a theory of corporate governance that is consistent with the neoclassical theory of the market economy. Like the theory of the market economy, however, the shareholder-value perspective lacks a theory of innovative enterprise (see Lazonick 2003b, 2006; O'Sullivan 2000a). As a result, the shareholder-value perspective on corporate governance fails to comprehend how and under what conditions the corporate allocation of resources supports investment in innovation at the level of the business enterprise and contributes to the achievement of stable and equitable growth at the level of the economy as a whole.

For adherents of the theory of the market economy, "market imperfections"—for example, "asset specificity" in the work of Oliver Williamson (1985, 1996)—necessitate managerial control over the allocation of resources, thus creating an "agency problem" for those "principals" who have made investments in the firm. The agency problem derives from two limitations, one cognitive and the other behavioral, on the human ability to make allocative decisions. The cognitive limitation is "hidden information" (also known as "adverse selection" or "bounded rationality") which prevents investors from knowing *a priori* whether the managers whom they have employed as their agents are good or bad resource allocators. The behavioral limitation is "hidden action" (also known as "moral hazard" or "opportunism") which reflects the proclivity, inherent in an individualistic society, of managers as agents to use their positions as resource allocators to pursue their own self-interests and not necessarily the interests of the firm's principals. These managers may allocate corporate resources to build their own personal empires regardless of whether the investments that they make and the people whom they employ generate sufficient profits for the firm. They may hoard surplus cash or near-liquid assets within the corporation, thus maintaining control over uninvested resources, rather than distributing these extra revenues to shareholders. Or they may simply use their control over resource allocation to line their own pockets. According to agency theory, in the absence of corporate governance institutions that promote the maximization of shareholder value, one should expect managerial control to result in the inefficient allocation of resources.

The manifestation of a movement toward the more efficient allocation of resources, it is argued, is a higher return to shareholders. But why is it shareholders for whom value should be maximized? Why not create more value for creditors by making their financial investments more secure, or for employees by paying them higher wages and benefits, or for communities in which the corporations operate by generating more corporate tax revenues? Neoclassical financial theorists argue that among all the stakeholders in the business corporation only shareholders are "residual claimants." The amount of returns that shareholders receive depends on what is left over after other stakeholders—all of whom, it is argued, have guaranteed contractual claims—have been paid for their productive contributions to the firm. If the firm incurs a loss, the return to shareholders is negative, and vice versa.

By this argument, shareholders are the only stakeholders who have an incentive to bear the risk of investing in productive resources that may result in superior economic performance (O'Sullivan 2000b, 2002). As residual claimants, moreover, shareholders are the only stakeholders who have an interest in monitoring managers to ensure that they allocate resources efficiently. Furthermore, by selling and buying corporate shares on the stock market, public shareholders, it is argued, are the participants in the economy who are best situated to reallocate resources to more efficient uses. The agency problem—the fact that public shareholders, as the (purported) principals who bear risk, are obliged to leave the corporate allocation of resources under the control of managers as their "agents"—poses a constant threat to the efficient allocation of resources.

Within the shareholder-value paradigm, the stock market represents the corporate governance institution through which the agency problem can be resolved and the efficient allocation of the economy's resources can be achieved. Specifically, the stock market can function as a "market for corporate control" that enables shareholders to "disgorge"—to use Michael Jensen's evocative term—the "free cash flow." As Jensen (1986, p. 323), a leading academic proponent of maximizing shareholder value, put it in a seminal 1986 article,

> Free cash flow is cash flow in excess of that required to fund all projects that have positive net present values when discounted at the relevant cost of capital. Conflicts of interest between shareholders and managers over payout policies are especially severe when the organization generates substantial free cash flow. The problem is how to motivate managers to disgorge the cash rather than investing it at below cost or wasting it on organization inefficiencies.

How can those managers who control the allocation of corporate resources be motivated, or coerced, to distribute cash to shareholders? If a company does not maximize shareholder value, shareholders can sell their shares and reallocate the proceeds to what they deem to be more efficient uses. The sale of shares depresses that company's stock price, which in turn facilitates a takeover by shareholders who can put in place managers who are willing to distribute the free cash flow to shareholders in the forms of higher dividends and/or stock repurchases. Better yet, as Jensen (1986, p. 324) argued in the midst of the 1980s corporate takeover movement, let corporate raiders use this "market for corporate control" for debt-financed takeovers, thus enabling shareholders to transform their corporate equities into corporate bonds. Corporate managers would then be "bonded" to distribute the "free cash flow" in the form of interest rather than dividends. Additionally, as Jensen and Murphy (1990), among others, contended, the maximization of shareholder value could be achieved by giving corporate managers stock-based compensation, such as stock options, to align their own self-interests with those of shareholders. Then, even without the threat of a takeover, these managers would have a personal incentive to maximize shareholder value by investing corporate revenues only in those "projects that have positive net present values when discounted at the relevant cost of capital" (Jensen 1986, p. 323) and distributing the remainder of corporate revenues to shareholders in the forms of dividends and/or stock repurchases.

A CRITIQUE OF THE SHAREHOLDER-VALUE PERSPECTIVE

During the 1980s and 1990s, maximizing shareholder value became the dominant ideology for corporate governance in the United States, and through a variety of institutional channels gained acceptance around the world. Top managers of U.S. industrial corporations became ardent advocates of this perspective; quite apart from their ideological predispositions, the reality of their stock-based compensation enticed them to maximize shareholder value (Lazonick and O'Sullivan 2000a; see also Chapter 2). The long stock market boom of the 1980s and 1990s combined with the remuneration decisions of corporate boards to create this bonanza for corporate executives. During the decade of the 1970s, the stock market had languished, and inflation had eroded dividend yields. In the 1980s and 1990s, however, as shown in Chapter 1 (see Table 1.2), high real yields on corporate stock characterized the U.S. corporate economy.

These high yields came mainly from stock-price appreciation as distinct from dividend yields, which were low in the 1990s despite high payout ratios. The form of yield is important to the mode of shareholding. A dividend yield provides the shareholder with an income by holding the stock, and hence promotes stable shareholding. A price yield, in contrast, can only be reaped if the shareholder sells his or her stock. When executives, or any other employees, exercise their stock options, they have an interest in selling the stock to lock in the gains. (Otherwise, unless they are at the end of the typical 10-year exercise period, they would have delayed the exercise of the options.) High price yields and high levels of executive stock-based compensation, therefore, go hand in hand.

It should be noted that, as a whole, U.S. corporations were not skimping on dividends in the 1980s and 1990s. It is simply that when a company's stock price increases, its dividend yield—the amount of dividends paid out as a percentage of the stock price—will fall unless the amount of dividends increases proportionately. In the 1980s dividends paid out by U.S. corporations increased by an annual average of 10.8 percent, while after-tax corporate profits increased by an annual average of 8.7 percent. In the 1990s these figures were 8.0 percent for dividends (including an absolute decline in dividends of 4.0 percent in 1999, the first decline since 1975) and 8.1 percent for profits. The payout ratio—the amount of dividends as a percentage of after-tax corporate profits (with inventory evaluation and capital consumption adjustments)—averaged 48.4 percent in the 1980s and 56.5 percent in the 1990s compared with 38.8 percent in the 1960s and 41.3 percent in the 1970s. From 2000 to 2007, the payout ratio was 60.5 percent, including a record 66.2 percent in 2007. During the first three quarters of 2008, the payout ratio shot up even higher, to 73.3 percent (U.S. Congress 2009, Table B-90).

High stock yields reflected a combination of three distinct forces at work in the U.S. corporate economy in the 1980s and 1990s: 1) manipulation of the distribution of income in favor of shareholders, especially by older corporations, through a combination of downsizing of the labor force and increased distributions to shareholders in the forms of cash dividends and stock repurchases; 2) innovation, especially by newer technology companies, that boosted earnings per share; and 3) speculation by stock market investors, encouraged, initially at least, by stock price increases due to the combination of manipulation and innovation. An understanding of these three determinants of stock-price movements is essential for a critical evaluation of the claim that maximizing shareholder value results in superior economic performance.

In the 1980s and 1990s, older companies, many with their origins in the late nineteenth century, engaged in a process of redistributing corporate revenues from labor incomes to capital incomes. Engaging in a downsize-and-distribute allocation regime, these companies downsized their labor forces and increased the distribution of corporate revenues to shareholders (Lazonick and O'Sullivan 2000a). As indicated earlier, this allocation regime represented a reversal of the retain-and-reinvest regime that had characterized these companies in the post–World War II decades. Companies had retained corporate revenues for reinvestment in organization and technology, expanding their labor forces in the process. Coming into the 1980s, employees—both managerial personnel and shop-floor workers—had expectations, based on over three decades of experience of a retain-and-reinvest regime, of long-term employment with these corporations (Lazonick 2004a, 2007e). Downsizing augmented the so-called free cash flow that could be distributed to shareholders. In the early and mid-1980s, this redistribution of corporate revenues often occurred through debt-financed hostile takeovers, which were favored by the proponents of the "market for corporate control." Posttakeover downsizing facilitated the servicing and retirement of the massive debt that a company had taken on (Blair 1993; Shleifer and Summers 1988).

Since the mid-1980s, the distribution of corporate revenues to shareholders increasingly has taken the form of corporate stock repurchases. As shown in Figure 6.1, net equity issues of nonfinancial business corporations as well as commercial banks and insurance companies, taken as a group, were negative in every year from 1994 through 2007. In the Internet boom years of 1997–2000, the extent of this "negative cash function" of the stock market increased markedly as many companies sought to use repurchases to augment the positive impact of stock-market speculation on stock prices. Measured in 2007 dollars, net equity issues for nonfinancial corporations, banks, and insurers combined bottomed out at about −$300 billion in 1998 before rising to −$49 billion in 2003, the highest level in real terms since 1993. Since then, however,

Figure 6.1 Net Corporate Equity Issues (billions of 2007 dollars) in the United States by Nonfinancial Corporate Business and by Selected Financial Sectors, 1980–2007

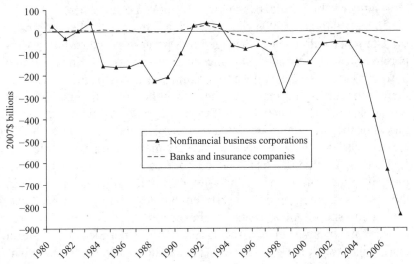

SOURCE: Board of Governors of the Federal Reserve System (2008).

net equity issues have plunged to unprecedented negative levels, reaching −$896 billion in 2007 (Figure 6.1).

This "disgorging" of the corporate cash flow manifests a decisive triumph of agency theory and its shareholder-value ideology in the determination of corporate resource allocation. Later, we shall look directly at the role of stock buybacks among the companies included in the S&P 500 Index in driving these massive distributions to shareholders. And then, by considering stock repurchases by leading ICT companies, I shall raise the question of whether the cash flow that has thus been disgorged has really been "free."

By creating new value, innovation also boosted company stock prices. In contrast, manipulation transferred value from labor incomes to capital incomes, raising the stock price as, for example, workers were laid off and wages and benefits were reduced, with no new value being created. During the 1980s and 1990s, newer technology companies such as Intel, Microsoft, Oracle, Sun Microsystems, and Cisco Systems experienced significant growth in both revenues and employment by means of a retain-and-reinvest allocation regime; they retained corporate revenues, paying little if any dividends (although most of them did some stock repurchases during the 1990s), and reinvested earnings in innovative products and processes. In general, both the revenues and employment levels of these companies grew over this period, especially during the 1990s, and these companies were highly profitable (see Lazonick 2007b). Steadily rising stock prices reflected the realization of the gains of innovative enterprise by these companies.

Sophisticated stock market investors recognized that the combination of manipulation and innovation provided a real foundation for stock price increases and speculated on further upward movements. Other, less knowledgeable investors followed suit. From the fourth quarter of 1985 to the third quarter of 1987, and then more significantly from the first quarter of 1995 to the third quarter of 2000, speculation became an increasingly important factor in the rise of stock prices. Professional insiders, within corporations and on Wall Street, encouraged and generally gained from this speculation because of the existence of a long queue of unprofessional outsiders who bought shares at inflated prices, implicitly assuming that "greater fools" than themselves remained ready to buy the overpriced shares on the market. At some point, however, the greatest fools were left holding these shares, as happened in the fourth quarter of 1987 and, more profoundly, in the fourth quarter of 2000 when stock prices fell precipitously. With the continued fall in stock prices in 2001, the speculation that helped to sustain the longest bull run in U.S. stock market history was put to rest.

The "behavioral" school in financial economics has recognized the importance of stock market speculation as a determinant of stock prices, but it has not in general embraced the greater fools perspective. For example, in a best-selling book published at the height of the Internet boom, financial economist Robert Shiller (2000) characterized the stock market bubble as "irrational exuberance." Shiller (p. 18) made the assumption that all players in the stock market, professionals and non-professionals, have access to the same information, implying that irrational exuberance is a general phenomenon among stock-market investors. Yet the assumption is contradicted by widespread use of inside information by professionals, as revealed in stock-fraud investigations in the aftermath of the Internet crash as well as in documents produced in numerous class action lawsuits by shareholders who bought shares and allegedly lost money because of false information provided by professional insiders. Investigations by the SEC have revealed the widespread corporate practices of backdating executive stock option awards to dates at which prices were lower and granting stock options to executives just ahead of good news announcements that could be expected to boost the company's stock price, both of which served to increase the gains of corporate executives from stock options (Forelle and Bandler 2006; Lie 2005). Insofar as insiders have the incentive and ability to manipulate stock market prices in these ways for their own personal gain, their exuberance is anything but irrational.

Under the heading "Cultural Changes Favoring Business Success or the Appearance Thereof," Shiller (2000, pp. 22–24) recognized, but in my view understated, the incentive that top corporate executives, as the ultimate professional insiders, had to contribute to speculation, given the importance of stock-based compensation to their pay packages. Ironically, after the crash, Michael Jensen chastised corporate executives for failing to say "no" to Wall Street, as, spurred on by the prospect of greater stock-based compensation, they had taken actions during the boom for the purpose of inflating stock prices (Fuller and Jensen 2002). Corporate insiders had much to gain, moreover, from the volatile stock market, not only as prices rose but also as they fell; while the outsiders continued to buy, the insiders sold (e.g., see Gimein et al. 2002).

Especially in high-tech companies, it was not only top executives who stood to gain from an ebullient stock market. As I have shown in Chapter 2, by the 1980s and 1990s broad-based employee stock option plans had become widespread among newer technology companies, and by the late 1990s had diffused to many older corporations, not only in the United States but also abroad, that competed for this highly mobile labor (Carpenter, Lazonick, and O'Sullivan 2003; Glimstedt, Lazonick, and Xie 2006). Although top executives continued to get highly disproportionate shares of the stock options that a company allocated, a broad base of the high-tech labor force, especially in high-tech industries, acquired a direct interest in corporate policies aimed at maximizing shareholder value.

But did this financial behavior lead to a more efficient allocation of resources in the economy, as the shareholder-value proponents claim? There are a number of flaws in agency theory's analysis of the relation between corporate governance and economic performance. These flaws have to do with three things: 1) a failure to explain how, historically, corporations came to control the allocation of significant amounts of the economy's resources; 2) the measure of free cash flow; and 3) the claim that only shareholders have "residual claimant" status. These flaws stem from the fact that agency theory, like the neoclassical theory of the market economy in which it is rooted, lacks a theory of innovative enterprise. These flaws are, moreover, amply exposed by the history of the industrial corporation in the United States, the national context in which agency theory evolved and in which it is thought to be most applicable.

Agency theory makes an argument for taking resources out of the control of inefficient managers without explaining how, historically, corporations came to possess the vast amounts of resources over which these managers could exercise allocative control. As far back as the first decades of the twentieth century, the separation of share owner-ship from managerial control characterized U.S. industrial corporations (Berle and Means 1932). This separation occurred because the growth of innovative companies demanded that control over the strategic allo-cation of resources to transform technologies and access new markets be placed in the hands of salaried professionals who understood the investment requirements of the particular lines of business in which the enterprise competed. At the same time, the listing of a company on a public stock exchange enabled the original owner-entrepreneurs to sell their stock to the shareholding public, and, thereby enriched, they were able to retire from their positions as top executives. The departing owner-entrepreneurs left control in the hands of senior salaried pro-fessionals, most of whom had been recruited decades earlier to help to build the enterprises. The resultant disappearance of family owners from positions of strategic control enabled the younger generation of salaried professionals to view the particular corporations that employed them as ones in which, through dedicated work effort over the course of a career, they could potentially rise to the ranks of top management.

With salaried managers exercising strategic control, innovative managerial corporations emerged as dominant in their industries dur-ing the first decades of the century (Chandler 1977, 1990). During the post–World War II decades, and especially during the 1960s conglom-erate movement, however, many of these industrial corporations grew to be too big to be managed effectively (Lazonick 2004a). Top managers responsible for corporate resource allocation became segmented, behaviorally and cognitively, from the organizations that would have to implement these strategies. Behaviorally, they came to see themselves as occupants of the corporate throne rather than as members of the corporate organization, and they became obsessed by the size of their own remuneration (e.g., see Crystal 1991; Patton 1988). Cognitively, the expansion of the corporation into a multitude of businesses made it increasingly difficult for top management to understand the particular investment requirements of any of them.

In the 1970s and 1980s, moreover, many of these U.S. corporations faced intense foreign competition, especially from innovative Japanese corporations (which also, it should be noted, were characterized by a separation of share ownership from managerial control). An innovative response required governance institutions that would reintegrate U.S. strategic decision makers with the business organizations over which they exercised allocative control. Instead, with their strategic decision makers guided by the ideology of maximizing shareholder value and rewarded with stock options, what these established corporations got were managers who had a strong personal interest in boosting their companies' stock prices, even if the stock-price increase was accomplished by a redistribution of corporate revenues from labor incomes to capital incomes and even if the quest for stock-price increases undermined the productive capabilities that these companies had accumulated from the past (Lazonick and O'Sullivan 2000a).

Agency theory also does not address how, at the time when innovative investments are made, one can judge whether managers are allocating resources inefficiently. Any strategic manager who allocates resources to an innovative strategy faces technological, market, and competitive uncertainty. Technological uncertainty exists because the firm may be incapable of developing the higher quality processes and products envisaged in its innovative investment strategy. Market uncertainty exists because, even if the firm succeeds in its development effort, future reductions in product prices and increases in factor prices may lower the returns that can be generated by the investments. Finally, even if a firm overcomes technological and market uncertainty, it still faces competitive uncertainty: the possibility that an innovative competitor will have invested in a strategy that generates an even higher-quality, lower-cost product that enables it to win market share.

One can state, as Jensen did, that the firm should only invest in "projects that have positive net present values when discounted at the relevant cost of capital." But, quite apart from the problem of defining the "relevant cost of capital," anyone who contends that, when committing resources to an innovative investment strategy, one can foresee the stream of future earnings required for the calculation of net present value knows nothing about the innovation process. It is far more plausible to argue that if corporate managers really sought to maximize shareholder value according to this formula, they would never contemplate investing in innovative projects, given their highly uncertain returns (Baldwin and Clark 1992).

Addressing the third point, it is simply not the case, as agency theory assumes, that all the firm's participants other than shareholders receive contractually guaranteed returns according to their productive contributions. The argument that shareholders are the sole residual claimants is a deduction from the theory of the market economy. It does not, however, accord with the reality of the innovative enterprise. The argument that a party to a transaction receives contractually guaranteed returns may hold when, in an open, competitive market, one firm purchases a physical commodity as a productive input from another firm. But, as I elaborate on below, one cannot assume contractually guaranteed returns when the inputs are made available to business enterprises by the state. Nor can one make this assumption when the inputs are made available to the business enterprise in the form of the labor services of employees. Finally, once one recognizes that the innovative enterprise cannot be understood as a "nexus of contracts," one can ask whether public shareholders actually perform the risk-bearing function that the proponents of agency theory claim.

Given its investments in productive resources, the state has residual claimant status. Any realistic account of economic development must take into account the joint role of the state in 1) making infrastructural investments that, given the required levels of financial commitment and the inherent uncertainty of economic outcomes, business enterprises would not have made on their own; and 2) providing business enterprises with subsidies that encourage investment in innovation. In terms of investment in new knowledge with applications to industry, the United States was the world's foremost developmental state over the course of the twentieth century. As a prime example, it is impossible to explain

U.S. dominance in computers, microelectronics, software, and data communications without recognizing the role of government in making seminal investments that developed new knowledge and infrastructural investments that facilitated the diffusion of that knowledge (e.g., see Abbate 2000; National Research Council 1999). Nor can one explain U.S. dominance in biotechnology without recognizing the persistent investments of the National Institutes of Health in the knowledge base and the government subsidies provided to companies through legislation such as the Orphan Drug Act of 1983 (see Lazonick and Tulum 2008).

The U.S. government has made investments to augment the productive power of the nation through federal, corporate, and university research labs that have generated new knowledge, as well as through educational institutions that have developed the capabilities of the future labor force. Business enterprises have made ample use of this knowledge and capability. Although these business enterprises may pay fees for these services—for example, the salary of an engineer whose education was supported in whole or in part by state funds—one would be hard put to show that there exists a nexus of contracts that guarantees the state a return on these investments for the productive contributions that the outputs of these investments make to the enterprises that use them. In effect, in funding these investments, the state (or more correctly, its body of taxpayers) has borne the risk that the nation's business enterprises would further develop and utilize these productive capabilities in ways that would ultimately redound to the benefit of the nation, but with the return to the nation in no way contractually guaranteed.

In addition, the U.S. government has often provided cash subsidies to business enterprises to develop new products and processes, or even to start new firms. Sometimes these subsidies have been built into the rates that firms in particular industries could charge as regulated monopolies. For selected industries, tariff protection has provided firms with the time to develop higher-quality, lower-cost products. The public has funded these subsidies through current taxes, by borrowing against the future, or by making consumers pay higher product prices for current goods and services than would have otherwise prevailed. By definition, a subsidy lies beyond the realm of a market-mediated contract and is, in fact, defined as "a grant paid by a government to an enterprise that benefits the public" (Dictionary.com 2008). Multitudes of business enterprises have benefited from these subsidies without having to enter into contracts with the public bodies that have granted them to remit a guaranteed return from the productive investments that the subsidies have helped to finance.

Similar to the government, workers can also find themselves in the position of having made investments in their own productive capabilities which they supply to firms without a guaranteed contractual return. In an important contribution to the corporate governance debate, Margaret Blair (1995) argued that, alongside a firm's shareholders, workers should be accorded residual claimant status because they make investments in "firm-specific" human capital at one point in time with the expectation—but without a contractual guarantee—of reaping returns on those investments over the course of their careers. Moreover, insofar as their human capital is indeed firm-specific, these workers are dependent on their current employer for generating returns on their investments. A lack of interfirm labor mobility means that the worker bears some of the risk of the return on the firm's productive investments, and hence can be considered a residual claimant. Blair goes on to argue that if one assumes, as the shareholder-value proponents do, that only shareholders bear risk and have residual claimant status, there will be an underinvestment in human capital to the detriment of not only workers but the economy as a whole.

For those concerned about the propensity of U.S. corporations to downsize-and-distribute, Blair's focus on investments in firm-specific human capital provides a stakeholder theory of the firm in which workers as well as shareholders should be viewed as principals for whose benefit the firm should be run. However, a corporate executive intent on downsizing his labor force could logically argue that the productive capabilities of workers in, say, their 50s who had made investments in firm-specific human capital earlier in their careers have now become old because of competition from equally adept but more energetic younger workers or, alternatively, have become obsolete because of technological change. The executive could then argue that, in making investments in firm-specific human capital in the past, these (now) older workers had taken on the risk-bearing function, and, like any risk-bearing investor, must accept the possibility that their investments would at some point lose their market value.

The workers could respond by arguing that the corporate executive is wrong—their accumulated capabilities are not old or obsolete, but rather, given a correct understanding of technological, market, and competitive conditions in the industry, remain critical to the innovation process. They might even, as principals, accuse the executive (as their agent) of acting opportunistically, perhaps because he has stock options that align his interests with shareholders. They might claim that what the proposed downsizing actually entails is a redistribution of income from labor to capital rather than a restructuring of the workforce for the purpose of innovation. Clearly, even from the workers' point of view, agency theory's concerns with hidden information and hidden action on the part of managers are relevant. The problem is that agency theory provides no guide to analyzing whether or not the executive is in fact acting innovatively or opportunistically, because agency theory, like neoclassical economic theory more generally, has no theory of innovative enterprise.

Investments that can result in innovation require the strategic allocation of productive resources to particular processes to transform particular productive inputs into higher-quality, lower-cost products than those goods or services that were previously available at prevailing factor prices. Investment in innovation is a direct investment that involves, first and foremost, a strategic confrontation with technological, market, and competitive uncertainty. Those who have the abilities and incentives to allocate resources to innovation must decide, in the face of uncertainty, what types of investments have the potential to generate higher-quality, lower-cost products. Then they must mobilize committed finance to sustain the innovation process until it generates the higher-quality, lower-cost products that permit financial returns (Lazonick 2006).

What role do public shareholders play in this innovation process? Do they confront uncertainty by strategically allocating resources to innovative investments? No. As portfolio investors, they diversify their financial holdings across the outstanding shares of existing firms to minimize risk. They do so, moreover, with limited liability, which means that they are under no legal obligation to make further investments of "good" money to support previous investments that have gone bad. Indeed, even for these previous investments, the existence of a highly liquid stock market enables public shareholders to cut their losses instantaneously by selling their shares—what has long been called the "Wall Street walk."

Without this ability to exit an investment easily, public shareholders would not be willing to hold shares of companies, the assets of which they exercise no direct allocative control over. It is the liquidity of a public shareholder's portfolio investment that differentiates it from a direct investment, and indeed distinguishes the public shareholder from a private shareholder who, for lack of liquidity of his or her shares, must remain committed to his or her direct investment until it generates financial returns. The modern corporation entails a fundamental transformation in the character of private property, as Berle and Means (1932) recognized. As property owners, public shareholders own tradable shares in a company that has invested in real assets; they do not own the assets themselves.

Indeed, the fundamental role of the stock market in the United States in the twentieth century was to transform illiquid claims into liquid claims on the basis of investments that had already been made, and thereby separate share ownership from managerial control. Business corporations sometimes do use the stock market as a source of finance for new investments, although the cash function has been most common in periods of stock market speculation, when the lure for public shareholders to allocate resources to new issues has been the prospect of quickly "flipping" their shares to make a rapid, speculative return (see Lazonick and Tulum 2008; O'Sullivan 2004). Public shareholders want financial liquidity; investments in innovation require financial commitment. It is only by ignoring the role of innovation in the economy, and the necessary role of insider control in the strategic allocation of corporate resources to innovation, that agency theory can argue that superior economic performance can be achieved by maximizing the value of those actors in the corporate economy who are the ultimate outsiders to the innovation process.

THE FIVE FUNCTIONS OF THE STOCK MARKET AND INNOVATIVE ENTERPRISE

A business enterprise seeks to transform productive resources into goods and services that can be sold to generate revenues. A theory of the firm, therefore, must, at a minimum, provide explanations for how this productive transformation occurs and how revenues are obtained. Further, if such a theory purports to capture the essential reality of a modern capitalist economy, it must explain how, in competing for the same product markets, some firms are able to gain sustained competitive advantage over others. For a perspective on corporate governance to have any claim to relevance for understanding how a firm achieves superior economic performance, it must be rooted in a theory of innovative enterprise (for elaborations, see Lazonick 2006; Lazonick and O'Sullivan 2000b; O'Sullivan 2000a).

The innovation process is uncertain, collective, and cumulative. As a result, innovative enterprise requires strategy, organization, and finance (Lazonick 2006; O'Sullivan 2000a). The role of strategy is to confront uncertainty by allocating resources to investments that, by developing human and physical capabilities, can enable the firm to compete for specific product markets. The role of organization is to transform technologies and access markets to generate products that buyers want at prices that they are willing and able to pay. The role of finance is to sustain the accumulation of capabilities from the time at which investments in productive resources are made to the time at which financial returns are generated through the sale of products.

Innovation is a social process supported in certain times and places by what I call "social conditions of innovative enterprise." Three distinct but interrelated social conditions—strategic control, organizational integration, and financial commitment—can transform strategy, finance, and organization into social processes that result in innovation. The social conditions of innovative enterprise manifest themselves as social relations that, embedded in the business enterprise, are central to the performance of the firm.

Strategic control gives decision makers the power to allocate the firm's resources to confront the technological, market, and competitive uncertainties that are inherent in the innovation process. For innovation to occur, those who occupy strategic decision-making positions must have both the abilities and incentives to allocate resources to innovative investment strategies. Their abilities to do so will depend on their knowledge of how the current innovative capabilities of the organization over which they exercise allocative control can be enhanced by strategic investments in new, typically complementary, capabilities. Their incentives to do so will depend on the alignment of their personal interests with the interests of the business organization in attaining and sustaining its competitive advantage.

Those who exercise strategic control must be capable of understanding the technological, market, and competitive characteristics of the industries in which their firms are competing as well as the learning capabilities of the business organizations upon which they rely to implement their innovative investment strategies. This integration of strategic decision makers into the business organization can break down because the firm overextends itself by expanding into too many lines of business, as happened in the U.S. conglomerate movement of the 1960s. Those who exercise strategic control may no longer understand the organizational and technological requirements of the innovation process. If so, the corporate governance challenge is to find ways of reintegrating strategic decision making with the learning organization.

The social condition that can make an organization innovative is organizational integration, which is a set of relations that creates incentives for people to apply their skills and efforts to generate higher-quality, lower-cost products than had previously been available. To develop high-quality products, participants in the innovation process must engage in organizational learning. The more this learning is collective and cumulative, the higher the fixed costs of the learning process. If investments in organizational learning are to be a source of competitive advantage rather than disadvantage, the enterprise must generate sufficient sales to transform the high fixed costs of these investments into low unit costs (Lazonick 2006). Modes of compensation (in the forms of promotion, remuneration, and benefits) are important instruments for integrating individuals into the organization. To generate innovation, however, a mode of compensation cannot simply manage the labor market by attracting and retaining employees. It must be part of a reward system that manages the productive processes that are the essence of innovation. Most importantly, the compensation system must motivate employees to engage in collective learning and to ensure a high level of utilization of the resultant productive capabilities.

The social condition that enables finance to support the innovation process is financial commitment, a set of relations that ensures the allocation of funds to sustain the cumulative innovation process until it can generate financial returns. What is often called "patient" capital enables the capabilities that derive from organizational learning to cumulate over time, notwithstanding the inherent uncertainty that the innovation process entails. Strategic control over internal revenues is the foundation of financial commitment. The size and duration of investments in innovation that are required may demand that such "inside capital" be supplemented by external sources of finance such as stock issues, bond issues, or bank debt. In different times and places, depending on varying institutional arrangements, different types of external finance may be more or less committed to sustaining the innovation process (Lazonick 2007d).

Control over internal funds, leveraged if need be by external funds, enables corporate executives to commit to innovative investment strategies of large size and long duration. Given the uncertain character of the innovation process, the full extent of financial commitment required to generate higher-quality, lower-cost products is not known at the outset of an investment strategy but only unfolds over time. There will be cases in which corporate executives squander corporate resources on ill-conceived investment strategies, as agency theorists contend. Given the cumulative character of the innovation process, however, an investment strategy that at any point in time entails costs without generating returns may turn out to be successful at a later point in time. The corporate governance challenge is to evaluate the often-escalating demands of corporate executives for financial commitment so that innovation is not nipped in the bud, while ensuring that good money is not thrown after bad.

Of central importance to the accumulation and transformation of capabilities in knowledge-intensive industries is the *skill base* in which the firm invests in pursuing its innovative strategy. Within the firm, different functional specialties and hierarchical responsibilities characterize the division of labor and define the firm's skill base. In the effort to generate collective and cumulative learning, those who exercise strategic control can choose how to structure the skill base, including how employees move around and up the enterprise's functional and hierarchical division of labor over the course of their careers. At the same time, however, the organization of the skill base will be constrained by both the particular learning requirements of the industrial activities in which the firm has chosen to compete and the alternative employment opportunities of the personnel whom the firm wants to employ.

The innovative enterprise requires that those who exercise strategic control be able to recognize the competitive strengths and weaknesses of their firm's existing skill base and, hence, the changes in that skill base that will be necessary to mount an innovative response to competitive challenges. These strategic decision makers must also be able to mobilize committed finance to sustain investment in the skill base until it can generate higher-quality, lower-cost products than were previously available. To build the types of organizations that can generate innovation, corporate governance institutions must concern themselves with financial commitment and strategic control.

What, then, is the role of the stock market in the innovative enterprise? Does it support or undermine the innovation process? How does the stock market influence strategic control, organizational integration, and financial commitment? A research agenda that seeks answers to these questions must consider the ways in which a business enterprise actually makes use of the stock market.

For the business enterprise, the stock market can perform five distinct functions, which I have labeled alliteratively as 1) creation, 2) control, 3) combination, 4) compensation, and 5) cash (Lazonick and O'Sullivan 2004).

- *Creation.* By providing a means to transform privately owned shares in a company into tradable securities, and thus facilitating the exit of financiers from further participation in the new firms that they have funded, the stock market can encourage a flow of finance into venture creation. By providing the prospect of financial liquidity at a later point in time, therefore, the stock market can induce financial commitment at an earlier point in time.

- *Control.* By enabling the selling and buying of shares, the stock market can affect the concentration or fragmentation of shareholding in a corporation, thus influencing the relation between ownership of corporate assets and control over the allocation of corporate resources. The stock market can therefore influence who exercises strategic control over corporate resource allocation.

- *Combination.* By giving corporate stock the status of an exchange currency, the stock market enables a corporation to tender its own stock, rather than cash, as a form of payment in mergers and acquisitions (M&A). The stock market can therefore influence the financial conditions that enable one company to gain strategic control over the resources of another company.

- *Compensation.* By giving corporate stock the status of an exchange currency, the stock market enables a corporation to use its own stock, most typically in the form of stock options, as a form of compensation that can attract, retain, motivate, and reward employees. The stock market can therefore serve as a means of organizational integration.

- *Cash.* By providing liquidity to investments in a company while also limiting the liability of the owners of shares for the investments they make, the stock market increases the sources from which a company can raise cash that can be used to fund capital expenditures, pay off debt, cover operating expenses, or augment the corporate treasury. The stock market can therefore function directly as a source of financial commitment.

The functions of the stock market have changed dramatically from OEBM, which prevailed among U.S. industrial corporations in the post–World War II decades, to NEBM, which evolved out of the Silicon Valley microelectronics industry of the 1960s and has consolidated its position as the predominant high-tech business model over the last decade or so (Carpenter, Lazonick, and O'Sullivan 2003; Lazonick 2007b,c,e; Lazonick and Tulum 2008; O'Sullivan 2004, 2007, forthcoming). For each of the five functions of the stock market, let us look at these transformations in the dominant U.S. business model.

Creation

The creation function of the stock market can support innovation by inducing investors to commit financial resources to highly uncertain new ventures with no immediate prospect of a financial return. The stock market enables equity holders to exit from their investments through an IPO. The number of venture-backed IPOs in the United States averaged 112 per year for 1987–1992, 180 for 1993–1998, 267 at the peak of the Internet boom in 1999–2000, and 55 for 2001–2007. Of these venture-backed IPOs, ICT accounted for 36 percent for 1987–1992, 50 percent for 1993–1998, 81 percent for 1999–2000, and 44 percent for 2001–2007.[1]

Alternatively, equity holders can sell the firm in which they have invested to an established company in an M&A deal. The number of venture-backed M&A deals in the United States averaged 27 per year for 1987–1992, 118 for 1993–1998, 289 for 1999–2000, and 357 for 2001–2007. Of these venture-backed M&A deals, ICT accounted for 49 percent for 1987–1992, 60 percent for 1993–1998, 73 percent for 1999–2000, and 78 percent for 2001–2007. Although a well-developed stock market is not a necessary condition for such a deal, the presence of an active IPO market tends to raise the sale price because equity holders also have the possibility of exiting via an IPO. A stock-market listing by the established company also provides the acquirer with the option to make the purchase with its tradable (and hence liquid) stock rather than with cash.

Since the 1960s the creation function of the stock market has served as a powerful inducement for venture capitalists to back high-tech start-ups. Well over two-thirds of the world's venture capital is invested in the United States. California's Silicon Valley is the world's leading district for venture capital, with 38 percent of the value of investments and 31 percent of the number of deals in the United States over the period from 2001 to 2007 (PricewaterhouseCoopers 2008b). The primacy of Silicon Valley in venture capital dates back to the 1960s and early 1970s when, as recounted in Chapter 2, it became involved in a proliferation of microelectronics start-ups. In 1973 the founding of the NVCA, with its main base in Silicon Valley, signaled that venture capital had emerged as an industry in its own right (Lazonick 2007b).

It has been most advantageous for new ventures to do IPOs during periods of rampant stock market speculation: in the late 1920s, when aviation issues were hot; in the early 1960s, when electronics yielded glamor stocks; in the early 1980s, when microelectronics and biotechnology issues were the rage; and in the late 1990s, when the Internet revolution generated the dot.com boom (Cassidy 2002; O'Sullivan 2007). During such periods, the prospect of a quick and lucrative IPO or M&A deal has generated too much of an inducement to venture creation, at the ultimate expense of the speculating public. The dot.com boom of the late 1990s was particularly problematic because of the extent to which U.S. households had become active participants in the highly liquid stock markets. Subsequent investigations by the New York State Attorney General and the SEC documented the extent to which Wall Street investment banks, as insiders, had privileged access to the new shares issued in IPOs and then quickly sold them to lock in gains, as outsiders clamored to buy the stocks once they became traded on the stock market (e.g., see Chaffin 2002a,b; Moore 2002; Teather 2002; Vickers and France 2002).

Speculation in dot.coms and other Internet-related new ventures resulted in a redistribution of income from the investing public as outsiders, be they day traders or unknowing households, who played the role of "greater fools" to Wall Street as insiders. In addition, on the supply side, such speculation caused problems for the accumulation of innovative capabilities. At technology start-ups, more effort was often devoted to getting to an IPO than to developing a commercializable product. Speculation could also disrupt the innovation process at established high-tech companies when key technical and administrative personnel jumped ship to join start-ups as well as when top executives of established companies acquired technology start-ups in an attempt to convince the investing public that their companies had become New Economy and hence were worthy of higher stock prices (Carpenter, Lazonick, and O'Sullivan 2003; Lazonick and March 2008).

Control

The integration of ownership and control in a new venture provides a powerful incentive for those who have an equity stake in the firm to succeed. These equity holders include not only founder-entrepreneurs and venture capitalists (who typically play an active role in determining the strategic direction of the company) but also employees who have equity stakes either in the form of shares or stock options. The stakes of these equity holders generally become much more valuable when the firm is able to do an IPO or M&A deal.

When a privately held company is acquired, asset ownership is separated from managerial control, although the former owner-managers of the company that is sold may stay on with the acquirer as executives and will often have equity stakes in the acquirer as a result of the sale. An IPO also inherently entails a degree of separation of ownership and control, with the extent of the separation depending on the dilution of the original stakes of the founder-entrepreneurs and venture capitalists both before and after going public, as well as on whether they retain their positions of strategic control. It is common for owner-managers of U.S. high-tech companies who have had their equity stakes diluted to a small minority share to stay on in positions of strategic control after an IPO. But now they cannot assume that they, or their descendants, will retain these positions by virtue of majority ownership. In most cases, after a generation—and often much sooner—strategic control passes to salaried managers who have never held substantial equity in the company.[2]

For those companies in which there remains an integration of ownership and control, the use of a company's stock as combination and compensation currencies will generally result in substantial dilution of the stakes of founders over time. Nevertheless, in younger companies, many founders who still maintain active roles in their companies owe the enormity of their wealth to the stock market. In addition, many top executives who occupy their positions of control solely as professional managers have accumulated considerable wealth by virtue of the stock-based compensation that their boards of directors have lavished on them. From their personal standpoint, these owners and managers have no reason to cast doubt on the ideology that the maximization of shareholder value benefits not only their corporations but also the economy and even the society in which they operate.

From the shareholder-value perspective, the separation of ownership and control poses the fundamental agency problem. But the notion that salaried managers will as agents rather than principals have a natural propensity to misallocate corporate resources begs the question of how, given the ubiquity of the separation of ownership and control, the U.S. corporate enterprise drove the development of the U.S. economy during the twentieth century (see Lazonick 1992). Moreover, it is incorrect to assume that the solution to the supposed agency problem is to give salaried executives an equity stake in the publicly traded corporation by, for example, granting them stock options. A volatile stock market provides these executives with ample opportunities to gain for themselves by selling their shares even when these gains are not warranted by the productive or competitive performance of the company.

The likelihood of such an event is all the greater if, as is generally the case in United States, the realization of gains from stock option grants does not depend on the superior performance of the company's stock over a sustained period of time relative to the performance of the industry in which the company competes. Moreover, especially when the stock market is highly speculative, as was the case in the late 1990s, or when corporate profits have been high, as was the case in the mid-2000s, there are ample opportunities for those who exercise strategic control to allocate corporate resources in ways that influence stock-price movements for their own personal gain. Stock repurchases, which I discuss in some detail below, represent one such mode of resource allocation.

There are many ways to govern the behavior of corporate executives to ensure that they take actions that enhance the productive and competitive performance of their companies, but giving them U.S.-style stock-based compensation is not, in my view, one of them. Indeed, as mentioned earlier, in the wake of the bursting of the Internet bubble, the excesses of the late 1990s even brought a critique of overvalued equities from Michael Jensen, who throughout the 1980s and 1990s had been the chief academic cheerleader for maximizing shareholder value. Jensen had argued in particular for the need to increase the stock-based pay of top executives to align their interests with those of shareholders (Jensen and Murphy 1990). In "Just Say No to Wall Street: Putting a Stop to the Earnings Game," Fuller and Jensen (2002) exhort CEOs to resist the demands of Wall Street financial analysts for companies to report higher earnings to justify higher stock prices. They blame corporate executives for collaborating with Wall Street in the overvaluation of their companies' shares, with a resultant misallocation of resources. As one of their two examples (the other being Enron), Fuller and Jensen (p. 44) find fault with the telecommunications equipment company Nortel Networks for spending more than $32 billion from 1997 to 2001 on acquisitions, purchased mainly with overvalued stock instead of cash, that subsequently had to be written off or shut down. Encouraging Nortel's top management in this behavior, Fuller and Jensen recognize, was "the incentive to maintain the value of managerial and employee stock options" (p. 44).

Combination

When one company acquires another, it has to account for the value of the acquisition on its balance sheet. In the last half of the twentieth century, many U.S. companies treated acquisitions as "pooling of interests," an accounting method that enabled the acquirer to put the book value of the acquisition on its balance sheet, and thus avoid recording goodwill—the difference between market value and book value—as an intangible asset. By not having to amortize goodwill, the acquirer would show higher earnings on its profit-and-loss statement over subsequent years than if it had recorded the acquisition at its actual purchase price. The prevailing notion among corporate executives was that higher reported earnings would result in higher stock prices.

During the conglomerate boom of the 1960s, many pooling-of-interests acquisitions were made with debt or with a combination of securities and cash (Brooks 1973, pp. 160–161; Editors of *Fortune* 1970). In 1970, in response to abuses of pooling-of-interests accounting during the conglomeration era, the Accounting Principles Board (replaced in 1973 by the Financial Accounting Standards Board [FASB]), ruled, among other things, that only acquisitions made entirely with common stock could use pooling of interests (Wallman, Wallman, and Aronow 1999, p. 26; more generally, Rayburn and Powers 1991; Seligman 1995, pp. 419–429). The Internet boom of the latter half of the 1990s raised the value of shares relative to cash, thus making stock a relatively more attractive combination currency. In the boom, pooling-of-interests accounting encouraged established companies to bid for relatively young companies, many of which were revenueless start-ups with low book values.

The use of stock instead of cash as an acquisition currency became much more prevalent in the United States in the late 1990s than it had been during the late 1980s. Rappaport and Sirower (1999, pp. 147–148) argued, "What is striking about acquisitions in the 1990s, however, is the way they're being paid for. In 1988, nearly 60% of the value of large deals—those over $100 million—was paid for entirely in cash. Less than 2% was paid for in stock. But just ten years later, the profile is almost reversed: 50% of the value of all large deals in 1998 was paid for entirely in stock, and only 17% was paid for entirely in cash." The collapse of stock prices that occurred in late 2000 and the first half of 2001 led to widespread criticism of pooling of interests, and the FASB banned the further use of this method of accounting for acquisitions in July 2001 (FASB 2001).

The use of stock to make acquisitions was particularly popular among ICT companies in the late 1990s, when the speculative boom provided them with a private currency that appeared to be more valuable than cash. As Steven Ballmer, then president of Microsoft, put it in an interview in early 1998 (quoted in Cusumano and Yoffie 1998, p. 302),

> We've had to step up and either make or not make big investments on Internet time. Like WebTV. Like Hotmail. Some of them, I think, will prove smart. Maybe some of them won't prove smart. But they're not huge decisions. We have a currency [with our stock price] that makes them relatively small decisions. These deals [WebTV and Hotmail] were both done for stock. I still think it's real money, whatever it is—$400 million or so per acquisition. But I can stop and say, "OK, that's half of one percent of Microsoft." That's probably a reasonable insurance policy to pay.

No company has made such systematic use of its stock as an acquisition currency as Cisco Systems. Founded in Silicon Valley in 1984, Cisco did its IPO in 1990, a year in which it had $70 million in revenues and 254 employees. Over the course of the 1990s Cisco came to dominate the Internet router market, reaching revenues $18.9 billion in fiscal 2000, with a year-end total of 34,000 employees. From 1993 through fiscal 2003, the company did 81 acquisitions for $38.1 billion, 98 percent of which was paid in stock.

From November 2003 through September 2008, however, Cisco did another 50 acquisitions for more than $15 billion, almost entirely in cash, with stock constituting partial payment in only two of these acquisitions. Why did Cisco reverse its practice of using stock as an acquisition currency? The outlawing of pooling-of-interests accounting in July 2001 meant that an all-stock acquisition could no longer serve to inflate future reported earnings. Cisco had made ample use of this accounting device when it was permitted (Donlan 2000). Yet this explanation of Cisco's shift from stock to cash as the dominant combination currency is clearly only a partial one since the company made 10 all-stock acquisitions between July 2001 and March 2003 when the new FASB ruling was in place. At best the ruling made Cisco indifferent, from an accounting point of view, to the question of whether to use cash or stock in acquisitions. In fact, Cisco's stock price was generally higher from November 2003 to December 2004 than it had been from July 2001 to October 2003, which, all other things being equal, should have encouraged the use of stock rather than cash for acquisitions—just the opposite of what Cisco actually did.

What probably tilted Cisco toward the use of cash were the facts that it had current assets of more than $14 billion on its balance sheet in fiscal 2004 and that, given its massive stock repurchase program, the use of stock to acquire companies would have just increased the number of shares it would then have had to repurchase to reduce dilution to a desired level (see Domis 2003). Cisco also paid much less on a per-employee basis for its cash acquisitions than it had paid for its stock-based acquisitions, reflecting perhaps a preference by the owners of the acquired firms for cash rather than volatile stock that might lose its value.

In late 2005 Cisco agreed to pay $6.9 billion for Scientific-Atlanta, a Georgia-based home-entertainment company with 7,500 employees. To complete the acquisition, in early 2006 Cisco did a $6.5 billion bond issue, the first time in its history that it had ever issued debt, and indeed the largest debt debut ever by a U.S. company. Cisco claimed that it had its cash tied up abroad (Aubin 2006). Cisco would not have wanted to pay U.S. taxes on repatriated profits. At the same time, Cisco wanted to preserve its U.S. cash for, as is discussed below, its massive annual stock repurchases.

Cisco became well known for its ability to integrate its acquisitions into its organization and for a relatively low level of employee turnover (Mayer and Kenney 2004; O'Reilly and Pfeffer 2000). During the 1990s, however, not all ICT companies used their stock as an acquisition currency as effectively as Cisco Systems. As shown in detail elsewhere (see Carpenter, Lazonick, and O'Sullivan 2003; Lazonick and March 2008; and Chapter 3 of this book), at the height of the Internet boom, in an effort to emulate the Cisco strategy, Lucent Technologies and Nortel Networks used billions of dollars worth of overvalued stock to acquire technology companies that brought little in real value to the acquirer. Nevertheless, in the fervor of the Internet boom, these acquisitions were hailed as the future of ICT and in the short run helped to boost the acquirer's stock price. At both Lucent and Nortel, the CEOs who approved these acquisitions made enormous gains from stock-based compensation and bonuses before being ousted as it became evident in the downturn that their New Economy behavior had brought their Old Economy companies to the brink of bankruptcy.

Compensation

As discussed in Chapter 2, from the 1950s on, executive stock options became a widespread mode of compensation in U.S. industrial corporations. In the 1960s, a very different type of firm began to make use of stock options for a very different purpose. High-tech start-ups began to use stock options to lure nonexecutive professional, technical, and administrative employees away from secure employment at established companies. As we have seen in Chapter 2, the use of nonexecutive stock options became particularly widespread in New Economy ICT companies.

The widespread distribution of the gains from stock options within a company serves to legitimize the enormous sums that top executives derive from this mode of employee compensation. The data that I presented in Chapter 2 suggest that, despite the sluggish stock market of the first half of the 2000s, the ability of these top executives to reap these rewards remained intact. It would appear that the same cannot be said for the average New Economy employee. In the 1980s and 1990s these nonexecutive employees in effect traded employment security in the Old Economy corporation for stock-based remuneration in the New Economy corporation. In the 2000s they have faced the insecurity of NEBM, exacerbated by the globalization of the ICT labor force (see Chapter 5), but with the gains from stock options much harder to come by.

Cash

If there is a conventional wisdom about the function of the stock market in the corporate economy, it is that firms issue stock to raise cash for investment in productive resources. This view of the main function of the stock market serves to support the ideology that public shareholders are risk bearers who finance economic growth without a guaranteed contractual return and hence have residual claimant status. Over the course of the twentieth century, however, the stock market was only a relatively minor source of cash for companies. Moreover, even when, as in the boom of the late 1920s, established companies sold large amounts of overpriced stock, they typically did so to take advantage of the speculative market to restructure their balance sheets rather than to make new investments (see O'Sullivan 2004). As a result of this financial restructuring, these companies were better positioned to withstand the subsequent stock market crash and downturn in economic activity.

In contrast, in the Internet boom of the late 1990s, it tended to be new ventures that took advantage of the speculative stock market to raise huge sums through initial and secondary public offerings that could then be used to fund investment in productive resources. A dramatic example is Sycamore Networks, an optical networking company founded in February 1998 in Massachusetts' Route 128 corridor by two men who had already built up and sold a highly successful data equipment company, Cascade. With one customer (whose top executives were given "friends and family" stock options in Sycamore), previous year revenues of $11 million, losses of $19 million, and 155 employees, Sycamore did its IPO in October 1999, raising $284 million for less than 10 percent of its outstanding shares (Bulkeley 1999; Carpenter, Lazonick, and O'Sullivan 2003; Warner 2000). In December 1999 Sycamore ranked one-hundred-seventeenth in market capitalization in the United States, just behind Emerson Electric, a company that was founded in 1890 and that had revenues of $14.3 billion and 117,000 employees! Sycamore then did a secondary offering in March 2000, at the very apex of the boom, with its stock at $150, netting another $1.2 billion for the corporate treasury. At the same time, top executives and board members of Sycamore sold a portion of their own stock holdings for $726 million (Gimein et al. 2002).

In effect, those who speculated in Sycamore's stock permitted the company's top executives and venture capitalists to gain huge returns from the company before what remained a start-up had gotten off the ground. The company did show a profit of $20.4 million in 2000, but from 2001 through 2008 (fiscal year ending July 31) rung up losses of $829 million. On September 27, 2001, Sycamore's stock price fell to $3.29, down from $107 a year earlier, and a year later it had fallen further, to $2.36. Since then, the stock price has fluctuated between $2.30 (October 9, 2002) and $6.29 (January 16, 2004), and on October 10, 2008, it stood at $2.70. Nevertheless, the extent of its fund-raising at the peak of the speculative boom plus some astute financial investments meant that, as of July 31, 2008, Sycamore was still sitting on $821 million in cash and short-term investments, down from $908 million a year earlier (Sycamore Networks 2008).[3]

Less speculative and more productive among New Economy ICT companies in the 1980s and 1990s was Nextel's 1999 stock offering of $2.4 billion as part of an externally financed "war chest" to fund its expansion in mobile phones (Knight 1999). Founded in 1987 as Fleet Call, a radio dispatch company, Nextel Communications had revenues of $3.3 billion and 15,000 employees in 1999, but it had sustained losses of $4.6 billion over the previous years. Indeed, the company was in the red in every year from 1990 through 2001, for a total loss of more than $9.2 billion. Nextel, however, steadily increased its revenues, and the company showed a $1.9 billion profit in 2002. By 2004 Nextel was one-hundred-fifty-seventh on the Fortune 500 list, with revenues of $13.4 billion, net income of $3.0 billion, and 19,000 employees. In 2005 Nextel merged with Sprint in a $35 billion deal.

Some New Economy start-ups of the 1980s and 1990s that experienced rapid growth in the 1990s had little if any resort to the stock market as a source of funds. For example, the only public stock issue that Cisco Systems has ever done was for $48 million when it went public in 1990. In that year the company had $70 million in revenues, net cash from operating activities of $10 million, and capital expenditures of $4 million. Subsequently, until its 2005 bond issue of $6.5 billion to acquire Scientific-Atlanta, Cisco relied entirely on internally generated funds to finance its growth. From 1991 through 2008 (fiscal year ending July 26), Cisco received payments totaling $18.3 billion for its shares, but these were sales to employees exercising their stock options and doing employee stock purchases, not public stock market issues.

Indeed, in the 2000s, Cisco has become a supplier of funds to the stock market rather than vice versa. Cisco did its first stock repurchases in 1995–1997 for a total of $508 million. Then, as speculators boosted Cisco's stock price from $8.51 on December 12, 1997, to $80.06 on March 27, 2000 (at which point the 16-year-old enterprise had the highest market capitalization of any company in the world), there was no reason for Cisco to do buybacks.[4] Over the next 30 months, however, Cisco's stock price plummeted so that on October 8, 2002, at $8.60, it was just 1 percent higher than it had been on December 12, 1997. In an effort to support its stock price, Cisco repurchased $1.9 billion worth of shares in 2002, $6.0 billion in 2003, $9.1 billion in 2004, $10.2 billion in 2005, $8.3 billion in 2006, $7.7 billion in 2007, and $10.4 billion in 2008, for a total of $53.6 billion over the seven years. A highly profitable company during these years, Cisco's stock price rose to a high of $34.08 on November 6, 2007, but fell to as low as $14.47 on November 20, 2008.

Cisco's expenditures on stock buybacks over the period 2002–2008 were almost double its expenditures of $27.0 billion on R&D. Over these seven years, buybacks were 144 percent of Cisco's net after-tax income. While Cisco remains an innovative and highly profitable company, one might hypothesize that Cisco's stock price was primarily driven by innovation from 1990 through 1997, by speculation and its collapse from 1998 through 2002, and by manipulation in the form of buybacks from 2003 through 2008 (see Chapter 7).

In the 2000s Cisco's financial behavior was typical of the largest U.S. companies, including those that, like Cisco, compete in high-tech industries. The overall trend of the "cash" function in major U.S. business corporations has been to give money to the stock market, not get money from it. For the 292 companies in the S&P 500 Index in January 2008 that were publicly traded in 1981, repurchases as a proportion of net income reached a local peak in 1987 when many companies sought to support their stock prices after the market crash in October of that year. Repurchases by these 292 companies rose sharply from 1995 on and surpassed dividends for the first time in 1997 (Dittmar and Dittmar 2004). On average, each of the 500 companies in the S&P 500 Index in January 2008 expended $513 million on cash dividends and $1,184 million on stock repurchases in 2007. In recent years stock repurchases have played a leading role as a manipulative mode of resource allocation that supports stock prices.

Figure 6.2 shows the payout ratios and mean payout levels for the 459 companies in the S&P 500 Index in January 2008 that were publicly traded in 1997.[5] Figure 6.2 includes such New Economy companies as Microsoft, Oracle, Cisco, and Dell, which were either not publicly listed or not in existence in 1980, but which have been big repurchasers of their own stock. Many New Economy companies (for example, Cisco, Dell, and Oracle) pay no dividends. Over the 11-year period shown in the figure, these 453 companies distributed a total of $1.7 trillion in cash dividends, an average of $3.8 billion per company, and spent $2.5 trillion on repurchases, an average of $5.5 billion per company. In 2007, as shown in Figure 6.2, these companies averaged $553 million in dividend payments and $1,194 million in stock repurchases. Combined, the

**Figure 6.2 Ratios of Cash Dividends and Stock Repurchases to
Net Income and Mean Dividend Payments and Stock
Repurchases among the S&P 500, 1997–2007**

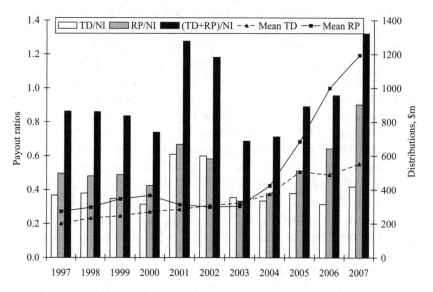

NOTE: Data for 453 corporations in the S&P 500 Index in January 2008 that were publicly traded in 1997. RP = repurchases, TD = total dividends (common and preferred),
and NI = net income (after tax with inventory evaluation and capital consumption
adjustments).
SOURCE: S&P Compustat database, 1997–2006; company 10-K filings, 2007.

500 companies in the S&P 500 Index in January 2008 repurchased $486
billion of their own stock in 2006 and $592 billion in 2007.

What kinds of companies are the largest repurchasers? Table 6.1
lists the top 50 repurchasers for the period of 2000–2007 among companies in the S&P 500 stock-market index for January 2008. From 2000
to 2003, the 50 top repurchasers for the years 2000–2007 averaged $1.8
billion–$1.9 billion in buybacks per year, but this expenditure steadily
climbed to $6.0 billion in 2007. As can be seen, these 50 companies are
distributed across a variety of industries, including 15 companies (in
italicized type) in financial services (which includes life and property
insurance), 10 companies (in bold type) in ICT, 4 companies in pharmaceuticals, and 3 companies in petroleum refining.

As shown in Table 6.2, 19 of the top 50 distributed more cash to shareholders in the form of stock buybacks than they generated in net after-tax income from 2000 to 2007, while another 7 companies repurchased stock equivalent to between 90 and 99 percent of their net income. The combined payouts for repurchases and dividends exceeded net income at 23 of the top 50 companies in this same period and were between 90 and 99 percent of net income at another 9 companies. From 2000 to 2007, repurchase payouts were greater than net income at 5 of the 10 ICT companies among the top repurchasers, while repurchase and dividend payouts were greater than net income at another 3.

How does the allocation of resources to stock repurchases affect the allocation of resources to other corporate objectives, including innovative investments that could result in higher-quality, lower-cost products? Given their technological, market, and competitive characteristics, the different industries represented in Table 6.1 raise different issues for business and government policy. In this discussion, I confine myself to the ICT industries whose major companies are well-represented among the largest repurchasers.[6]

Nine of the top 50, shown in bold in Table 6.2, had R&D expenditures that exceeded 10 percent of sales and hence can be classified as "high-tech." Five of these companies—Microsoft, Cisco, Intel, Oracle, and TI—are in ICT, with the other four in pharmaceuticals. Repurchase payouts exceeded R&D expenditures at all of these companies, as well as at the other five ICT companies—IBM, HP, Dell, AT&T Inc., and Comcast—whose R&D expenditures were under 10 percent of sales.

The case of Microsoft, which distributed 143 percent of its 2000–2007 net income to shareholders, is instructive in revealing how executives at even the most dominant high-tech companies have succumbed to demands from Wall Street that they use their earnings to boost stock prices. In June 2004, with a dividend yield of just 0.6 percent on its stock, Microsoft's corporate treasury was bursting with $56 billion in cash and short-term investments, and the balance sheet showed no debt. The highly profitable company, moreover, had generated almost $16 billion in cash flow in the previous year. Given these conditions, in mid-2004 Wall Street began to exert pressure on Microsoft to increase its distributions to shareholders and increase its stock price. A Goldman Sachs report by its software analyst suggested that, by borrowing $30 billion and using $70 billion in cash balances, Microsoft could do

Table 6.1 Top 50 Repurchasers of Stock, 2000–2007, among Corporations in the S&P 500 Index in January 2008

RP Rank 2000–2007	Company	Fortune industry classification, 2007	Fortune rank, 2007	RP ($m) 2006	RP ($m) 2007	RP ($m) 2000–2007
1	Exxon Mobil	Petroleum refining	2	29,558	31,822	108,304
2	**Microsoft**	Computer software	44	19,207	27,575	81,747
3	**IBM**	Information technology services	15	8,022	18,828	62,318
4	*Bank Of America*	Commercial banks	9	13,660	3,790	55,674
5	Pfizer	Pharmaceuticals	47	6,979	9,994	50,132
6	*General Electric*	Diversified financials	6	10,512	14,913	48,263
7	**Cisco Systems**	Network/communications equipment	71	8,295	7,681	43,129
8	**Intel**	Semiconductors/electronic components	60	4,593	2,788	41,575
9	*Citigroup*	Commercial banks	8	7,125	663	37,141
10	Procter & Gamble	Household & personal products	23	16,830	5,578	36,324
11	**Hewlett-Packard**	Computers, office equipment	14	7,779	10,887	33,721
12	*Goldman Sachs*	Securities	201	7,817	8,956	30,186
13	Johnson & Johnson	Pharmaceuticals	35	6,722	5,607	26,694
14	**Dell**	Computers, office equipment	34	3,026	3,026	25,545
15	Time Warner	Entertainment	49	13,660	6,231	25,165
16	**Oracle**	Computer software	137	2,067	3,937	23,939
17	*Wells Fargo*	Commercial banks	41	1,965	7,418	23,243
18	**AT&T Inc.**	Telecommunications	10	2,678	10,390	21,628
19	*JPMorgan Chase*	Commercial banks	12	3,938	8,178	21,248
20	*Merrill Lynch*	Securities	30	9,088	5,272	21,028
21	PepsiCo	Food, consumer products	59	3,010	4,312	20,704
22	UnitedHealth Group	Health care: insurance & managed care	25	2,345	6,599	20,678

23	Amgen	Pharmaceuticals	173	2,000	5,100	20,361
24	Wal-Mart Stores	General merchandisers	1	3,580	1,718	19,633
25	*Morgan Stanley*	Securities	21	3,376	3,753	19,050
26	Chevron	Petroleum refining	3	5,033	7,036	18,815
27	Altria Group	Tobacco	61	1,254	0	18,213
28	Walt Disney	Entertainment	67	6,898	6,923	17,815
29	*American Express*	Diversified financials	75	4,093	3,572	17,643
30	United Parcel Service	Mail, package, freight delivery	46	2,460	2,639	17,374
31	*Lehman Brothers*	Securities	37	2,678	2,605	16,672
32	CBS	Entertainment	181	6	3,351	16,519
33	Home Depot	Specialty retailers	22	3,040	6,684	16,388
34	**Texas Instruments**	Semiconductors/electronic components	185	5,302	4,886	16,296
35	Merck	Pharmaceuticals	101	1,002	1,430	15,984
36	*Wachovia*	Commercial banks	38	4,513	1,196	15,664
37	3M	Miscellaneous	100	2,351	3,239	13,521
38	*Washington Mutual*	Savings institutions	97	3,039	3,497	13,271
39	McDonald's	Food services	106	2,959	3,943	12,878
40	Boeing	Aerospace and defense	27	1,698	2,775	12,876
41	*Allstate*	Insurance: property & casualty	64	1,770	3,606	12,334
42	*US Bancorp*	Commercial banks	122	2,798	1,983	12,313
43	Anheuser-Busch	Beverages	149	746	2,707	11,909
44	WellPoint	Health care: insurance & managed care	33	5,439	6,151	11,591
45	*Prudential Financial*	Insurance: life, health	74	2,512	3,000	10,889
46	Coca-Cola	Beverages	83	2,416	1,838	10,589
47	Kimberly-Clark	Household & personal products	136	762	2,813	10,002

236

Table 6.1 (continued)

RP Rank 2000–2007	Company	*Fortune* industry classification, 2007	*Fortune* rank, 2007	RP ($m) 2006	RP ($m) 2007	RP ($m) 2000–2007
48	ConocoPhillips	Petroleum refining	5	925	7,001	9,850
49	**Comcast**	Telecommunications	79	2,347	3,102	9,489
50	Cigna	Health care: insurance & managed care	141	2,765	1,185	9,434

NOTE: RP = repurchases of common and preferred stock. Bold indicates ICT companies, and italics indicate financial services companies. Data are for the 2007 fiscal year of the companies.

SOURCE: S&P Compustat database, 2000–2006; company 10-K filings, 2007; *Fortune* (2008).

Table 6.2   Payout Ratios and R&D Intensity Compared with Repurchases Intensity for the Top 50 Repurchasers of Stock, 2000–2007, among Corporations in the S&P 500 Index in January 2008

RP Rank 2000–07	Company	RP/ NI (%)	TD/ NI (%)	(TD+RP)/ NI (%)	R&D/ sales (%)	RP/ sales (%)
1	Exxon Mobil	47	29	75	0.3	5.1
2	**Microsoft**	80	63	143	**15.9**	29.1
3	IBM	99	16	115	5.6	8.7
4	Bank Of America	55	49	104	0.0	9.4
5	**Pfizer**	76	61	137	**17.9**	14.8
6	General Electric	35	50	85	1.7	4.2
7	**Cisco Systems**	151	0	151	**16.2**	22.8
8	**Intel**	93	18	110	**14.4**	15.8
9	Citigroup	31	36	68	0.0	4.4
10	Procter & Gamble	80	44	124	3.1	8.7
11	Hewlett-Packard	128	33	160	4.7	5.8
12	Goldman Sachs	72	8	80	0.0	8.8
13	**Johnson & Johnson**	39	37	76	**12.6**	7.6
14	Dell	136	0	136	1.0	8.4
15	Time Warner	−56	−4	−60	0.4	8.4
16	**Oracle**	92	0	92	**12.4**	28.4
17	Wells Fargo	46	43	89	0.0	7.9
18	AT&T Inc.	25	65	90	0.1	4.8
19	JPMorgan Chase	36	51	87	0.0	3.9
20	Merrill Lynch	56	17	74	0.0	6.0
21	PepsiCo	64	35	99	0.2	8.8
22	UnitedHealth Group	95	1	95	0.0	4.3
23	**Amgen**	126	0	126	**27.6**	27.7
24	Wal−Mart Stores	31	20	51	0.0	1.2
25	Morgan Stanley	46	23	69	0.0	4.6
26	Chevron	17	35	52	0.2	1.5
27	Altria Group	26	56	82	1.1	3.4
28	Walt Disney	92	27	118	0.0	7.6
29	American Express	69	18	87	0.0	8.3
30	United Parcel Service	64	34	99	0.0	5.8
31	Lehman Brothers	92	10	102	0.0	6.9
32	CBS	−70	−9	−78	0.0	10.3
33	Home Depot	54	16	70	0.0	5.1
34	**Texas Instruments**	108	10	119	**16.3**	17.7
35	**Merck**	34	53	87	**11.1**	6.3

Table 6.2 (continued)

RP Rank 2000–07	Company	RP/ NI (%)	TD/ NI (%)	(TD+RP)/ NI (%)	R&D/ sales (%)	RP/ sales (%)
36	Wachovia	44	55	100	0.0	6.0
37	3M	58	43	101	6.3	8.8
38	Washington Mutual	62	51	113	0.0	8.3
39	McDonald's	64	30	94	0.0	8.8
40	Boeing	69	33	102	4.1	2.9
41	Allstate	55	26	81	0.0	4.7
42	US Bancorp	44	53	98	0.0	9.9
43	Anheuser–Busch	69	37	106	0.0	10.3
44	WellPoint	99	0	99	0.0	5.0
45	Prudential Financial	75	16	90	0.0	4.6
46	Coca–Cola	30	53	83	0.0	5.9
47	Kimberly–Clark	62	43	105	1.7	8.2
48	ConocoPhillips	17	18	35	0.1	1.2
49	Comcast	112	0	112	0.0	6.4
50	Cigna	133	13	147	0.0	6.6

NOTE: RP = repurchases of common and preferred stock, TD = common and preferred cash dividends, NI = net after-tax income, and R&D = research and development expenditure. Bold indicates companies with R&D expenditures that exceeded 10 percent of sales.

SOURCE: S&P Compustat database, 2000–2006; company 10-K filings, 2007.

a $100 billion stock repurchase (Bishop 2004). A month later, in July 2004, the Microsoft board approved a $30 billion repurchase plan to take place over four years, a doubling of the dividend from $0.16 per annum to $0.08 quarterly, and a special one-time dividend that, at $3 per share (over 12 percent of the current share price), totaled $32.64 billion.

The company press release that announced these distributions assured the public that "this payout will not affect Microsoft's commitment to research and development to fuel growth in the years ahead" (Microsoft 2004). In support of this commitment, it quoted Chairman Gates: "We see incredible potential for our innovation to help businesses, individuals and governments around the world accomplish their goals, and we will continue to be one of the top innovators in our industry—as evidenced by the fact that we will file for more than 3,000 patents this fiscal year." The press release also quoted CEO Ballmer: "We will continue to make major investments across all our businesses and maintain our position as a leading innovator in the industry, but we can now also provide up to $75 billion in total value to shareholders over the next four years."

Just over a year and a half later, on April 27, 2006, Microsoft announced that it would be making major new technology investments, including a large-scale commitment of resources to its online business to confront Google and Yahoo!. The company predicted earnings per share of $1.36 to $1.41 for fiscal 2007, well below the expectations of Wall Street analysts of $1.57. Rick Sherland, the same Goldman Sachs analyst who had previously encouraged Microsoft to do a $100 billion repurchase, was not pleased with the Microsoft announcement: "It's bad to surprise the Street. It's harmful to the stock because investors are looking for the rewards of this big product cycle next year flowing through to earnings" (quoted in Romano 2006). The next day Microsoft's stock price fell by more than 11 percent, reducing the company's market capitalization by some $30 billion. The stock price continued to decline during most of May, amid criticism from Wall Street's top-rated software analysts that Microsoft was a mature firm that had attracted "value investors" who wanted returns from dividends and buybacks. An article from *Bloomberg News* (Bass 2006a) quoted Richard Pzena, head of an investment company that held 14.3 million Microsoft shares, as saying, "They are not managing the business with an acknowledgment the shareholders have changed. People expecting 25 percent annual growth don't own the stock anymore."

On May 31 Ballmer defended the company's "big, bold bets" on Internet technology at a conference at Sanford C. Bernstein & Company, the Wall Street investment research firm (Bass 2006b). Wall Street remained critical of Microsoft's technology strategy (*New York Times* 2006).[7] Microsoft's stock price, which had trended downward during May but had moved upward in the days before the Bernstein conference, resumed its decline, reaching a low on June 13 at almost 21 percent down from its level on April 27. Finally, on July 20, Microsoft announced that it was accelerating by two years the completion of its $30 billion buyback program. At the same time, Microsoft also announced a plan to repurchase another $20 billion in stock from 2007 to 2011. Over the next four days, Microsoft's stock price rose by almost 7 percent.

The Microsoft example illustrates the pressure that Wall Street can exert on even the most powerful high-tech company to allocate its cash flow to "create" shareholder value. Wall Street's argument is that Microsoft is now a mature company that has lost its innovative capability, at least relative to the start-ups that the U.S. economy is adept at spawning. As a mature company, the analysts argue, Microsoft should disgorge its cash flow to shareholders. As far as these "old" New Economy companies are concerned, the Wall Street consensus is that what I call manipulation, not innovation, should be driving the stock market.

Should U.S. high-tech companies be allocating more of their financial resources to R&D rather than stock repurchases? During the 2000s, the Semiconductor Industry Association and its leading company, Intel, have been lobbying the U.S. government to spend more on nanotechnology research (Electronic News 2005). Yet on its Web site, Intel touts the cumulative $63.2 billion in stock repurchases that it has done since 1990 (Intel 2008b). Given that companies like Intel have benefited greatly from government investments in the high-tech knowledge base in the past, why should not a portion of Intel's buyback expenditures be devoted instead to supporting the U.S. national nanotechnology research effort?[8]

Since the 1980s U.S. corporate executives have embraced the ideology that the performance of their companies and the economy are best served by the maximization of shareholder value. It is an ideology that, among other things, says that any attempt by the government to interfere in the allocation of resources can only undermine economic performance. In practice, what shareholder ideology has meant for corporate resource allocation is that, when companies reap more profits, they spend a substantial proportion of them on stock repurchases in an effort to boost their stock prices.

There are many alternative ways that corporate executives could productively allocate these massive amounts of resources. They could use these funds to sustain the employment of experienced employees who currently are being let go, sometimes to be hired back at lower wages as contractors. Such expenditures should not be make-work but rather should reflect innovative thinking on the part of corporate executives as to how the productive resources available to the firm can be utilized to generate higher-quality, lower-cost goods and services. Money spent on buybacks could be allocated to provide much-needed public services in the communities in which the companies have grown up. Or, as already indicated, instead of doing buybacks, companies could pay higher taxes to support government initiatives to invest in the technologies of the future. In short, rather than a "take the money and run" approach pursued through stock repurchases and stock-option exercises, corporate executives could allocate resources to support sustainable prosperity.

WHY DO COMPANIES REPURCHASE THEIR OWN STOCK?

Toward the beginning of this chapter, I critiqued the ideology of maximizing shareholder value. Shareholders are not the only class of participants in the corporation who make investments without a contractually guaranteed return. Indeed, given the ease with which a public shareholder can create and sever her relation with any particular company by simply buying and selling shares, it can be questioned whether the investments that she makes contribute to the development and utilization of the company's productive resources, and if so how. I have argued that, to answer this question, we need a theory of innovative enterprise on the basis of which we can analyze the productive functions that the stock market actually performs in the publicly traded corporation.

The most obvious way in which the public shareholder can contribute to the development and utilization of a company's productive capabilities is by providing the company with cash that it can use to invest in such capabilities. Yet the evidence suggests that, in the U.S. case at least, the stock market has been a relatively unimportant source of cash for corporate investment, except possibly in periods of rampant stock market speculation. In biotechnology, for example, at certain points since 1980, through IPOs, young companies that are still years away from developing a commercial product and that face fundamental uncertainty about whether these products will ever emerge have been able to raise substantial cash from the stock market for investment in drug development (Lazonick and Tulum 2008). For more mature companies, however, the stock market has become a "use" rather than a "source" of funds as stock repurchases have become a systematic and widespread feature of corporate resource allocation.

Why do companies repurchase their own stock?[9] The agency theory argument is that these distributions to shareholders represent "free cash flow." The notion that corporations should distribute the free cash flow to shareholders is central to the agency theory argument that the economy is run more efficiently when corporate executives seek to maximize shareholder value. The massive stock repurchases that have characterized the 2000s manifest the triumph of this shareholder value ideology.

Ideology apart, there are problems with the free cash flow argument for the allocation of corporate resources. Given technological, market, and competitive uncertainty, we cannot expect that even the most informed corporate decision maker will be able to make a reasonably accurate forecast of the company's stream of earnings over a period as short as, say, five years. Yet without such an accurate forecast, one cannot determine, at any point in time, the extent to which the cash flow available is in fact free. As the recent subprime mortgage debacle illustrates, a series of profitable years can give way to a period of losses during which the cash flow that seemed to be free can suddenly be sorely needed.

Even if one could accept a forecast of a future stream of earnings as being reasonably accurate, the determination of the relevant cost of capital with which to derive the present value of those earnings is a subjective measure set by those who make allocation decisions. Given that top executives, with their stock-based compensation, stand to gain from repurchases, we can expect that they will tend to set the relevant cost of capital high, thus biasing their decisions against making investments in productive capabilities for an uncertain future and hence designating a larger proportion of the company's cash flow as free. In contrast, if corporate decision makers were to recognize, and choose to confront, the technological, market, and competitive uncertainties inherent in the innovation process, they would understand the need to conserve the company's cash flow to respond to such fundamental exigencies as changes in technology, fluctuations in market demand, and the rise of new competitors.

A corporate executive who rejects agency theory and accepts innovation theory might want to argue that her company does buybacks so that its stock will be attractive as a combination and compensation currency, which in turn will support the accumulation of innovative capabilities. There are, however, problems with such an argument.[10]

When stock is used as a combination currency to acquire other companies, there is no doubt that a company with a soaring stock price will have a competitive edge. But that soaring stock price will tend to be the result of innovation or speculation rather than manipulation through stock repurchases. As we have seen for the case of Cisco Systems, it is likely that companies that are doing large-scale stock repurchases will refrain from using stock as a combination currency. Otherwise, all other things being equal, stock repurchases would have to be even greater to offset dilution from stock-based acquisitions.

Companies often state explicitly in their financial statements that they are doing stock repurchases to offset dilution from their stock option programs.[11] Even from a shareholder-value perspective, the economic rationale for this argument is not clear. If a company that seeks to maximize shareholder value deems it worthwhile to partially remunerate employees with stock options, it should see that remuneration as adding to rather than subtracting from earnings per share. True, these additions to earnings per share may only accrue in years to come, but then, from the shareholder-value perspective, the issue is simply one of whether remuneration in the form of stock options (or any other mode of compensation) is expected to yield positive net present value of future earnings at the appropriate discount rate.

From the perspective of innovation theory, employees are supposed to reap the rewards from stock options in future years, when the company's stock price has risen as the innovative investments of the company generate profits. Given the prospects of a rising stock price, innovative companies can make use of employee stock options as a form of remuneration to attract, retain, motivate, and recognize employees.[12] Systematic stock repurchases, such as those that Intel advertises on its Web site, may aid this remuneration strategy by convincing employees that the company is committed to keeping its stock price high and on the rise. Alternatively, however, employees who understand the investment requirements of innovative enterprise may take the view that, in allocating resources to stock repurchases, the company has foregone critical investments in innovation required to make it competitive in the future. If so, they may see systematic repurchases as a sign that it is time to cash in their vested options and leave the company. Objectively, the critical question (for both academic researchers and long-term corporate employees) is whether a company can use its cash flow to do repurchases and boost stock prices today without undermining the financial commitment that, particularly in highly competitive global industries, is required to fund innovation for tomorrow.

Top executives often simply argue that, in doing stock repurchases, they, as corporate decision makers, are "signaling" confidence that their company's stock price will rise over the long term (Louis and White 2007; Vermaelen 2005, chap. 3). Yet, from a financial point of view, such an investment would only make sense if one could expect that at some point in the future when speculation has resulted in an overvalued stock the corporation would turn from being a purchaser to a seller of its own stock. Otherwise, corporate executives are taking the position that their stock can never be overvalued, even in a highly speculative boom. According to the "signaling" argument, we should have seen massive sales of corporate stock in the speculative boom of the late 1990s, as was the case with U.S. industrial corporations in the speculative boom of the late 1920s. Instead, in the boom of the late 1990s, corporate executives, as personal investors, sold their own stock to reap speculative gains (often to the tune of tens of millions, and in some cases even hundreds of millions, of dollars). Yet, if anything, these same corporate executives, as corporate decision makers, used corporate funds to repurchase shares, thus attempting to push speculative stock prices even higher, to their own personal gain. Given the extent to which stock repurchases have become a systematic mode of corporate resource allocation, and given the extent to which through this manipulation of their corporation's stock price top executives have enriched themselves personally in the process, there is every reason to believe that, in the absence of legislation that restricts both stock repurchases and gains from stock options, executive behavior that places personal interests ahead of corporate interests will continue in the future.[13]

Stock repurchases are, in my view, central to a massive redistribution process that in the United States has made the rich even richer at the expense of stable and equitable economic growth. It is a process that received ample encouragement from the Jobs and Growth Tax Relief Reconciliation Act of 2003, which reduced tax rates on dividends from 38.6 percent (the top tax on ordinary income) to 15 percent and on capital gains (including of course those derived from selling stock) from 20 percent to 15 percent (McNamee and Scherreik 2003). Despite the fact that the 2003 act reduced the tax on dividends even more than the tax on capital gains, since 2002, as we have seen, U.S. corporations have increased stock repurchases even more than they have increased dividends (Blouin, Raedy, and Shackleford 2007).[14]

The main reason, in my view, is that repurchases tend to boost stock prices, which in turn increases the returns from stock options (see Fenn and Liang 2001; Grullon and Ikenberry 2000, pp. 41–42; Hsieh and Wang 2006; Jolls 1998; Kahle 2002; Weisbenner 2000).[15] As I have shown for the case of leading ICT companies in Table 2.4, the gains from stock options of the people at the top of the corporation are typically hundreds of times, and often thousands of times, the average gains per employee in their company. Certainly, as in the late 1990s, when the stock market moved up rapidly, millions of nonexecutive employees who held stock options benefited, and at companies like Cisco and Microsoft smaller numbers of nonexecutive employees benefited immensely. For many if not most nonexecutive employees, however, the gains from stock options were ephemeral, as the decline of the early 2000s was followed by the jobless recovery of 2003 in which the acceleration of offshoring played an important role.

There has been virtually no public policy debate in the United States over the practice of buybacks, its acceleration in recent years, or the implications for both the distribution of income and economic growth. In the summer of 2008, however, changes seemed to be afoot. On July 31, 2008, after Exxon Mobil—by far the largest repurchaser of stock (see Table 6.1)—had announced record second quarter profits of $11.7 billion and stock buybacks of $8.8 billion, prominent congressional Democrats took aim at stock repurchases by the big oil companies (Menendez 2008).[16] Senator Charles Schumer (D-NY) was quoted as saying, "They [the big oil companies] tell us they want to do more domestic production. They tell us they need to drill offshore. They tell us that they can find oil on the mainland. And what do they do with their profits? They buy back stock, simply to increase their share price" (Hays and Ivanovich 2008).

As we have seen, it is not only the oil companies that are doing multibillion dollar buybacks. The practice pervades the U.S. economy. Are top executives who spend much of their time and energy thinking about how to manipulate the stock market through stock repurchases devoting sufficient time and energy to thinking about how to confront the technological, market, and competitive uncertainties with which, in a globalized economy, even the most powerful companies must be concerned?

From a public policy perspective, should the people who exercise strategic control over the corporate allocation of resources have such overwhelming personal incentives to allocate resources for the sole purpose of boosting their companies' stock prices? Should high-tech companies be doing massive and systematic repurchases while appealing to the government to finance investment in the technologies of the future? Should companies that make high profits by charging high oil prices or high drug prices be using these profits to make massive and systematic buybacks instead of spending more on discovering oil and developing drugs? Or should the prices that these oil and drug companies charge be regulated along with a prohibition on stock repurchases? As in the cases of the Wall Street banks, should the government be in the business of bailing out companies that run into trouble when these companies would be better positioned to bail themselves out but for the massive and systematic repurchases that they have done in recent years?

To ask these questions is to raise the larger public policy issue of how many resources should go into propping up the stock market, and indeed, the questions of why the stock market has become so central to the operation of the U.S. economy and whether, if we wish to have sustainable prosperity, it should remain so. A vital first step in addressing these questions is to jettison the ideology that maximizing shareholder value leads to the highest common good. The rejection of the ideology of shareholder value is, in my view, a prerequisite for the formulation and implementation of the policies for sustainable prosperity that I shall discuss in the concluding chapter of this book.

Notes

1. Venture-backed IPO and M&A data are from Thomson Financial Venture Xperts. See also Lazonick (2007d, pp. 1001–1004).
2. For documentation of the separation of ownership and control in the Old Economy and New Economy ICT companies in Tables 1.6 and 1.7, see Lazonick (2007d, pp. 1008–1009).
3. In 2005 Sycamore showed a gain from the sale of investments of $467 million, increasing its cash and near-cash on hand from $45 million at the end of fiscal 2004 to $508 million at the end of fiscal 2005 (Sycamore Networks 2006, pp. 24–25).

4. In any case, given Cisco's pace of acquisitions for 1998–2000 and the extent to which it used the pooling-of-interests method to account for their cost, Cisco was prevented from doing buybacks because of an SEC rule that prohibited stock repurchases within six months of a pooling-of-interests acquisition (McCarthy 1999, p. 94). FASB outlawed pooling-of-interests accounting in July 2001, and the Cisco board authorized a $3 billion stock repurchase on September 13, 2001 (Nguyen 2001). The press viewed the Cisco buyback plan as a patriotic move to prevent a collapse of stock prices when the stock market reopened on September 17 after being closed for four sessions in the wake of the 9/11 terrorist attacks (e.g., Rapoport 2001). Indeed, the SEC relaxed the rules on the timing of buybacks during a stock-trading session to encourage companies to repurchase their shares when the stock market reopened (Gordon 2001). Following Cisco's lead, many companies responded by announcing buyback programs (see Reuters News 2001).

5. For each company, I treat the fiscal year as the calendar year in which its fiscal year ends. For example, I regard the $7.691 billion in stock repurchases that Wal-Mart did in its fiscal year ending on January 31, 2008, as having been made in 2008, and the $1.718 billion that it did in the fiscal year ending on January 31, 2007, as having been made in 2007.

6. Currently I am engaged in statistical research that seeks to identify the industry- and firm-level determinants of stock repurchases across the S&P 500 companies as well as case-study research to assess the impacts of stock repurchases on the productive capabilities of the companies that make them. For a preliminary discussion of the implications of stock buybacks for the oil, financial services, and pharmaceutical industries, see Lazonick (2008d).

7. The full text of the Bernstein and Co. conference is available from Factiva, including Ballmer's complete remarks (Voxant FD Wire 2006).

8. A similar type of question can be asked of the U.S. pharmaceutical industry. The four pharmaceutical companies in Tables 6.1 and 6.2 are among those that argue that they need to charge higher drug prices in the United States than in other parts of the world to fund R&D. Yet, as can be seen in Table 6.2, these companies have used substantial proportions of their earnings to do repurchases (Lazonick 2008c; Lazonick and Tulum 2008).

9. For alternative hypotheses posed by the considerable academic literature on the topic, see Dittmar (2000); Jun, Jung, and Walking (2008); and Kahle (2002).

10. For an in-depth analysis, in the context of the Internet boom and bust of the late 1990s and early 2000s, of the conditions under which the use of stock as a combination and compensation currency can support or undermine the innovation process, see Carpenter, Lazonick, and O'Sullivan (2003).

11. Through fiscal year 2004, Dell stated explicitly that the purpose of its share repurchase program was "to manage the dilution resulting from shares issued under Dell's equity compensation plans" (Dell 2005, p. 23). In 2005 and 2006, however, the company stated that the purposes of repurchases were "both to distribute cash to shareholders and to manage dilution resulting from shares issued under Dell's equity compensation plan" (Dell 2006, p. 16; Dell 2007, p. 18). Similarly, prior to 2001 Sun explicitly tied repurchases to stock-based compensation plans, but

in 2001 the firm introduced "a new opportunistic stock repurchase program to acquire shares in the open market at any time" (Sun Microsystems 2004, p. 84). Of the value of shares that Sun repurchased in 2001, 2002, and 2003, 47 percent, 25 percent, and 100 percent, respectively, were bought under the opportunistic plan. HP has stated that it repurchases shares "to manage the dilution created by shares issued under employee stock plans as well as to repurchase shares opportunistically" (HP 2006, p. 30). In fact, for most of the ICT companies in Table 2.1, the number of shares repurchased was well in excess of the number of stock options exercised over the period 2000–2007; at IBM this ratio was 4.32, at Texas Instruments 3.26, HP 2.80, Intel 2.78, Oracle 2.59, Cisco Systems 2.14, Dell 1.89, Motorola 1.67, Microsoft 1.36, Sun Microsystems 1.34, AMD 0.10, and Lucent (for 2000–2006) 0.00.

12. For an in-depth analysis of the attraction, retention, motivation, and recognition functions of employee stock options, and the labor-market conditions under which they might perform different functions, see Glimstedt, Lazonick, and Xie (2006).

13. Many countries do not permit stock repurchases (Grullon and Michaely 2002, p. 1677). Indeed, until 1982 in the United States, the SEC had at times viewed stock repurchases as a manipulation of a company's stock price. As Grullon and Michaely (p. 1649) put it, "Until 1982, there were no explicit rules directly regulating share repurchase activity in the United States. This situation exposed repurchasing firms to the risk of triggering an SEC investigation and being charged with illegal market manipulation." In that year, however, as part of the general deregulation of financial institutions that had been taking place since the late 1970s, the SEC "made it easier for companies to buy back their shares on the open market without fear of SEC stock-manipulation charges" (Hudson 1982). Specifically, under Rule 10b-18, the SEC assured companies that manipulation charges would not be filed if each day's open-market repurchases were not greater than 25 percent of the stock's average daily trading volume (Grullon and Michaely 2002, pp. 1676–1682; McCarthy 1999).

14. Also slowing the growth of dividends relative to repurchases is the fact that insofar as a company that pays dividends reduces its shares outstanding through repurchases, it automatically reduces the total amount of dividends that it pays out.

15. An article in the *Journal of Applied Financial Economics* (Billett and Xue 2007) titled "Share Repurchases and the Need for External Finance" opens with the statement, "One of the best-documented findings in the corporate finance literature is that stock prices go up when companies announce their intent to buy back shares" (p. 42).

16. Senator Schumer first raised the issue in January 2006 in reaction to the fact that Exxon Mobil had spent more on repurchases than on development and exploration in the previous year. Schumer was quoted as saying "the federal government has a responsibility to make sure that these companies continue to innovate instead of just profiting from the status quo" (Piller 2006). Representative Ed Markey (D-MA) took up the issue in May 2008, when he was quoted as saying "Big Oil is spending their profits to prop up their stock price rather than on discovering and delivering alternatives to $4 gas" (Souder 2008).

7
Prospects for Sustainable Prosperity

"MARKET FORCES" ARE NOT NATURAL PHENOMENA

Driven by the microelectronics revolution, the United States has been a highly innovative economy over the past three decades. The resultant economic growth, however, has been unstable, and the distribution of income has become significantly more unequal. In this book, I have shown that the change from OEBM to NEBM in the ICT industries has contributed to this instability and inequity. Gone is the collective security that the corporatist OEBM once offered its employees. In its place is a far more individualized relation between employer and employee. The employment and incomes of even the most highly educated members of the U.S. labor force are now much more susceptible to the pressures and vagaries of "market forces" than they were a few decades ago. In particular, as I have shown in Chapters 5 and 6, global labor markets and national financial markets now exert preponderant influences on the conditions of high-tech employment in the United States.

In the regulation of the employment relation, market forces are not natural phenomena. Rather the policies and decisions of corporations and governments shape how and in whose interests capital and labor markets function (Lazonick 1991, 2003b). Since the late 1970s corporate strategies and government policies in the United States have combined to define the ways in which NEBM allocates resources, employs labor, and finances investments. Given the political will, government legislation can proscribe those corporate strategies that result in instability and inequity and can enable those corporate strategies that promote sustainable prosperity.

When U.S. corporate executives systematically offshore as much productive activity as possible to lower-wage regions of the world, they will argue that the forces of market competition compel them to do so. Yet, in making these decisions, these executives are generally unaccountable to current U.S.-based employees who have helped to build the organizations that are capable of globalization, and they rarely consult with these employees—as, for example, they once did at Xerox (see Chapter 4)—about alternative strategies for maintaining and extending the competitiveness of the company. Indeed, the United States is unique among the advanced economies in according so little voice or protection to incumbent labor in this regard.

When U.S. corporate executives systematically allocate billions of dollars to stock repurchases, they argue that the stock market requires them to do so. Yet, in the 2000s, the powerful corporations that have the financial resources to engage in this practice are actually using their financial might to manipulate the stock market—to the direct benefit of those executives who make resource-allocation decisions. Armed with the ideology of maximizing shareholder value, U.S. corporate executives who control the allocation of their companies' resources now simply take it for granted that they are responsible to shareholders alone.

The U.S. federal government has played a significant role in aiding and abetting the modes of resource allocation that prevail under NEBM. It continues to devote tax revenues to fund the nation's high-tech knowledge base, but it demands little if any accountability from so-called private enterprises about how or for whose benefit this knowledge base is used. If the top executives of U.S. corporations that have benefited from government largesse in the past now say they have to offshore jobs to remain competitive, then the U.S. government will not stand in the way or demand a quid pro quo. Through its immigration legislation, the U.S. government has accommodated, until recently at least, the demands of the high-tech lobby for more nonimmigrant work visas, while providing little in the way of effective oversight of the use, and abuse, of these visas. In failing to intervene to regulate the remuneration of corporate executives, the U.S. government has been a party to an unwarranted and unseemly, and many would say obscene, explosion in top executive pay that the United States has witnessed over the past three decades.

U.S. corporate executives claim that they have a fiduciary responsibility to maximize shareholder value—a perspective that, as I have shown in Chapter 6, fails to address the conditions under which business enterprises are in fact innovative. Yet, even as corporate executives spout this ideology and enrich themselves in the process, they are far from shy in appealing to the U.S. government for increased spending on knowledge creation and lower burdens of taxation to keep "America" competitive. Nor, in the financial meltdown of 2008, have these corporate executives had any problem in invoking their responsibility to shareholders to justify the excessive remuneration that they received for mismanaging companies that, at a great cost to the public, ultimately failed. For example, Richard S. Fuld, CEO of Lehman Brothers, told the House Oversight and Government Reform Committee in October 2008 that the $300 million in remuneration he admitted to having received since 2000 was bestowed upon him by "a compensation committee that spent a tremendous amount of time making sure that the interests of the executives and the employees were aligned with shareholders" (Davis 2008).

A nation needs innovation to generate economic growth. When, however, corporate executives use stock-based compensation to skew the distribution of income in their favor, and when they decide to terminate the employment of qualified people even as the company is reaping the returns on its past investments in innovation in which these very people participated, then it may well be that many U.S. citizens will lose, even as the companies for which they work, or used to work, remain highly profitable. Moreover, as I have suggested in Chapter 6, as we stand at the end of the first decade of the twenty-first century, it may well be that corporate adherence to the goal of maximizing shareholder value is undermining the innovative capabilities of some of America's most successful business enterprises.

Earning a living in the United States has never been easy for those who are poorly educated and lack work experience. In the 2000s, however, even well-educated Americans with substantial work experience face far greater employment insecurity than they did in the past. In documenting the instability and inequity inherent in NEBM, I am not advocating a return to OEBM. There is a need, however, to recognize the collective functions that OEBM performed in providing security in employment and retirement to a significant proportion of the U.S. labor force. The fact that, in the Old Economy, U.S. business corporations performed these functions greatly reduced the need for the government to be directly involved in ensuring stable and equitable growth. Indeed, I would argue that because business corporations performed these collective functions for such a substantial portion of the population by the 1960s, the U.S. government could contemplate launching a "War on Poverty" to upgrade the employment prospects of those segments of the U.S. population for whom business corporations did not provide economic security. In a variety of ways, OEBM provided a foundation, including a consensus among an economic elite, for the government to intervene in the economy to deal with problems of instability and inequity. With the decline of OEBM, and its replacement by NEBM, from where will such a new consensus come?

THE LIMITED ROLE OF THE STOCK MARKET IN THE OLD ECONOMY

An understanding of the historical context in which OEBM performed these collective functions in the post–World War II decades is critical for analyzing both the power of OEBM to provide a foundation for stable and equitable growth and its ultimate limits. The historical context was marked by the following:

- government spending on World War II which resuscitated the U.S. economy in the first half of the 1940s, thus lifting the United States out of the Great Depression, which spanned the 1930s;

- the U.S. government's enormous investment in the high-tech knowledge base after World War II in the context of the Cold War, including national research efforts and a system of higher education to disseminate this knowledge;

- the existence of powerful corporate research labs, many of them dating back to the beginning of the twentieth century, that could absorb and further develop that knowledge; and

- a progressive tax regime that enabled the U.S. government to intervene both to bolster the corporate foundations of sustainable prosperity and, when pushed by social movements, to try to spread the gains of prosperity through equal opportunity to those segments of the population that the corporate economy was leaving behind.

The provision of career employment with one company underpinned OEBM's contribution to stable and equitable growth in the U.S. economy. Oligopolistic market positions and proprietary technology strategies enabled and encouraged Old Economy corporations to offer career employment to their personnel. The presence in many Old Economy companies of industrial unions with their emphasis on employment security reinforced this corporate commitment to "the organization man." For managers and workers, a clear manifestation of the expectation of career employment with one company was the inclusion, as integral to the employment relation, of a nonportable DB pension plan that rewarded longevity.

In the New Economy, pensions, along with much else, are heavily dependent on the performance of the stock market. In historical retrospect, a major reason why OEBM was able to contribute to stable and equitable growth was the limited role of the stock market, in its creation, control, combination, compensation, and cash functions, in the operations of its constituent corporations. In OEBM the prime role of the stock market was to separate share ownership and managerial control, a key social condition for the managerial revolution that permitted experienced salaried employees to run established companies and rendered dispersed public shareholders powerless to intervene in the corporate allocation of resources. By facilitating the separation of ownership and control, this "noncontrol" function of the stock market promoted stable and equitable economic growth under OEBM in the immediate post–World War II decades. That record stands quite in contrast to the destabilizing influence of the shareholder-value-driven "market for corporate control" that sought to unwind OEBM in the 1980s by "disgorging" corporate cash flows that were allegedly "free" (Lazonick 1992).

Under OEBM, as a rule, even established companies with listed shares did not make use of the stock market to fund new investment in productive assets. The period in which the stock market was an important source of cash under OEBM was during the speculative boom of the late 1920s, when corporations sold stock at inflated prices to strengthen their balance sheets by paying off debt or building up their cash reserves—quite the opposite of what U.S. industrial corporations did in the Internet boom at the end of the twentieth century (Carpenter, Lazonick, and O'Sullivan 2003; O'Sullivan 2004).

In the era of OEBM, it was only in the context of the "hot issues" market in the late 1950s and early 1960s that the over-the-counter (OTC) markets began to perform the creation function of the stock market by inducing investment in start-ups (O'Sullivan 2007). In historical perspective, this speculative boom provided a glimpse into the role that new-venture IPOs would come to play in NEBM. Indeed the appearance of hot issues on the OTC markets triggered the SEC's *Special Study of the Securities Markets* (SEC 1963) which resulted eight years later in the formation of NASDAQ (Ingebretsen 2002, chap. 4; O'Sullivan, forthcoming).

In the 1950s and 1960s, as we have seen, the stock market also began to perform a compensation function under OEBM, but only for top executives—a special privilege designed for tax avoidance that opened up this use of corporate stock to public criticism. In historical retrospect, we can see the introduction of executive stock options as the first stage in the opportunistic separation of the rewards of top executives from the pay structures of the organizations over which they exercised strategic control. The next stage in segmenting the interests of top executives from the organizations that they headed came in the 1960s when many of these top executives built corporate empires through conglomeration, a movement that made OEBM unstable as corporations diversified into too many unrelated lines of business to be managed effectively. Here too, as in the case of executive stock options, corporate stock performed a major function—what I have called the "combination" function—under OEBM, but one that contributed to instability and inequity in the economy and eventually contributed to the demise of OEBM.

In both its compensation and combination functions, therefore, the stock market under OEBM fostered a separation in major corporations between the strategic allocation of resources and the processes of organizational learning. Yet the integration of strategy and learning is a *sine qua non* of innovative enterprise (Lazonick 2004a, 2006, 2007a; Lazonick and O'Sullivan 2000b; O'Sullivan 2000a,b). This separation of strategy and learning rendered the U.S. industrial corporation vulnerable to innovative competitors from abroad. During the 1970s and continuing in the 1980s, U.S. companies found that they were losing competitive advantage to foreign corporations in a number of key industries in which U.S. manufacturers had been the world's leading producers. Foreign companies had been able through licensing agreements, multinational investments, and military contracts to gain access to the U.S. knowledge base. Given their highly integrated skill bases, Japanese companies were the most adept among foreign competitors at absorbing this knowledge and improving upon it through a process of indigenous innovation. It is of significance that the business model that enabled Japanese companies to outcompete their U.S. counterparts entailed more highly collectivized forms of OEBM that, through the institutions of cross-shareholding, lifetime employment, and main-bank lending, permitted the superior development and utilization of technology (Lazonick 1998, 1999, 2005).

THE STOCK MARKET IN NEBM: FROM INNOVATION TO SPECULATION TO MANIPULATION

The rise of NEBM in the 1960s and 1970s was only minimally influenced by the transformation that was taking place at the same time in the Japanese industrial economy. Nevertheless, in the 1980s and 1990s, NEBM emerged as, in effect, the U.S. response to Japanese competition. As was shown in Chapter 2, the U.S. stock market supported the reallocation of capital and labor from OEBM to NEBM through its creation and compensation functions, while it supported the rapid growth of young high-tech firms through its combination function.

Through its creation and compensation functions, the stock market reallocated capital and labor from Old Economy wealth holders to New Economy start-ups. The existence of a highly liquid stock market with lax listing requirements—namely, NASDAQ—enhanced the prospect of an early and successful IPO and thereby induced venture capital to invest in high-tech start-ups. As shown in Chapter 2, venture capital played a central role in the reallocation of resources from OEBM to NEBM by enabling start-ups to tap entrepreneurship and knowledge that may have otherwise remained locked up in established corporations. If venture capital reallocated financial resources from the Old Economy to the New Economy, stock options played a complementary role in the reallocation of labor. The stock market enabled high-tech start-ups to offer stock options to well-educated personnel as an inducement for them to forgo secure employment with established Old Economy companies. These stock options could become valuable with an IPO or an M&A deal with a listed company. Once a new venture had done an IPO, the combination function then became important for the growth of New Economy firms, as epitomized by Cisco's growth-through-acquisition strategy, discussed in Chapter 6.

In the 1990s the creation, compensation, and combination functions of the stock market were central to the expansion of NEBM. Entrepreneurs, venture capitalists, and high-tech employees could claim that they were contributing their resources to an innovative economy and reaping the rewards for these contributions through their stock holdings. At the same time, however, the augmented role of the stock market in NEBM has rendered U.S. economic growth both unstable and inequitable since the 1980s. While the stock market can facilitate the reallocation of capital and labor to innovative start-ups, it can also enable speculation, which engenders instability, and manipulation, which engenders inequity.

In the late 1990s the U.S. stock market became highly speculative indeed, as the public discovered the existence of highly innovative New Economy firms and then began making bets on many dot.com start-ups that had little in the way of innovative capability. The extent of the speculative bubble is displayed in Figure 7.1. The rise and fall of the NASDAQ Composite Index between 1998 and 2001 make the movements of the Dow Jones Industrial Average (DJIA), which at the time included Intel and Microsoft as the NASDAQ representatives among its 30 stocks, and the S&P 500 Index look like mere blips. Between March 1998 and March 2000, the NASDAQ Composite Index of more than 3,000 stocks rose by 149 percent, compared with 21 percent for the DJIA and 36 percent for the S&P 500.

This speculative bubble followed a long period since the early 1980s in which stock-price movements were driven much more by a combination of manipulation, as Old Economy companies restructured their organizations and balance sheets, and innovation, as New Economy companies pumped back virtually all of their earnings into enterprise growth. In the 2000s, however, as I have shown in Chapter 6, manipulation reemerged with a vengeance as a driver of stock-price movements, with stock buybacks as the main manipulative mechanism.

One of the high-fliers on NASDAQ in the late 1990s was Cisco Systems. In October 1998, Charles O'Reilly (1998, p. 1), a professor at Stanford Business School, published a case that began with the sentence, "Cisco is a $6 billion high technology stealth company, largely unknown to the general public." Just 17 months later this "largely

Figure 7.1 DJIA, S&P 500, and NASDAQ Composite Indices, July 1986–October 2008 (monthly data)

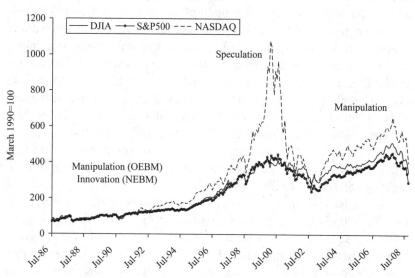

NOTE: As of August 2009, the Dow Jones Industrial Average (DJIA) consists of 30 stocks, of which 27 are listed on the New York Stock Exchange (NYSE) and 3 on NASDAQ; the S&P 500 Index consists of 500 stocks, of which 410 are NYSE and 90 are NASDAQ; and the NASDAQ Composite Index consists of 2,809 stocks.

SOURCE: Yahoo! Finance, http://finance.yahoo.com, *Historical Prices*, monthly data.

unknown" company sported the highest market capitalization in the world. In May 2000, Thomas Donlan (2000, p. 34), a *Barron's* editor, calculated that to justify its stock price, which stood at 190 times earnings, Cisco would have to increase its 1999 profits of $2.5 billion to $2.5 trillion by 2010!

Cisco remains highly successful in the 2000s, but given a relative absence of speculation, it has required massive stock repurchases to prop up its stock price. Figure 7.2, Panel A, depicts the movement of Cisco's stock price as having passed through an innovation stage from 1990 to 1998 characterized by reinvestment of most of its earnings,[1] followed by a speculation stage from 1998 to 2000 in which market exuberance drove up its stock price at an extremely rapid rate, and then a manipulation stage in the 2000s in which buybacks (as detailed in Chapter 6) supported the price of the company's stock.

Panel A of Figure 7.2 also shows the stock-price movements of Intel and Microsoft, which when charted on the Cisco scale give the appearance of having been flat in the Internet boom. But, as Panel B shows, they too experienced stock-price movements that reflect the innovation, speculation, and manipulation phases. And the main mode of manipulation is, again, stock buybacks. These three companies, mainstays of the U.S. ICT industries, together spent $113 billion on R&D from 2000 through 2007. Over those years, however, these three also spent $164 billion on stock buybacks. In fiscal 2008, Cisco (year ended July 26) spent $10.4 billion on stock repurchases and $5.1 billion on R&D, Microsoft (year ended June 30) $12.5 billion on repurchases and $11.6 billion on R&D, and Intel (year ended December 31) $7.1 billion on repurchases and $5.4 billion on R&D.[2]

As we have seen, these companies are leaders of a larger trend that saw the 500 companies that are included in the S&P 500 Index spend well over $2 trillion to buy back their own stock in the first eight years of the twenty-first century. These buybacks are a measure of the grip that shareholder-value ideology has on corporate America, and hence on the ways in which financial resources are allocated in the U.S. economy. The shareholder-value perspective that I critiqued in Chapter 6 provides a simplistic answer to a complex problem: how to reward stakeholders so that their contributions raise living standards and provide economic gains that can be shared equitably. In the 2000s, the problem has not been addressed, and instability and inequity are the result.

THE RISE OF ECONOMIC INSECURITY

The result of this redistributive quest for shareholder value in the U.S. ICT industries has been growing economic insecurity for the U.S. ICT labor force. High-tech personnel already found themselves vulnerable to changes in markets, technology, and enterprise strategies because of the end of career employment in the 1990s. In its place was substituted interfirm labor mobility, especially in the "high velocity" labor markets of Silicon Valley (Benner 2002; Hyde 2003).

For many ICT employees, the power of individual labor mobility served them well in the Internet boom of the late 1990s, especially

Figure 7.2 Stock-Price Movements for (Panel A) Cisco Systems (March 1990–October 2008) and Intel and Microsoft (July 1986– October 2008) and for (Panel B) Intel and Microsoft (July 1986–October 2008)

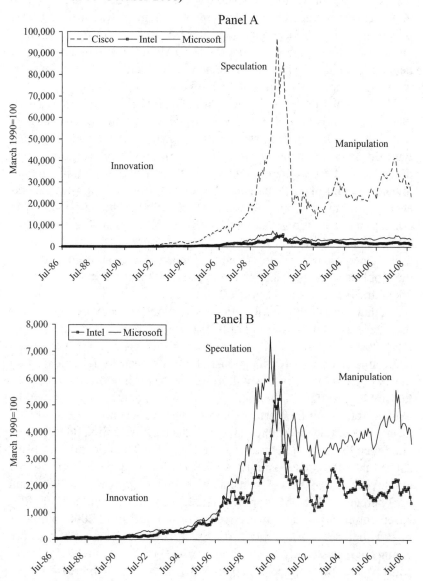

SOURCE: Yahoo! Finance, http://finance.yahoo.com, *Historical Prices*, monthly data.

when they entered into employment at companies with generous stock-option plans (see Chapter 2). The growth of NEBM, culminating in the tight labor markets of the late 1990s, and the very real and often realized possibilities for substantial gains from stock options, inured high-tech employees to an employment system in which their career prospects would be dependent on interfirm labor mobility rather than on the movement up and around the hierarchy of one company. By the beginning of the 2000s, the expectation of such career employment with one company had disappeared in U.S. ICT industries.

It was inherent in the transition from OEBM to NEBM in the 1990s that older members of the ICT labor force faced much greater insecurity than they had in the past. Career employment with one company typically meant that one's salary rose with length of tenure and that the accrual of the value of traditional DB pensions was much greater toward the end of one's career. The position of older high-tech workers became much more vulnerable in the 2000s. The deterioration in employment conditions that faced high-tech labor in the first half of the 2000s extended beyond the downturn in economic activity in 2001–2002. Unemployment rates among engineers and programmers rose in the "jobless recovery" that began in late 2002 (Hira 2003; IEEE-USA 2004a,b; Khatiwada and Sum 2004).

A major part of the explanation for the jobless recovery in ICT was the acceleration of offshoring of ICT jobs from the United States in the early 2000s (Groshen and Potter 2003; Houseman 2007), with India and China as the favored locations. There is a need for reliable data on the extent and locations of offshoring, the proportion of offshored jobs that are high skill, and the impacts of offshoring on employment in the United States and the performance of the U.S. economy as a whole.[3] Data collected by the Semiconductor Industry Association on engineers employed by large- and medium-sized U.S.-based semiconductor firms show that offshored positions accounted for 12.3 percent of 56,995 employees in 1997, 20.8 percent of 96,093 employees in 2000, and 33.7 percent of 125,360 employees in 2005. While the number of U.S.-based engineers at these firms declined from 76,129 in 2000 to 66,851 in 2004 before rising sharply to 83,167 in 2005, the number of offshore engineers rose steadily from 19,964 in 2000 to 42,193 in 2005 (Brown and Linden 2008a, p. 5).[4] It appears that most of this increase in offshore employment has been at semiconductor manufacturing facilities in China and chip design centers in India (Brown and Linden 2008a; see also Ernst 2005).

What is clear is that, in the 2000s, U.S. companies have been able to access growing supplies of high-tech labor in India and China with the capabilities to perform increasingly sophisticated work that had previously been done in the United States (Chapter 5). Moreover, as we have also seen, U.S.-based companies can access this labor in the United States through nonimmigrant H-1B and L-1 visas. The H-1B program has come under heavy criticism from those who see the influx of nonimmigrant labor into the United States as subverting the remuneration and work conditions of permanent members of the U.S. labor force (Matloff 2004).

In principle, employers are supposed to pay workers on H-1B visas "at least the local prevailing wage or the actual wage level paid by the employer to others with similar experience and qualifications, whichever is higher." The law also stipulates that an employer can only engage someone on an H-1B visa, if such employment "will not adversely affect the working conditions of workers similarly employed" (U.S. Department of Labor 2007). In practice, it is difficult to ensure the preservation of these labor conditions since there is little if any enforcement of compliance on the part of the employer.[5]

Even when the employer complies with the letter of the law, moreover, the H-1B worker is not in the same position of power vis-à-vis her employer as a U.S. citizen or permanent resident. Under NEBM, the power of the employee resides in her ability to switch jobs. An H-1B worker can only leave her employer and remain in the United States if she can find another employer with a vacant H-1B visa who is ready to hire her. An employer may use his leverage over H-1B employees to demand that they be reassigned to different geographic locations within the United States that regular members of the U.S. labor force might be unwilling to accept. The dependency of the H-1B worker on her employer will be even greater, moreover, when the employer has sponsored the employee for U.S. permanent residency, the acquisition of which may be a long, drawn-out process (Chakravartty 2006).

Recall from Chapter 5 that the annual new H-1B visa cap was 65,000 through 1998, 115,000 in 1999 and 2000, and 195,000 in 2001 through 2003, before reverting back to 65,000 in 2004, plus an additional 20,000 for foreigners with a graduate degree from a U.S. university.

There has been an excess demand for these 85,000 visas since 2004, and high-tech employers have been clamoring for a substantial increase in the cap that would alleviate, so they claim, a shortage of high-tech labor in the United States. The Comprehensive Immigration Reform Bill that was passed in the Senate in May 2006 would have raised the H-1B cap to 115,000 and instituted an automatic increase of 20,000 per year whenever the previous year's quota was reached.[6] In 2007 and 2008, however, legislative approval for an increase was stalled in the House of Representatives, not over the H-1B question, but rather over the treatment of illegal foreign entrants to the U.S. labor force.

ICT employers argue that more H-1B visas are needed because there is a shortage of high-tech labor in the United States. Absent a remedy that includes an expansion of the H-1B visa program in the short run and an upgrading of the U.S. K–12 education system in the long run, they warn of a deterioration of innovative capabilities in the United States and a further acceleration of offshoring of high-tech jobs.

In an influential op-ed piece, Bill Gates (2007) said that the U.S. schooling system had to be improved to enable "young Americans [to] enter the workforce with the math, science and problem-solving skills they need to succeed in the knowledge economy." He cited a 2003 report that found that U.S. high school students ranked twenty-fourth out of 29 developed economies in math scores.[7] Gates called upon business and government to work together to improve the delivery of science and math education in the U.S. K–12 system. He also counseled that the United States should make it "easier for foreign-born scientists and engineers to work for U.S. companies." Indeed, the shortage of computer science graduates in the United States had reached, Gates argued, a "crisis point." He called for an increase in the quota of H-1B visas as well as a faster and simpler process for acquiring permanent residency. Given that foreigners constitute half of the doctoral candidates in computer sciences in the United States, an important impact of these changes would be to increase the number of foreign graduates from U.S. universities who remain in the United States after completion of their studies.

Not surprisingly, the United States branch of the Institute of Electrical and Electronics Engineers (IEEE), which "promotes the careers and public-policy interests of more than 220,000 engineers, scientists and allied professionals" (IEEE-USA 2006a) is far from enthusiastic about changes in immigration law that would expand the supply of high-tech workers in the United States. After the U.S. Senate passed the Comprehensive Reform Bill in May 2006, IEEE-USA President Ralph W. Wyndrum, Jr., commented, "The bill opens the spigot on numerous skilled visa categories. The question is how many high-tech workers can the United States absorb annually without driving up unemployment and driving down wages?" (IEEE–Cedar Rapids Section 2006).

There is considerable debate over whether a shortage or a surplus of high-tech labor exists in the United States in the 2000s (Gordon 2007). Responding generally to claims of crisis in the reproduction and expansion of the STEM (science, technology, engineering, mathematics) workforce in the United States, a 2004 study by the RAND Corporation for the U.S. Office for Science and Technology Policy and the Alfred P. Sloan Foundation argued that "many of these claims of shortfalls are suspect or are based on metrics that must be taken in context" (Kelly et al. 2004, p. 5).[8] Writing during the jobless recovery of 2003, Michael S. Teitelbaum (2004, p. 13), a demographer and program director (now vice president) at the Alfred P. Sloan Foundation, observed: "The profound irony of many such claims [of labor shortage] is the disjuncture between practice in the scientific and engineering professions—in which accurate empirical evidence and careful analyses are essential—and that among promoters of 'shortage' claims in the public sphere, where the analytical rigor is often, to be kind, quite weak."

Rhetoric of crises aside, given rapid changes in technology and the high degree of specialization of high-tech workers, these two very different perspectives on the adequacy of the supply of high-tech personnel in the United States are two sides of an age-related coin. In any market for skilled labor, there may be at any point in time a labor market "mismatch" between the skill set of the extant supply of high-tech employees and the demand for new skills inherent in new high-tech jobs (see Levy and Murnane 1992; Morris and Western 1999; Powell and Snellman 2004). For members of the ICT labor force generally, one's age may have an inverse relation to the relevance of one's learned skills to meet new demands for ICT labor. If companies are systematically employing younger workers, ostensibly with up-to-date skills, and systematically laying off older workers, ostensibly with obsolete skills, it is quite possible that there will exist, simultaneously, a shortage of the new workers that companies want to hire and a surplus of the old workers that companies have decided to fire.

Such a scenario is entirely consistent with everything we know about the transition from OEBM to NEBM. A key characteristic of NEBM is a lack of commitment by companies to career employment. Under NEBM, companies continue to value the productivity that emanates from the experience of many of their existing employees, and, for employees, the prospect of promotion within the organizational hierarchy still can serve as a powerful inducement for supplying more and better effort in making productive contributions to the firm. At the same time, however, under NEBM there are no institutional constraints to terminating some employees even as, or often because, the company seeks to take advantage of new profitable opportunities that result from changes in its industry's technological, market, and competitive conditions. When such opportunities present themselves—and in the fast-changing, globalizing ICT industries such events are regular and continuous phenomena—the company will be apt to replace older workers with younger workers.

One need only look at the transformation in employment relations at IBM between 1990 and 1994, as I have done in Chapter 3, to see how older employees could be made redundant as the company restructured with a bias toward hiring younger employees. A central purpose of IBM's massive restructuring in the 1990s was to rid itself of its decades-old system of lifelong employment. Indeed, about 3,500 IBM employees filed a class action lawsuit against the Internal Revenue Service in 1994, claiming that IBM should not have withheld taxes on their severance pay, since these awards represented a legal settlement obtained in return for signing an agreement in which they waived their right to sue IBM for age discrimination (DeBare 1997; Ramstad 1994b,c; see also Associated Press 1994; *Raleigh News and Observer* 1996). As we have seen in Chapter 4, in 1995 and 1999 IBM made fundamental changes in its pension system for the expressed purpose of making the company more attractive to younger employees. In the process, many midcareer IBM employees who were not able to remain on the traditional DB plan experienced substantial reductions in their expected pensions.

Given its size, reputation, and central position in the ICT industries, IBM's transformation from OEBM to NEBM marked a fundamental juncture in the transition from employment security to employment insecurity in the U.S. corporate economy. Indeed, in line with the IBM experience, for the period of 1992–1997, Abowd and his coauthors (2007) found a general shift in U.S. employment from older experienced workers to younger skilled workers related to the adoption of computer technologies. Using Current Population Survey data, Schultze (1999, pp. 10–11) discovered that "middle-aged and older men, for whatever reason, are not staying as long with their employers as they once did." He goes on to show, moreover, that the job displacement rate for white-collar workers relative to blue-collar workers rose substantially in the 1980s and 1990s, starting at 33 percent in 1981–1982 and rising to about 80 percent in the 1990s.

In late 1998, as the Internet boom gained momentum and as Congress stood ready to increase the H-1B visa cap from 65,000 to 115,000, the IEEE-USA published its "MisFortune 500"—"a parody of *Fortune* magazine's annual listing of top profit-making companies," according to the Web site www.misfortune500.org, which posted letters from hundreds of experienced engineers who had lost their jobs and could not find work as engineers during the boom (PR Newswire 1998).[9] In IEEE-USA surveys of unemployed engineers, age was listed as the primary barrier to getting a new job by 67 percent of respondents in 2004 and 72 percent in 2006 (IEEE-USA 2006b).[10]

While anecdotal information abounds on the displacement of senior ICT personnel in the 1990s and 2000s (e.g., see Hira 2007), there remains a deficiency of systematic research on this phenomenon. For example, HP's "churning" of its labor force in the 2000s, subsequent to the merger with Compaq, presumably reduced the average age of employees (Wong 2006). It would be of interest to know how older employees fared relative to younger employees when thousands of positions were eliminated in the aftermath of the merger. In the absence of firm evidence, it is also debatable whether the displacement of older workers in favor of younger workers reflects the need of companies to employ people with different skills sets or simply a way to save money by getting rid of long-time employees who have traditionally received a pay premium for their seniority. The substitution of younger for older personnel for the purpose of cost reduction and not for the purpose of skill acquisition is particularly likely when the change in the age-composition of employment is achieved through offshoring to lower-wage regions.

In their book on "turbulence" in employment, which compares the financial services, retail food, semiconductor, software, and trucking industries, Brown, Haltiwanger, and Lane (2006, p. 108) suggest that both factors may be at work in ICT, thus posing a double whammy for older, higher-paid employees. They find that the most common career path in semiconductors is the "job switcher," who works for two different companies, and the most common career path in software is the "job hopper," who works for more than two companies (pp. 84–86). For personnel at all levels of education in these industries, workers who change jobs more earn less (see also C. Brown 2005; Brown and Linden 2008b). Based on intensive research on the U.S. semiconductor industry, Brown and Linden (p. 22) have concluded that "the labor market situation is especially difficult for older engineers, who face rapid skill obsolescence....When companies claim they face a shortage of engineers, they usually mean that they face a shortage of young, relatively inexpensive engineers with the latest skills, even when they have a queue of experienced engineers who want retraining."

More research is needed on what skills older employees actually lack in an NEBM setting. Under NEBM, companies want to retain workers who have, or are willing to learn, the requisite skills, and who, in a highly competitive environment with "time to market" as a key to profitability, are willing to work long and hard. At a company like Microsoft, for example, software programming is a highly collective and cumulative process in which the generation of a faster, better, and cheaper product depends on the integration of the work of hundreds of individual contributors (Cusumano 2000). A high level of productivity at a company like Microsoft depends on a relatively low level of labor turnover, which in turn reflects a relatively high level of dependence of a particular employee on his or her current employer for remunerative work. The greater the available labor supply, the greater this dependence.

Long work hours are the norm under NEBM. High-tech workers at New Economy companies are generally salaried workers who are exempt from the requirement under the Fair Labor Standards Act that companies pay them overtime at one-and-a-half times the hourly rate when they work more than 40 hours a week. Exempt workers may find themselves working very long hours with little if any increase in remuneration. For Internet bloggers, a particularly well-known example of such work conditions in ICT was that of an Electronic Arts (EA) software engineer whose spouse (female, as it turned out) posted an anonymous open letter on LiveJournal in November 2004 titled "EA: The Human Story."[11] Her complaint was that, under a permanent "crunch" to meet video-game publishing deadlines, EA compelled game developers like her spouse to work 85-hour weeks: "9am to 10pm—seven days a week—with the occasional Saturday evening off for good behavior (at 6:30 pm)." For working these long hours, game developers received no overtime pay, extra time off, or sick days.

Within a month of publication of the open letter, more than 4,000 people had posted comments on LiveJournal, almost all in support of the "EA Spouse," with many advising that EA employees should join a union. As it happened, under California law, many of the game developers had a claim to overtime pay. EA agreed to the settlement of two class action lawsuits for overtime pay, one by its graphic designers for $15.6 million in October 2005 and the other by its programmers for $14.9 million in April 2006. In both cases, EA then transformed those of its employees who were nonexempt under the California law into hourly employees who would henceforth be paid time-and-a-half for overtime hours. As part of this change, EA gave these workers a one-time grant of EA stock but ruled them ineligible for EA stock options (Maragos 2005; Jenkins 2006).

It will be remembered from Chapter 3 that in 1958 IBM sought to "blur the distinction between white-collar and blue-collar workers" (to repeat the words of CEO Thomas Watson, Jr.) by paying all 89,000 of its employees on a salaried basis. Almost a half-century later, in early 2006, with IBM operating on the basis of a totally different business model, systems administrators, network technicians and other technical staff throughout the United States launched a class action lawsuit against IBM for "depriving its employees who install, maintain, and support computer software and hardware by unlawfully characterizing them as 'exempt' from state and federal labor law protections" (Business Wire 2006a,b). In November 2006, IBM settled the lawsuit with a payment of $65 million, but without admitting any wrongdoing or liability (Konrad 2006). Then, in January 2008, IBM announced that 7,600 technical-support workers would be reclassified as nonexempt, and that their base pay for a 40-hour work week would be cut by 15 percent because they would now be eligible for overtime pay (Bergstein 2008).

Meanwhile, as we have also seen, from 2000 through 2007 IBM increased its worldwide employment by more than 72,000 people while cutting its U.S. employment by almost 27,000. Nevertheless, insofar as high-tech companies like IBM, Microsoft, Intel, and Cisco still employ people in the United States, their executives want to find labor in abundant supply in this country. ICT executives lobby the U.S. government for an expansion in the H-1B visa program not simply, or even primarily, because the availability of more high-tech workers will help to keep down wage costs. If these companies want to lower their wage bills, they can offshore more routine activities to India or China, as indeed they have done and will continue to do. For work that is kept in the United States, however, the problem for ICT companies is not the wages of labor but rather the productivity of labor.

Labor productivity depends on effort as well as skill, and tight labor markets reduce the power of employers to demand that their employees deliver high levels of work effort (see Lazonick 1990). An exclusive focus on wage rates as the equilibrating mechanism in the labor market misunderstands the nature of the problem from an employer's point of view, especially in a high-wage, high-skill sector of the economy. The key issue for ICT employers operating in the United States is not the level of remuneration per se but the lack of control over the work effort of a highly mobile labor force. Employees at these companies—well aware that changes in corporate strategy could bring a career within a particular company to an end, and supported by a labor market that encourages interfirm mobility—are on the lookout for employment opportunities with other companies that might be beneficial to their personal careers. All other things being equal, the larger the available high-tech labor supply, the more dependent the high-tech worker on employment with his or her current company, and the greater the power of the employer to demand that the employee work long and hard.

Here then is the significance of Bill Gates' demand for unlimited H-1B visas. Besides increasing the labor supply, the holders of H-1B visas are much more dependent on their current employer for continuing employment. Moreover, they also tend to be younger than citizen members of the U.S. ICT labor force (U.S. General Accounting Office 2003, pp. 14, 42). Among electrical/electronic engineers, the median age of H-1B workers approved in 2002 was 32 years, compared with 41 years for U.S. citizen workers, while among systems analysts/programmers these median ages were 31 and 37, respectively. The combination of youth and dependence makes H-1B personnel able and willing to work long and hard (see Matloff 2006a). Moreover, these H-1B visa holders are ideal recruits for a company operating in the United States that may want its employees to pursue global career paths as it decides to offshore higher value-added activities. With years of experience in the United States, still-young former H-1B holders from places like China and India can be very valuable to a company as, through the company's offshored operations, they follow their global career paths back to the countries from whence they came.

THE PROBLEM OF MINORITY EDUCATION AND EMPLOYMENT

Major U.S. ICT companies could deal with a high-tech labor "crisis" if they would retrain and employ greater numbers of older employees on reasonable conditions of work and pay. These companies could pay for any additional cost of such employment by eschewing stock repurchases, which have no other purpose than to boost the price of the company's stock. To take this high road to solving its labor shortage, a company would, however, in effect be rejecting the modes of employing labor and allocating capital that are characteristic features of NEBM. Instead these companies will doubtless continue to look to in-migration and offshoring to find the types of younger high-tech workers consistent with NEBM.

Given that the education systems of China and India have been generating massive numbers of potential ICT workers, both in-migration and offshoring have become the most viable solutions in the here and now of the 2000s. It has been estimated that, for the academic year 2003–2004, U.S. universities awarded (in round numbers) 137,000 four-year bachelor's degrees in engineering, computer science, and information technology, compared with 139,000 in India and 361,000 in China (Wadhwa et al. 2007, p. 75). The U.S. number for 2003–2004 was up sharply from 109,000 in 1999–2000, but it declined to 134,000 in 2004–2005. The increase in these bachelor's degrees awarded in China and India exhibited a much steeper trajectory from 1999–2000 to 2003–

2004, and grew further in 2004–2005. Large numbers of these Indian and Chinese college graduates subsequently migrate abroad, especially to the United States, for graduate education or work experience.

The greatly increased availability in the 2000s of a global supply of high-quality high-tech labor, via either in-migration or offshoring, has raised concerns in the United States about the adequacy of the U.S. K–12 education system to prepare the next generation of homegrown entrants to the U.S. labor force to compete in the global high-tech labor market. While the massive flow abroad of high-skill, high-tech jobs is a phenomenon of the 2000s, the concern with the adequacy of the K–12 system for preparing U.S. youth for a new world of work is not new. Since the early 1980s, various interests, including business associations, civil society organizations, and government agencies, have expressed concern with the adequacy of the U.S. K–12 education system to provide students with the levels of proficiency in math and science needed to pursue college degrees in the STEM disciplines (CPGE 2007; National Commission on Excellence in Education 1983; New Commission on the Skills of the American Workforce 2007).

The United States currently participates in the OECD's Programme for International Student Assessment (PISA), which has done three rounds of data collection and analysis on literacy in reading, mathematics, and science of 15-year-old students around the world. The first assessment, done in 2000, focused on reading; the second (2003) on mathematics; and the third (2006) on science. In PISA 2000, the reading performance of U.S. students was just above the average for the 27 participating OECD nations, among which the United States ranked fifteenth, or just below the median (Lemke et al. 2001, p. 7). In PISA 2003, the mathematics performance of U.S. students was significantly below the OECD average, as the United States ranked twenty-fourth out of 29 OECD countries (Lemke et al. 2004, pp. 14–15).[12] In PISA 2006, the science performance of U.S. students was significantly below the OECD average, as the United States ranked twenty-first of 30 OECD countries (Baldi et al. 2007, p. 6).

The roots of the problem of the performance of the U.S. system of mass education are deeply embedded in the nation's social structure (see Berliner 2006). In all cases, blacks and Hispanics in the United States did significantly worse on these assessments than whites and Asians (Baldi et al. 2007, p. 55; Lemke et al. 2001, p. 50; Lemke et al. 2004, p.

38). In the PISA 2000 reading rankings, U.S. non-Hispanic whites had a score that would have placed them (as a hypothetical nation) second after Finland and just ahead of Canada, while U.S. blacks had a score that would have placed them twenty-fifth, leading only Luxembourg and Mexico. In the PISA 2003 math rankings, U.S. non-Hispanic whites scored above the OECD average and would have placed thirteenth out of 29 OECD countries, while U.S. blacks would have ranked twenty-eighth, ahead of Mexico. In the PISA 2006 science rankings, U.S. non-Hispanic whites would have been seventh among 30 OECD nations, while U.S. blacks would have been last, just behind Mexico.

In each case, U.S. Hispanics performed better than U.S. blacks but well below the OECD average. U.S. Asians did less well than U.S. non-Hispanic whites and were above the OECD average in reading and math but just below it in science. Much of the poor showing of the United States as an actual nation in PISA, therefore, can be attributed to deficiencies in the K–12 educations of blacks and Hispanics. During this period, of the U.S. population aged 15–19, non-Hispanic whites made up 63 percent, blacks 15 percent, Hispanics 16 percent, and Asians 4 percent (U.S. Census Bureau 2004, 2005, pp. 14–15).

An inadequate education places one at a great disadvantage in the global competition for good jobs. Even for well-educated whites, the employment trends under NEBM that I have documented do not give cause for optimism. For blacks and Hispanics the problem is far worse. Increasing proportions of the black and Hispanic populations have attained university degrees at the bachelor's level or higher. Nevertheless, their numbers still lag far behind those of the white population (National Center for Education Statistics 2008, Table 8). In 2007 blacks and Hispanics were also still lagging behind whites at the associate's degree level, which includes qualifications for entry into many ICT technician jobs (ibid., Table 9).

While some progress has been made, thus far blacks and Hispanics are not well represented in the STEM occupations—in sharp contrast not only to whites but also to people of Asian origin in the U.S. population (Lowell and Regets 2006, pp. 16–18). Much of the progress that blacks and Hispanics made in the STEM occupations in the last decades of the twentieth century was at the lower-paid technician levels (U.S. Census Bureau 2008f, p. 388), and these occupations are among the most likely to be offshored.

The lack of representation of black and Hispanic workers in the ICT industries is evident in those cases (all too rare) in which companies make data public on the changing composition of their U.S. labor forces by race, ethnicity, and gender. Exceptionally, IBM has provided detailed employment data by race, ethnicity, and gender for eight occupational categories, from officials/managers to operatives, for the years 1996 through 2008.[13]

In 1996, 9.9 percent of IBM's 125,618 employees were black. In 2008 IBM had 120,227 U.S. employees, but the proportion who were black had fallen to only 7.5 percent. On net, blacks had 3,439 fewer U.S. jobs at IBM in 2008 than in 1996, while Asians had 5,281 more jobs. Hispanics saw their numbers increase slightly, but they represented only 4.0 percent of IBM's U.S. labor force in 1996 and 4.2 percent in 2008.

The main reason for the decline in black employment at IBM was the reduction of employment in the types of jobs that blacks had occupied in 1996, when over 43 percent of blacks were clustered in the operative and office/clerical categories. In 2008, as the combined result of divestments of manufacturing facilities and offshoring, IBM employed only 78 black operatives in the United States, down from 3,474 in 1996. In 2008 there were 885 black employees in office/clerical work, but in 1996 that number had been 1,905. In 2008 IBM employed 3,347 blacks as professionals, but that number was 8 percent less than the number employed in 1996. Blacks benefited from the growth of marketing positions at IBM, with the number of positions they held rising substantially, from 1,248 in 1996 to 2,853 in 2008. Nevertheless, the proportion of all marketing employees who were black declined, from 7.9 percent in 1996 to 7.2 percent in 2008.

Overall, then, in this age of high-tech global competition, the data on education and employment by race and ethnicity in the United States strongly suggest that significant groups within American society will still face tough times in the years and indeed decades to come unless public policy knocks down the systemic socioeconomic barriers to advancement that still face large proportions of blacks and Hispanics in the United States. Besides confronting the substantial supply-side problem of the transformation of the K–12 education system, public policymakers must also consider the types of policies that can deal with the demand-side problem of the expansion and augmentation of high-tech employment in the United States in the face of the apparently irreversible tendency for U.S. jobs of ever higher quality to go abroad. The challenge of sustainable prosperity in the United States is not simply to replace the jobs that disappear but to generate an ever-expanding number of high-quality jobs that can draw members of previously excluded groups into remunerative and meaningful work.

To have any chance of success, legislators must desist from viewing the resource allocation decisions of companies such as Cisco, HP, IBM, Intel, and Microsoft as market forces that are presumably outside the purview of legitimate government policy. The analysis that I have presented in this book argues that, for government investment in the U.S. science and technology infrastructure to have any chance of resulting in prosperity for most Americans, blacks and Hispanics included, over the next generation, the government will have to intervene strategically to influence the allocation of resources by business corporations, U.S.-based and foreign, in a way that would make use of the high-tech knowledge and highly qualified people that government investment would generate.

CORPORATE GOVERNANCE FOR SUSTAINABLE PROSPERITY

The critical area for strategic policy intervention—yet one that has been virtually absent from the U.S. policy debate in the 2000s—is corporate governance, by which I mean the institutions and mechanisms that determine and regulate the ways in which business corporations allocate resources. More specifically, for the sake of sustainable prosperity, government policy must focus on the role of the stock market in the corporate allocation of resources. I have argued that stock-price movements can be driven by innovation, speculation, and manipulation. The general objective of government policy in the area of stock-market regulation should be to eliminate the forces of speculation and manipulation in the determination of stock-price movements so that the stock market can function to support, and stock-price movements reflect, innovation.

A prelude to such policy intervention is a rejection of the overwhelmingly dominant ideology that maximizing shareholder value results in superior economic performance. A rejection of this ideology will not be easy, to say the least. Shareholder-value ideology derives its credibility from the theory of the market economy that dominates the thinking of academic economists. It is, however, a theory that, as I have argued in many contexts, cannot come to grips with the role of the developmental state and the innovative enterprise in the process of economic growth (e.g., see Lazonick 2008b). In practice, moreover, as I have also shown in this book, the financial affairs of U.S. households, businesses, and governments have become tied up with the stock market. Powerful financial interests, including the top executives of major U.S. corporations, who profit enormously from the willingness of households to speculate on the stock market, will vigorously oppose any significant policies that threaten to bring their party to an end.

One might argue that, given that they are so invested in the stock market, U.S. households also benefit from the boosts to stock prices that stock buybacks generate. There are problems with this argument, however. Insiders who know when buybacks are actually to occur (as distinct from when the authorization of a repurchase amount is announced) will be best positioned to take advantage of subsequent stock-price increases (see Fried 2000, 2001; Netter and Mitchell 1989). More generally, households, as outsiders, lack the sophistication and knowledge of corporate executives and money managers as insiders to gain from stock-price volatility. Moreover, even before the financial turmoil of 2008, the evidence on pension assets suggested that working households had not been well served by corporate securities markets in the 2000s in terms of their expected retirement earnings (Munnell and Sundén 2006; Sorokina, Webb, and Muldoon 2008). The best way to ensure income security in retirement is to have well-paid employment as long as one can be productive. Yet in the 2000s, even for the best educated and most experienced middle-aged workers, such sustained employment has become hard to find.

Corporate stock repurchases and executive stock options must be brought under control if stable and equitable economic growth is to become a possibility over the next generation. The government needs to enact legislation that restricts, and indeed even forbids, the practice of corporate stock repurchases. It is a practice that only serves to manipulate the stock market in the interests of those with the power to allocate corporate resources. If economics is about the "optimal" allocation of resources to achieve superior economic performance, stock buybacks on the scale to which corporate executives and Wall Street have become accustomed represent a gargantuan misallocation of resources in the U.S. economy.

As shown in Chapter 6, the obsession with buybacks pervades the U.S. corporate economy (see Lazonick 2008d). U.S. companies that profit from offshoring buy back stock rather than augment the quality and quantity of jobs available in the United States (see Milberg 2008). Leading ICT companies do huge buybacks even as they demand that the government invest in the knowledge base, and they cut back on U.S. employment even as they expand abroad. Leading oil companies do huge buybacks even as U.S. households find their real incomes shrinking because of rising energy prices. Leading pharmaceutical companies do huge buybacks even as they argue in Congress against the regulation of U.S. drug prices because they ostensibly need as much of their profits as possible to pump back into drug research. Leading health-care providers do huge buybacks even as Americans face ever-mounting costs for health care. Leading Wall Street banks did huge buybacks even as they speculated on credit default swaps and collateralized debt obligations to such an extent that they brought the global financial system to its knees. U.S. government–sponsored financial entities Fannie Mae and Freddie Mac did huge buybacks even as they embroiled themselves in the subprime mortgage mess to the point where the government had to bail them out. And if bailed-out General Motors had banked the $20.4 billion distributed to shareholders as buybacks from 1986 through 2002 (with a 2.5 percent after-tax annual return), it would have had $33.8 billion of its own cash to help keep it afloat and respond to global competition in 2008.

The government also needs to enact legislation that drastically reins in top executive pay, which means placing restrictions on stock-based remuneration, especially stock options. The greatest gains from stock options come in periods of stock-market speculation, when holders of options benefit from the fact that in the United States there is virtually never any requirement that option gains can only be reaped if a company's stock does better than similar companies in its industry. And when the market is less speculative, corporate executives can allocate resources to stock buybacks to give a boost to the company's stock price. Presto, the "performance" of the company improves, and it is time for executives to exercise their abundant options once again. Is it a surprise, as investigations into the 2008 financial crisis have revealed, that top corporate executives are prone to speculate with other people's money and to manipulate earnings per share when they are remunerated in ways that encourage them to speculate with other people's money and manipulate earnings per share?

The problem of exploding executive pay has been around for a long time, and virtually nothing has been done about it. The last serious challenge to the legitimacy of executive stock options in the U.S. Congress was in the 1960s, when Senator Albert Gore (D-TN) was engaged in a battle with corporate tax-dodgers (Gore 1965). Congress did not go as far as Gore would have liked, but until the Tax Reform Act of 1976 there was a legislative movement toward restricting the tax advantages of stock options. All of that changed in the latter half of the 1970s as the newly organized high-tech lobby swung into action and got the capital-gains tax reduced, got accounting rules changed, and ensured that stock repurchases would be freely permitted to enhance the benefits of employee stock options.

The one attempt in the 1990s by Democrats to control the rise of executive pay ended up doing just the opposite. In 1993, after Bill Clinton assumed the presidency, his administration implemented a campaign promise to legislate a cap of $1 million on the amount of nonperformance-related, top-executive compensation that could be claimed as a corporate tax deduction. One perverse result of this law was that companies that were paying their CEOs less than $1 million in salary and bonuses raised these components of CEO pay toward $1 million, which was now taken as the government-approved "CEO minimum wage" (Byrne 1994). The other perverse result was that companies increased CEO stock option awards, for which tax deductions were not in any case being claimed, as an alternative to exceeding the $1 million salary-and-bonus cap (Byrne 1995).

A further irony of the Clinton-driven legislation was that the high-tech lobby at the time was fighting against an attempt by FASB to require companies to expense stock options (see PR Newswire 1994; World Accounting Report 1994). Especially for companies with broad-based stock option plans, this prospective regulatory change would have resulted in lower reported earnings that, it was thought, would result in lower stock prices. Hence, even though the proposed FASB regulation (which was ultimately enacted in 2004) would have reduced the corporate tax bill, corporate executives were against it. Why would these same executives give much thought to the fact that there would be no corporate tax deductions for personal pay that exceeded the million-dollar cap?

Now, as then, it is futile to talk about placing restrictions on executive compensation without limiting the extent to which executives can reap gains from stock options that result from either speculation or manipulation. Besides making stock repurchases illegal, legislation is needed to place limits on stock option grants to individuals and to make the gains from the exercise of stock options dependent on achieving a variety of performance goals, including first and foremost ongoing contributions to job creation in the United States.

Finally, to pay for the many things that the United States needs, taxes on stock-based income, whether in the form of dividends or capital gains, need to be raised substantially. By lowering both the capital-gains and dividend tax rates to 15 percent, the Jobs and Growth Tax Relief Reconciliation Act of 2003 further enriched those who receive stock-based income, including income from the exercise of qualified stock options that can receive capital-gains tax treatment. The dubious rationale behind these tax cuts for the rich was that they would spawn real investment and economic growth. The result, however, has been to give corporate executives even greater incentives to do stock repurchases, a mode of resource allocation that reduces the number of productive jobs that U.S. corporations can generate for the U.S. labor force.

The OEBM was hardly perfect, but it did provide employment security, health coverage, and retirement benefits to tens of millions of people whose work was at the heart of the economy. Under NEBM, the corporate economy no longer assumes these collective functions. In an era of open standards, rapid technological change, convergence of technologies, and intense global competition, business enterprises do need to be flexible in the deployment of capital and labor. One way of attaining this flexibility is by giving the organized labor force a major role in enterprise governance, as for example the Japanese, Germans, and Swedes have done, each in their own particular ways (Lazonick 2005, 2007d). In such a system, there is the possibility of an interaction between business and government to provide widespread economic security in employment and retirement while permitting business enterprises to remain innovative and competitive on a global scale.

The other way is the American way in the era of NEBM, which, in an updated version of what I have called "the myth of the market economy" (Lazonick 1991), works under the pretense that the collective provision of economic security is not required. Just get enough education to be "employable" in a well-paid job, and individual initiative will provide one with the lifetime of security that one needs. From the NEBM perspective, the only legitimate function of the government is to invest in the knowledge base, and even then with no notion that, through taxation, a substantial proportion of the gains from innovative enterprise that this knowledge base makes possible should be returned to the government to support the ongoing development of the economy as a whole.

In the United States in the 2000s, the quest for economic security evades even a substantial portion of the better educated population. In its stead stands the quest for shareholder value; the worship of wealth in the 2000s has rewritten the 1980s' motto "greed is good" to read "greed is god." The small minority of the population that controls the allocation of corporate resources is reaping unprecedented wealth—even when some among them cause a financial meltdown—while demanding that the government spend more of the taxpayers' money on knowledge creation and warning that only lower taxes on their wealth can keep the spirit of innovation alive. With the aid of a compliant government, the NEBM may continue to generate respectable U.S. economic growth—although, given global competition and the U.S. financial crisis, even that outcome is in doubt. What does seem certain is that for a growing majority of Americans, the stock market–oriented political economy that has NEBM as its foundation will continue to generate instability and inequity as a normal way of life.

Notes

1. During this period, Cisco paid no cash dividends but did a total of $508 million in stock repurchases from 1995 through 1997, which represented 21.0 percent of its net income for 1995–1997 and 11.5 percent of its net income for 1990–1998.

2. In September 2008, having completed a $40 billion stock repurchase program, Microsoft announced that its board had approved another $40 billion program through September 2013. Microsoft's board also authorized debt financing of up to $6 billion, some of which could be used for buybacks (Associated Press Newswires 2008).

3. For an attempt to use newspaper articles and press releases to track the number of offshored jobs and the companies that are doing the offshoring, see the TechsUnite offshore tracker at http://www.techsunite.org/offshore/.

4. Brown and Linden point out that the data are not strictly comparable from year to year but nevertheless capture the general trend in the location of the employment of engineers in the U.S.-based semiconductor industry.

5. For a list of problems with the H-1B program from the perspecitve of an anti-H-1B Web site, see ZaZona.com (2008). See also hireamericansfirst.org, launched in January 2008.

6. For more information, see http://en.wikipedia.org/wiki/Comprehensive_Immigration_Reform_Act_of 2006.

7. Gates was undoubtedly referring to the 2003 International Student Math Assessment, sponsored by the OECD Programme for International Student Assessment (PISA) (OECD 2004), which is discussed below.

8. For a critique of the argument that there is a shortage of qualified science and engineering graduates in the United States, see Lowell and Salzman (2007).

9. According to Norman Matloff (2006b), who is among the most vocal critics of corporate and government policies that have generated surpluses of experienced engineers, in 2000 "IEEE-USA came under heavy pressure from the IEEE parent organization, which is dominated by industry and academia and thus is highly pro-H-1B. So IEEE-USA suddenly changed its stance. It still was critical of the H-1B program, but it started extolling 'instant green cards' for foreign workers instead of H-1B visas. It ignored member complaints that the green card idea would be just as harmful to IEEE-USA members as H-1B. The Misfortune 500 Web page was taken down."

10. Hyde (2003, chap. 12) argues that employment discrimination law, including that which relates to age discrimination, is based on "an assumption of stable long-term careers inside individual firms," and hence employment discrimination is very difficult to prove in the context of what he calls "a high-velocity labor market" such as exists in Silicon Valley.

11. The article can be found at http://ea-spouse.livejournal.com/; see also http://en.wikipedia.org/wiki/Erin_Hoffman.

12. Trailing the United States were Portugal, Italy, Greece, Turkey, and Mexico.

13. IBM's diversity employment data for 1996–2008 are available at http://www-03.ibm.com/employment/us/diverse/employment_data.shtml.

References

Abbate, Janet. 2000. *Inventing the Internet*. Cambridge, MA: MIT Press.

Abowd, John, John Haltiwanger, Julia Lane, Kevin L. McKinney, and Kristin Sandusky. 2007. "Technology and the Demand for Skill: An Analysis of Within and Between Firm Differences." NBER Working Paper no.13043. Cambridge, MA: National Bureau of Economic Research.

Adams, Walter, ed. 1968. *The Brain Drain*. New York: Macmillan.

Affleck, John. 2000. "IBM Shareholders Reject Return to Traditional Pension Plan." Associated Press Newswires, April 25.

AFL-CIO. 2007. "2007 Trends in CEO Pay." http://www.aflcio.org/ corporatewatch/paywatch/pay/index.cfm (accessed February 25, 2009).

AFX International Focus. 2005. "Intel to Build 2nd Chip Test and Package Plant in Southwest China." AFX International Focus, March 23.

Agence France-Press. 2002. "Hewlett-Packard Launches Research Lab in India." Agence France-Press, February 22.

Albright, Robert C. 1964, "Senate Democrats Optimistic about Tax Bill Chances." *Washington Post*, January 15.

Allegretto, Sylvia. 2006. "Dow's All-Time High Inconsequential for Most Americans." Economic Snapshots. Washington, DC: Economic Policy Institute. http://www.epi.org/content.cfm/webfeatures_snapshots_20061011 (accessed October 21, 2008).

Alliance@IBM. 2008. http://www.allianceibm.org/ (accessed February 25, 2009).

Alterio, Julie Moran. 2007. "IBM Authorizes Buy Back of $15 Billion in Shares." *White Plains (NY) Journal News*, April 25.

Amighini, Alessia. 2004. "China in the International Fragmentation of Production: Evidence from the ICT Industry." *European Journal of Comparative Economics* 2(2): 203–219.

Amparano, Julie. 1988. "US West and Nynex to Stick with Plans to Boost Research." *Wall Street Journal*, January 11.

Amsden, Alice. 1989. *Asia's Next Giant: South Korea and Late Industrialization*. New York: Oxford University Press.

Amsden, Alice, and Wan-wen Chu. 2003. *Beyond Late Development: Taiwan's Upgrading Policies*. Cambridge, MA: MIT Press.

Anand, Vineeta. 1994. "New IRS Rules Anticipated: Cash Balance Sponsors to Get Long-Awaited Help." *Pensions and Investments*, April 18.

———. 1999. "Big Blues: IBM's Conversion Draws Watchdogs: Switch to Cash Balance Plan Raises Concern from Lawmakers about Age Discrimination." *Pensions and Investments*, September 6.

Anders, George. 1999. "Packard Children to Split Efforts in Running Entity." *Wall Street Journal*, July 14, B:6.

Anderson, William. 1991. *Corporate Crisis: NCR and the Computer Revolution*. Santa Fe, NM: Landfall Press.

Arditi, Lynn. 2004. "Angry Shareholders, Workers, Retirees Speak Out at IBM's Annual Meeting." *Providence Journal*, April 28.

Arnold, Jay. 1990. "FCC Adopts Price-Cap Regulations for Eight Local Phone Companies." *Washington Post*, September 20, E:3.

Arnold, Walter. 1988. "Science and Technology Development in Taiwan and South Korea." *Asian Survey* 28(4): 437–450.

Arnst, Catherine. 1991. "Poor Nations Seen Aiding Rich by Brainpower Export in Billions." Reuters News, April 7.

Asia in Focus. 2004. "China's Lenovo to Use AMD Chips in Two New PCs." Asia in Focus, June 11.

Asiainfo Daily China News. 2000. "Intel to Set Up R&D Umbrella Program." Asiainfo Daily China News, November 6.

AsiaPort Daily News. 2001. "Intel to Reinvest US$302,000,000 to China." AsiaPort Daily News, September 26.

Asia Pulse. 2000. "Intel Expands IC Chip Production in China." Asia Pulse, September 8.

Associated Press.1994. "Lotus Development Ordered to Pay $275,000 in Age Discrimination Suit." Associated Press, November 30.

Associated Press Newswires. 2005. "Lenovo Ranked Top Chinese Computer Maker in 2004." Associated Press Newswires, March 9.

———. 2008. "Microsoft to Buy Back $40 Billion of Stock." Associated Press Newswires, September 22.

AT&T Corp. 1984. *10-K Filing to the U.S. Securities and Exchange Commission*. Dallas: AT&T Corp.

———. 1999. *1998 Annual Report*. Dallas: AT&T Corp.

Aubin, Dena. 2006. "Cisco Sells $6.5 Billion in Record U.S. Debt Debut." Reuters News, February 14.

Auten, Gerald. 1999. "Capital Gains Taxation." In *The Encyclopedia of Taxation and Tax Policy*, Joseph J. Cordes, Robert D. Ebel, and Jane G. Gravelle, eds. Washington, DC: Urban Institute, pp. 58–61.

Autor, David H., Lawrence F. Katz, and Melissa S. Kearney. 2008. "Trends in U.S. Wage Inequality: Revising the Revisionists." *Review of Economics and Statistics* 90(2): 300–325.

Avnimelech, Gil, Martin Kenney, and Morris Teubal. 2005. "A Life Cycle Model for the Creation of National Venture Capital Industries." In *Clusters Facing Competition: The Importance of External Linkages*, Elissa Giuliani, Roberta Rabellotti, and Meine Pieter van Dijk, eds. Alsershot, UK and Burlington, VT: Ashgate, pp. 195–214.

Bachman, Justin. 2002. "BellSouth Call Centers Consolidating." AP Online, February 5.

Bacon, David. 2006. "Organizing Silicon Valley's High-Tech Workers." *California Labor and Employment Law Review* 20(4): 3–4, 22–23.

Bacon, Kenneth H. 1981. "Lobbyists Say Options Tax Break Is Needed to Spur Innovation and Congress Responds." *Wall Street Journal*, July 1.

Bahr, Morton. 1999. "Federal Pension Plans." Congressional Testimony. Federal Document Clearing House, September 21.

Bailey, Brandon. 2008. "HP to Cut 24,600 Jobs in EDS Integration." *San Jose Mercury News*, September 16.

Baily, Martin Neil, and Daniel E. Sichel. 2003. "Exploding Productivity Growth: Context, Causes, and Implications: Comments and Discussion." *Brookings Papers on Economic Activity* 2: 280–298.

Baker, John C. 1963. "Stock Options at the Crossroads." *Harvard Business Review* 41(1): 22–29, 164–166.

Baldi, Stéphane, Ying Jin, Melanie Skemer, Patricia J. Green, and Deborah Herget. 2007. *Highlights from PISA 2006: Performance of U.S. 15-Year-Old Students in Science and Mathematics Literacy in an International Context.* NCES 2008-016. Washington, DC: National Center for Education Statistics, Institute of Education Sciences, US Department of Education. http://nces.ed.gov/pubs2008/2008016.pdf (accessed October 22, 2008).

Baldwin, Carliss, and Kim Clark 1992. "Capabilities and Capital Investment: New Perspectives on Capital Budgeting." *Journal of Applied Corporate Finance* 5(2): 67–87.

Barro, Robert J., and Jong-Wha Lee. 2000. "International Data on Educational Attainment: Updates and Implications." Harvard Center for International Development Working Paper no. 42, Appendix Data Files. Cambridge, MA: Harvard University. http://www.cid.harvard.edu/ciddata/ciddata.html (accessed October 22, 2008).

Barry, Kenneth. 1988. "FCC Price Plan to Have Major Impact on AT&T." Reuters News, May 11.

Bass, Dina. 2006a. "Ballmer Pressured to Buy Back Shares of Microsoft Stock." *Seattle Times*, May 13.

———. 2006b. "Sagging Stock Sends Ballmer to Wall Street to Quell Critics." *Seattle Times*, May 30.

Bassett, Ross Knox. 2002. *To the Digital Age: Research Labs, Start-Up Companies, and the Rise of MOS Technology.* Baltimore, MD: Johns Hopkins University Press.

———. 2005. "Facing Two Ways: The Indian Institute of Technology Kanpur, American Technical Assistance, and the Indian Computing Community, 1961–1980." Paper presented at the Society of the History of Technology meetings, held in Minneapolis, MN, November 5.

Baton Rouge Advocate. 2002. "Officials Say PSC Can't Stop Call-Center Closures." *Baton Rouge Advocate*, March 22.

Batt, Rosemary. 1995. "Performance and Welfare Effects of Work Restructuring: Evidence from Telecommunications Services." PhD dissertation. Cambridge, MA: Massachusetts Institute of Technology.

———. 1996. "From Bureaucracy to Enterprise? The Changing Jobs and Careers of Managers in Telecommunications Service." In *Broken Ladders: Managerial Careers in the New Economy*, Paul Osterman, ed. New York: Oxford University Press, pp. 55–80.

———. 1999. "Work Organization, Technology, and Performance in Customer Service and Sales." *Industrial and Labor Relations Review* 52(4): 539–564.

———. 2001. "The Economics of Teams among Technicians." *British Journal of Industrial Relations* 39(1): 1–24.

Beckman, Sara L. 1996. "Evolution of Management Roles in a Networked Organization." In *Broken Ladders: Managerial Careers in the New Economy*, Paul Osterman, ed. New York: Oxford University Press, pp. 155–184.

Behrman, Jack N., and Harvey W. Wallender. 1976. *Transfers of Manufacturing Technology within Multinational Enterprises*. Cambridge, MA: Ballinger.

Bell Atlantic. 1997. *10-K Filing to the U.S. Securities and Exchange Commission*. New York: Bell Atlantic.

Bellinger, Bob. 1989. "The Spark of Silicon Valley." *Electronic Engineering Times*, March 13.

BellSouth. 1994. *1993 10-K*. Atlanta: BellSouth.

Benner, Chris. 2002. *Work in the New Economy: Flexible Labor Markets in Silicon Valley*. Oxford: Blackwell.

Berg, Eric. 1985. "New Phone Research Giant." *New York Times*, July 15.

Bergstein, Brian. 2001a. "Computer Maker to Cut 3,000 Jobs, Miss Earnings Expectations." Associated Press State and Local Wire, April 18.

———. 2001b. "Hewlett-Packard Buying Compaq for $25 Billion to Create Technology Giant." Associated Press State and Local Wire, September 4.

———. 2006a. "IBM Ups Dividend 50 Percent in Bid to Boost Stock." Associated Press State and Local Wire, April 25.

———. 2006b. "IBM's Freeze Is a Stronger Move Toward 401(k)s." *Newark Star-Ledger*, January 8.

———. 2008. "IBM Riles Employees with Base Pay Cuts." Associated Press Online, January 23.

Berle, Adolf A., and Gardiner Means. 1932. *The Modern Corporation and Private Property*. New York: Macmillan.

Berlin, Leslie. 2001. "Robert Noyce and Fairchild Semiconductor, 1957–1968." *Business History Review* 75(1): 63–102.

————. 2005. *The Man Behind the Microchip*. New York: Oxford University Press.

Berliner, David C. 2006. "The State versus the Poor." Occasional Paper 13. Potsdam, Germany: Liberal Institute of the Friedrich Naumann Foundation.

Berman, Dennis K. 2003. "New Calling: At Bell Labs, Hard Times Take Toll on Pure Science." *Wall Street Journal*, May 23, A:1.

Best, Michael H. 2001. *The New Competitive Advantage: The Renewal of American Industry*. New York: Oxford University Press.

Billett, Matthew T., and Hui Xue. 2007. "Share Repurchases and the Need for External Finance." *Journal of Applied Financial Economics* 19(2): 42–55.

Bindra, Ashok. 1997. "Silicon Influx Puts India on World Electronics Map." *Electronic Engineering Times*, April 7.

Bishop, Todd. 2004. "Microsoft Wants to Reduce Its Cash Balance and Improve Its Share Price, Analyst Says; Stock Buyback May Be in the Works." *Seattle Post-Intelligencer*, June 16.

Blair, Margaret, ed. 1993. *The Deal Decade: What Takeovers and Leveraged Buyouts Mean for Corporate Governance*. Washington, DC: Brookings Institution.

————. 1995. *Ownership and Control: Rethinking Corporate Governance for the Twenty-First Century*. Washington, DC: Brookings Institution.

Bloom, Martin. 1992. *Technological Change in the Korean Electronics Industry*. Paris: Organisation for Economic Co-Operation and Development.

Blouin, Jennifer L., Jana Smith Raedy, and Douglas A. Shackleford. 2007. "Did Firms Substitute Dividends for Share Repurchases after the 2003 Reductions in Shareholder Tax Rates?" NBER Working Paper no. 13601. Cambridge, MA: National Bureau of Economic Research.

Board of Governors of the Federal Reserve System. 2008. "Flow of Funds Accounts of the United States—Z1 Release." Federal Reserve Statistical Release. Washington, DC: Board of Governors of the Federal Reserve System. http://www.federalreserve.gov/RELEASES/z1/Current/ (accessed October 22, 2008).

Boehner, John. 2006. "Looking Back at 2006's Top Employee Benefits Newsmakers." *Business Insurance*, December 25. http://www.businessinsurance.com/cgi-bin/article.pl?articleId=20685&a=a&bt=employee+benefits+newsmakers (accessed October 22, 2008).

Borrus, Michael, and John Zysman. 1997. "Wintelism and the Changing Terms of Global Competition: Prototype of the Future?" BRIE Working Paper no. 96B. Berkeley, CA: University of California, Berkeley.

Bozman, Jean. 1990. "U.S. Plight: Factory Flight." *Computerworld*, March 19.

Bradbury, Katharine L. 1996. "The Growing Inequality of Family Incomes: Changing Families and Changing Wages." *New England Economic Review* (July–August): 55–82.

Branscomb, Lewis, and Young-Hwan Choi, eds. 1996. *Korea at the Turning Point: Innovation-Based Strategies for Development.* Westport, CT: Praeger.

Braun, Ernest, and Stuart MacDonald. 1982. *Revolution in Miniature: The History and Impact of Semiconductor Electronics*, 2d ed. Cambridge: Cambridge University Press.

Breznitz, Dan. 2007. *Innovation and the State: Political Choice and Strategies for Growth in Israel, Taiwan, and Ireland.* New Haven, CT: Yale University Press.

Brody, David. 1980. *Workers in Industrial America.* New York: Oxford University Press.

Brooks, John. 1973. *The Go-Go Years: The Drama and Crashing Finale of Wall Street's Bullish 60s.* New York: Dutton.

Brown, Clair. 2005. "Career Paths and Job Ladders." Sloan-LEHD working paper. http://www.economicturbulence.com/data/papers/CareerPaths JobLaddersWorkingPaper.pdf (accessed October 22, 2008).

Brown, Clair, John Haltiwanger, and Julia Lane. 2006. *Economic Turbulence: Is a Volatile Economy Good for America?* Chicago: University of Chicago Press.

Brown, Clair, and Greg Linden. 2005. "Offshoring in the Semiconductor Industry: A Historical Perspective." In *Brookings Trade Forum, 2005: Offshoring White-Collar Work*, Lael Brainard and Susan M. Collins, eds. Washington, DC: Brookings Institution, pp. 279–333.

———. 2008a. "Semiconductor Capabilities in the U.S. and Industrializing Asia." Paper presented at the Sloan Annual Industry Studies Conference "Building Capacity for High Wage Employment," held in Boston, May 1–2.

———. 2008b. "Is There a Shortage of Engineering Talent in the U.S.?" Center for Work, Technology, and Society working paper. Berkeley, CA: University of California, Berkeley.

Brown, Ken Spencer. 2005. "HP Turning a Page with its Business." *Investor's Business Daily*, July 12.

Brown, Warren. 1992. "AT&T, Unions Work Late on Contract." *Washington Post*, May 31, A:5.

Browning, Larry D., and Judy C. Shetler. 2000. *Sematech: Saving the U.S. Semiconductor Industry.* College Station, TX: Texas A&M Press.

Brumfiel, Geoff. 2008. "Bell Labs Bottoms Out." *Nature* 454(7207): 927.

Brynjolfsson, Eric, and Loren Hitt. 2003. "Computing Productivity: Firm-Level Evidence." *Review of Economics and Statistics* 85(4): 793–808.

Bulkeley, William M. 1999. "Sycamore Networks' Gain of 386% Ranks as the 4th-Best IPO Performance." *Wall Street Journal*, October 25, B:10.

Bureau of Economic Analysis (BEA). 2009. *1998–2008 NAICS Data: GDPbyInd_VA_NAICS: Value Added by Industry, Gross Output by Industry, Intermediate Inputs by Industry, the Components of Value Added by Industry, and Employment by Industry.* Washington, DC: Bureau of Economic Analysis. http://www.bea.gov/industry/gdpbyind_data.htm (accessed February 25, 2009).

Burgelman, Robert A. 1994. "Fading Memories: A Process Theory of Strategic Exit in Dynamic Environments." *Administrative Science Quarterly* 39(1): 24–56.

Burgess, John. 1993. "IBM Eliminates 200 Jobs in Montgomery County." *Washington Post*, April 23, F:1.

Burlingame, Harold W., and Michael J. Gulotta. 1998. "Case Study: Cash Balance Pension Plan Facilitates Restructuring the Workforce at AT&T." *Compensation and Benefits Review* 30(6): 38–45.

Burns, Judith. 2000. "SEC Tells IBM It Can't Stop Vote on Pension Plan." Dow Jones News Service, February 16.

Burrows, Peter, and Peter Elstrom. 1999. "The Boss: Hewlett-Packard's New CEO." *BusinessWeek*, August 2, pp. 76–80.

Business Insurance. 1998. "Unions Ratify AT&T Pact." *Business Insurance*, July 13: 1.

Business Korea. 1994. "Key Contributor to Korea's Semiconductor Industry Exported $3.2 Billion of Semiconductors, Communications Equipment." *Business Korea*, February 1: 53.

Business Line. 2002. "India to Increase Staff Strength." *Business Line*, March 11.

Business Standard. 2005. "Juniper Sets Eye on Indian Telecom Market." *Business Standard*, November 24.

Business Times. 2003. "Intel to Expand Capacity with RM152m Investment." *Business Times*, August 27.

Business Wire. 1992. "IBM, Solectron Sign Contracts for Transfer of Some Operations in Bordeaux and Charlotte." Business Wire, August 18.

———. 1994. "SP Telecom Acquires Qwest Communications." Business Wire, February 22.

———. 1996. "Home Market and Color Inkjets Spur U.S. Printer Market to 14 Percent Growth." Business Wire, February 5.

———. 1997. "Lucent Technologies Appoints Chief Operating Officers, Organizes Business around Fastest Growth Opportunities." Business Wire, October 23.

———. 2005. "Intel Establishes $200 Million China Venture Fund." Business Wire, June 13.

———. 2006a. "Plaintiffs' Counsel Announces IBM Tech Workers File Nationwide Overtime Pay Class Action Lawsuit in Federal Court." Business Wire, January 24.

———. 2006b. "Landmark Overtime Pay Class Action Lawsuit against IBM by Tech Workers Expands." Business Wire, March 14.

Business World. 2003. "Geek Haven: Texas Instruments." *Business World,* September 1: 28.

BusinessWeek. 1959. "The Death of Equities." *BusinessWeek,* August 13: 54.

———. 1960. "Blue-Ribbon Venture Capital." *BusinessWeek,* October 29.

———. 1975. "How IBM Avoids Layoffs Through Retraining." *Business-Week,* November 10.

———. 1976. "The LCD Digital Makes a Comeback." *BusinessWeek,* April 19.

———. 1977. "NCR's New Strategy Puts It in Computers to Stay." *Business-Week,* September 26.

———. 1981a. "Intel's Leap into Computers." *BusinessWeek,* November 16.

———. 1981b. "After the Qualified Stock Option." *BusinessWeek,* May 25.

———. 1983. "A Chipmaker Learns a Lesson in Humility." *BusinessWeek,* February 21.

———. 1984. "How Xerox Speeds Up the Birth of New Products." *Business-Week,* March 19.

Byrne, John A. 1994. "That's Some Pay Cap, Bill." *BusinessWeek,* April 25, p. 57.

———. 1995. "CEO Pay: Ready for Takeoff." *BusinessWeek,* April 24, pp. 88–90.

Byun, Byung Moon. 1994. "Growth and Recent Development of the Korean Semiconductor Industry." *Asian Survey* 34(8): 706–720.

Campbell, Erwin D. 1961. "Stock Options Should Be Valued." *Harvard Business Review* 39(4): 52–58.

Carbone, James. 2000. "Growth Means More Consolidation, More Services." *Purchasing* 129(7): 48–55.

———. 2002. "Design Moves into EMS Spotlight." *Purchasing* 131(1): 36, 38, 40.

———. 2004. "Targeting Design." *Purchasing* 133(17): 30, 32, 34, 36.

Carpenter, Marie, and William Lazonick. 2008. "Alcatel-Lucent as a Global Competitor: How a Century-Old French Conglomerate Became a Leader in the Communications Equipment Industry, Survived the Telecom Crash, and Recovered to Absorb a One-Time American Giant." Revision of a paper presented at the INSEAD Conference "Innovation and Competition in the Global Communications Technology Industry," held in Fontainebleau, France, August 23–24.

Carpenter, Marie, William Lazonick, and Mary O'Sullivan. 2003. "The Stock Market and Innovative Capability in the New Economy: The Optical Networking Industry." *Industrial and Corporate Change* 12(5): 963–1034.

Cassidy, John. 2002. *Dot.con: The Greatest Story Ever Sold.* New York: HarperCollins.

Cauley, Leslie. 1996. "SAIC Seen Near Agreement to Buy Bellcore." Capital Markets Report, September 23.

Chaffin, Joshua. 2002a. "SEC Launches Investigation into Wall Street Banks." *Financial Times*, April 25.

———. 2002b. "Lawyers Agog as the Banks Spill the IPO Beans." *Financial Times*, September 18.

Chakravartty, Paula. 2006. "Symbolic Analysts or Indentured Servants? Indian High-Tech Migrants in America's Information Economy." *Knowledge, Technology, and Policy* 19(3): 27–43.

Chandler, Alfred D., Jr. 1977. *The Visible Hand: The Managerial Revolution in American Business.* Cambridge, MA: Harvard University Press.

———. 1990. *Scale and Scope: The Dynamics of Industrial Capitalism.* Cambridge, MA: Belknap Press.

———. 2001. *Inventing the Electronic Century: The Epic Story of the Consumer Electronic and Computer Industries.* New York: Free Press.

Chang, Y.S. 1971. "The Transfer of Technology: Economics of Offshore Assembly: The Case of the Semiconductor Industry." UNITAR Research Report no. 11. Geneva: United Nations Institute for Training and Research.

Chase, Marilyn. 1983. "The Chip Race." *Wall Street Journal*, February 4, A:1.

Chatterjee, Julie. 1994. "Bangalore Woos the Technocrat." *Straits Times*, January 21.

Chesbrough, Henry. 2003. *Open Innovation: The New Imperative for Creating and Profiting from Technology.* Boston: Harvard Business School Press.

Chester, John S., Jr. 1990. "BellSouth Offers Retirement Package." *Communications Week,* November 19.

Chicago Daily Tribune. 1901. "Model Factory Closed by Strike." *Chicago Daily Tribune,* June 6.

China Daily. 2007. "AMD Eats into Intel's Market Share in China." *China Daily,* September 6. http://www.chinadaily.com.cn/china/2007-09/06/content_6086152.htm (accessed February 25, 2009).

China Industry Daily News. 2006. "Intel (China) Ltd. Forges Innovation Alliance with 22 Chinese Enterprises." China Industry Daily News, January 13.

Chira, Susan. 1985. "Korea's Chipmakers Race to Catch Up." *New York Times*, July 15.

Clark, Don. 1990. "National Semi to Trim 2,000 Jobs in Cutback." *San Francisco Chronicle*, August 22, C:1.

————. 1991. "3000 Workers OK Buyouts at Hewlett-Packard." *San Francisco Chronicle*, October 19, B:1.

CMP TechWeb. 2005. "Cisco Pledges $50 Million More for Bangalore Campus." CMP TechWeb, October 21.

————. 2006. "HP Outsourcing Chief Wants to Take It Offshore." CMP TechWeb, November 8.

Cohen, Edward S. 1964 "New Revenue Act Reduces Charm of Stock Options for Executives." *Washington Post*, February 28.

Cohen, Stephen S., and John Zysman. 1987. *Manufacturing Matters: The Myth of the Post-Industrial Economy*. New York: Basic Books.

Compete America. 2008. *Compete America Coalition Members*. http://www.competeamerica.org/whoweare/coalition/index.html (accessed February 26, 2009).

Computer Reseller News. 2005. "Intel Announces $1 Billion Investment Plan for India." *Computer Reseller News*, December 15.

Conference Board. 2008. "Total Economy Database." New York: Conference Board. http://www.conference-board.org/economics/database.cfm (accessed December 3, 2008).

Conroy, Richard. 1992. *Technological Change in China*. Development Centre Studies. Paris: Organisation for Economic Co-Operation and Development.

Cooke, Sandra D. 2003. "Information Technology Workers in the Digital Economy." In *Digital Economy 2003*. Washington, DC: U.S. Department of Commerce, Economics and Statistics Adminstration. https://www.esa.doc.gov/reports/DE-Chap2.pdf (accessed October 22, 2008).

Costanza, Anthony. 1989. "Participatory Action Research: A View from the ACTWU." *American Behavioral Scientist* 32(5): 566–573.

Coughlin, Kevin. 2006. "Lucent, Retirees at Odds over Exec Pay." *Newark Star-Ledger*, February 15.

Cowan, Lynn. 2006. "SAIC Is Poised to Gain from the War on Terror." *Wall Street Journal*, October 9, C:4.

Committee on Prospering in the Global Economy of the 21st Century (CPGE). 2007. *Rising Above the Gathering Storm: Energizing and Employing America for a Brighter Economic Future*. Washington, DC: National Academies Press.

Crenshaw, Albert B. 2004. "IBM Stops Offering Cash-Balance Pension." *Washington Post*, December 9, E:5.

Crenshaw, Albert B., and Amy Joyce. 2006. "IBM Adds Its Name to List of Firms Freezing Pensions." *Washington Post*, January 6, A:1.

Crystal, Graef. 1978. *Executive Compensation: Money, Motivation, and Imagination*. New York: American Management Association.

———. 1991. *In Search of Excess: The Overcompensation of American Executives*. New York: W. W. Norton.

Curran, Lawrence J. 1997. "An Expanding Universe (Growth of Electronics Contract Manufacturers)." *Electronic Business Today*, 23(August 1): 57–58.

Cusumano, Michael. 2000. "Making Large Teams Work Like Small Teams: Product Development at Microsoft." In *New Product Development and Production Networks. Global Industrial Experience*, Ulrich Jürgens, ed. Berlin and Heidelberg: Springer-Verlag, pp. 85–104.

Cusumano, Michael, and David Yoffie. 1998. *Competing on Internet Time: Lessons from Netscape and Its Battle with Microsoft*. New York: Free Press.

Cutcher-Gershenfeld, Joel. 1991. "The Impact on Economic Performance of a Transformation in Workplace Relations." *Industrial and Labor Relations Review* 44(2): 241–260

———. 1992. "Xerox and the ACTWU: Tracing a Transformation in Industrial Relations." In *Human Resources Management: Cases and Text*, 2d ed., Fred K. Foulkes and E. Robert Livernash, eds. Englewood Cliffs, NJ: Prentice Hall, pp. 348–373.

Dale, Arden. 2004a. "Judge Rules IBM Must Make Back Payments in Pension Case." Dow Jones Newswires, February 18.

———. 2004b. "Update: IBM Pension Settlement Leaves Unresolved Issues." Dow Jones News Service, September 30.

Danziger, Sheldon, and Peter Gottschalk. 1995. *America Unequal*. Cambridge, MA: Harvard University Press.

Dash, Eric. 2006. "Off To the Races Again, Leaving the Many Behind." *New York Times*, April 9, C:1.

Dataquest. 2002. "DQ Top 20: Hewlett-Packard." Indian Business Insight Database, August 31.

———. 2003. "Hewlett-Packard India." *Indian Business Insight*, August 31.

Davis, Julie Hirschfeld. 2008. "Congress Opens Hearings on Financial Meltdown." CNSNews.com, October 6. http://www.cnsnews.com/public/content/article.aspx?RsrcID=36962 (accessed February 26, 2009).

Davis, Warren E., and Daryl G. Hatano. 1985. "The American Semiconductor Industry and the Ascendancy of East Asia." *California Management Review* 27(1): 128–143.

Dayton Daily News. 2000. "Last Remaining UAW Workers Lose Jobs at Dayton, Ohio, Infotech Firm." *Dayton Daily News*, August 18.

DeBare, Ilana. 1997. "WORKWAYS—Labor Laws Offer Protection for Live-In Workers." *San Francisco Chronicle*, September 8, B:1. http://www.sfgate.com/cgi-bin/article.cgi?f=/c/a/1997/09/08/BU24846.DTL&type=printable (accessed October 23, 2008).

Deffree, Suzanne. 2008. "Acer Overcomes Lenovo as No. 3 PC OEM, Nips at Dell's Heels for No. 2 Spot." Electronic News, March 6.

Dell. 2005. *2004 10-K*. Round Rock, TX: Dell.

———. 2006. *2005 10-K*. Round Rock, TX: Dell.

———. 2007. *2006 10-K*. Round Rock, TX: Dell.

DeNavas-Walt, Carmen, Bernadette D. Proctor, and Jessica C. Smith. 2008. *Income, Poverty, and Health Insurance Coverage in the United States: 2007*. Current Population Reports: Consumer Income. P60-235. Washington, DC: U.S. Census Bureau.

Dennis, Reid. 2000. "Institutional Venture Partners." In *Done Deals: Venture Capitalists Tell their Stories*, Udayan Gupta, ed. Boston: Harvard Business School Press, pp. 179–190.

Dennis, William. 1990. "Intel to Start MPU Production in Malaysia." Electronic World News, April 9.

DePalma, Anthony. 1990. "Graduate Schools Fill with Foreigners." *New York Times*, November 29, A:1.

Deutschman, Alan. 1994. "How H-P Continues to Grow and Grow." *Fortune* 129(May 2): 90–100.

DiCarlo, Lisa. 1999. "IBM Cashes In: Wielding a Massive Arsenal of Patents, Big Blue Shakes Up the High-Tech Industry." *PC Week* 16(38): 1.

Dictionary.com. 2008. *Subsidy*. http://dictionary.reference.com/search?q= subsidy (accessed February 26, 2009).

Dittmar, Amy K. 2000. "Why Do Firms Repurchase Stock?" *Journal of Business* 73(3): 331–354.

Dittmar, Amy K., and Robert F. Dittmar. 2004. "Stock Repurchase Waves: An Explanation of the Trends in Aggregate Corporate Payout Policy." Business school working paper. Ann Arbor, MI: University of Michigan. http://webuser.bus.umich.edu/adittmar/Stock_Repurchase_Waves.pdf (accessed October 23, 2008).

Domis, Olaf de Senerpont. 2003. "Latitude for Change." *Daily Deal*, December 1.

Donlan, Thomas G. 2000 "Cisco's Bids: Its Growth by Acquisition Will Cause Problems." *Barron's* 80(19): 31–34.

Dow Jones International News. 2008. "Tata Consultancy To Hire 30,000–50,000 Staff This FY." Dow Jones International News, April 21.

Dreyfack, Kenneth, and Otis Port. 1986. "Even American Knowhow is Headed Abroad." *BusinessWeek*, March 3, pp 60–63.

Drury, Allan. 2005. "Shareholders Taking IBM to Task." *White Plains (NY) Journal News*, April 26.

Dudley, Brier. 2004. "Microsoft Research Lab is Opening in India." *Seattle Times*, December 1.

Economist. 1986. "Has IBM Abandoned Full Employment?" *Economist* 300(September 20): 73–74.

———. 1991. "India's Electronics Industry: Skills Exporter." *Economist* 319(May 4): 69–70.

Editors of *Fortune.* 1970. *The Conglomerate Commotion.* New York: Viking.

EFA Global Monitoring Report. 2007. *Strong Foundations: Early Childhood Care and Education.* Paris: UNESCO.

Electronic Buyers' News. 1989. "Union Flare-Up Cools at Korean Motorola Site." *Electronic Buyers' News*, January 9: 2.

Electronic News. 2005. "U.S. Could Lose Race for Nanotech Leadership, SIA Panel Says." Electronic News, March 16.

Electronic Times. 1986."The Recession in the Semiconductor Industry Has Added Another 500 Workers to the Ranks of the Unemployed and Caused Two of Silicon Valley's Premium Chip Makers to Lose a Combined $161 Million in the Past Three Months." *Electronic Times*, October 16.

———. 1992a. "Intel to Move Microcontroller Operations to Penang Plant." *Electronic Times*, July 30.

———. 1992b. "Malaysian Unit to Look at Intel Moves Into China." *Electronic Times*, September 3.

———. 1994. "A Golden Deal for Intel." *Electronic Times*, November 3.

Electronic World News. 1989. "National Semiconductor Closes Plant in S. Korea." Electronic World News, May 15.

Electronics Weekly. 1987. "Electronics Weekly Concludes Its Look at U.S. Semiconductors in '86." *Electronics Weekly*, January 28.

———. 1990. "New Visa Limit Could Restrict Companies' Employment of Foreign Staff." *Electronics Weekly*, October 24: 8.

Elmore, Charles. 1987a. "Early-Retirement Plan's Cost Contributes to Drop in BellSouth Profits." *Atlanta Journal-Constitution*, July 21.

———. 1987b. "BellSouth Says 2,400 OK'd Early Retirement." *Atlanta Journal-Constitution*, August 8.

Elstrom, Peter. 2007. "Gates to Senate: More Visas." *BusinessWeek*, March 8. http://www.businessweek.com/bwdaily/dnflash/content/mar2007/db20070308_624948.htm (accessed October 23, 2008).

Endlich, Lisa. 2004. *Optical Illusions: Lucent and the Crash of Telecom.* New York: Simon and Schuster.

Engen, Eric M., and Andreas Lehnert. 2000. "Mutual Funds and the U.S. Equity Market." *Federal Reserve Bulletin* 86(12): 797–812.

Ernst, Dieter. 2002. "Global Production Networks and the Changing Geography of Innovation Systems: Implications for Developing Countries." *Economics of Innovation and New Technology* 11(6): 497–523.

————. 2005. "Complexity and Internationalisation of Innovation—Why Chip Design is Moving to Asia." *International Journal of Innovation Management* 9(1): 47–73.

ESP Report on Engineering Construction and Operations in the Developing World. 1995. *China: Initial Investment of $30,000,000 to Build Microchip Plant Is to Be Followed by Significant Additional Outlays, Intel (USA)*. ESP Report on Engineering Construction and Operations in the Developing World, July 1.

Evers, Joris. 2006. "Lenovo Expands Use of AMD Chips." ZDNet UK, August 8.

Farber, Henry. 2007. "Job Loss and the Decline of Job Security in the United States." Princeton University Industrial Relations Section Working Paper no. 520. Princeton, NJ: Princeton University. http://www.irs.princeton.edu/pubs/pdfs/520revised.pdf (accessed October 23, 2008).

Federal Communications Commission (FCC). 2007. "Trends in Telephone Service." Washington, DC: Industry Analysis and Technology Division, Wireline Competition Bureau, Federal Communications Commission. http://www.fcc.gov/wcb/iatd/trends.html (accessed October 23, 2008).

Feng, Kaidong, and Ming Zhang. 2008. "Governance and Technological Learning in a Transition Economy: The Case of the Chinese Telecommunications Equipment Sector." Revision of a paper presented at the INSEAD conference "Innovation and Competition in the Global Communications Technology Industry," held in Fontainebleau, France, August 23–24.

Fenn, George W., and Nellie Liang. 2001. "Corporate Payout Policy and Managerial Stock Incentives." *Journal of Financial Economics* 60(1): 45–72.

Financial Accounting Standards Board (FASB). 2001. "FASB Issues Two Statements on its Business Combinations Project." News release, July 20. http://72.3.243.42/news/nr072001.shtml (accessed February 26, 2009).

Fisher, Lawrence M. 1999. "Hewlett Trims Its Forecast for Quarter." *New York Times*, October 2, C:1.

Flamm, Kenneth. 1985. "Internationalization in the Semiconductor Industry." In *The Global Factory: Foreign Assembly in International Trade*, Joseph Grunwald and Kenneth Flamm, eds. Washington, DC: Brookings Institution, pp. 38–136.

————. 1987. *Targeting the Computer: Government Support and International Competition*. Washington, DC: Brookings Institution.

————. 1988. *Creating the Computer: Government, Industry, and High-Technology*. Washington, DC: Brookings Institution.

Flannery, Russell. 1999. "Advanced Semiconductor to Buy 2 Motorola Plants." *Asian Wall Street Journal*, February 8, 3.

Forbes. 2007. "The World's Billionaires." http://www.forbes.com/lists/2007/10/07billionaires_The-Worlds-Billionaires_Rank.html (accessed February 26, 2009).

Forelle, Charles, and James Bandler. 2006. "The Perfect Payday: Some CEOs Reap Millions by Landing Stock Options When They are Most Valuable; Luck—Or Something Else?" *Wall Street Journal*, March 18, A:1.

Foremski, Tom. 1990. "Jobs for Thousands of UK Programmers/Analysts Threatened by Immigration Bill Limiting Work Visas." *Computing*, October 25.

Fortney, Judith. 1970. "International Migration of Professionals." *Population Studies* 24(2): 217–232.

Fortune. 2006. "Fortune 500 Largest U.S. Corporations." *Fortune* 153(7): F1–F20.

———. 2008. "Fortune 500 Largest U.S. Corporations." *Fortune* 157(9). http://money.cnn.com/magazines/fortune/fortune500/2007/full_list/index.html (accessed February 26, 2009).

Freund, Bob. 2002. "IBM Stockholders Reject Pension Proposal." *Post-Bulletin*, April 30.

Frey, Carol. 1999a. "IBM Makes Pension Plan More Attractive to Younger Workers." *Raleigh (NC) News and Observer*, May 4.

———. 1999b. "IBM's Pension Concession Doesn't Stop Union Movement." *Raleigh (NC) News and Observer*, September 22, D:3.

Fried, Jesse M. 2000. "Insider Signaling and Insider Trading with Repurchase Tender Offers." *University of Chicago Law Review* 67(2): 421–477.

———. 2001. "Open Market Repurchases: Signaling or Managerial Opportunism?" *Theoretical Inquiries in Law* 2(2): 1–30.

Fukasaku, Tohiko. 1992. *Technology and Industrial Development in Pre-War Japan: Mitsubishi Nagasaki Shipyard, 1884–1934*. New York: Routledge.

Fuller, Joseph, and Michael C. Jensen. 2002. "Just Say No to Wall Street: Putting a Stop to the Earnings Game." *Journal of Applied Corporate Finance* 14(4): 41–46.

Fulman, Ricki. 1998. "AT&T Unions Move to Cash Balance Plan." *Pensions and Investments*, June 15.

Fuscaldo, Donna. 2001. "IBM Shareholders Vote on Proposal Attacking Pension Plan." Dow Jones News Service, April 24.

Garr, Doug. 1999. *IBM Redux: Lou Gerstner and the Business Turnaround of the Decade*. New York: HarperBusiness.

Gartner Incorporated. 2008. "Worldwide Semiconductor Revenue Increased 4 Percent in 2007, According to Final Results by Gartner." Press release, March 31. Stamford: CT: Gartner. http://www.gartner.com/it/page.jsp?id=635207 (accessed February 26, 2009).

Gates, Bill. 2007. "How to Keep America Competitive." *Washington Post*, February 25, B:7.

Geisel, Jerry. 1995. "Pension Equity Plans Another Option When Traditional Pension Doesn't Fit." *Business Insurance*, August 14.

———. 1999. "IBM Debuts Innovative Health Plan for Retirees." *Business Insurance*, May 24.

Gerstner, Louis V., Jr. 2002. *Who Says Elephants Can't Dance?* New York: HarperBusiness.

Ghilarducci, Teresa. 1992. *Labor's Capital: The Economics and Politics of Private Pensions*. Cambridge, MA: MIT Press.

Gilson, Ronald J. 1999. "The Legal Infrastructure of High-Technology Industrial Districts: Silicon Valley, Route 128, and Covenants Not to Compete." *New York University Law Review* 74(3): 575–629.

Gimein, Mark, Eric Dash, Lisa Munoz, and Jessica Sung. 2002. "You Bought. They Sold." *Fortune* 146(4): 64–68, 72, 74.

Glimstedt, Henrik, William Lazonick, and Hao Xie. 2006. "Evolution and Allocation of Stock Options: Adapting U.S.-Style Compensation to the Swedish Business Model." *European Management Review* 3(3): 1–21.

Goldin, Claudia, and Lawrence F. Katz. 2008. *The Race between Education and Technology*. Cambridge, MA: Harvard University Press.

Gompers, Paul, and Josh Lerner. 2002. *The Venture Capital Cycle*. Cambridge, MA: MIT Press.

Gonsalves, Antone. 2008. "PC Market Rises on Notebook Sales: HP, Dell, Acer Hold Top Rankings." *InformationWeek*, June 27. http://www.informationweek.com/news/hardware/desktop/showArticle.jhtml?article ID=208801463 (accessed October 23, 2008).

Gordon, Bart. 2007. "U.S. Competitiveness: The Education Imperative." *Issues in Science and Technology*, Spring. http://www.issues.org/23.3/gordon .html (accessed November 6, 2008).

Gordon, Marcy. 2001. "Wall Street to Reopen with Relaxed Rules." Associated Press, September 15.

Gordon, Robert J. 2003. "Exploding Productivity Growth: Context, Causes, and Implications." *Brookings Papers on Economic Activity* 2: 207–279.

Gore, Albert. 1965. "How to Be Rich without Paying Taxes." *New York Times*, April 11.

Government Of India. 2002. *Statistical Abstract India*. New Delhi: Government of India, Ministry of Statistics and Programme Implementation.

———. 2003. *Statistical Abstract India*. New Delhi: Government of India, Ministry of Statistics and Programme Implementation.

Green, Milford B. 2004. "Venture Capital Investment in the United States, 1995–2002." *Industrial Geographer* 2(1): 2–30.

Grindley, Peter C., David C. Mowery, and Brian Silverman. 1994. "SEMAT-ECH and Collaborative Research: Lessons in the Design of High-Technology Consortia." *Journal of Policy Analysis and Management* 13(4): 723–758.

Grindley, Peter C., and David J. Teece. 1997. "Managing Intellectual Capital: Licensing and Cross-Licensing in Semiconductors and Electronics." *California Management Review* 39(2): 8–41.

Griswold, Erwin N. 1960. "Are Stock Options Getting Out of Hand?" *Harvard Business Review* 38(6): 49–55.

Groshen, Erica, and Simon Potter. 2003. "Has Structural Change Contributed to a Jobless Recovery?" *Current Issues in Economics and Finance* 9(8): 1–7.

Grove, Andrew S. 1996. *Only the Paranoid Survive: How to Exploit the Crisis Points That Challenge Every Company*. New York: Doubleday Business.

Grullon, Gustavo, and David L. Ikenberry. 2000. "What Do We Know about Stock Repurchases?" *Journal of Applied Corporate Finance* 13(1): 31–51.

Grullon, Gustavo, and Roni Michaely. 2002. "Dividends, Share Repurchases, and the Substitution Hypothesis." *Journal of Finance* 57(4): 1649–1684.

Gu, Shulin. 1999. *China's Industrial Technology: Market Reform and Organizational Change*. London: Routledge.

Guarisco, Tom. 1995. "BellSouth to Cut Up to 11,000 Jobs." *Baton Rouge Advocate*, May 19.

Gutchess, Jocelyn. 1985a. "Employment Security and Productivity? It Can Be Done." *National Productivity Review* 4(3): 275–286.

———. 1985b. *Employment Security in Action: Strategies That Work*. Oxford, UK: Pergamon Press.

Hall, Brian J., and Jeffrey B. Leibman. 1998. "Are CEOs Really Paid Like Bureaucrats?" *Quarterly Journal of Economics* 113(3): 653–691.

Hall, Brian J., and Kevin Murphy. 2003. "The Trouble with Options." *Journal of Economic Perspectives* 17(3): 49–70.

Halperin, Morton P. 1961. "The Gaither Committee and the Policy Process." *World Politics* 13(3): 360–384.

Hambrecht, William R. 1984. "Venture Capital and the Growth of Silicon Valley." *California Management Review* 26(2): 74–82.

Harden, Blain. 2003. "Microsoft Millionaires Grapple with Wealth: Stock Option Riches Leave Some Uneasy." *Washington Post*, August 23, A:1.

Harrison, Bennett, and Barry Bluestone. 1988. *The Great U-Turn: Corporate Restructuring and the Polarizing of America*. New York: Basic Books.

Hays, Kristen, and David Ivanovich. 2008. "Politicians Fume as Exxon Profits; Firm Buys Back $8 Billion in Shares." *Houston Chronicle*, August 1, A:1.

Hays, Laurie. 1994a. "IBM's Czarnecki Resigns No. 3 Post After Less Than Year." *Wall Street Journal*, April 27, A:3.

————. 1994b. "IBM Aide Quit under Pressure, Executives Say." *Wall Street Journal*, April 28, A:3.

Head, Beverley. 1989. "Bodyshopping Boom Eases Australia's Skill Shortage." *Australian Financial Review*, September 4.

Hearn, Edward T. 1991. "Baby Bells Seek OK to Manufacture." *Chicago Tribune*, March 10.

Heim, Kristi. 2004. "U.S. High-Tech Giants Invest in Future Competitor." *San Jose Mercury News*, March 15.

Henderson, Jeffrey. 1989. *The Globalisation of High Technology Production: Society, Space, and Semiconductors in the Restructuring of the Modern World*. London: Routledge.

Henry, David, and Donald Dalton. 2003. "Information Technology Producing Industries—Hopeful Signs in 2003." In *Digital Economy 2003*, U.S. Department of Commerce, Economics and Statistics Administration, ed. http://www.esa.doc.gov/reports/DE-Chap1.pdf (accessed November 6, 2008).

Hewlett-Packard (HP). 1985. *1984 Annual Report*. Palo Alto, CA: Hewlett-Packard.

————. 2006. *2005 10-K*. Palo Alto, CA: Hewlett-Packard.

————. 2008. *Global Citizenship Report 2007*. Palo Alto, CA: HP.

Hiltzik, Michael A. 2000. *Dealers of Lightning: Xerox PARC and the Dawn of the Computer Age*. New York: HarperCollins.

Hira, Ron. 2003. "Global Outsourcing of Engineering Jobs: Recent Trends and Possible Implications." Testimony to the Committee on Small Business, U.S. House of Representatives, June 18.

————. 2007. "Policy and the STEM Workforce System." STEM Workforce Data Project Report No. 9. Washington, DC: Commission on Professionals in Science and Technology. http://www.cpst.org/STEM/STEM9_Report.pdf (accessed November 6, 2008).

Hira, Ron, and Anil Hira. 2005. *Outsourcing America*. New York: American Management Association.

Hira, Ron, and Philip E. Ross. 2007. "The R&D 100: A Company's Research Budget Tells You Very Little about Its Prospects." *IEEE Spectrum*, December.

Hirschman, Albert O. 1970. *Exit, Voice, and Loyalty: Responses to Decline in Firms, Organizations, and States*. Cambridge, MA: Harvard University Press.

Ho, Samuel P.S. 1975. "Industrialization in Taiwan: Recent Trends and Problems." *Pacifica* 48(1): 27–41.

Hobday, Michael. 1995. *Innovation in East Asia: The Challenge to Japan*. Cheltenham, UK: Edward Elgar.

Holbrook, Daniel, Wesley M. Cohen, David A. Hounshell, and Steven Klepper. 2000. "The Nature, Sources, and Consequences of Firm Differences in the Early History of the Semiconductor Industry." *Strategic Management Journal* 21(10–11): 1017–1041.

Holland, Daniel M., and Wilbur G. Lewellen. 1962. "Probing the Record of Stock Options." *Harvard Business Review* 40(2): 132–150.

Hollinger, Peggy, Frédéric Schaeffer, Guillaume de Calignon, and Andrew Parker. 2007. "Deadline for Alcatel-Lucent." *Financial Times*, September 28. http://www.ft.com/cms/s/0/735b7e0c-6d60-11dc-ab19-0000779fd2ac .html (accessed November 6, 2008).

Holmes, Stanley. 1996. "Unionizing the Nerds." *PC Week*, October 28.

Holusha, John. 1989. "Stress on Quality Lifts Xerox's Market Share." *New York Times*, November 9, D:1.

Hopfner, Jonathan. 2007. "Intel Readies Vietnam Facility for Fall 2009 Launch." *EETimes*, August 9.

Horwitt, Elisabeth. 1996. "For Whom the Bells Toll: As Competition among RBOCs Heats Up, Joint Ownership of Bellcore Has Become Dicey." *ComputerWorld*, November 1.

Hou, Mingjuan. 2000. "Intel Boosts R&D in China." *China Daily*, October 26.

Houseman, Susan N. 2007. "Outsourcing, Offshoring, and Productivity Measurement in U.S. Manufacturing." Upjohn Institute Working Paper no. 06-130. Kalamazoo, MI: W.E. Upjohn Institute for Employment Research. http://www.upjohninstitute.org/publications/wp/06-130.pdf (accessed November 7, 2008).

Howells, Thomas F. III, and Barefoot, Kevin B. 2007. "Annual Industry Accounts: Advance Estimates for 2006." *Survey of Current Business* 88(10): 12–25. www.bea.gov/scb/pdf/2007/05%20May/0507_annual_industry_accounts.pdf (accessed November 7, 2008).

Hsieh, Jim, and Qinghai Wang. 2006. "Insiders' Tax Preferences and Firm's Choice between Dividends and Share Repurchases." Finance Group Working Paper no. 41. Atlanta, GA: Georgia Tech University, College of Management. http://papers.ssrn.com/sol3/papers.cfm?abstract_id=925350 (accessed November 7, 2008).

Hsu, David H., and Martin Kenney. 2005. "Organizing Venture Capital: The Rise and Demise of American Research & Development Corporation, 1946–1973." *Industrial and Corporate Change* 14(4): 579–616.

Hudson, Richard L. 1982. "SEC Eases Way for Repurchase of Firms' Stock." *Wall Street Journal*, November 10.

Husted, Bill. 1991. "BellSouth Hopes Early Retirement Can Trim Payroll." *Atlanta Journal and Constitution*, May 14.

Hyde, Alan. 2003. *Working in Silicon Valley: Economic and Legal Analysis of a High-Velocity Labor Market.* Armonk, NY: M.E. Sharpe.

IBM. 2004. *2003 Annual Report.* Armonk, NY: IBM.

———. 2006. *IBM Notice of 2006 Annual Meeting and Proxy Statement.* Armonk, NY: IBM.

———. 2007. *IBM Annual Meeting of Stockholders, Final Stockholder Voting Results.* Armonk, NY: IBM.

———. 2008. *2007 Annual Report.* Armonk, NY: IBM. http://www.ibm.com/annualreport/2007/index.shtml (accessed February 26, 2009).

IEEE–Cedar Rapids Section 2006. "IEEE-USA Disappointed with Senate Bill Increasing H-1B Visas." Press release, May 26. http://www.ieee-cr-section.org/content.asp?ID=1296&I=5169 (accessed February 26, 2009).

IEEE–Central Texas Section. 2008. "Employment Opportunities for CTS Members." http://ewh.ieee.org/r5/central_texas/employment.html (accessed February 26, 2009).

IEEE-USA 2004a. "Employed Number of Electrical Engineers, Computer Scientists Declines, Unemployment Rate Increases from Fourth Quarter '03 to First Quarter '04." Press release, May 4. Washington, DC: IEEE-USA. http://www.ieeeusa.org/communications/releases/2004/050404pr.html (accessed February 26, 2009).

———. 2004b. "High-Tech Employment Shrinks in Second Quarter, Despite Positive Signs on Unemployment Rates." Press release, July 26. Washington, DC: IEEE-USA. http://www.ieeeusa.org/communications/releases/2004/072604pr.html (accessed February 26, 2009).

———. 2006a. *IEEE-USA 2006 Annual Report.* Washington, DC: IEEE-USA. http://www.ieeeusa.org/about/Annual_Report/2006.pdf (accessed February 26, 2009).

———. 2006b. *2006 IEEE-USA Unemployment Survey Results.* Washington, DC: IEEE-USA. http://www.ieeeusa.org/careers/pdf/Employment Survey2006Report.pdf (accessed February 26, 2009).

IFI Patent Intelligence. 2008. "IFI Patent Intelligence Announces 2007's Top U.S. Patent Assignees." Press release, January 14. Wilmington, DE: Wolters Kluwer Health. http://www.ificlaims.com/IFI Patent Release 1-9-08.htm (accessed February 26, 2009).

Ilchman, Warren F. 1969. "'People in Plenty': Educated Unemployment in India." *Asian Survey* 9(10): 781–795.

Immigration and Naturalization Service. 1999. *1997 Statistical Yearbook of the Immigration and Naturalization Service.* Washington, DC: Immigration and Naturalization Service. http://www.dhs.gov/xlibrary/assets/statistics/yearbook/1997YB.pdf (accessed July 13, 2009).

————. 2000. *1998 Statistical Yearbook of the Immigration and Naturalization Service*. Washington, DC: Immigration and Naturalization Service. http://www.dhs.gov/xlibrary/assets/statistics/yearbook/1998/1998yb.pdf (accessed July 13, 2009).

————. 2002a. *1999 Statistical Yearbook of the Immigration and Naturalization Service*. Washington, DC: Immigration and Naturalization Service. http://www.dhs.gov/xlibrary/assets/statistics/yearbook/1999/FY99 Yearbook.pdf (accessed July 13, 2009).

————. 2002b. *2000 Statistical Yearbook of the Immigration and Naturalization Service*. Washington, DC: Immigration and Naturalization Service. http://www.dhs.gov/xlibrary/assets/statistics/yearbook/2000/Yearbook 2000.pdf (accessed July 13, 2009).

————. 2003. *2001 Statistical Yearbook of the Immigration and Naturalization Service*. Washington, DC: Immigration and Naturalization Service. http://www.dhs.gov/xlibrary/assets/statistics/yearbook/2001/yearbook2001.pdf (accessed July 13, 2009).

Index Mundi. 2008. *Malaysia GDP—Real Growth Rate*. http://indexmundi .com/malaysia/gdp_real_growth_rate.html (accessed February 26, 2009).

Indo-Asian News Service. 2007. "Texas Instruments to Focus R&D in India." Indo-Asian News Service, April 3.

Industrial Union Department, AFL-CIO. 1959. *The Stock Option Scandal*. Washington, DC: AFL-CIO.

Industry Updates. 2006. "Lenovo Sees More Market Share Growth." Industry Updates, June 1.

Infosys. 2008. *Annual Report, 2007–2008*. Bangalore: Infosys.

Ingebretsen, Mark. 2002. *NASDAQ: A History of the Market That Changed the World*. Rosedale, CA: Prima Publishing.

Institute of International Education. 2005. *Open Doors: Report on International Educational Exchange, 1948–2004*. New York: Institute of International Education.

Intel. 1973. *1972 Annual Report*. Santa Clara, CA: Intel.

————. 2008a. *Intel China Research Center*. Beijing: Intel. http://www.intel .com/cd/corporate/icrc/apac/eng/167066.htm (accessed February 26, 2009).

————. 2008b. *Stock Data—Stock Buyback Summary*. Santa Clara, CA: Intel. http://www.intc.com/stockBuyBack.cfm (accessed February 26, 2009).

International Labour Organization. 1999. "Americans Work Longest Hours among Industrialized Countries, Japanese Second Longest. Europeans Work Less Time, but Register Faster Productivity Gains. New ILO Statistical Volume Highlights Labour Trends Worldwide." Press release, September 6. Geneva: ILO. http://www.ilo.org/global/About_the_ILO/Media_and_public _information/Press_releases/lang--en/WCMS_071326 (accessed February 26, 2009).

Ismail, Izwan. 2005. "Intel Steps Up Local Investment." *New Straits Times*, December 12.

Ismail, Mohd Nazai. 1999. "Foreign Firms and National Technological Upgrading: The Electronics Industry in Malaysia." In *Industrial Technology Development in Malaysia*, K.S. Jomo, Greg Fulker, and Rajah Rasiah, eds. New York: Routledge, pp. 21–37.

Jackson, Tim. 1997. *Inside Intel: Andy Grove and the Rise of the World's Most Powerful Chip Company*. New York: Dutton.

Jacobson, Gary. 1988. "Employee Relations at Xerox: A Model Worth Copying." *Management Review* 77(2): 22–23, 27.

Jacobson, Gary, and John Hillkirk. 1986. *Xerox American Samurai: The Behind the Scenes Story of How a Corporate Giant Beat the Japanese at Their Own Game*. New York: Scribner.

Jander, Mary. 2000. "Lucent Shares Hammered by $125M Goof." *Light Reading*, November 21.

———. 2001. "SEC Knocking on Lucent's Door." *Light Reading*, February 9.

Jenkins, David. 2006. "Programmers Win EA Overtime Settlement, EA Spouse Revealed." *Gamasutra News*, April 26. http://www.gamasutra.com/php-bin/news_index.php?story=9051 (accessed February 26, 2009).

Jensen, Michael C. 1986 "Agency Costs of Free Cash Flow, Corporate Finance, and Takeovers." *American Economic Review* 76(2): 323–329.

Jensen, Michael C., and Kevin J. Murphy. 1990. "Performance Pay and Top Management Incentives." *Journal of Political Economy* 98(2): 225–264.

Jensen, Michael C., Kevin J. Murphy, and Eric G. Wruck. 2005. "CEO Pay… and How to Fix It." Harvard Business School NOM Working Paper no. 04-28. Boston: Harvard Business School. http://www.nber.org/~confer/2005/si2005/cg/jensen.pdf (accessed November 7, 2008).

Johns, Brian. 1994. "Chip Maker Intel Signs China Partnership Agreement." *Journal of Commerce*, March 30.

Johnson, Jean, and Mark Regets. 1998. "International Mobility of Scientists and Engineers to the United States—Brain Drain or Brain Circulation?" Division of Science Resources Studies Issue Brief, NSF 98-316. Arlington, VA: National Science Foundation.

Johnson, Tom. 2000. "Lucent Target of Lawsuits Over 4th-Quarter Earnings." *Star-Ledger*, November 29.

Jolls, Christine. 1998. "Stock Repurchases and Incentive Compensation." NBER Working Paper no. 6467. Cambridge, MA: National Bureau of Economic Research.

Jomo, K.S., Greg Fulker, and Rajah Rasiah, eds. 1999. *Industrial Technology Development in Malaysia*. New York: Routledge.

Jones, Arthur F. Jr., and Daniel H. Weinberg. 2000. *The Changing Shape of the Nation's Income Distribution, 1947–1998.* Current Population Report P60-204. Washington, DC: U.S. Census Bureau. http://www.census.gov/prod/2000pubs/p60-204.pdf (accessed November 7, 2008).

Jorgenson, Dale W. 2001. "Information Technology and the U.S. Economy." *American Economic Review* 91(1): 1–32.

Jun, Sang-Gyung, Mookwan Jung, and Ralph A. Walking. 2008. "Share Repurchase, Executive Options, and Wealth Changes to Stockholders and Bondholders." LeBow College of Business Working Paper. Philadelphia: Drexel University.

Kahle, Kathleen M. 2002. "When a Buyback Isn't a Buyback: Open Market Repurchases and Employee Options." *Journal of Financial Economics* 63(2): 235–261.

Ke, Wei. 1998. "First U.S. JV Now Reaps Rewards." *Business Weekly*, June 28.

Kehoe, Louise. 1991. "Lumbering Giant Starts to Stir." *Financial Times*, July 5.

———. 1994. "Intel in Chinese Partnership." *Financial Times*, March 29.

Keller, Greg. 2008. "Salvaging Alcatel-Lucent Deal a Job for New Blood." Associated Press, July 29.

Kelly, Terence K., William P. Butz, Stephen Carroll, David M. Adamson, and Gabrielle Bloom, eds. 2004. *The U.S. Scientific and Technical Workforce: Improving Data for Decisionmaking.* Santa Monica, CA: RAND Corporation.

Kelly, Tracey Elizabeth. 1997. "Productivity of the Regional Bell Operating Companies Under Rate-of-Return and Price-Cap Regulation." Master's thesis. Blacksburg, VA: Virginia Polytechnic Institute and State University.

Kenney, Martin, ed. 2000. *Understanding Silicon Valley: The Anatomy of an Entrepreneurial Region.* Palo Alto, CA: Stanford University Press.

Kenney, Martin, and Richard Florida. 2000. "Venture Capital in Silicon Valley: Fueling New Firm Formation." In *Understanding Silicon Valley: The Anatomy of an Entrepreneurial Region*, Martin Kenney, ed. Palo Alto, CA: Stanford University Press, pp. 98–123.

Khatiwada, Ishwar, and Andrew Sum. 2004. "Labor Market Problems in Massachusetts from the End of the Labor Market Boom in 2000 through 2003." Boston: Northeastern University, Center for Labor Market Studies. http://www.massworkforce.com/files/Recession_in_Massachusetts_2000_2003April2004.pdf (accessed November 7, 2008).

Kim, Dong-Won, and Stuart W. Leslie. 1998. "Winning Markets or Winning Noble Prizes? KAIST and the Challenges of Late Industrialization." *Osiris*, 2d. series. 13: 154–185.

Kim, Linsu. 1997a. *Imitation to Innovation: The Dynamics of Korea's Technological Learning.* Boston: Harvard Business School Press.

———. 1997b. "The Dynamics of Samsung's Technological Learning in Semiconductors." *California Management Review* 39(3): 86–100.

Kirby, Carrie. 2000. "Sweeping Proposal: Janitors Look to Silicon Valley Giants for Help in Pay Dispute." *San Francisco Chronicle,* May 20, A:1.

———. 2001. "Hewlett-Packard Asks Workers to Take Pay Cut, Vacation Days." *San Francisco Chronicle,* June 30, E:1.

Klayman, Ben. 2002. "Lucent's New CEO to Get Double Chairman's 2001 Pay." Reuters News, February 14.

Knight, Jerry. 1999. "Nextel Builds War Chest." *Washington Post,* November 11, E:1.

Koike, Kazuo, and Takenori Inoki, eds. 1990. *Skill Formation in Japan and Southeast Asia.* Tokyo: University of Tokyo Press.

Konrad, Rachel. 2005. "Hewlett-Packard Ousts CEO Fiorina." *Seattle Times,* February 10.

———. 2006. "IBM Settles Overtime Lawsuit." Associated Press Online, November 23.

Korea Economic Weekly. 1999. "ASE Group to Beef Up Korean Operation." *Korea Economic Weekly,* November 1.

Korea Herald. 1998. "Motorola Korea Opens Software R&D Center." *Korea Herald,* July 23.

Korea Times. 1999. "Motorola Vows Continued Commitment to Korea." *Korea Times,* April 19.

Kornblut, Anne E. 1999. "IBM Relents on Pension Plan Revision." *Boston Globe,* September 18, F:1.

Kotkin, Joel. 1985. "Is IBM Good for America?" *Washington Post,* October 6.

Krishnan, Anne. 2003. "IBM Shareholders Reject Pension Choice Proposal for Third Time." *Durham (NC) Herald-Sun,* April 30.

Kulkarni, Vishwanath. 2008. "EDS Buy Gives HP Services India Edge." *Mint,* May 14.

Lane, Randall. 1994. "Venture Capital Heaven." *Forbes* 154(July 18): 130.

Langlois, Richard N. 1992 "External Economies and Economic Progress: The Case of the Microcomputer Industry." *Business History Review* 66(1): 1–50.

LaPedus, Mark. 1997. "China: Sleeping Giant is Stirring." *Electronic Buyers' News,* January 13.

Lazes, Peter, Leslie Rumpeltes, Ann Hoffner, Larry Pace, and Anthony Costanza. 1991. "Xerox and ACTWU: Using Labor-Management Teams to Remain Competitive." *National Productivity Review* 10(3): 339–349.

Lazonick, William. 1990. *Competitive Advantage on the Shop Floor*. Cambridge, MA: Harvard University Press.

———. 1991. *Business Organization and the Myth of the Market Economy*. New York: Cambridge University Press.

———. 1992. "Controlling the Market for Corporate Control: The Historical Significance of Managerial Capitalism." *Industrial and Corporate Change* 1(3): 445–488.

———. 1998. "Organizational Learning and International Competition." In *Globalization, Growth and Governance: Creating an Innovative Economy*, Jonathan Michie and John Grieve Smith, eds. New York: Oxford University Press, pp. 204–238.

———. 1999. "The Japanese Economy and Corporate Reform: What Path to Sustainable Prosperity?" *Industrial and Corporate Change* 8(4): 607–633.

———. 2003a. "Stock Options and Innovative Enterprise: The Evolution of a Mode of High-Tech Compensation." Center for Industrial Competitiveness and INSEAD Working Paper. Lowell, MA: University of Massachusetts Lowell, Center for Industrial Competitiveness.

———. 2003b. "The Theory of the Market Economy and the Social Foundations of Innovative Enterprise." *Economic and Industrial Democracy* 24(1): 9–44.

———. 2004a. "Corporate Restructuring." In *The Oxford Handbook of Work and Organization*, Stephen Ackroyd, Rose Batt, Paul Thompson, and Pamela Tolbert, eds. New York: Oxford University Press, pp. 577–601.

———. 2004b. "Indigenous Innovation and Economic Development: Lessons from 'China's Leap into the Information Age.'" *Industry and Innovation* 11(4): 273–298.

———. 2005. "The Institutional Triad and Japanese Development." In *The Contemporary Japanese Enterprise*, vol.1, Glenn Hook and Akira Kudo, eds. Tokyo: Yuhikaku Publishing, pp. 55–82.

———. 2006. "Innovative Enterprise and Economic Development." INSEAD working paper. Fontainebleau, France: INSEAD.

———. 2007a. "Varieties of Capitalism and Innovative Enterprise." *Comparative Social Research* 24: 21–69.

———. 2007b. "Evolution of the New Economy Business Model." In *Internet and Digital Economics*, Eric Brousseau and Nicola Curien, eds. New York: Cambridge University Press, pp. 59–113.

———. 2007c. "Globalization of the ICT Labor Force." In *The Oxford Handbook of Information and Communication Technologies*, Robin Mansell, Christanthi Avgerou, Danny Quah, and Roger Silverstone, eds. New York: Oxford University Press, pp. 75–99.

————. 2007d. "The U.S. Stock Market and the Governance of Innovative Enterprise." *Industrial and Corporate Change* 16(6): 983–1035.

————. 2007e. "Economic Institutional Change and Employer Pensions." In *Employee Pensions: Policies, Problems and Possibilities*, Teresa Ghilarducci and Christian E. Weller, eds. Ithaca, NY: Cornell University Press, pp. 29–68.

————. 2008a. "Comment on 'Technological Revolutions and the Evolution of Industrial Structures' (by Giovanni Dosi, Alfonso Gambardella, Marco Grazzi, and Luigi Orsenigo)." *Capitalism and Society* 3(1): Article 3.

————. 2008b. "Entrepreneurial Ventures and the Developmental State: Lessons from the Advanced Economies." World Institute of Development Economics Research Discussion Paper dp2008-01. Helsinki: World Institute of Development Economics. http://www.wider.unu.edu/ publications/working-papers/discussion-papers/2008/en_GB/dp2008-01/_ files/78805634425684379/default/dp2008-01.pdf (accessed November 11, 2008).

————. 2008c. "Everyone Is Paying the Price for Share Buy-Backs." *Financial Times*, September 26.

————. 2008d. "The Quest for Shareholder Value: Stock Repurchases in the U.S. Economy." *Louvain Economic Review* 74(4): 479–540.

Lazonick, William, Michael Fiddy, and Steven Quimby. 2002. "'Grow Your Own' in the New Economy? Skill-Formation Challenges in the New England Optical Networking Industry." In *Globalization, Universities, and Sustainable Human Development*, Robert Forrant and Jean Pyle, eds. Cheltenham, UK: Edward Elgar, pp. 233–259.

Lazonick, William, and Edward March. 2008. "The Rise and Fall of Lucent Technologies." Center for Industrial Competitiveness Working Paper. Lowell, MA: University of Massachusetts Lowell, Center for Industrial Competitiveness.

Lazonick, William, and Mary O'Sullivan. 2000a. "Maximizing Shareholder Value: A New Ideology for Corporate Governance." *Economy and Society* 29(1): 13–35.

————. 2000b. *Perspectives on Corporate Governance, Innovation, and Economic Performance*. Report prepared for the project on Corporate Governance, Innovation, and Economic Performance under the Targeted Socio-Economic Research Programme of the European Commission. Fountainbleau, France: INSEAD. http://www.insead.edu/v1/projects/cgep/Research/ Perspectives/PCGIEPFinalCorrected%200201.pdf (accessed November 11, 2008).

———. 2004. "Corporate Governance, Innovation, and Economic Performance in the EU: Final Report," Targeted Socio-Economic Research (TSER) Report to the European Commission (DGXII) under the Fourth Framework Programme. Fountainbleu, France: INSEAD. http://www.insead.edu/v1/projects/cgep/Research/NationalSystems/GermanSystem310101.pdf (accessed November 11, 2008).

Lazonick, William, and Steven Quimby. 2007. "Transitions of a Displaced High-Tech Labor Force." In *The Future of Work in Massachusetts*, Tom Juravich, ed. Amherst, MA: University of Massachusetts Press, pp. 111–134.

Lazonick, William, and Oner Tulum. 2008. "U.S. Biopharmaceutical Finance and the Sustainability of the Biotech Boom." Paper presented at the Business History Conference, held in Sacramento, CA, April 10–12.

Leachman, Robert C., and Chien H. Leachman. 2004. "Globalization of Semiconductors: Do Real Men Have Fabs, or Virtual Fabs?" In *Locating Global Advantage: Industry Dynamics in the International Economy*, Martin Kenney with Richard Florida, eds. Palo Alto, CA: Stanford University Press, pp. 203–231.

Lécuyer, Christophe. 2000. "Fairchild Semiconductor and Its Influence." In *The Silicon Valley Edge: A Habitat for Innovation and Entrepreneurship*, Chong-Moon Lee, William Miller, Marguerite Hancock, and Henry Rowen, eds. Palo Alto, CA: Stanford University Press, pp. 158–183.

———. 2006. *Making Silicon Valley: Innovation and the Growth of High Tech, 1930–1970*. Cambridge, MA: MIT Press.

Lee, Charles S. 1998. "Remaking Korea, Inc." *Far Eastern Economic Review* (April 30): 10–14.

Lee, Chong-Moon, William F. Miller, Marguerite Gong Hancock, and Henry S. Rowen, eds. 2000. *The Silicon Valley Edge: A Habitat for Innovation and Entrepreneurship*. Palo Alto, CA: Stanford University Press.

Lee, Dal Hwan, Zong-Tae Bae, and Jinjoo Lee. 1991. "Performance and Adaptive Roles of the Government-Supported Research Institute in South Korea." *World Development* 19(10): 1421–1440.

Lee, Susan. 1991. "Train 'em Here: Foreign Students Crowd Our Schools for Advanced Scientific and Engineering Education." *Forbes* 147(11): 110–116.

Lemke, Mariann, Christopher Calsyn, Laura Lippman, Leslie Jocelyn, David Kastberg, Yan Yun Liu, Stephen Roey, Trevor Williams, Thea Kruger, and Ghedam Bairu. 2001. *Outcomes of Learning: Results from the 2000 Program for International Student Assessment of 15-Year-Olds in Reading, Mathematics, and Science Literacy*. Washington, DC: U.S. Department of Education, National Center for Education Statistics.

Lemke, Mariann, Arindita Sen, Erin Pahlke, Lisette Partelow, David Miller, Trevor Williams, David Kastberg, and Leslie Jocelyn. 2004. *International Outcomes of Learning in Mathematics Literacy and Problem Solving: PISA 2003 Results from the U.S. Perspective.* Washington, DC: U.S. Department of Education, National Center for Education Statistics.

Lenoir, Timothy, Nathan Rosenberg, Henry Rowen, Christophe Lécuyer, Jeannette Colyvas, and Brent Goldfarb. 2003. "Inventing the Entrepreneurial University: Stanford and the Co-Evolution of Silicon Valley." Paper presented at the Stanford University Social Science and Technology Seminar Series, held in Stanford, CA, November 19. http://siepr.stanford.edu/programs/SST_Seminars/Lenoir.pdf (accessed November 11, 2008).

Lent, George E., and John A. Menge. 1962. "The Importance of Restricted Stock Options in Executive Compensation." *Management Record* (June): 6–13.

Leow, Claire. 1992. "Intel Corp Plans US$80m Investment in Penang Plant." *Business Times Singapore*, November 13.

Lerner, Josh. 2002. "Boom and Bust in the Venture Capital Industry and the Impact on Innovation." *Economic Review* 87(4): 25–39.

Leslie, Stuart W. 1993a. "How the West Was Won: The Military and the Making of Silicon Valley." In *Technological Competitiveness: Contemporary and Historical Perspectives on the Electrical, Electronics, and Computer Industries*, William Aspray, ed. Los Alamitos, CA: IEEE Press, pp. 75–89.

———.1993b. *The Cold War and American Science: The Military-Industrial-Academic Complex at MIT and Stanford.* New York: Columbia University Press.

———. 2000. "The Biggest 'Angel' of Them All: The Military and the Making of Silicon Valley." In *Understanding Silicon Valley: The Anatomy of an Entrepreneurial Region*, Martin Kenney, ed. Palo Alto, CA: Stanford University Press, pp. 48–67.

Leslie, Stuart W., and Robert H. Kargon. 1996. "Selling Silicon Valley: Frederick Terman's Model for Regional Advantage." *Business History Review* 70(4): 435–472.

Levy, Frank, and Richard J. Murnane. 1992. "U.S. Earnings Levels and Earnings Inequality: A Review of Recent Trends and Proposed Explanations." *Journal of Economic Literature* 30(3): 1333–1381.

Lewellen, Wilbur. 1968. *Executive Compensation in Large Industrial Corporations.* New York: Columbia University Press.

Lewis, Anthony. 1956. "AT&T Settles Antitrust Case; Shares Patents." *New York Times*, January 25, A:1.

Lewis, Diane E. 1999. "Change in Pension Plan Stirs Union Talk at Big Blue." *Boston Globe*, July 25, G:1.

Lie, Erik. 2005. "On the Timing of CEO Stock Option Awards." *Management Science* 51(5): 802–812.

Lohr, Steve. 1994. "IBM Struggling with Task of Keeping Its Best People." *Austin American-Statesman*, January 23.

———. 2004. "I.B.M. Sought a China Partnership, Not Just a Sale." *New York Times*, December 13, C:1.

Loomis, Carol J. 2003. "The Whistleblower and the CEO." *Fortune* 148(1): 88–92, 94, 96.

Louis, Henock, and Hal White. 2007. "Do Managers Intentionally Use Repurchase Tender Offers to Signal Private Information? Evidence from Firm Financial Reporting Behavior." *Journal of Financial Economics* 85(1): 205–233.

Lowell, B. Lindsay. 2000. "H-1B Temporary Workers: Estimating the Population." Center for Comparative Immigration Studies Working Paper no. 12. San Diego, CA: University of California, San Diego, Center for Comparative Immigration Studies. http://www.ccis-ucsd.org/publications/wrkg12 .PDF (accessed November 11, 2008).

Lowell, B. Lindsay, and Mark Regets. 2006. *A Half-Century Snapshot of the STEM Workforce, 1950–2000*. Commission on Professionals in Science and Technology, STEM Workforce Data Project, White Paper no. 1. Washington, DC: Commission on Professionals in Science and Technology.

Lowell, B. Lindsay, and Hal Salzman. 2007. "Into the Eye of the Storm: Assessing the Evidence on Science and Engineering Education, Quality, and Workforce Demand." Urban Institute Working Paper. Washington, DC: The Urban Institute. http://www.urban.org/UploadedPDF/411562_Salzman_ Science.pdf (accessed November 11, 2008).

Lu, Qiwen. 2000. *China's Leap into the Information Age*. New York: Oxford University Press.

Lu, Qiwen, and William Lazonick. 2001. "The Organization of Innovation in a Transitional Economy: Business and Government in Chinese Electronic Publishing." *Research Policy* 30(1): 35–54.

Lucent Technologies. 2000. "Lucent Technologies Selects Massachusetts Site to become Global Optical Systems Integration Center." Press release, June 7. Murray Hill, NJ: Lucent Technologies.

———. 2002. *2001 10-K*. Murray Hill, NJ: Lucent Technologies.

———. 2003. *2002 10-K*. Murray Hill, NJ: Lucent Technologies.

Lynn, Kathleen. 1999. "For Older Workers, Cash-Balance Pension Plans Can Hurt." *Hackensack (NJ) Record*, May 20.

M2 Presswire. 1995. "Bell Atlantic Introduces 'Portable' Pension Plan for Management Employees." M2 Presswire, October 26.

————. 2005. "Intel Expands Research and Development in China." M2 Presswire. September 15.

Maddison, Angus. 2007. "Historical Statistics, World Population, GDP, and Per Capita GDP, 1–2003 AD." http://www.ggdc.net/maddison/Historical_ Statistics/horizontal-file_03-2007.xls (accessed November 11, 2008).

Mailman, Stanley, and Stephen Yale-Loehr. 2003. "Foreign Nurses: Dealing with the Shortage." *New York Law Journal*, December 22.

Main, Frank. 1991. "BellSouth Has Several Options in Cutting La. Work Force, Spokesman Says." *Baton Rouge State-Times*, March 8.

Malone, Michael. 1985. "Union Worries Add New Cloud to High-Tech Industry's Horizon." *Dallas Morning News*, August 10.

Mandel, Michael, Anderson Forest, and Gary McWilliams. 1992. "No Help Wanted: Ongoing Layoffs are Hobbling the Recovery." *BusinessWeek*, September 21: 26–29.

Manners, David. 1997. "Hero of Our Time." *Electronics Weekly*, March 26.

Maragus, Nick. 2005. "Electronic Arts Settles Overtime Suit, Will Reclassify Entry-Level Artists." *Gamasutra News*, October 5. http://www.gamasutra .com/php-bin/news_index.php?story=6747 (accessed February 26, 2009).

Maremont, Mark D. 1984. "The New AT&T Struggles to Get to Its Feet." *BusinessWeek*, December 3.

Mathews, John A. 1997. "A Silicon Valley of the East: Creating Taiwan's Semiconductor Industry." *California Management Review* 39(4): 26–54.

Mathews, John A., and Dong-Sung Cho. 2000. *Tiger Technology: The Creation of a Semiconductor Industry in East Asia*. New York: Cambridge University Press.

Matloff, Norman. 2004. "On the Need for Reform of the H-1B Non-Immigrant Work Visa in Computer-Related Occupations." *University of Michigan Journal of Law Reform* 36(4): 1–99.

————. 2006a. "The Adverse Impact of Work Visa Programs on Older U.S. Engineers and Programmers." *California Labor and Employment Law Review* 20(4): 5–6, 24, 34.

————. 2006b. "IEEE-USA Hastening the Demise of the American Engineer." E-mail to H-1B/L-1/offshoring newsletter, April 10. http://heather.cs.ucdavis .edu/Archive/IEEEUSAHastensDemise.txt (accessed July 21, 2009).

Matsumoto, Miwao. 1999. "Reconsidering Japanese Industrialization: Marine Turbine Transfer at Mitsubishi." *Technology and Culture* 40(1): 74–97.

Maury, Mary, and Victoria Shoaf. 2001. "The Effects of Adopting Cash-Balance Pension Plans." *Business Horizons* 44(2): 67–74.

May, Jeff. 1998a. "AT&T Staff is Torn over Buyout Offer." *Newark Star-Ledger*, May 20.

———. 1998b. "Managers Denied Retirement Buyouts Sue AT&T." *Newark Star-Ledger*, September 9.

———.1999. "U.S. Judge Throws Out AT&T Managers' Suit." *Newark Star-Ledger*, October 16.

Mayer, David, and Martin Kenney. 2004. "Economic Action Does Not Take Place in a Vacuum: Understanding Cisco's Acquisition and Development Strategy." *Industry and Innovation* 11(4): 299–325.

McCabe, Kathy. 2007a. "Union Fights to Retain 250 Telecom Jobs." *Boston Globe*, October 7. http://www.boston.com/news/local/articles/2007/10/07/union_fights_to_retain_250_telecom_jobs/ (accessed December 1, 2008).

———. 2007b. "Workers Mourn 'Death of Ma Bell' as Plant Closes." *Boston Globe*, December 16. http://www.boston.com/news/local/massachusetts/articles/2007/12/16/workers_mourn_death_of_ma_bell_as_plant_closes/?page=1 (accessed December 1, 2008).

McCarthy, Ed. 1999. "Stock Buybacks: The Rules." *Journal of Accountancy* 187(5): 91–97.

McCash, Vicki. 1993. "BellSouth Announces More Cuts by 1996." *Fort Lauderdale Sun-Sentinel*, November 11.

McEnaney, Maura. 1985. "Semiconductors: Fear and Loathing on the Comeback Trail." *Computerworld*, December 30.

McKay, Martha. 2006. "Lucent Stockholders OK Pay Proposals." *Hackensack (NJ) Record*, February 16.

McNamee, Mike, and Susan Scherreik. 2003. "What the Cuts Mean to You." *BusinessWeek*, June 9: 40–42.

McNerney, Donald. 1996. "HR Practices: HR Adapts to Continuous Restructuring." *HR Focus* 73(May): 1, 4–6.

Mehran, Hamid, and Joseph Tracy. 2001. "The Impact of Employee Stock Options on the Evolution of Compensation in the 1990s." NBER Working Paper no. 8353. Cambridge, MA: National Bureau of Economic Research.

Menendez, Robert. 2008. "Democrats Tell Big Oil: Spend More on Production and Renewable Energy, Less on Stock Buybacks before Making Demands for New Drilling Leases." Press release, July 31. Washington, DC: Senator Robert Menendez, U.S. Senate. http://menendez.senate.gov/newsroom/record.cfm?id=301639 (accessed February 26, 2009).

Merritt, Rick. 2004. "Political Winds Hit Offshoring." *Electronic Engineering Times*, March 26, 66.

Microsoft. 2004. "Microsoft Outlines Quarterly Dividend, Four-Year Stock Buyback Plan, and Special Dividend to Shareholders." Press release, July 20. Redmond, WA: Microsoft. http://www.microsoft.com/presspass/press/2004/jul04/07-20boardPR.mspx (accessed February 26, 2009).

Milberg, William. 2008. "Shifting Sources and Uses of Profits: Sustaining U.S. Financialization with Global Value Chains." *Economy and Society* 37(3): 420–451.

Miller, Michael W. 1984. "Unions Curtail Organizing in High Tech." *Wall Street Journal*, November 13.

———. 1993. "IBM is Planning $2 Billion Charge to Slash Jobs." *Wall Street Journal*, July 2, A:3.

Mills, C. Wright. 1951. *White Collar: The American Middle Classes*. New York: Oxford University Press.

Mitchell, Jim. 1986. "TI Grasping the Future with Both Hands." *Dallas Morning News*, September 26.

Mitra, Raja M. 2007. "India's Emergence as a Global R&D Center." ITPS Working Paper R2007:012. Östersund, Sweden: Swedish Institute for Growth Policy Studies. http://www.itps.se/Archive/Documents/Swedish/ Publikationer/Rapporter/Arbetsrapporter%20(R)/R2007/R2007_012_ webb.pdf (accessed December 1, 2008).

Molloy, Chuck. 1989. "Hitachi Ltd. and Electronic Data Systems Form Hitachi Data Systems." Business Wire, May 1.

Monthly Labor Review. 1965. "Developments in Industrial Relations." *Monthly Labor Review* 88(5): 571.

Moore, Heidi. 2002. "High Stakes in N.Y. Suits Over IPOs." *National Law Journal*, April 22.

Morganthaler Ventures. 2008. *About Morganthaler*. Menlo Park, CA: Morganthaler Ventures. http://www.morgenthaler.com/about.asp (accessed February 26, 2009).

Morikawa, Hidemasa. 2001. *History of Top Management in Japan: Managerial Enterprises and Family Enterprises*. New York: Oxford University Press.

Morris, Martina, and Bruce Western. 1999. "Inequality in Earnings at the Close of the Twentieth Century." *Annual Review of Sociology* 25: 623–657.

Morrison, Scott. 2005. "HP to Launch 'Breakthrough' Inkjets." *Financial Times*, July 11, 27.

Morrow, David J. 2000a. "Talks Stall at Boeing, and Engineers Go on Strike." *New York Times*, February 10, C:1.

———. 2000b. "No Direct Talks Set by 2 Sides in Boeing Strike." *New York Times*, February 22, C:1.

Moskowitz, Milton. 1985. "Firms Do Like Their Employees." *San Francisco Chronicle*, August 28.

Moss, Philip. 2002. "Earnings Inequality and the Quality of Jobs: Current Research and a Research Agenda." In *Corporate Governance and Sustainable Prosperity*, William Lazonick and Mary O'Sullivan, eds. New York: Palgrave, pp. 183–225.

Mowery, David, and Richard Langlois. 1996. "Spinning Off and Spinning On(?): The Federal Government Role in the Development of the U.S. Computer Software Industry." *Research Policy* 25(6): 947–966.

Moxon, Richard. 1974. "Offshore Production in the Less Developed Countries: A Case Study of Multinationality in the Electronics Industry." Institute of Finance Bulletin nos. 98–99. New York: New York University.

Mulqueen, John T. 1989a. "Industry Watch: The Data Communications 100: A Year of Waiting for Another to Begin So Something Significant Could Happen." *Data Communications*, January 1.

———. 1989b. "Industry Watch: Connecting Nets, A Growth Business. T1 Links Take Bridge and Router Sales to New, and Brighter, Horizons." *Data Communications*, July 1.

Munnell, Alicia H., and Annika Sundén. 2006. "401(k) Plans Are Still Coming Up Short." Center for Retirement Research Issues in Brief no. 43. Chestnut Hill, MA: Center for Retirement Research at Boston College.

Murray, Andy. 2003a. "Lucent Property Sold." *Lawrence (MA) Eagle-Tribune*, September 3.

———. 2003b. "Breakup Haunts Lucent Workers." *Lawrence (MA) Eagle-Tribune,* April 20.

———. 2003c. "Lucent Trims 110 Jobs." *Lawrence (MA) Eagle-Tribune*, April 30.

National Center for Education Statistics. 2008. *Digest of Education Statistics, 2007*. Washington, DC: National Center for Education Statistics. http://nces.ed.gov/pubs2008/2008022.pdf (accessed December 1, 2008).

National Commission on Excellence in Education (NCEE). 1983. *A Nation at Risk: The Imperative for Educational Reform*. Washington, DC: Government Printing Office. http://www.ed.gov/pubs/NatAtRisk/risk.html (accessed December 1, 2008).

National Research Council. 1999. *Funding a Revolution: Government Support for Computing Research*. Washington, DC: National Academies Press.

National Science Board. 2004. *Science and Engineering Indicators 2004*. Arlington, VA: National Science Foundation. http://www.nsf.gov/statistics/seind04/ (accessed December 1, 2008).

———. 2008. *Science and Engineering Indicators 2008*. Arlington, VA: National Science Foundation. http://www.nsf.gov/statistics/seind08/ (accessed December 1, 2008).

National Science Foundation. 1993. "Human Resources for Science and Technology: The Asian Region." Surveys of Science Resources Series, Special Report, NSF 93-303. Arlington, VA: National Science Foundation.

————. 2003. *Survey of Industrial Research and Development*. Arlington, VA: National Science Foundation, Division of Science Resources Statistics. http://www.nsf.gov/statistics/srvyindustry/ (accessed December 1, 2008).

Netter, Jeffrey M., and Mark L. Mitchell. 1989. "Stock Repurchase Announcements and Insider Trading after the October 1987 Stock Market Crash." *Financial Management* 18(3): 84–96.

New Commission on the Skills of the American Workforce. 2007. *Tough Choices or Tough Times: The Report of the New Commission on the Skills of the American Workforce*. Washington, DC: National Center on Education and the Economy. http://skillscommission.org/report.htm (accessed December 1, 2008).

New York Times. 1959. "Investment Firm Formed in West." *New York Times*, August 14.

————. 1967. "Low Wages in Korea Attracting Foreign Investors." *New York Times,* January 20, 45.

————. 1968. "National Cash Register Strike Ends 67 Years of Labor Peace." *New York Times*, November 25, 34.

————. 1986. "Hewlett-Packard Retirement Plan." *New York Times*, June 13.

————. 2006. "Microsoft to Use Cash for Development, Not Share Buybacks." *New York Times*, June 1, C:11.

Newsbytes. 1995. "China-Intel Plans Assembly Plant in Shanghai." Newsbytes, June 7.

Nguyen, Thi. 2001. "Cisco's $3Bln Stock Buyback May Usher in Other Plans." Reuters News, September 14.

Nikkei Weekly. 2005. "Profit Streak Continues at Canon." *Nikkei Weekly*, March 14.

Niland, Powell. 1976. "Reforming Private Pension Plan Administration." *Business Horizons* 19(1): 25–35.

Noble, Kenneth B. 1981. "Stock Option Plans: Clouds on Horizon." *New York Times*, December 31, D:1.

Noone, Charles M., and Stanley M. Rubel. 1970. *SBICs: Pioneers in Organized Venture Capital*. Chicago: Capital Publishing Corp.

North, David S. 1995. *Soothing the Establishment: The Impact of Foreign-Born Scientists and Engineers on America*. Lanham, MD: University Press of America.

Nossiter, Bernard D. 1961. "Gore Seeks to Plug Stock Option Loophole." *Washington Post*, July 21.

Okimoto, Daniel I., and Yoshio Nishi. 1994. "R&D Organization in Japanese and American Semiconductor Firms." In *The Japanese Firm: The Sources of Competitive Strength*, Masahiko Aoki and Ronald Dore, eds. New York: Oxford University Press, pp.178–208.

Oliner, Stephen D., and Daniel E. Sichel. 2002. "Information Technology and Productivity: Where Are We Now and Where Are We Going?" *Federal Reserve Bank of Atlanta Economic Review* 87(3): 15–43.

O'Neill, Mark. 1998. "Legend Gives Intel Chief Millionth PC." *South China Morning Post*, May 7.

O'Reilly, Brian. 1992. "Your New Global Work Force." *Fortune* 126(December 14): 52–54.

O'Reilly, Charles A. 1998. "Cisco Systems: The Acquisition of Technology is the Acquisition of People." Stanford Business School Case HR10. Palo Alto, CA: Graduate School of Business, Stanford University.

O'Reilly, Charles A., and Jeffrey Pfeffer. 2000. "Cisco Systems: Acquiring and Retaining Talent in Hypercompetitive Markets." *Human Resource Planning* 23(3): 38–52.

Organisation for Economic Co-operation and Development (OECD). 2004. *Learning for Tomorrow's World: First Results from PISA 2003*. Paris: Programme for International Student Assessment, OECD.

O'Sullivan, Mary. 2000a. "The Innovative Enterprise and Corporate Governance." *Cambridge Journal of Economics* 24(4): 393–416.

———.2000b. *Contests for Corporate Control: Corporate Governance and Economic Performance in the United States and Germany*. New York: Oxford University Press.

———. 2002. "Corporate Control." In *The IEBM Handbook of Economics*, William Lazonick, ed. London: Thomson, pp. 129–155.

———. 2004. "What Drove the U.S. Stock Market in the Last Century?" INSEAD Working Paper. Fontainebleau, France: INSEAD.

———. 2007. "Funding New Industries: A Historical Perspective on the Financing Role of the U.S. Stock Market in the Twentieth Century." In *Financing Innovation in the United States, 1870 to the Present*, Naomi Lamoreaux and Kenneth Sokoloff, eds. Cambridge, MA: MIT Press, pp. 163–216.

———. Forthcoming. "The Deficiencies, Excesses and Control of Competition: The Development of the U.S. Stock Market from the 1930s to 2001." In *Balancing Public and Private Control: Germany and the U.S. in the Postwar Era*, Louis Galambos and Caroline Fohlin, eds. New York: Cambridge University Press.

Oyer, Paul, and Scott Schaefer. 2005. "Why Do Some Firms Give Stock Options to All Employees? An Empirical Examination of Alternative Theories." *Journal of Financial Economics* 76(1): 99–133.

Pace, Larry, and Dominick Argona. 1989. "Participatory Action Research: A View from Xerox." *American Behavioral Scientist* 32(5): 552–565.

Pace, Larry, and Eileen Kelly. 1998. "TQM at Xerox: Lessons Worth Duplicating." *International Journal of Technology Management* 16(4-6): 326–335.

Packard, David. 1995. *The HP Way: How Bill Hewlett and I Built Our Company*. New York: HarperBusiness.

Parker, Jeffrey. 1994a. "Intel's First China Chip Project Challenges Curbs." Reuters News, March 25.

———. 1994b. "Intel Pushes Software in China." *Reuters News*, December 5.

Patterson, William Pat. 1981. "Gathering Storm Clouds for Semiconductors." *Industry Week*, January 26.

———. 1982. "It's Semiconductors' Turn to Fight the Japanese." *Industry Week*, Feb 22.

Patton, Arch. 1988. "The Executive Pay Boom is Over." *Harvard Business Review* 66(5): 154–155.

Pearson, Drew. 1950. "Big Business Gets Tax Loopholes." *Washington Post*, September 5.

Pei, Jianfeng. 1994. "Intel May Produce Chips in Shanghai." *Business Weekly*, September 11.

Pension Benefit Guaranty Corporation. 2007. *Pension Insurance Data Book 2006, No. 11*. Washington, DC: Pension Benefit Guaranty Corporation.

Pensions and Investment Age. 1987. "Profiles." *Pensions and Investment Age*, January 26.

———. 1988. "Letters." *Pensions and Investment Age*, March 21.

———. 1989. "Profiles." *Pensions and Investment Age*, January 13.

Perkins, Anthony. 1994. "Venture Pioneers." *Red Herring*, February 1.

Pernia, Ernest M. 1976. "The Question of the Brain Drain from the Philippines." *International Migration Review* 10(1): 63–72.

Pierson, John, 1978, "Trend of Higher Levies on Capital Gains is Reversed as President Signs Tax Bill." *Wall Street Journal*, November 9.

Piketty, Thomas, and Emmanuel Saez. 2003. "Income Inequality in the United States, 1913–1998." *Quarterly Journal of Economics* 118(1): 1–39.

———. 2006. "The Evolution of Top Incomes: A Historical and International Perspective." *American Economic Review* 96(2): 200–205.

Piller, Dan. 2006. "Exxon Mobil Sets Record for Profits." *Fort Worth Star-Telegram*, January 31.

Pimentel, Benjamin. 2002a. "HP Tells Details of Layoff Scheme." *San Francisco Chronicle*, April 10, B:1.

———. 2002b. "As Tech Jobs Decrease, Interest in Unions Is Up." *San Francisco Chronicle*, July 18, B:1.

———. 2003. "The HP-Compaq Merger: One Year Later." *San Francisco Chronicle*, May 4, I:1.

Pirtle, Caleb III. 2005. *Engineering the World: Stories from the First 75 Years of Texas Instruments*. Dallas, TX: Southern Methodist University Press.

Poletti, Therese. 2001a. "Hewlett-Packard Workplace Philosophy Hits a Rough Patch." *San Jose Mercury News*, February 1.

———. 2001b. "Hewlett-Packard Announces Plans to Trim 3,000 Management Positions." *San Jose Mercury News*, April 19.

———. 2004. "IBM to Sell Majority Stake in PC Business to Chinese Firm." *San Jose Mercury News*, December 8.

Pollack, Andrew. 1985a. "The Daunting Power of IBM." *New York Times*, January 20, 3:1.

———. 1985b. "US–Korea Chip Ties Grow." *New York Times*, July 15, D:1.

Poole, Shelia M. 1991. "BellSouth Creates Management Unit." *Atlanta Journal-Constitution*, March 5, C:1.

Potter, Joseph C. 1953. "Good 'Human Relations' Keep Employees Happy and Put IBM at the Top of Its Field." *Wall Street Journal*, February 11.

Powell, Walter W., and Kaisa Snellman. 2004. "The Knowledge Economy." *Annual Review of Sociology* 30: 199–220.

PR Newswire. 1988. "American Immigration Lawyers Association Elects New President." PR Newswire, July 19.

———. 1989. "Xerox Wins National Quality Award." PR Newswire, November 2.

———. 1991. "BellSouth Reports about 3,100 Managers Elect Early Retirement." PR Newswire, August 13.

———. 1994. "FASB Drops Controversial Stock Option Proposal; Elects Footnote Disclosure." PR Newswire, December 14.

———. 1998. "IEEE-USA Releases 'Misfortune 500' List of Displaced High-Tech Workers." PR Newswire, October 12.

———. 1999a. "Communications Workers to 14 Western Governors: Qwest Takeover Would Further Undermine Phone Services, Slash Jobs and Investment." PR Newswire, June 21.

———. 1999b. "IBM Employees Forming Nationwide Organization: Alliance@IBM/CWA." PR Newswire, September 21.

———. 2001. "Hewlett Family Members and William R. Hewlett Revocable Trust to Vote against Hewlett-Packard/Compaq Merger." PR Newswire, November 6.

———. 2003. "Lucent Technologies Reaches Agreement to Settle Shareowner Class Action." PR Newswire, March 28.

Prencipe, Loretta W. 2001. "Lucent's Early-Out Brings Questions." Info-World, August 10. http://www.infoworld.com/articles/pe/xml/01/08/13/010813peknow.html (accessed December 2, 2008).

Press Trust of India. 2007. "Two Indian BPO Firms in World's 'Hot Growth' Companies List." Press Trust of India, May 28.

PricewaterhouseCoopers. 2008a. *MoneyTree Report*. London: Pricewater-houseCoopers.   https://www.pwcmoneytree.com/MTPublic/ns/index.jsp (accessed February 26, 2009).

———. 2008b. *MoneyTree Report–Historical Trend Data*. London: Pricewa-terhouseCoopers.   https://www.pwcmoneytree.com/MTPublic/ns/nav.jsp? page=historical (accessed February 26, 2009).

Prokesch, Steven. 1985. "Xerox Halts Japanese March." *New York Times*, No-vember 6, D:1.

Pryor, Frederic L. 2007. "The Anatomy of Increasing Inequality of U.S. Fam-ily Incomes." *Journal of Socio-Economics* 36(4): 595–618.

Rai, Saritha. 2003. "In India, a High-Tech Outpost for U.S. Patents." *New York Times*, December 15, C:4.

Raleigh News and Observer. 1996. "Ex-IBMers File Redux of Suit against Severance Tax." *Raleigh News and Observer*, March 29, C:9.

Ramirez, Anthony. 1992. "BellSouth to Cut 8,000 from Work Force." *New York Times*, November 7, A:37.

Ramstad, Evan. 1994a. "IBM's Year Marked by Series of Upheavals." *Austin American-Statesman*, January 1.

———. 1994b. "Ex-IBMers Confront IRS Over Taxes." Associated Press, May 24.

———. 1994c. "Ex-IBM Workers Battle IRS." *San Francisco Chronicle*, June 1.

Ramstad, Evan, and Qin Juying. 2006. "Intel Pushes Chip Production Deep into China." *Wall Street Journal*, May 23, B:1.

Rankin, Deborah. 1981. "Applause for the 'Incentive' Stock Option." *New York Times*, August 16, 3:15.

Rapoport, Michael. 2001. "Stock Buybacks Could Help Bolster Market When It Reopens." Dow Jones News Service, September 14.

Rappaport, Alfred, and Mark L. Sirower. 1999. "Stock or Cash? The Trade-Offs for Buyers and Sellers in Mergers and Acquisitions." *Harvard Busi-ness Review* 77(6): 56–58.

Rayburn, Frank, and Ollie Powers. 1991. "A History of Pooling of Interests Accounting for Business Combinations in the United States." *Accounting Historians Journal* 18(2): 155–192.

Reid, T.R. 1985. *The Chip: How Two Americans Invented the Microchip and Launched a Revolution*. New York: Random House.

Reiner, Martha L. 1989. "The Transformation of Venture Capital: A History of Venture Capital Organization in the United States." PhD diss., University of California, Berkeley.

Reuters News. 1988. "Workers Occupy Computer Room of Motorola Factory." Reuters News, December 29.

————. 1999a. "Qwest, U.S. West See $4.4 Bln in Cost Savings." Reuters News, July 18.

————. 1999b. "Legend, Intel to Boost China Internet Use." Reuters News, March 8.

————. 2001. "Table—Company Share Buybacks Announced Since U.S. Attacks." Reuters News, September 18.

Ribbing, Mark. 1998. "AT&T to Cut as Many as 18,000 Jobs." *Baltimore Sun*, January 27, 1:C.

Riley, James. 1994. "Intel Out to Expand China PC Activities." *South China Morning Post*, September 6.

Riley, Sheila. 2001. "Tech Slowdown: HP Tries Range of Cost-Cutting Plans amid Shortfall." *Investor's Business Daily*, August 2.

Roach, Stephen S. 2003. "The Index of Missing Economic Indicators: The Productivity Paradox." *New York Times*, November 30, 4:9.

Robertson, Jordan. 2008. "HP Surprises Wall Street with Size of EDS Job Cuts." Associated Press, September 16.

Rock, Arthur. 2000. "Arthur Rock and Co." In *Done Deals: Venture Capitalists Tell Their Stories*, Udayan Gupta, ed. Boston: Harvard Business School Press, pp. 139–148.

Rohrer, Julie. 1995. "IBM Rethinks Pensions." *Institutional Investor*, March 1.

Romano, Benjamin J. 2006. "Ballmer Defends Microsoft's Spending Increase." *Seattle Times*, May 1. http://community.seattletimes.nwsource.com/archive/?date=20060502&slug=microsoft02 (accessed December 2, 2008).

Rosegrant, Susan, and David R. Lampe. 1992. *Route 128: Lessons from Boston's High-Tech Community*. New York: Basic Books.

Rosenbloom, Richard. 2000. "Leadership, Capabilities, and Technological Change: The Transformation of NCR in the Electronic Era." *Strategic Management Journal* 21(10/11): 1083–1103.

Ross, Nancy L. 1979. "New Law Gives Money Managers Breathing Space." *Washington Post*, July 15, G:4.

Rugaber, Christopher S. 2007. "Supreme Court Refuses to Hear IBM Pension, Workplace Retaliation Cases." Associated Press, January 16.

Ryan, Margaret. 1990. "Cuts to Affect Engineers." *Electronic Engineering Times*, February 5.

Sabin, Russell. 1986. "Intel's Man in China Chips Away at Vast Market." *San Francisco Chronicle*, April 28.

Sabow, Steven, and Erin Milligan. 2000. "Trends in Broad-Based Stock Option Plans." *Journal of Employee Ownership, Law, and Finance* 12(2): 99–105.

Saez, Emmanuel. 2005. "Top Incomes in the United States and Canada over the Twentieth Century." *Journal of the European Economic Association* 3(2–3): 402–411.

Sahlman, William A. 1990. "The Structure and Governance of Venture Capital Organizations." *Journal of Financial Economics* 27(2): 473–521.

Salih, Kamal, and Mei Ling Young. 1987. "Social Forces, the State, and the International Division of Labour: The Case of Malaysia." In *Global Restructuring and Territorial Development*, Jeffrey Henderson and Manuel Castells, eds. London: Sage Publications: pp. 168–202.

San Francisco Chronicle. 2002. "HP to Begin Worker Cuts." *San Francisco Chronicle*, May 13, E:1.

Sawyer, Kathy. 1984. "Unions Striking Out in High-Tech Firms." *Washington Post*, March 18.

Saxenian, AnnaLee. 1994. *Regional Advantage: Culture and Competition in Silicon Valley and Route 128*. Cambridge, MA: Harvard University Press.

———. 2006. *The New Argonauts: Regional Advantage in a Global Economy*. Cambridge, MA: Harvard University Press.

Saxenian, AnnaLee, and Jinn-Yuh Hsu. 2001. "The Silicon Valley-Hsinchu Connection: Technical Communities and Industrial Upgrading." *Industrial and Corporate Change* 10(4): 893–920.

Schmeck, Harold M., Jr. 1973. "Asia Biggest Source of Brain Drain to U.S." *New York Times*, January 13, A:28.

Schultz, Ellen E. 2000 "Pension Cuts 101: Companies Find Subtle Ways to Pare Retirement Benefits." *Wall Street Journal*, July 27, A:1.

Schultz, Ellen E., and Theo Francis. 2006. "IBM Ruling Paves Way for Changes to Pensions: Appeals Court's Reversal of Discrimination Finding to Aid Cash Balance Plans." *Wall Street Journal*, August 8, A:3.

Schultze, Charles L. 1999. "Downsized and Out: Job Security and American Workers." *Brookings Review* 17(4): 9–17.

Schuyten, Peter J. 1979. "To Clone a Computer: Neophyte National Semiconductor Has Jolted the Industry." *New York Times*, February 4, F:1.

Scott, A.J. 1987. "The Semiconductor Industry in South-East Asia: Organization, Location, and the International Division of Labour." *Regional Studies* 21(2): 143–160.

Sebaly, Kim Patrick. 1972. "The Assistance of Four Nations in the Establishment of the Indian Institutes of Technology, 1945–1970." PhD dissertation. Ann Arbor, MI: University of Michigan.

Securities and Exchange Commission (SEC). 1963. *Report of the Special Study of the Securities Markets of the Securities and Exchange Commission*. H.R. Doc. no. 95, 88th Cong., 1st sess. Washington, DC: Government Printing Office.

Seipel, Tracy. 2001. "Co-Founder's Son is Displeased with Direction of Hewlett-Packard." *San Jose Mercury News*, November 7.

Seipel, Tracy, and Therese Poletti. 2002. "Hewlett Files Suit over Merger Vote." *San Jose Mercury News*, March 29.

Seligman, Joel. 1995. *The Transformation of Wall Street: A History of the Securities and Exchange Commission and Modern Corporate Finance*, 2d. ed., rev. Boston: Northeastern University Press.

Semiconductor Equipment and Materials International (SEMI). 1995. "Silicon Valley Genealogy Chart." San Jose, CA: SEMI.

Sesil, J., M. Kroumova, J. Blasi, and D. Kruse. 2002. "Broad-Based Employee Stock Options in U.S. 'New Economy' Firms." *British Journal of Industrial Relations* 40(2): 273–294.

Shabecoff, Philip. 1970. "South Korea's Economy Booming with Cheap Labor." *New York Times*, May 12, 57.

Shanghai Star. 1994. "Intel to Help Set Up PC Standards." *Shanghai Star*, September 9.

Sharma, Dinesh. 2004. "AMD to Open Engineering Center in India." CNET-News.com, April 22.

Sharpston, Michael. 1975. "International Sub-Contracting." *Oxford Economic Papers* 27(1): 94–135.

Shenkman, Albert S. 1954. "Higher Education in India." *Far Eastern Survey* 23(2): 24–28.

Shiller, Robert. 2000. *Irrational Exuberance*. Princeton, NJ: Princeton University Press.

Shleifer, Andre, and Lawrence Summers. 1988. "Breach of Trust in Hostile Takeovers." In *Corporate Takeovers: Causes and Consequences*, Alan J. Auerbach, ed. Cambridge, MA: National Bureau of Economic Research, pp. 33–56.

Siegel, Jeremy J. 2008. *Stocks for the Long Run: The Definitive Guide to Financial Market Returns and Long-Term Investment Strategies*, 4th ed. New York: McGraw-Hill.

Sigurdson, Jon. 1980. *Technology and Science in the People's Republic of China*. New York: Oxford University Press.

Simison, Robert. 1985. "Texas Instruments Hopes for Better Times." *Wall Street Journal*, June 14, A:6.

Solow, Robert S. 1987. "We'd Better Watch Out." *New York Times Book Review*, July 12, 36.

Sorokina, Olga, Anthony Webb, and Dan Muldoon. 2008. "Pension Wealth and Income: 1992, 1998, and 2004." Center for Retirement Research Issue in Brief no. 8-1. Chestnut Hill, MA: Center for Retirement Research at Boston College.

Souder, Elizabeth. 2008. "Exxon's 17% Gain Disappoints, Irritates." *Dallas Morning News*, May 2. http://www.dallasnews.com/sharedcontent/dws/bus/industries/energy/stories/DN-exxon_02bus.ART.State.Edition1.4626ce1.html (accessed December 2, 2008).

Spaeth, Anthony. 1984. "Korean Companies Set Expensive Plans to Make Microchip Plants Competitive." *Wall Street Journal*, February 8.

Sporck, Charles E., with Richard L. Molay. 2001. *Spinoff: A Personal History of the Industry That Changed the World*. Saranac Lake, NY: Saranac Lake Publishing.

Sprout Group. 2009. *Our Team*. New York: Sprout Group. http://www.sproutgroup.com/janet_hickey.shtml (accessed February 26, 2009).

Stark, Louis. 1940. "Say NLRB Dragged Case to Aid CIO." *New York Times*, May 1, 17.

Starobin, Paul. 1989. "Democrats Unlikely to Block FCC's Price-Cap Plan." *Congressional Quarterly Weekly Report*, March 4.

Stone, Katherine V.W. 2004. *From Widgets to Digits: Employment Regulation for the Changing Workplace*. New York: Cambridge University Press.

Stroud, Jerri. 1988. "SW Bell Sets Up Technology Unit." *St. Louis Post-Dispatch*, October 30.

Sturgeon, Timothy J. 2002. "Modular Production Networks: A New American Model of Industrial Organization." *Industrial and Corporate Change* 11(3): 451–496.

Subramanyam, R. 2005. "Intel Sets Up Circuit Research Lab in B'lore." *Economic Times*, May 25.

Sun Microsystems. 2004. *2003 10-K*. Santa Clara, CA: Sun Microsystems.

Suttmeier, Richard P. 1975. "Science Policy Shifts, Organizational Change, and China's Development." *China Quarterly* 62: 207–241.

Swoboda, Frank. 1992. "Cooperation Worth Copying? In N.Y., Xerox and Its Union Team to Keep U.S. Jobs from Moving to Mexico." *Washington Post*, December 13, H:1.

Sycamore Networks. 2006. *2005 10-K*. Chelmsford, MA: Sycamore Networks.

———. 2008. "Sycamore Networks, Inc., Reports Fourth Quarter and Fiscal Year 2008 Financial Results." Press release, September 5. Chelmsford, MA: Sycamore Networks. http://media.corporate-ir.net/media_files/irol/94/94677/sycamore2008q4.pdf (accessed February 26, 2009).

Szabo, Joan C. 1989. "Opening Doors for Immigrants." *Nation's Business*, August 1: 48.

Taiwan Industry Semiconductor Association. 2007. *Overview on Taiwan Semiconductor Industry (2007 Edition)*. Chutung, Hsinchu, Taiwan: Taiwan Industry Semiconductor Association. http://www.tsia.org.tw/eng/Files/Publication/2007%20Overview%E8%8B%B1%E6%96%87.pdf (accessed December 3, 2008).

Takahashi, Dean. 2003. "Hewlett-Packard Reports Profit Boost as Employees Lose Jobs." *San Jose Mercury News*, May 21.

———. 2004. "Hewlett-Packard to Add 1,400 Jobs." *San Jose Mercury News*, June 10.

Tarrant, Bill. 1991. "IBM Set to Return to India." *Reuters News*, August 28.

Tata Consultancy Services (TCS). 2008. *Annual Report, 2007–2008*. Mumbai: TCS.

Teal, Gordon K.. 1991. "Gordon K. Teal: An Interview Conducted by Andrew Goldstein." New Brunswick, NJ: IEEE History Center, Rutgers University. http://www.ieee.org/portal/cms_docs_iportals/iportals/aboutus/history_center/oral_history/pdfs/Teal136.pdf (accessed October 23, 2008).

Teather, David. 2002. "'Flipping' Goldman Fingered." *Guardian*, October 4, 22.

Teitelbaum, Michael S. 1996. "Too Many Engineers, Too Few Jobs." *New York Times*, March 19, A:23.

———. 2004. "Do We Need More Scientists?" In *The U.S. Scientific and Technical Workforce: Improving Data for Decisionmaking*, Terence K. Kelly, William P. Butz, Stephen Carroll, David M. Adamson, and Gabrielle Bloom, eds. Santa Monica, CA: RAND Corporation, pp. 11–20.

Tenorio, Vyvyan. 1985. "The Big Computer Catch-Up Begins." *Australian Financial Review*, July 31, 13.

Tilton, John E. 1971. *International Diffusion of Technology: The Case of Semiconductors*. Washington, DC: Brookings Institution.

Tripathi, Salil. 1992. "India Approves Seven Foreign Investment Plans Worth S$685m." *Business Times Singapore*, January 15.

Tully, Shawn. 1993. "Managing the Modular Corporation." *Fortune* 127(3): 106–115.

Tumulty, Brian. 2003. "Age Bias Claim Tested in IBM Pension Conversion Case." Gannett News Service, June 5.

Tyler, David. 2005. "Health Plan Still in Xerox Contract." *Rochester Democrat and Chronicle*, March 15.

Uchitelle, Louis. 1990. "Unequal Pay Widespread in U.S." *New York Times*, August 14, D:1.

United Press International. 1985. "Texas Inst. Looks to Grab Fast-Growing Asia Market." United Press International, August 19.

U.S. Bureau of Labor Statistics. 2007. *BLS Collective Bargaining Agreements File: Online Listings of Private and Public Sector Agreements*. Washington, DC: U.S. Bureau of Labor Statistics. http://www.dol.gov/esa/olms/regs/compliance/cba/index.htm (accessed February 26, 2009).

———. 2008a. *Table 2. Retirement Benefits: Access, Participation, and Take-Up Rates, Private Industry Workers, National Compensation Survey, March 2008*. Washington, DC: U.S. Bureau of Labor Statistics. http://www.bls.gov/ncs/ebs/benefits/2008/ownership/private/table02a.pdf (accessed December 3, 2008).

————. 2008b. "Union Members in 2007." Economic News Release USDL-08-0092, January 25. Washington, DC: U.S. Bureau of Labor Statistics. http://www.bls.gov/news.release/union2.nr0.htm (accessed December 3, 2008).

U.S. Census Bureau. 1976. *Historical Statistics of the United States from the Colonial Times to the Present.* Washington, DC: U.S. Government Printing Office.

————. 1997. *1997 NAICS and 1987 SIC Correspondence Tables.* Washington, DC: U.S. Census Bureau. http://www.census.gov/epcd/www/naicstab .htm (accessed February 26, 2009).

————. 2004. *Statistical Abstract of the United States, 2004.* Washington, DC: U.S. Government Printing Office.

————. 2005. *Statistical Abstract of the United States, 2005.* Washington, DC: U.S. Government Printing Office.

————. 2008a. *Censtats: County Business Patterns Data (SIC & NAICS).* Washington, DC: U.S. Census Bureau. http://censtats.census.gov/ (accessed February 26, 2009).

————. 2008b. *Foreign Trade Statistics, Advanced Technology Product Data—Imports and Exports.* Washington, DC: U.S. Census Bureau. http://www.census.gov/foreign-trade/statistics/product/atp/select-atpctry .html (accessed February 26, 2009).

————. 2008c. "Annual Capital Expenditure Surveys, 1994–2006." Washington, DC: U.S. Census Bureau. http://www.census.gov/csd/ace/pubs.html (accessed December 3, 2008).

————. 2008d. *International Data Base—Country Summaries.* Washington, DC: U.S. Census Bureau. http://www.census.gov/ipc/www/idb/summaries .html (accessed February 26, 2009).

————. 2008e. "Foreign Trade Statistics—Country and Product Trade Data." Washington, DC: U.S. Census Bureau. http://www.census.gov/foreign-trade/ statistics/country/index.html (accessed February 26, 2009).

————. 2008f. *Statistical Abstract of the United States, 2008.* Washington, DC: U.S. Government Printing Office. http://www.census.gov/compendia/ statab/ (accessed December 3, 2008).

————. 2009. *Historical Income Tables—Families: Table F-4, Gini Ratios for Families, by Race and Hispanic Origin of Householder: 1947 to 2007.* Washington, DC: U.S. Census Bureau. http://www.census.gov/hhes/www/ income/histinc/f04.html (accessed February 26, 2009).

U.S. Citizenship and Immigration Services. 2005. "USCIS Reaches H-1B Cap." Press Release, August 12. Washington, DC: U.S. Citizenship and Immigration Services. http://www.uscis.gov/files/pressrelease/H-1Bcap_ 12Aug05.pdf (accessed February 26, 2009).

U.S. Congress. 2009. *Economic Report of the President*. Washington, DC: U.S. Government Printing Office.

U.S. Department of Commerce. 2003. *Digital Economy 2003*. Washington, DC: U.S. Department of Commerce, Economics and Statistics Administration. http://www.esa.doc.gov/2003.cfm (accessed December 3, 2008).

U.S. Department of Homeland Security. 2003a. *2002 Yearbook of Immigration Statistics*. Washington, DC: U.S. Department of Homeland Security, Office of Immigration Statistics. http://www.dhs.gov/xlibrary/assets/statistics/yearbook/2002/Yearbook2002.pdf (accessed July 13, 2009).

———. 2003b. Characteristics of Specialty Occupation Workers (H-1B): Fiscal Year 2002. Washington, DC: U.S. Department of Homeland Security, Office of Immigration Statistics. http://www.uscis.gov/files/article/FY2002Charact.pdf (accessed July 13, 2009).

———. 2004a. *2003 Yearbook of Immigration Statistics*. Washington, DC: U.S. Department of Homeland Security, Office of Immigration Statistics. http://www.dhs.gov/xlibrary/assets/statistics/yearbook/2003/2003Yearbook.pdf (accessed July 13, 2009).

———. 2004b. Characteristics of Specialty Occupation Workers (H-1B): Fiscal Year 2003. Washington, DC: U.S. Department of Homeland Security, Office of Immigration Statistics. http://www.uscis.gov/files/article/FY-03H1BFnlCharRprt.pdf (accessed July 13, 2009).

———. 2006a. *2004 Yearbook of Immigration Statistics*. Washington, DC: U.S. Department of Homeland Security, Office of Immigration Statistics. http://www.dhs.gov/xlibrary/assets/statistics/yearbook/2004/Yearbook2004.pdf (accessed July 13, 2009).

———. 2006b. *2005 Yearbook of Immigration Statistics*. Washington, DC: U.S. Department of Homeland Security, Office of Immigration Statistics. http://www.dhs.gov/xlibrary/assets/statistics/yearbook/2005/OIS_2005_Yearbook.pdf (accessed July 13, 2009).

———. 2006c. Characteristics of Specialty Occupation Workers (H-1B): Fiscal Year 2004. Washington, DC: U.S. Department of Homeland Security, U.S. Citizenship and Immigration Services. http://www.uscis.gov/files/nativedocuments/H1B_FY04_Characteristics.pdf (accessed July 13, 2009).

———. 2007. *2006 Yearbook of Immigration Statistics*. Washington, DC: U.S. Department of Homeland Security, Office of Immigration Statistics. http://www.dhs.gov/xlibrary/assets/statistics/yearbook/2006/OIS_2006_Yearbook.pdf (accessed July 13, 2009).

———. 2008. *2007 Yearbook of Immigration Statistics*. Washington, DC: U.S. Department of Homeland Security, Office of Immigration Statistics. http://www.dhs.gov/xlibrary/assets/statistics/yearbook/2007/ois_2007_yearbook.pdf (accessed July 13, 2009).

U.S. Department of Labor. 2007. *Labor Condition Applications and Requirements for Employers Using Nonimmigrants on H-1B Visas in Specialty Occupations and as Fashion Models, and Labor Attestation Requirements for Employers Using [04/01/2005].* Washington, DC: U.S. Department of Labor. http://www.dol.gov/eta/regs/fedreg/proposed/2005006454.htm (accessed February 26, 2009).

———. 2008. "Occupational Employment Statistics." Washington, DC: U.S. Department of Labor. http://www.bls.gov/oes/home.htm (accessed February 26, 2009).

U.S. Department of State. 2009. *Visa Statistics: Reports of the Visa Office, 2000–2008.* Reports for years 1997–1999 available from State Department upon request. Washington, DC: U.S. Department of State, Bureau of Consular Affairs. http://travel.state.gov/visa/frvi/statistics/statistics_1476.html (accessed July 15, 2009).

U.S. General Accounting Office. 2003. *H-1B Foreign Workers: Better Tracing Needed to Help Determine H-1B Program's Effects on U.S, Workforce.* Report to the Ranking Minority Member, Subcommittee on Environment, Technology, and Standards, Committee on Science, House of Representatives. GAO-03-883. Washington, DC: U.S. Government Accounting Office. http://www.gao.gov/new.items/d03883.pdf (accessed December 4, 2008).

U.S. House of Representatives. 1990. "Joint Hearings before the Subcommittee of Immigration, Refugees, and International Law of the Committee on the Judiciary and the Immigration Task Force of the Committee on Education and Labor." 101st Congress, Second Session, on S. 358, H.R. 672, H.R. 2448, H.R. 2646, and H.R 4165, Immigration Act of 1989, February 21, March 1, 7, 13, and 14. Washington, DC: U.S. House of Representatives.

U.S. Newswire. 1992. "'Justice for Janitors' Campaign Adds Hewlett-Packard to Victory List." *U.S. Newswire,* August 6.

Van der Kroef, Justus M. 1968. "Asia's 'Brain Drain': The Causes Are Complex and Not Wholly Economic." *Journal of Higher Education* 39(5): 241–253.

Van Jaarsveld, Danielle D. 2004. "Collective Representation among High-Tech Workers at Microsoft and Beyond: Lessons from WashTech/CWA." *Industrial Relations* 43(2): 364–385.

Vaughan, Jessica. 2003. "Shortcuts to Immigration: The 'Temporary' Visa Program is Broken." *Backgrounder* (January): 1–15. http://www.cis.org/articles/2003/back103.pdf (accessed December 4, 2008).

Vermaelen, Theo. 2005. *Share Repurchases: Foundations and Trends in Finance.* Hanover, MA: Now Publishers.

Vickers, Marcia, and Mike France. 2002. "How Corrupt is Wall Street?" *BusinessWeek*, May 13: 36–42.

Vosti, Curtis. 1992. "Hybrids Are Taking Root: IRS Nod Provides Boon to Popular Cash Balance Plans." *Pensions & Investments* 20(1): 17, 20.

Voxant FD (Fair Disclosure) Wire. 2006. "Microsoft at Sanford C. Bernstein and Co. Strategic Decisions Conference—Final." Herndon, VA: Voxant.

Wade, Robert. 1990. *Governing the Market: Economic Theory and the Role of Government in East Asian Industrialization*. Princeton, NJ: Princeton University Press.

Wadhwa, Vivek, Gary Gereffi, Ben Rissing, and Ryan Ong. 2007. "Where the Engineers Are." *Issues in Science and Technology* 23(3): 73–84.

Wall Street Journal. 1958. "IBM Puts Hourly-Rated Workers on a Salary Basis." *Wall Street Journal*, January 31.

———. 1959. "Fairchild Camera Acquires All Common of Semiconductor Firm." *Wall Street Journal*, October 9: 20.

———. 1974a. "SEC Moves Closer to Goal of Ending Fixed Fees by May 1." *Wall Street Journal*, October 25, A:4.

———. 1974b. "Intel Closes Two Plants in California for Week Due to Slowing Business." *Wall Street Journal*, September 4.

———. 1984. "Intel Begins Shipment under Chinese Contract." *Wall Street Journal*, December 12.

Wallace, Richard. 2005. "Intel Spies Opportunities Aplenty for China Growth." *Electronic Engineering Times*, August 8, 1.

Wallman, S, K. Wallman, and G. Aronow. 1999. "Pooling-of-Interests Accounting and High Growth Economy Companies." Submitted to the Financial Accounting Standards Board. Great Falls, VA: Wallman Consulting. http://www.wallman.com/pdfs_etc/fasb.pdf (accessed December 4, 2008).

Warner, Melanie. 2000. "Friends and Family: Sycamore Gave Lots of 'Directed Shares' To a Key Customer." *Fortune* (March 20). http://money.cnn.com/magazines/fortune/fortune_archive/2000/03/20/276388/index.htm (accessed December 4, 2008).

Washington Post. 1963. "Text of Special Message on Tax Reduction and Reform." *Washington Post*, January 25, A:12.

———. 1982. "Kodak, Xerox Layoffs Set." *Washington Post*, August 24, D:8.

WashTech. 2008. *About WashTech*. Seattle, WA: WashTech. http://www.washtech.org/about/ (accessed February 26, 2009).

Watson, Lloyd. 1988. "Another S.F. First—A Consumer Data Bank." *San Francisco Chronicle*, January 27.

Watson, Thomas J., Jr., and Peter Petre. 1990. *Father, Son and Co.: My Life at IBM and Beyond*. New York: Bantam Books.

Weinstein, Eric. 1998. "How and Why Government, Universities, and Industry Create Domestic Labor Shortages of Scientists and High-Tech Workers." NBER/PEAT working paper. Cambridge, MA: National Bureau of Economic Research. http://www.nber.org/~peat/PapersFolder/Papers/SG/NSF.html (accessed December 4, 2008).

Weisbenner, Scott J. 2000. "Corporate Share Repurchases in the 1990s: What Role Do Stock Options Play?" FEDS Working Paper 2000-29. Washington, DC: Federal Reserve Board of Governors. http://www.federalreserve.gov/pubs/feds/2000/200029/200029pap.pdf (accessed July 20, 2009).

Wells, Rob. 2004. "U.S. House Backs Court Cash Balance Pension Plan Decision." Dow Jones International News, September 22.

Wharton, John. 1990. "Top 10 List: Intel's Technological Detours en Route to Success." InfoWorld, April 9.

Whyte, William H. 1956. The Organization Man. New York: Simon & Schuster.

Williams, Fred. 1995. "3 Baby Bells Select Cash Balance Plans." Pensions and Investments 23(23): 1, 55.

———. 1997. "SBC Picks Cash Balance: Company is 6th RBOC to Modify Its Pension Plan." Pensions and Investments 25(11): 3, 46.

Williamson, Oliver E. 1985. The Economic Institutions of Capitalism. New York: Free Press.

———. 1996. The Mechanisms of Governance. New York: Oxford University Press.

Wilson, Gretchen, and Mike Blain. 2001. "Organizing in the New Economy: The Amazon.com Campaign." Working USA 5(2): 32–58.

Wilson, John W. 1986. The New Venturers: Inside the High-Stakes World of Venture Capital. Reading, MA: Addison-Wesley.

Wohn, Dong-Hee. 2005. "Chip Developers See Korea as Ideal for R&D Centers." Joins.com, May 20.

Wong, Nicole C. 2006. "HP Uses Worker 'Churn' to Hone Its 'Edge.'" Oakland Tribune, December 26.

World Accounting Report. 1994. "Congress Threatens to Overrule FASB." World Accounting Report, February 23.

World Bank. 1993. The East Asian Miracle: Economic Growth and Public Policy. New York: Oxford University Press.

Wyatt, Lindsay. 1996. "Hybrid Plans Fit Evolving Workforce." Pension Management 32(3): 12–19.

Xerox. 2006. 2006 Report on Global Citizenship. Norwalk, CN: Xerox. http://www.xerox.com/downloads/usa/en/c/citizenshipreport06.pdf   (accessed July 8, 2009).

Xie, Wie, and Steven White. 2004. "Sequential Learning in a Chinese Spin-Off: The Case of Lenovo Group Ltd." R&D Management 34(4): 407–422.

Xinhua Financial Network. 2003. "Intel, China's Legend Group Set Up Technology Center in Beijing." Xinhua Financial Network, August 28.

Xinhua News Agency. 1991. "State Councillor Meets U.S. Businessman." Xinhua News Agency, March 8.

———. 2006. "HP China to Hire over 1,000 People, Biggest Ever." Xinhua News Agency, May 13.

Yale-Loehr, Stephen. 2003a. "Testimony of Mr. Stephen Yale-Loehr, Cornell Law School, September 16." U.S. Congress. Senate Committee on the Judiciary. Examining the Importance of the H-1B Visa to the American Economy, 108th Cong., 1st sess. http://judiciary.senate.gov/hearings/testimony.cfm?id=913&wit_id=2611 (accessed December 4, 2008).

———. 2003b. "Testimony of Mr. Stephen Yale-Loehr, Adjunct Professor, Cornell Law School, July 29." U.S. Congress. Senate Committee on the Judiciary. Subcommittee on Immigration and Border Security. The L-1 Visa and American Interests in the 21st Century, 108th Cong., 1st sess. http://judiciary.senate.gov/hearings/testimony.cfm?id=878&wit_id=2520 (accessed December 4, 2008).

Yang, Dori Jones, and Laxmi Nakarmi. 1989. "Is the Era of Cheap Asian Labor Over?" *BusinessWeek*, May 15: 45–46.

Yee, Ho Siew. 2005. "Intel to Spend RM800m on New Centres." *Business Times*, December 9, 1.

Yoder, Stephen Kreider. 1989. "Costly Exports: Reverse 'Brain Drain' Helps Asia but Robs U.S. of Scarce Talent." *Wall Street Journal*, April 18.

Yonekawa, Shin-ichi. 1984. "University Graduates in Japanese Enterprises before the Second World War." *Business History* 26(3): 193–218.

Yoon, Bang-Soon L. 1992. "Reverse Brain-Drain in South Korea: State-Led Model." *Studies in Comparative International Development* 27(1): 4–26.

Young, Doug. 2003. "Interview: Intel Sees China PC Market Overtaking U.S. by 2010." Reuters News, October 15.

Young, Doug, and David Lin. 2006. "Interview: Intel Aims for Increased Market Share in China." Reuters News, March 16.

Zachary, G. Pascal. 1994. "Trading Places: Malaysians Become Stars at U.S. Electronic Firms." *Asian Wall Street Journal*, October 3.

ZaZona.com. 2008. *H-1B FAQs*. Chandler, AZ: ZaZona.com/JobDestruction.info. http://www.zazona.com/ShameH1B/H1BFAQs.htm#IfH-1BAbolished (accessed February 26, 2009).

ZDNet UK. 2003. "HP Marks Indian Employment Milestone." *ZDNet UK*, December 4.

Zerega, Blaise. 1999. "Real Men Hire Fabs: Chip Companies Are Cutting Costs by Outsourcing." *Red Herring*, March 1.

Zintner, Aaron. 1993. "More U.S. Software Jobs Going to Foreign Workers." *Boston Globe*, July 5, 1.

The Author

William Lazonick is a professor in the Department of Regional Economic and Social Development at the University of Massachusetts Lowell and director of UMass Lowell's Center for Industrial Competitiveness. He is also affiliated with the Centre National de la Recherche Scientifique's (CNRS) Groupe de Recherche en Économie Théorique et Appliquée of the Université Montesquieu-Bordeaux IV on a European Commission project on finance, innovation, and growth. Previously, he was assistant and associate professor of economics at Harvard University (1975–1984); professor of economics at Barnard College, affiliated with Columbia University (1985–1993); and distinguished research professor at INSEAD (1996–2007). He has also served on the faculties of the University of Toronto (1982–1983), Harvard Business School (1984–1986), and the University of Tokyo (1996–1997), and was a visiting member of the Institute for Advanced Study at Princeton (1989–1990). He holds a Bachelor of Commerce degree from the University of Toronto (1968), a Master of Science degree in economics from the London School of Economics (1969), and a Doctor of Philosophy degree in economics from Harvard University (1975). In 1991, Sweden's Uppsala University awarded him an honorary doctorate for his work on the theory and history of economic development.

Index

The italic letters *f, n,* and *t* following a page number indicate that the subject information of the heading is within a figure, note, or table, respectively, on that page. Double italics indicate multiple but consecutive elements.

About the Institute

The W.E. Upjohn Institute for Employment Research is a nonprofit research organization devoted to finding and promoting solutions to employment-related problems at the national, state, and local levels. It is an activity of the W.E. Upjohn Unemployment Trustee Corporation, which was established in 1932 to administer a fund set aside by Dr. W.E. Upjohn, founder of The Upjohn Company, to seek ways to counteract the loss of employment income during economic downturns.

The Institute is funded largely by income from the W.E. Upjohn Unemployment Trust, supplemented by outside grants, contracts, and sales of publications. Activities of the Institute comprise the following elements: 1) a research program conducted by a resident staff of professional social scientists; 2) a competitive grant program, which expands and complements the internal research program by providing financial support to researchers outside the Institute; 3) a publications program, which provides the major vehicle for disseminating the research of staff and grantees, as well as other selected works in the field; and 4) an Employment Management Services division, which manages most of the publicly funded employment and training programs in the local area.

The broad objectives of the Institute's research, grant, and publication programs are to 1) promote scholarship and experimentation on issues of public and private employment and unemployment policy, and 2) make knowledge and scholarship relevant and useful to policymakers in their pursuit of solutions to employment and unemployment problems.

Current areas of concentration for these programs include causes, consequences, and measures to alleviate unemployment; social insurance and income maintenance programs; compensation; workforce quality; work arrangements; family labor issues; labor-management relations; and regional economic development and local labor markets.